Readings From
FUTURES

Readings From
FUTURES

edited by **RALPH JONES**

A collection of articles from the journal **FUTURES, 1974–80**

Westbury House

Published by Westbury House, the books division
of IPC Science and Technology Press Limited, PO
Box 63, Bury Street, Guildford, Surrey GU2 5BH,
England

© IPC Business Press Limited, 1981, unless otherwise stated

British Library CIP Data

Readings from Futures.
    1. History, Modern – 1945–
    I. Futures
    909.82   DA840

    ISBN 0-86103-040-0

Printed in Great Britain

Futures is published quarterly by IPC Science and
Technology Press Limited.

CONTENTS

The articles reprinted originally appeared in the following issues of FUTURES:

Cole *et al*, Feb. 1978, Vol 10, pp. 3–20
Marien, Oct. 1977, Vol 9, pp. 415–431

Freeman, Dec. 1974, Vol 6, pp. 450—462
Gershuny, April 1977, Vol 9, pp. 103–114
Marsh, April 1979, Vol 11, pp. 91–103
Pym, April 1980, Vol 12, pp. 142—150
Powell, Aug. 1979, Vol 11, pp. 338—341
Vickers, Oct. 1979, Vol 11, pp. 371—382

Otway and Pahner, April 1976, Vol 8, pp. 122—134
Haveman, Oct. 1977, Vol 9, pp. 365–374
Taylor, Oct. 1977, Vol 9, pp. 404–414
Waddington, April 1977, Vol 9, pp. 139–146
Atkin, Dec. 1978, Vol 10, pp. 492–499

Forrester, June 1976, Vol 8, pp. 195–214
Hughes and Mesarovic, Aug. 1978, Vol 10, pp. 267–282
Roberts, Feb. 1977, Vol 9, pp. 3–16
Norse, Oct. 1979, Vol 11, pp. 412–422

Briggs, Dec. 1978, Vol 10, pp. 445–451
Blish, April 1979, Vol 11, pp. 155–160
Barnett, Aug. 1975, Vol 7, pp. 335–340
Wise, Oct. 1976, Vol 8, pp. 411–419
Chapman, June 1976, Vol 8, pp. 254–260
Brown and Sheriff, Dec. 1978, Vol 10, pp. 500–506

Ray, April 1978, Vol 10, pp. 91–108
Pavitt, Dec. 1979, Vol 11, pp. 458–470
       Feb. 1980, Vol 12, pp. 35–44
Pirie, Dec. 1976, Vol 8, pp. 509–516
Wiener, June 1977, Vol 9, pp. 182–193
Fuhrmann, June 1979, Vol 11, pp. 216–223
Caudle, Oct. 1978, Vol 10. pp. 361–379
Surrey and Thomas, Feb. 1980, Vol 12, pp. 3–17
Williams, Aug. 1978, Vol 10, pp. 293–302
Kelly, Aug. 1977, Vol 9, pp. 324–334

PREFACE

In the early 1970s forecasters looked at the future of the world and decided that it didn't have one. The conclusions were reinforced by the post 1973 stagflation (itself a seventies word) which 'proved' that the limits to growth were at hand: resources were running out, food was short, and economic growth was bad.

Today forecasters look at the future of the world and see not one but several possible futures. And the conventional wisdom of the 1970s has been challenged—not just the arithmetic of material reserves but the concepts underlying resource consumption or post-industrial society. This book is a collection of some of those challenges.

Futures studies is a field without boundaries. Its jargon is inherited from a dozen different disciplines and languages. This can be confusing for the new-comer, particular when, as Michael Marien shows, one word can have two very different meanings. Sam Cole *et al*, provide some reference points for those trying to disentangle the different viewpoints on global development.

In his article, Christopher Freeman questions the climate of despair that was generated, in part, by the conclusions of the first global models. The second generation of world models, such as SARUM, did not present such clear-cut pessimism. And by the time SARUM was adapted for use in the OECD study INTERFUTURES, the result was a set of scenarios.

Some forecasters see the use of scenarios as evidence of increasing sophistica-tion; many users see them as a cop-out. Few private companies allow their forecasters the luxury of producing a set of contrasting scenarios. And even then the forecaster should take the precaution of taking two or four (not three) scenarios. With an odd number decision makers invariably focus on the middle one, and the rest, along with the work that went into them, are discarded.

The decade closed with the qualified pessimism of the INTERFUTURES study. The end of the world was not at hand. But there were plenty of things in the industrialized West that needed changing if it was to help itself, and the Third World.

As Gershuny points out, post-industrialised society is not a panacea for all the ills that beset industrial society. The service economy won't automatically mop up all the unemployment created by the decline of traditional industries. And Keith Pavitt warns that even strong manufacturing sectors can be laid low by a failure in product (as opposed to process) innovation.

Three consecutive articles deal with politics, management and morality, though with scarcely a mention of power, money, or sex.

Enoch Powell explains why politicians are not thinking the same things as they are saying, Denis Pym looks at why managers play truant, and Sir Geoffrey Vickers shows why the quest for rights is a sign, and a weakness, of the 'permissive' society.

The lack of boundaries in futures studies has attracted academics from other fields. The methods they have introduced reflect their backgrounds: e.g., Robert Haveman (economics), Asa Briggs (history), Ron Atkin (mathematics), Alan Marsh (sociology). This gives the prospective researcher a wide choice of methods. No one method guarantees success—a fact highlighted by the retro-spective studies. Even the most careful and comprehensive economic analysis can go badly awry, as Brown and Sheriff show in their evaluation of a forecast for the UK economy.

The forecasts themselves, set out in the last section of this collection, contain a strong retrospective element. Peter Caudle looks back to some of the chemical pathways, discarded in the era of cheap energy, that may make a comeback in the chemical industry of the 1990s. Surrey and Thomas review the performance of nuclear power stations to see how the promises worked out in practice. Jill Williams' article is underpinned by a trend that goes back centuries—the rise in global CO_2 concentration caused by man's industrial activity.

The articles here are taken from the pages of *Futures*, 1974–1980. This collection is not a handbook of futures studies, it does not define the field, neither does it present one picture of the future. What it does do is round up some of the best work in the field. The studies are not perfect—but they will be of interest and help to anyone concerned with the future. Those who do not learn from the mistakes of futures studies are destined to repeat them.

Acknowledgements

The contents of Futures, and hence of this collection, reflect the help and advice given by the journal's advisory board and by Dr Ivan Klimeš, publishing director, Neil Stamper, assistant editor, and Stephen Wood of IPC Science and Technology Press Ltd. Special thanks to Rosalind Bradley, Jan Holloway, and Sally Miller.

Ralph Jones
January, 1981

OVERVIEWS

SCENARIOS OF WORLD DEVELOPMENT

Sam Cole, Jay Gershuny, and Ian Miles

This article looks at 16 recent studies of global futures and examines their conclusions within a sociopolitical framework.† Three idealised worldviews—conservative, reformist, radical—are constructed from this framework; they are then married with a classification based upon the two parameters of high growth–low growth and equality–inequality. This allows for the concise mapping of existing scenarios and, by the elucidation of the major differences in sociopolitical forecasts, provides a simple but effective technique for comparative analysis. Two quality-of-life issues, the future of work, and of political development and change, are used as concrete examples of how the method can be used to create a series of scenarios which cover the whole sociopolitical spectrum of alternative futures.

In the last few years, as readers of *Futures* will be well aware, a number of long-term forecasts of possibilities for global economic growth have caught the attention of the media and the public. Most of these have called for dramatic new thinking about the possibilities for the long-term future and for a reorientation of present trends in world development. However, their authors disagree both over proposals and over prospects.

By comparing the content and prescriptions of the major studies, the assumptions upon which they are based can be set out, and the comparison between these assumptions and the different methods employed gives some guidance for our own thinking about the future. Several of these futures studies received much publicity, some have achieved notoriety, and some are believed to have an influence on government policies. Table 1 summarises these forecasts.

The authors are all members of the Science Policy Research Unit at the University of Sussex, Brighton, Sussex, UK. The methodological approach described in this article was developed as part of a study—supported by the Social Science Research Council and the Leverhulme Trust—at SPRU which will be published as *World Futures: The Great Debate* (London, Martin Robertson, forthcoming 1978) under the editorship of Professors Chris Freeman and Marie Jahoda. The figures and tables in this article are based on those which will appear in the published study.
† These studies are referenced in a short bibliography at the end of the article.

TABLE 1. SIXTEEN RECENT WORLD FUTURES STUDIES

	Outlook	Diagnosis
Spengler (1965)	Current prospect for less-developed countries (LDC) definitely Malthusian; income gap grows	Economic size facilitates growth; seek optimum population; "technology, prudence, and reason"
Kahn/Wiener (1967)	Qualified optimism; continued upward trend; era of political stability; but, "islands of wealth in a sea of poverty"	Step-wise progression to worldwide post-industrial society; change and continuity of the multifold trend
Ehrlich (1970)	World is already over-developed; ecological collapse possible; living standards in LDCs likely to fall	Population control essential; theoretical limit to LDCs' development; bring into line with resource realities; individual attitude change is the key
Forrester (1971)	"Overshoot and collapse" of world system through resource shortage	Industrialisation is more dangerous than population; urgent task is to face issues; "hard choices must be made"; low-level inegalitarian equilibrium
Meadows (1972)	Limits reached in next 100 years	Only safe way is to slow down; population growth is greatest impediment to redistribution, must achieve equilibrium or face overshoot and collapse
Schumacher (1973)	The world will face environmental degradation, energy shortage, and reduced quality of life unless we mend our ways	Essential problem facing mankind is the choice of organisations; giantism complexity, capital maturity, violence; redirect to R and D
Dumont (1974)	With present trends inequalities will remain indefinitely and give rise to serious revolt	Distribution of population is the basic cause of injustice; stop the population explosion; solution through economic adjustment; continued confrontation and struggle
Modrzhinskaya (1974)	Refute neo-Malthusian theories; socialist post-industrial society conjectured	Prosperity is limited by social structure (especially capitalism), not by technical possibilities or financial resources
Heilbroner (1974)	Grim Malthusian outcome in LDCs; worldwide totalitarianism or anarchy	Only major disaster will slow the pace of growth; danger that "Malthusian checks" will be offset; central issue is to deal with the environment; may be possible to ease long-term adjustments
Mesarovic and Pestel (1974)	Developing world crisis; regional resource catastrophes could spread worldwide, and paralyse future orderly development	Survival of world system is in question; need technological restraint with social, institutional, and lifestyle reforms
Kaya (1975)	Developing countries could run into an impasse	Alleviating poverty is the greatest problem today; advanced nations must take steps to reform structure of industry; new type of international division of industry

TABLE 1—*continued*

	Outlook	Diagnosis
Fundacion Bariloche (1976)	Catastrophe is an everyday reality in LDCs; extreme economic difficulty predicted in Asia and Africa by 2000	Scarcity is not due to physical limits; population growth is not the major factor; must achieve basic needs in LDCs, but without help, this will not happen in a reasonable time
Kosolapov (1976)	The next quarter century promises to be turbulent and dynamic; finally society will become a global association of people	The future today is being moulded in the struggle for communism, with the world revolutionary process and the scientific and technological revolution going on simultaneously
Tinbergen (1976)	World becoming increasingly complex politically; cornucopia of growth turning into Pandora's box; Third world turning from defence to defiance; no sane person could seriously envisage a world in which the world's poor live like today's affluent minority	Rich and poor have unparalleled problems which cannot be solved independently; dependency relationships of Third world must be reduced; equitable order requires changes in the distribution of power; political changes have not been reflected in institutions
Kahn, Brown, and Martel (1976)	Things are going rather well; 6 : 1 chance that all serious long-term problems will be successfully dealt with in due course; superindustrial society to emerge in late 20th and early 21st century	Roughly 100–200 years from now world population and economic growth will level off in a more or less natural and comfortable way; closing of the gap will not occur soon
Leontief (1977)	Second development decade strategy does not provide for sufficiently rapid closing of income gap between developing and developed countries; the gap will not diminish by the year 2000	Significant changes in economic relations between developed and developing countries; high growth rates in LDCs, coupled with slightly lower rates in developed countries, are needed

The global futures debate

The futures debate of the last decade has taken place against a background of rapidly changing world conditions. The late 1960s and early 1970s saw the postwar economic boom slipping into "stagflation". Alienation and environmental degradation became major issues—which, for some commentators, reflected a more general disillusion with industrial society.

In addition, many observers argue that there has been a shift in the global balance of power. The humiliation of the USA in South East Asia and the success of OPEC have added weight to calls for a new international economic order. Forecasters have certainly been influenced by these events, but it is not clear in what way their prognoses have influenced the course of affairs.

While the futures literature shows the impact of social and political turmoil, forecasters themselves have introduced significant changes in their methods. One new aspect of the world futures debate is the highly controversial application of computer models to the analysis of global trends. Those who have constructed mathematical world models argue that the complex interactive nature of the modern world makes such a device essential for analysis.[1]

The futures debate has become all embracing in scope, and accordingly confused in nature. Different authors use the same words to express different ideas, often adapting their language to the jargon of the day: such phrases as "radical institutional and social change", "appropriate technology", "self-reliance", or "the new international economic order" encompass a wide range of meanings, varying according to who uses them.

Profiles of world development

But whatever their differences, the writers do have some common concerns— including, notably, a concern to achieve a broad, comprehensive view of all the social sciences[2]—and indeed they share some general assumptions about the future. For example, *if* present population and economic trends continue, a widening gap between rich and poor countries is likely: most authors offer reasons why these trends should not or cannot continue. However, while agreeing that population growth must end eventually, they disagree about the constraints that resource and environmental factors may impose on population and income, and on whether income gaps can be narrowed or closed.

Population

Forecasters present a wide range of estimates of world population trends. Typically, these studies involve two kinds of question: what might happen if the present trends continue unabated, and what might happen if various measures to slow down population growth are introduced.

The most critical assumption is whether and when the "demographic transition" (essentially a change from high to low rates of population growth) will occur in the poor countries. For periods after the year 2000 forecasts diverge, reflecting the differing assumptions about growth rates, fertility, and the effectiveness of population policies. In fact, the population forecasts for the year 2100 differ by almost an order of magnitude, even though all authors see some levelling off as inevitable.

Wealth

Two crucial aspects of the world forecasts are the growth of total world product and its distribution between currently rich and poor countries.

Figure 1 indicates how different authors view their *normative* futures, that is the futures expected *if* the measures they each advocate were implemented, in terms of average world income per head *and* its global distribution between rich and poor nations. In some cases their *expectations* for these variables are considerably less hopeful.

Four wealth–equity profiles

Indicators such as these can only provide limited information about social welfare and social justice; economic growth need not necessarily lead to improved living standards, and international equality levels tell us nothing directly about economic equality within nations.

Nevertheless, they are useful for structuring the analysis. The two criteria of wealth and equity yield four alternative profiles of the world's future: a high-growth, more-equal world; a low-growth, more-equal world; a low-growth, less-equal world; and a high-growth, less-equal world.

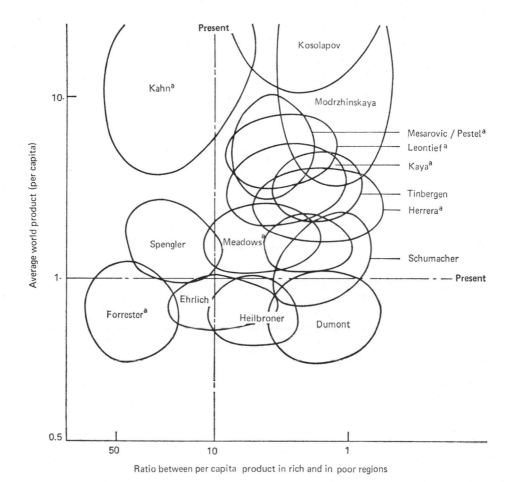

Figure 1. Distribution of wealth in preferred futures. Herrera was the Project Director for the Fundacion Bariloche model—the area enclosed represents the Bariloche preferred future. Quantified forecasts are indicated [a].

Worldviews

Forecasters have often failed to make explicit their underlying social and political philosophies, and in consequence they frequently talk at cross-purposes. Underlying the futures debate are unrecognised differences in assumptions concerning the processes of social, economic, and political change. The existence of such competing theories must be taken into account in attempting to evaluate alternative paths of world development.

However, an adequate consideration of all the subtle shades of opinion in different accounts of the evolution of the world system would be a lifetime's work. To simplify the task we have grouped different accounts into three broad categories—three "worldviews".

We have labelled these worldviews according to the different political standpoints: conservative, reformist, and radical. Each standpoint may be defined by a mixture of analytic and prescriptive statements about how the world operates and what should be done to influence its operation. The three

TABLE 2. THE THREE WORLDVIEWS: SOURCES

	Economic theory	Sociological theory	Political theory
Conservative	Neoclassical economics	Structural-functionalism	Pluralism
Reformist	Keynesianism, structural economics	Post-industrial society, liberal sociology	Elite theory
Radical	Marxist political economy, dependency theory	Class theory, conflict theory, Marxism	Class analysis

worldviews should not be thought of as simply different points on a single "left–right" dimension of political orientation—there are surprising convergences and divergences between their approaches. Table 2 summarises the sources from which these three worldviews were derived.[3]

The three worldviews: some areas of conflict

Management and intervention
The worldviews differ on the question of whether desirable social changes may be brought about by planned social intervention. The conservative view is that managerial intervention upsets the "natural justice" of the existing social and distributive order. The state should simply play the role of referee, ensuring that the rules of the game are not breached by powerful interests.

Reformist writers see unregulated market economics as yielding heavy social costs—unemployment, pollution, poverty. They accordingly advocate government intervention to direct the development of the market along the lines dictated by pluralist decision making.

Radicals hold fundamental change to be desirable, but consider that social injustice can only ultimately be rectified by a revolutionary restructuring of social relations, by replacing the market system with democratic planning.

Technical diffusion and change
The important question here is the *suitability* of technological change. To conservatives the process of development may be largely seen as a matter of the diffusion of better technologies from more-developed countries to the less developed. Reformists accept the importance of technical efficiency in promoting welfare, but also accept the desirability of a measure of technical choice according to the culture within which the technology is to be employed. Radicals claim that technologies are shaped by class interests both in developed economies and in less-developed countries, where the introduction of Western technologies often creates dependency on developed economies and reproduces the inequalities of the developed world in a more extreme form.

Evolution and development
Conservatives see the ideal process of development as a continuous evolution towards a more efficient and hence richer society. Social systems at any level of efficiency may be destabilised by technical or institutional innovations, but will normally return to an equilibrium position at a higher level of efficiency. Inventions, in this view, tend to drive social welfare upwards.

Reformists have a less optimistic view; social and technical evolution is simply change, and not necessarily progress towards a higher or better state.

Social engineering and technology assessment may, however, at least ensure that change tends to be in a positive direction.

Radicals see all past and present social systems as containing inherent contradictions that tend to undermine their most basic foundations; attempts to resolve these contradictions simply move them to higher levels, creating crisis after crisis, doing nothing to remove the basic relationships of exploitation and oppression (which only social revolution can do).

Political views and the Malthusian debate

Figure 2 shows how the forecasters considered earlier might be placed both in terms of their political views and their positions in the Malthusian debate (as technological optimists or pessimists).[4] Authors have only been assigned approximate positions, given the ambiguity and sometimes inconsistency of much of their work in terms of our three "ideal" worldviews. Classifying authors in this way is nevertheless of value in understanding their differing pronouncements.

Figures 1 and 2 show highly suggestive similarities: the major difference between these two figures is that both reformist and radical authors believe that their proposals would bring about fairly equitable futures. The profiles of their forecasts in terms of international equality thus tend to converge even where their political prescriptions diverge. While a discussion of Malthusian attitudes clearly plays a role in forecasters' assessments of future world economic growth, their views of the international distribution of incomes in the future is more closely bound to a different set of political attitudes.

Scenarios for the future

The three worldviews imply very different accounts of historical trends in world growth and inequality, and make very different prescriptions for the future.

In the conservative view growth can best be assured by freeing the market system from constraint; in the reformist view a substantial degree of government control is necessary; and in the radical view only a total transformation away from capitalism will permanently free the world from crisis and major conflict.

By combining the four alternative growth–equality profiles derived earlier with these three world views, we have constructed 12 alternative scenarios. While it is unlikely that the course of future history will closely follow any one of the specific courses depicted below, the scenarios should provide a framework in terms of which world development may be monitored.

High-growth, inegalitarian scenarios (HI)
In this profile, represented in Figure 3, the alternative sociopolitical scenarios rest on the continuation of technological changes which make available sufficient food, energy, and raw materials. In some cases very great changes in the technological structure of society, especially in the efficiency of use of basic materials, are probable.

A future with high rates of growth in the world economy and with larger gaps between the rich and poor nations might be derived by projecting postwar trends in world development, although the experience of the last few years has led to

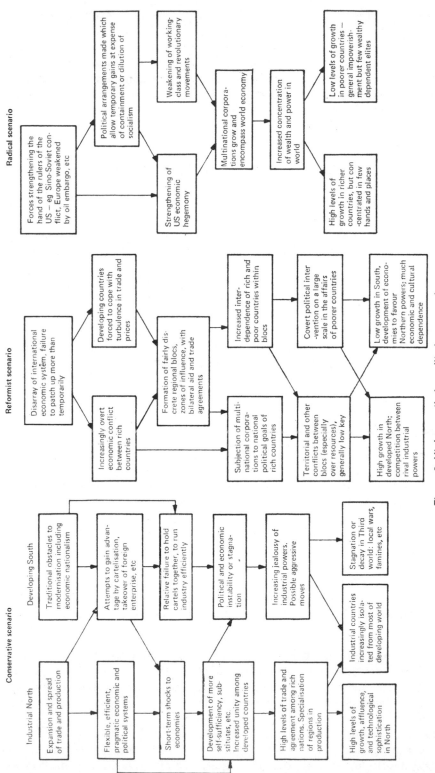

Figure 3. High-growth, inegalitarian scenarios

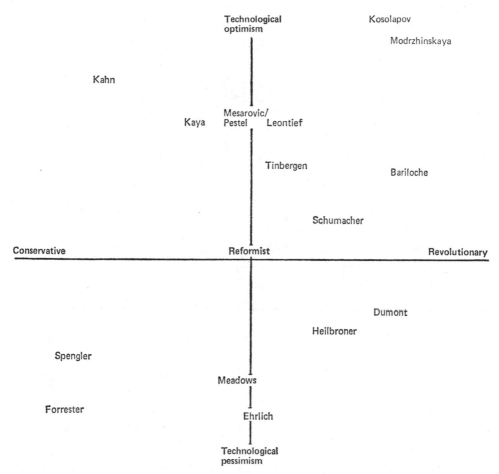

Figure 2. Mapping forecasters according to their political views and their positions in the Malthusian debate. They are positioned by reference to their international rather than domestic outlook.

more pessimistic expectations on the part of many commentators. The differences among the three worldviews relate particularly to the role of the state *vis-à-vis* private interests and to patterns of world trade.

For conservatives, an extremely uneven pattern of world development might suggest that there is some barrier between the poor and the rich countries (the economists' principle of comparative advantage alone, however, gives little clue as to the distribution of gains between trading partners). Rich countries would be achieving high levels of economic activity, while poor countries would be insulated from or impervious to modern economic practices. This suggests a future in which there is extensive trade and mobility only among the industrial nations, whose political strategies are presumably fairly united.

From a reformist perspective a period of disturbance and threat in economic affairs might stimulate competition among industrial countries to form stable trading alliances with poor countries. An HI scenario could thus consist of the development of regional blocs, in which superpowers stake out distinct zones of economic influence around the world.

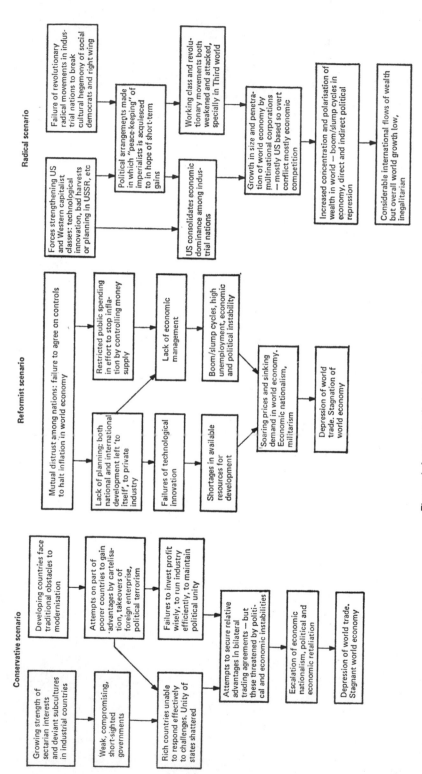

Figure 4. Low-growth, inegalitarian scenarios

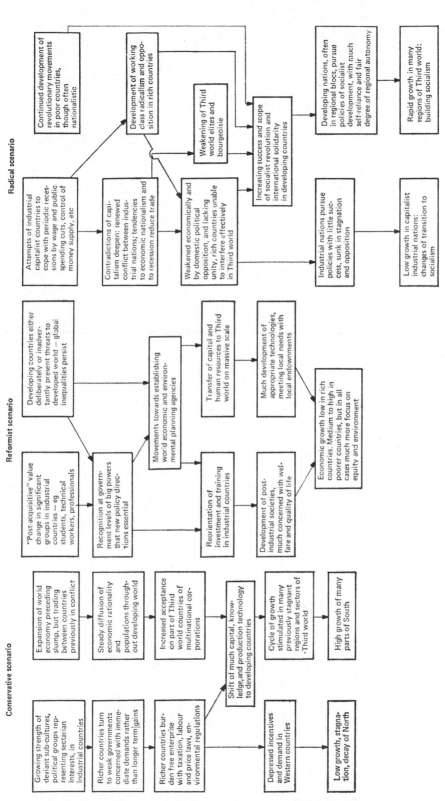

Figure 5. Low-growth, more-equal scenarios

Radicals would probably assign a greater role in the HI scenario to multinational corporations—supported by political intervention both nationally and internationally—in the concentration of wealth and power within the richer nations.

Low-growth, inegalitarian scenarios (LI)
Low-growth scenarios are more likely to involve what will appear to be Malthusian shortages, due to failures to apply technology to release the potentials of the physical world, often because of institutional and political factors.

A future in which world growth rates are low, and present international inequalities prevail, might appear at first glance to be a respectably wealthy world; at growth rates of only 1% per annum, gross world product would more than double in 80 years. But with population growth, this could result in declining living standards. As Figure 4 indicates, the LI scenarios superficially appear similar: they all include high inflation, economic nationalism, and failures of technology, for example. But again, the processes that are singled out are very different.

Low-growth, more-equal scenarios (LE)
Here (Figure 5) the poorer countries display rapid rates of economic growth, while growth rates in richer countries are much reduced. If this rapid growth of poorer countries gradually slows as they approach income levels found in the industrial nations, overall world product would grow slowly. This is a favoured profile for several of the more radical world forecasters. Among these authors, reasons for preferring low growth differ, as do the final levels of consumption regarded as ideal.

For conservatives this future could come about through the operation of extraeconomic factors in the industrial countries, whose effect would be to transfer income and opportunity to the poorer regions of the world. Several such factors might be involved—wars or debilitating political conflict among European countries, major mistakes in technological development, even climatic change, or, perhaps more commonly, the role of political and cultural minorities such as powerful union movements, environmentalist pressure groups, and deviant subcultures.

Reformists envisage this scenario as either coming about through conflict or mistake or as the result of a deliberate policy.

Radicals would be likely to see this profile as being on the verge of world revolution, and thus potentially a transitional stage to an HE pattern of socialist growth.

High-growth, more-equal scenarios (HE)
One common characteristic of the three worldviews is the expectation of a fairly high level of world trade and interchange in the HE profile (figure 6). For conservatives world development would be best accomplished by free trade.

Reformists, however, would argue that while it is necessary to remove those restrictions upon trade which discriminate against the poorer countries, world development requires a considerable restructuring of the existing world economy —which cannot be entirely left to market forces. Trade relationships would be expanded on a planned basis and linked with multilateral aid programmes.

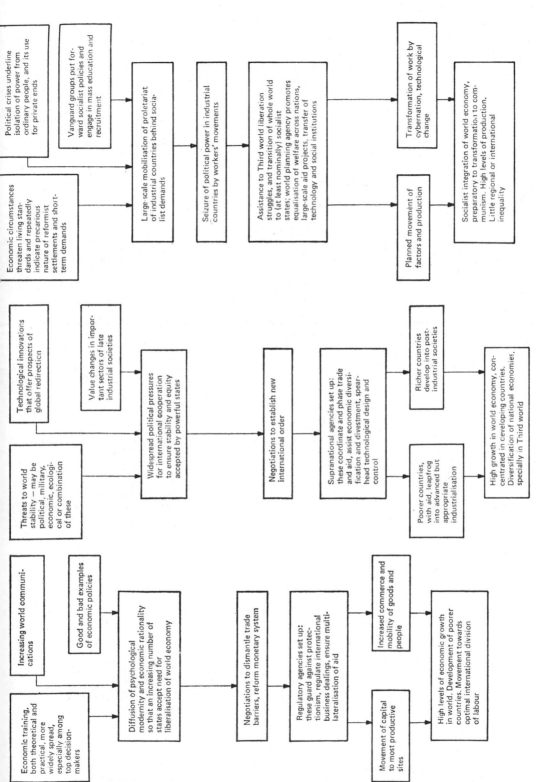

Figure 6. High-growth, more-equal scenarios

TABLE 3. IMAGES OF THE FUTURE

	High-growth egalitarian	High-growth inegalitarian
Political development and change		
Conservative	(1) The global trend is towards establishment of liberal pluralist states. In many poor countries the emphasis of regimes may be puritan, with religious overtones. In rich countries there would be much more tolerance of differing life-styles. State regulates unions and other interest groups, ensures welfare of infirm and aged, and prevents discrimination against individuals or products.	(4) Rich countries: liberal-pluralist states, possibly linked in loose federation. Important policies decided consensually among Northern countries. Poor countries: varieties of totalitarian regime in many countries; some communistic, some nationalistic, and many small millenarian, separatist movements. Some exceptions, with probable links to the North and effective exploitation of local resources.
Reformist	(2) Rich countries: political power balance affected by pressures from the young, from professionals and technical workers, etc. Decentralisation promotes growth and permits redistribution of wealth. Poor countries: progressive forces and sectors of society challenge traditional elites, development proceeds with more attention to local accumulation and less cost to the poorer sections of society.	(5) Rich countries: governments very concerned with economic efficiency and maintaining stability, but social welfare needs also the focus of social engineering. Poor countries: variety of dependent political regimes. Some aspire to paternal liberalism, some have the wherewithal to develop along social democratic lines, some simply repressive.
Radical	(3) Rich countries: worker's states, with national goals determined by delegates from workers and community councils. Strong central governing bodies, but under public control and scrutiny, and with much regional autonomy. Poor countries: socialist states, possibly with some remnants of state capitalism being phased out; development towards communism.	(6) Rich countries: highly repressive, manipulative regimes in West, possibly masquerading as democratic with two-party system but no real choice. High degree of surveillance of public. Poor countries: often puppet military regimes, corruption rife, strong links between state and organised crime, terrorism against dissenters.
Work and industrial organisation		
Conservative	(1) Automation is being or has been introduced on a grand scale; in rich countries, employment may even be seen as a privilege for the highly educated. Poor countries more labour-intensive, particularly in primary sectors.	(4) Many jobs in the richer countries would have been automated, but local need for primary and secondary production might place limits on this. Poor countries mix traditional patterns and factory work.
Reformist	(2) In industrial countries the most wearing and boring tasks automated, emphasis on job enrichment. Attempts to integrate work and leisure. In poor countries technologies would be less sophisticated: factories resemble an agglomeration of labour-intensive craft workshops.	(5) Many of the more unpleasant or polluting jobs would be done by migrant labour or exported from rich to poor countries. The work-force resident in poor countries would be divided between an industrial sector for export, and other employment in traditional and informal sectors.
Radical	(3) Considerable emphasis on automation as a means of reducing the differences between manual and mental work; technologies chosen in order to maximise worker control and choice. A fundamental change in the nature of work, away from alienated wage-labour, underway; process at different stages of development in different areas.	(6) Rich countries: work and leisure increasingly unsatisfying. Threatened by economic uncertainty, and ignorant of alternatives, deskilled workers engage in monotonous production. Poor countries' peasantry either pursue traditional lifestyle or are coerced into plantation or industrial labour.

Low-growth inegalitarian	Low-growth egalitarian
(7) Rich countries: many states in various stages of decline. Failed welfare states, now heavily over-bureaucratised, discouraging enterprise and trade. Possibly some military regimes, probably much regional separatism. Poor countries as in (4), but lacking enclaves of development.	(10) Rich countries: domestic policies **Conservative** may resemble scenario (7), but possibly less conflict between Northern countries. Poor countries: stresses of rapid social change need containment, so possibly the most stable governments in the short-term would be military regimes aligned with business interests, giving way to more pluralistic states as development proceeds. In some cases, a Japanese model?
(8) Rich countries: degenerate pluralist states, now non-meritocratic and largely governed by ruling elites (in name of socialism, nationalism, or whatever). Poor countries: some strictly dependent as in scenario (5); others pursuing autarchic policies with little success and under continual military threats.	(11) Rich countries: resemble either (5) **Reformist** or (8), plus conservation, decentralisation, collectivisation. Poor countries: many are networks of village or commune republics, integrated by states based on a middle-class backbone, regulating regional trade and technological development.
(9) Rich countries: much as in scenario (6), but with some states less successful and possibly propped up by the major powers. Socialist countries probably recovering from economic setbacks. Poor countries: much as in scenario (6), but less nonmilitary assistance from rich countries and likelihood of guerila and peasant warfare recurring in many areas.	(12) Rich countries: socialist countries **Radical** fairly affluent, others range from totalitarian to early stages of socialism. Poor countries: again a variety of states and much conflict: the most successful are, however, socialist or left-inclined state capitalist, acting together in preservation of mutual interests.
(7) In rich countries life reminiscent of Great Depression: public works, over-manning, machinery unproductive. Associated social problems. Poor countries: as in (4), but less success in industrialisation.	(10) Situation in industrial countries as **Conservative** in (7). In poor countries there would be a massive growth in employment opportunities, and a large expansion of the secondary and tertiary sectors.
(8) Despite technological innovations at the workplace, labour productivity in rich countries is low; workers reject poor conditions, and machines idle in face of low levels of effective demand. Conflicts over "scabbing" and unemployment. In poor countries work conditions would vary enormously: many unemployed, subsistence farmers; small industrial labour force.	(11) In rich countries product life would **Reformist** be lengthened, and other strategies adopted to reduce energy and resource requirements. High unemployment in some countries. In poor countries, there would be labour-intensive appropriate technology as the backbone of development, supported by local manufacture and imports of capital goods (eg simple machine tools).
(9) In industrial countries the circumstances for workers would probably closely resemble those described in scenario (6), with more automation and unemployment probable. In the poorer countries (including, possibly, declining industrial nations), totalitarianism might be attempting to revive production with forced labour gangs, conscription, etc.	(12) For some rich countries this would **Radical** resemble scenario (9), for others, with a more socialist pattern of development, there would be moves towards worker control of industry and increasing production via selective automation. In poor countries the pattern would tend to be one of communal self-reliance and hard work.

Radicals would argue that such planning on a world scale would be subverted (if, indeed, it were allowed in the first place) by commercial interests, unless backed by powerful socialist forces.

Images of the future, and the quality of life

In describing alternative futures we need to distinguish and understand many issues associated with the "quality of life". What would it feel like to be living in the future world emerging from one of these 12 scenarios? It is an enormously complex issue to evaluate living conditions and lifestyles.

But the 12 scenarios can be elaborated into more detailed images of the future. Based on our interpretation of the worldviews, ideas from other forecasters, and social-science literature, we have chosen a set of variables which jointly influence quality of life, and analysed these in the light of our four profiles and three worldviews. The three worldviews were especially valuable in structuring fundamental issues of social choice, and hence in setting up scenarios and the quality of life criteria.

In Table 3 we give a summary of our analysis for two quality of life issues, political development and change, and work and industrial organisation. The 12 different futures are contrasted by taking the four profiles as the columns and the three worldviews as the rows of each table. This condensed presentation sets out the "ideal types" in a given future. In particular, the distinctions made here between rich and poor countries are rather gross ones, concealing many divergences.

Methodology: conclusions

The debate about economic growth in the future—often incoherent and confusing—tends to support the illusion that long-term forecasting is concerned solely with technical issues. But there exists among forecasters a wide variety of interests and values, and these are embedded in the assumptions which shape future studies.

Like the classical economists, today's futurologists all expect that world economic growth and population growth will eventually stop or be transformed out of all recognition—but they differ enormously about when and at what levels or how this will or should happen. These differences are fundamental to the debate and they can be traced back to *three* problem areas: resources and technical change; the desirable political objectives and norms for society; and the economic, social, and political processes whereby society evolves and changes.

Very little that is not ambiguous can be said about the long-term future, and the horizons of the "near-term" future (ie that for which we have sufficient information to make relatively accurate assessments of the impact of current trends or policies) are close.

Every previous world forecaster has attempted to direct the agenda of the global futures debate. Kahn, with his continuing belief in the panacea of world economic growth, the Ehrlichs and the authors of *The Limits to Growth* with their concentration on ecological constraints and population growth, the Bariloche group with their concept of basic needs, the Club of Rome with their world *problematique*; all those who have considered the problem have tried to exert some such influence. The method outlined here refocuses the debate, by highlighting issues of technological change and dependence, and discussing these issues in explicitly sociopolitical terms.

Notes and references

1. The STAFF team at the Science Policy Research Unit have identified how and where these models have made a specific contribution to the debate about the future; see Sam Cole, *Global Models and the International Economic Order* (Oxford, Pergamon, 1977) and John Clark and Sam Cole, with Ray Curnow and Mike Hopkins, *Global Simulation Models: A Comparative Study* (Chichester, John Wiley, 1976). Sam Cole and Ian Miles take up this analysis in *World Futures: The Great Debate*.

2. It is notable that recently many leading orthodox economists have returned to an interest in the relations between economics, politics, and sociology. This rebirth of political economy has produced influential essays like Tibor Scitovsky's *The Joyless Economy* (London, Oxford University Press, 1977) and Fred Hirsch's *Social Limits to Growth* (London, Routledge and Kegan Paul, 1977). Some forecasters, like Galtung, are also explicitly concerned with sociopolitical factors in futures studies.

3. For accounts of different worldviews in economics, see Michael Barret-Brown, *The Economics of Imperialism* (Harmondsworth, Penguin Books, 1975) and Robert Gilpin, *US Power and the Multinational Corporations* (London, Macmillan, 1975). For worldviews in sociology and social policy, see David and Ruth Elliot, *The Control of Technology* (London, Wykeham, 1976) and Paul Lazarsfeld, *Main Trends in Sociology* (London, George Allen and Unwin, 1973). For political theory worldviews, see Robert Alford, *Political Sociology* (Englewood Cliffs, New Jersey, Prentice-Hall, 1976) and R. Lindberg *et al*, *Stress and Contradiction in Modern Capitalism* (Lexington, Mass, Lexington Books, 1975).

4. Figure 2 deals with *international* political analysis and does not necessarily depict the authors' position on domestic matters. It is by no means uncommon, for example, to find an advocate of revolutionary change in the world economy simultaneously supporting reactionary policies at home, or vice versa. Kosolapov and Modrzhinskaya may be examples of the former. Our account of the three worldviews, then, imposes a degree of order on political and theoretical controversies which, although useful for an analysis of alternative futures, loses a great deal of their characteristic diversity.

Bibliography

R. Dumont, *Utopia or Else* (London, Deutsch, 1974).

A. Ehrlich and P. Ehrlich, *Population, Resources, Environment* (San Francisco, Freeman, 1970).

P. Ehrlich and R. Harriman, *How to be a Survivor* (London, Pan/Ballantine, 1971).

J. W. Forrester, *World Dynamics* (Cambridge, Mass, MIT Press, 1971).

R. Heilbroner, *An Inquiry into the Human Prospect* (New York, Norton, 1974).

R. Heilbroner, *Business Civilisation in Decline* (London, Boyars, 1976).

A. Herrera *et al*, *Catastrophe or New Society?* (Ottawa, IDRC, 1976)—the Bariloche report.

H. Kahn and A. Wiener, *The Year 2000* (London, Macmillan, 1969).

H. Kahn and B. Bruce-Briggs, *Things to Come* (New York, Macmillan, 1972).

H. Kahn, "Things are going rather well", *The Futurist*, December 1975, IX (6), pages 290–292.

H. Kahn, W. Brown, and L. Martel, *The Next 200 Years* (New York, Morrow, 1976; London, Associated Business Programmes, 1977).

Y. Kaya *et al*, *On the Future Japan and the World—A Model Approach* (Japan Techno-Economics Society, 1973).

Y. Kaya and Y. Suzuki, "Global constraints and a new vision for development", *Technological Forecasting and Social Change*, May and July 1974, 6 (3 and 4).

V. Kosolapov, *Mankind and the Year 2000* (Moscow, Progress Publishers, 1976).

W. Leontief *et al*, *The Future of the World Economy* (Oxford, Oxford University Press, 1977).

D. Meadows *et al*, *The Limits to Growth* (New York, Universe Books, 1972).

M. Mesarovic and E. Pestel, *Mankind at the Turning Point* (New York, Dutton/Readers Digest Press, 1974).

M. Mesarovic and E. Pestel, "Multilevel world model project", IIASA, Schloss Laxenburg 2361, Austria (mimeo), 1974.

Y. Modrzhinskaya and C. Stephanyan, *The Future of Society* (Moscow, Progress Publishers, 1973).

E. Schumacher, *Small is Beautiful: A Study of Economics as if People Mattered* (New York, Harper and Row, 1973).

E. Schumacher, "Economics should begin with people not goods", *The Futurist*, December 1974, *VIII* (6).

J. Spengler, "The population question", *American Economic Review*, March 1966.

J. Spengler, *Population Change, Modernisation, and Welfare* (New Jersey, Prentice Hall, 1974).

J. Tinbergen, *Reshaping the International Order: A Report to the Club of Rome* (New York, Dutton, 1976).

THE TWO VISIONS OF POST-INDUSTRIAL SOCIETY

Michael Marien

The author discusses and contrasts two different usages of the phrase "post-industrial society". The independent development of these two usages has culminated in the present distinction between post-industrial society as a technological, affluent, service society, and post-industrial society as a more decentralised and ecologically conscious agrarian society. This new global version of the old Jefferson–Hamilton debate—a political continuum best viewed at right angles to the familiar left–right political spectrum —may become the dominant political struggle of our time. A useful synthesis of the two visions is possible, though, if our intellectual segregation, exemplified by the two visions, can be overcome.

NEARLY two decades ago, the British novelist and essayist, C. P. Snow, gave a famous lecture entitled *The Two Cultures and the Scientific Revolution*. His central lament was that "the intellectual life of the whole of Western society is increasingly being split into two polar groups",[1] most readily represented by literary intellectuals and physical scientists. Snow asserted that each has a distorted image of the other, and this loss of a common culture makes it "difficult or impossible for us to take good action".[2] This paper will attempt to demonstrate the truth of Snow's statement, while tentatively pointing to some possibilities for "good action".

Snow, however, considered two representative poles of academic life, each preoccupied with very dissimilar subject matter. I would like to consider the two representative poles on a single subject: the condition of highly developed —or overdeveloped—societies. (The choice of adjectives is a critical one, hinting at the points of difference which will be explored here.)

The variety of views on where our society is and where it is headed is remarkable, and no doubt overwhelming to those who have been content to develop their societal image within the confines of a single discipline or ideology. My recent survey of the literature, *Societal Directions and Alternatives*,[3] documents more than 1000 books and articles published this century. Many of the

The author is Director of Information for Policy Design, LaFayette, New York 13084, USA.

authors identified in this guidebook use some title for our society or era, and an examination of these labels can serve as a convenient introduction to the basic questions about our society. The guidebook identifies a total of 350 titles for modern societies—and there are certainly more that could be identified, as well as continual additions from new books and articles.

The identified titles are categorised in three indexes: titles for our present society, titles of evolutionary stage theories describing our present social transition, and titles for desired societies—what our society ought to be and can be. For example, our present condition is described by Michael Harrington as "the accidental century", by French sociologist Michel Crozier as "the stalled society", by Hazel Henderson as "the entropy state", and by Donald Michael as "the unprepared society". The next social stage that we are evolving to has been described by Kenneth Boulding as "post-civilised society", by Margaret Mead as "pre-figurative culture", by Lewis Mumford as "the age of equilibrium", and by Charles Reich as "consciousness III".

Candidates for the desirable society that we could attain (utopias no longer being a viable form of social criticism and prescription) include Ralf Dahrendorf's very modest vision of "the improving society", Dennis Gabor's "mature society", Lester Brown's "world without borders", Erich Fromm's "sane society", and Amitai Etzioni's "active society". I have previously referred to this cacophonous collection as "The banners of Babel",[4] for it is noteworthy how each observer/advocate promulgates his or her unique title with little or no reference to competing ideas.

But I agree with Snow in answer to his critics that there is an "excessive unsimplicity" to "the two thousand and two cultures school of thought".[5] Among all of these titles, there is one that clearly emerges as the frontrunner in usage: the "post-industrial society" notion widely attributed to Daniel Bell. However, there are two completely different modes of usage: "post-industrial society" as a technological, affluent, service society, and "post-industrial society" as a decentralised agrarian economy following in the wake of a failed industrialism.

The first and better-known meaning of "post-industrialism" is the vision of the future that is held by the most respectable social scientists, and, not unimportantly, it serves as the ideology of the established order.[6] This article will provide a short history of the concept beyond that offered by Bell in *The Coming of Post-Industrial Society*. A brief history will also be provided of the antithetical view, which is reappearing in this decade with notable force. These two visions of post-industrial society may very well be the poles of the dominant ideological debate in forthcoming decades.

Snow warned that the number "two" is a dangerous number, and that "attempts to divide anything into two ought to be regarded with much suspicion".[7] This point is well-taken, but an equal amount of suspicion should be directed to any single vision of what our future will be, "post-industrial" or otherwise.

Post-industrial society as a service society

Daniel Bell acknowledges Arthur J. Penty, a British guild socialist, as the first writer to use the post-industrial label in a 1917 book, *Old Worlds for New:*

A Study of the Post-Industrial State.[8] But a few additional words, at least, can be added to this history. Penty published a book in 1922 entitled *Post-Industrialism*, in which he credits the term to Ananda K. Coomaraswamy, a British-educated Indian who was influenced by Ruskin and who later became a well-known expert in Eastern art at the Boston Museum of Fine Arts.

The earliest reference to post-industrialism that I have been able to find is in an advertisement for an anthology, *Essays in Post-Industrialism* edited by Coomaraswamy and Penty, that appeared in the end pages of a 1913 edition of Hilaire Belloc's *The Servile State*.[9] However, I have been unable to find any evidence that this book was ever published. In any event, Penty's definition of post-industrialism—"the state of society that will follow the break-up of Industrialism, and might therefore be used to cover the speculations of all who recognize Industrialism is doomed"[10]—is not the one that is normally used today. As we all know, Penty was wrong . . . or was premature by half a century.

The conventional usage of post-industrialism is to designate a shift in the occupational structure, so that the majority of the labour force is engaged in services. A pre-industrial society is characterised by agriculture as the dominant economic activity; industrial society or industrialism (a term introduced by Carlyle in the 1830s)[11] is characterised by mechanical production and the manufacture of goods; in a post-industrial society, there is affluence and leisure and the majority of the labour force is engaged in services such as government, health care, education, entertainment, and sales.

According to Bell, his first use of "post-industrialism" was at the Salzburg Seminar in 1959, and the first publication (without his permission) was in 1962. Official statements from Bell appeared in 1967,[12] culminating in the publication of *The Coming of Post-Industrial Society* in 1973. Bell deserves credit for being the first writer to use the post-industrial label to describe a service society, and for writing the greatest number of words in its behalf. But he is far from being the first person to describe the service society as the next stage of societal evolution.

Service-sector growth

There were many early intimations of a change in social structure beyond that of an industrial society. In 1882, for example, Herbert Spencer cautiously offered a "parenthetical suggestion" of a future type of society with a fully-developed sustaining system devoted to the carrying on of higher activities: "the multiplication of institutions and appliances for intellectual and aesthetic culture and for kindred activities not of a directly life-sustaining kind".[13]

In 1899, Thorstein Veblen examined "the leisure class" engaged in non-industrial occupations such as government, warfare, religious observances, and sports.[14] In 1901 Charles A. Conant, having noted the increase in public expenditure and arguing that "increased social wealth permits additions to the office-holding and professional classes",[15] predicted that this modern social development would open new means of comfort and luxury to the mass of men. In 1920, R. H. Tawney devoted an entire chapter of his famous essay on *The Acquisitive Society* to "The Position of the Brain Worker", a "new class of officials" almost unknown fifty years ago.[16] In contrast to Conant's cheerful optimism, Tawney foresaw the growth of an intellectual proletariat resulting

from the concentration of business, the spread of organisation, and the application of science to industry.

Two prominent American social thinkers both identified, in 1934, the shift
to services. Stuart Chase, in advocating a further evolution to *The Economy of
Abundance*, noted that "While industrial and agricultural labor will steadily
decline, we may expect a great increase in service occupations . . ."[17] and that
this is necessary to allow the powers of abundance to function freely on our
behalf. George Soule noted that as capitalism and mechanical civilisation
advances, "There develops a new class of employees—those engaged in professional and service occupations. They show signs of outnumbering in the not-
distant future those engaged in production of actual physical goods".[18] To
solidify this argument with data, Colin Clark provided an extensive cross-
national analysis of "The flow of labor to tertiary production" in 1940.[19]

Characterisation of a service state
The first writer to use the title of "the service state" was a British economist,
Roy Glenday, in 1944. In his view, the industrial age was drawing to a close:
"The immediate future of countries destined to continue to advance would
seem to lie with what I have broadly termed 'services'".[20] Glenday continued
with long-term speculations about Britain, envisaging it as an organising
point for new types of leisure services like tourism, science, and culture. And he
also raised a number of questions which have become important current
concerns—population and environment, problems of appropriate scale, the
need for greater attention to the agricultural sector, and "the irresistible logic
of technical evolution which is driving the world to build ever-larger productive
units, and to impose an ever-increasing caste-like bureaucracy".[21]

The first American to employ a "service state" label was the distinguished
jurist, and Dean of the Harvard Law School, Roscoe Pound, who warned in a
1949 address that the service state—his term for the welfare state—has been
creeping up on us in the present century. It "takes the whole domain of human
welfare for its province and would solve all economic and social ills through its
administrative activities". Furthermore, "it is characteristic of the service state
to make lavish promises of satisfying desires which it calls rights".[22]

This conservative caution is the polar opposite of Galbraith's pronouncements
on *The Affluent Society*, made nearly a decade later in 1958, where scarcity
economics was announced as obsolete, and the "New Class" of well-educated
people who enjoy their occupations was identified, extolled, and encouraged
to expand as a design for progress: as "investment in human as distinct from
material capital".[23] In 1960, W. W. Rostow published his well-known theory
on *The Stages of Economic Growth*, with its view of the USA, in "the era of high
mass consumption", moving towards an abundant era "beyond consumption".[24] Also in 1960, Stuart Chase reappeared, announcing that more than
half of the labour force was in the tertiary trades, and that we were moving
from "era three, the economy of abundance" to "era four, a time to live".[25]
This announcement was followed in 1965 by the official findings of Victor
Fuchs and the National Bureau of Economic Research that "We are now a
'service economy'".[26]

Considerably more attention was paid to the nature of the social transition in the late 1960s, perhaps sparked by the Commission on the Year 2000, formed in 1965 and chaired by Daniel Bell. The working groups of the Commission, according to Bell, "take as predicate the assumption that the United States is becoming a post-industrial society . . .".[27] One of the great classics of future studies, *The Year 2000*, by Herman Kahn and Anthony Wiener, served as a conceptual baseline for the Commission; it included a chapter on "Postindustrial society in the standard world", and also discussed the concept of the "basic, long-term multifold trend", a mainstay of this and subsequent volumes from the Hudson Institute.

Post-industrial society as a technological, affluent, service society was widely used in 1968. For example, sociologist William Faunce, without any reference to Bell or the Commission on the Year 2000, used the term to designate a transition to automation.[28] A 1968 Delphi survey among corporate executives and liberal professors, conducted by the National Industrial Conference Board, concluded that the US was in a period of major transition to a post-industrial society.[29] And a 1968 seminar at Princeton, bringing together "the world's leading social scientists", devoted one of the four sections of its proceedings to examining post-industrial society.[30]

Semantic and analytical alternatives
Other generally interchangeable labels were proposed in the late 1960s and early 1970s. Zbigniew Brzezinski, now foreign affairs adviser to President Carter, wrote of the emergence of "technetronic society" in 1967, and elaborated on this notion in his 1970 book, *Between Two Ages*.[31] Peter F. Drucker's 1969 book, *The Age of Discontinuity*, stressed society's increasing reliance on knowledge and information, and predicted that the knowledge industries would account for half the US national product in the late 1970s.[32] Alvin Toffler's 1970 best-seller, *Future Shock*,[33] suggested "super-industrialism" as a more appropriate term than post-industrialism; in 1971, sociologist Paul Meadows argued that "neo-industrialism" was a more accurate label to describe the transition from mechanisation to cybernation.[34] In 1972, political scientist Heinz Eulau offered the "consultative commonwealth" as a "more persuasive" construct of the future for its suggestion that the human services would be technologised, but not ruled by technologists.[35] In a 1974 address, sociologist Frederick L. Bates explained the transition from the unmanaged *laissez-faire* society to a managed global society.[36] Alan Gartner and Frank Riessman described two developmental continua: the transition from industry to services, and from capitalism to some form of socialism. They expressed indecision about whether to call the emerging society a service society or a consumer society.[37] Sociologists Carl Gersuny and Rosengren did not hesitate to call their book *The Service Society*.[38]

Despite these challenges, post-industrial society appears to persist as the favoured title for the vision of an emerging service society, perhaps because it is so vague and innocuous, unlike Brzezinski's jarring and explicit "technetronic society". The quasi-official adaptation of the phrase is suggested by the December 1976 report of the Advisory Committee on National Growth Policy Processes, which announced a "post-industrial revolution" whereby two-thirds of the nation's manpower would be concentrated in services by 1980.[39]

The most long-range and most optimistic statement about post-industrialism came in 1976 from Herman Kahn, William Brown and Leon Martel of the Hudson Institute, who saw us in a superindustrial economy moving toward a truly post-industrial society in the distant future:

At the midway mark in the 400-year period we have just seen in the most advanced countries the initial emergence of superindustrial economies (where enterprises are extraordinarily large, encompassing and pervasive forces in both the physical and societal environments), to be followed soon by postindustrial economies (where the task of producing the necessities of life has become trivially easy because of technological advancement and economic development.) We expect that almost all countries will develop the characteristic of super- and postindustrial societies.[40]

Moreover, the Hudson Institute forecasted a topping out of world population growth over the next 200 years at 15 billion "give or take a factor of two (that is, a range of 7·5 to 30 billion)", and a per capita product of $20 000, give or take a factor of three. This "guardedly optimistic" technology-and-growth position was contrasted to the pessimism of the neo-Malthusians, "the limits-to-growth position which creates low morale, destroys assurance, undermines the legitimacy of governments everywhere, erodes personal and group commitment to constructive activities and encourages obstructiveness to reasonable policies and hopes".[41]

Philosophical unity
The remarkable fact about all these views of the emerging service society is that, like it or not, there is no question about the direction of evolution. With the exception of the 1976 book by Kahn *et al*, not a single author considered the possibility of limited natural resources. Even the critics of the technological service society—notably Glenday in 1944 and Pound in 1949—conceded that it is an inexorable development. Jacques Ellul published his scathing critique *The Technological Society* in 1954,[42] while his fellow countryman, Jean Meynaud, warned of the expansion of technocracy in 1964.[43] In 1971, Bertram M. Gross envisioned the grand alternatives of the emerging service society as "techno-urban fascism" (also described as "friendly fascism") or "humanist reconstruction", and the outlines of a truly civilised "post-service society" were sketched, where the bulk of the employed population would be involved in non-routine informational activities.[44] Also in 1971, historian W. Warren Wagar, in a consciously utopographic exercise in response to the "totalizing crisis" of world civilisation, outlined a post-industrial world civilisation which would also be to a large extent a post-economic civilisation, a generally socialist and essentially classless society, with an "expansion and improvement of services of every kind".[45] Christopher Lasch also took a socialist stance, admitting that scarcity is no longer a problem under the capitalist industrial system of post-industrial society, and that all basic human needs are satisfied.[46]

In sum, the most widely employed vision of our general future has been promulgated by many social scientists throughout this century. Although Daniel Bell is associated with the post-industrial concept, there are many others who can share credit or blame for advancing the notion (only a few of whom are acknowledged by Bell). In some instances, such as Chase's *Economy of Abundance* in 1934 and the Hudson Institute's "technology-and-growth" vision in 1976, there is forthright advocacy and approval. In most instances, the expression of this vision has been in neutral and passive tones, with any overt expression of values overshadowed by the sense of inexorable development, for better or worse. Even critics such as Ellul and Meynaud, who fear the coming technological society, are still resigned to this direction of evolution.

The notable attribute of the other vision of post-industrial society is that it is not resigned to this extrapolation as either viable or desirable. Indeed, the other vision describes and prescribes an opposite course of development.

Post-industrial society as decentralisation

The less-recognised vision of post-industrial society is critical of industrialism in both capitalist and socialist forms, advocating a more decentralised and agrarian society. Invidious descriptions of advocates of this position include traditionalist, romantic, Luddite, irrationalist, anarchist, Malthusian, and pessimist. More positive labels as used by the advocates themselves have included decentralist, distributist, agrarian, populist, Jeffersonian democrat, anarchist socialist, guild socialist, and minarchist.

Whatever the label, I feel strongly that this view, diametrically opposed to that of an emerging service society, has never been given a fair hearing. There are many reasons for the obscurity of this vision, some of which will be subsequently discussed, but the major reason may very well be the "flat earth" view of political taxonomy that has characterised our assessment of ideologies, at least throughout this century. We have all been conditioned to array socio-economic preferences along a left–right, liberal–conservative (or radical–liberal–conservative) political axis. And it is certainly true that much of the debate in this century has been along this axis, between labour and capital, and between government control and *laissez-faire*.

But there is another axis which was dominant long ago in the USA in, for example, the debate between Jefferson and Hamilton as to whether we should have an essentially agrarian society, with minimal government, or a managed society that would encourage commercial enterprise.[47] This axis is best understood as a separate continuum at right angles to the conventional left–right continuum.[48] It is contended here that the Jefferson–Hamilton debate is reappearing with a global relevance and may well be the dominant political debate of our time.

It is difficult to recognise this, however, because we are conditioned (among many influences, by sociological questionnaires) to view political opinions and our political selves as left, right, or centre. But there have been some strange developments recently: we can no longer readily categorise some US political leaders, such as Governor Jerry Brown of California; political decisions taken in the name of environmental preservation, by those apparently on the progressive left, are often in fact reactionary; business leaders who were once characterised as reactionaries are now the leading advocates of progress or growth. Our present paradigm for the political world simply cannot explain the coalition of six Reaganite Republicans and six eco-activist Democrats into the recently formed Decentralist League of Vermont.[49]

The decentralist vision should not be confused with the "growth–no growth" debate that has surfaced in recent years. Among futurists, this division might be called "The Herman–Harman debate" in that Herman Kahn and Willis Harman are major figures.[50] Kahn pictures Harman as a neo-Malthusian, while Harman describes his perspective as "transformational", advocating frugal technology, a changing social contract for corporations, a redefinition of growth in less economic and material terms, and more emphasis on social innovation.[51] But Harman does not deal with basic questions about where we live and how we will satisfy our basic needs, nor do many of the other limits-to-growth thinkers. The contrast between the liberal, no-growth position and the decentralist position is exemplified by a comparison of *The Limits to Growth* volume,[52] sponsored by the Club of Rome, with *A Blueprint for Survival*, issued at virtually the same time in 1972 by a British group associated with *The Ecologist* magazine. The former advocated a state of global equilibrium, shifting economic preferences of society toward more services, while the latter attacks the industrial way of life itself and advocates decentralisation of polity and economy at all levels.

Harman asserts that "almost all forecasts currently advanced by practising futurists lie in one of two groups",[53] essentially, the basic long-term multifold trend of the Hudson Institute, and a "bend" in this trend—a transformation into something different. Such a conceptualisation limits the terms of debate, for decentralists do not advocate a "bend" in the course of direction of social development, but, in certain respects, a 180° reversal. Either Harman does not recognise this distinction or, possibly, those persons who are "practising futurists" do not include any decentralists. Do decentralists have anything of value to contribute, either to help dispassionate forecasts of what might happen, or to add to the consideration of what constitutes the good society? I contend that they do, and, to paraphrase C. P. Snow, that the absence of any understanding of their position makes it "difficult or impossible for us to take good action".

The historical sources

An understanding of the modern decentralist position could profitably begin with *The Servile State*, published in 1912, by Hilaire Belloc. This still provides a basic theoretical foundation, arguing that capitalism is unstable and the line of least resistance for reformers is the collectivist solution, or socialism, which inadvertently leads to the servile state. "Collectivism promises employment to the great masses who think of production only in terms of employment".[54] The more difficult but rewarding path of reform, according to Belloc, would be to distribute property and restore the free society of the Middle Ages, or "the distributive state". Arthur J. Penty's *Old Worlds for New: A Study of the Post-Industrial State* was influenced by Belloc, and it provides a valuable chapter that contrasts the leisure state and the work state, arguing that the former vision (essentially that of Kahn's "post-industrial" society) is an "utterly impossible dream so far as the majority are concerned".[55] Another leading thinker in British distributist thinking was the renowned essayist, G. K. Chesterton, whose sympathies are best expressed in *The Outline of Sanity* (1927), which asserts that "the cure for centralisation is decentralisation",[56] and that to stake everything on the state's justice is to put all the eggs in one basket.

Shortly before the onset of the great depression, a nonacademic American economist, Ralph Borsodi, published *This Ugly Civilization*,[57] a prophetic work which argued in great detail that true organic homesteads organised to function biologically, socially, and economically, could enable a material well-being equal to that which we now enjoy, with less unpleasant effort and greater security—essentially the message promulgated today in *The Mother Earth News* and *Organic Gardening and Farming*, the two leading popular decentralist periodicals.

In 1930, twelve Southern men of letters published a famous anthology entitled *I'll Take My Stand*,[58] which argued against industrialism and defended an agrarian society. In 1935, historian Herbert Agar's *Land of the Free*[59] stated that we must choose between the true American culture of self-government, equality, and freedom, and a Hamiltonian plutocracy. Along with Allen Tate, Agar issued an important anthology in 1936 entitled *Who Owns America? A New Declaration of Independence*,[60] which attacked both capitalism and socialism, and advocated an American form of distributism. Many of the leading decentralist intellectuals, notably Agar and Borsodi, came together in the 1937–1947 period to publish a monthly journal, *Free America*, which offered many eloquent statements of the decentralist position that could still be relevant today.

This brief history of pre-World War 2 decentralist thinking touches on only some of the major documents. Except for occasional references to soil depletion, there was no mention of environmental or resource problems; the decentralist argument was essentially confined to the concern of maintaining human scale. There is no evidence, to my knowledge, that this argument ever entered into the consciousness of any social scientist. Perhaps, viewed on the left–right spectrum, it was dismissed as right-wing. Or, more probably, it was a tiny voice, never heard at all. In any event, after World War 2, when the market economy flourished and there was little thought of basic alternatives, decentralist thinking virtually disappeared.

Resurgence and reappearance
An explicit home for decentralist thought reappeared in a British bimonthly, *Resurgence*, which began publication in 1966 and is notable for having regularly published the essays of E. F. Schumacher. In 1969, *Resurgence* added a subtitle, "Journal of the Fourth World", defined as "the world of decentralized, small-scale forms of organization, structured organically rather than mechanically and directed towards the fulfilment of human values rather than materialist objectives". Today there are more than a dozen decentralist periodicals (not including right decentralist or libertarian periodicals, which are closely related), but none adhere to a formal academic style.

Theodore Roszak, widely known for his earlier work, *The Making of a Counter Culture*, published in 1972 a work entitled *Where the Wasteland Ends: Politics and Transcendence in Postindustrial Society*. This extensive—but neglected—analysis argued that urban industrialism had reached a dead end. Roszak maintained that the fate of the soul was at stake: "Only those of us who have reached the horizon of the technocratic society are ready for that postindustrial society".[61]

Ivan Illich, who had already made a big stir in 1970 by attacking the growth of schooling in society, argued in his 1973 *Tools for Conviviality* that tools were basic for participatory justice and that the present structure of tools must be inverted to form a "convivial" or "postindustrial" society.[62] A similar argument was made in 1970 by Paul Goodman on the need for technological simplification,[63] and in 1974 by Robert Heilbroner who advocated abandoning the techniques and lifeways of industrial civilisation and aiming toward a "post-industrial society" of parsimonious attitudes to production and consumption.[64] Also in 1974, *The Ecologist*, a British periodical first issued in 1970, added a subtitle: *Journal of Postindustrial Society*.

In the preface to his 1976 anthology on *Radical Agriculture*, Richard Merrill proposes farmlands for "small growers and postindustrial communities".[65] Nor is the vision of decentralisation confined to capitalist countries, for a recent book of essays by Alexander Solzhenitsyn and six dissidents still living in the Soviet Union harshly criticises contemporary socio-economic systems, both capitalist and socialist, as well as "the arrogant insensitivity of the modern trend in the social sciences".[66]

Two major developments have been overlooked by the observers/advocates of the service society, but eagerly underscored by decentralists. The first development is the relative growth of population in non-metropolitan areas in the early 1970s. This "new ruralism", hailed by William N. Ellis as "the tool of the post-industrial age",[67] clearly represents a check in the continued trend towards urbanisation which had been widely—and confidently—predicted in earlier years. The second development is perhaps of even greater significance: the growth of the household economy relative to the market economy. As described by neo-Borsodian economist Scott Burns, the transition from a "maturing industrial" society to a "post-industrial" society involves "the inevitable maturation and decline of the market economy", with the household revitalised as a powerful and productive unit.

It must be acknowledged that the conventions of economic and social measurement developed in advanced industrial societies tacitly serve the interests of large institutions by omitting the household as a productive unit. Yet, from three separate studies, Burns estimated that "the value of household labour amounts to nearly a third of the gross national product and about one half of disposable consumer income",[68] and he concludes that the market economy "will account for no more than 50% of our economic activity by the end of the century",[69] and will perhaps be as low as 25%. This is clearly a biased forecast, but not more biased than the Hudson Institute's forecast of post-industrial affluence, 200 years hence.

A major problem of the service society or welfare state notion is that little or no attention is given to the proper balance between dependence and independence, under conditions of either scarcity or affluence. It has simply been assumed that the only possible and desirable direction for the evolution of society is towards an ever-growing portion of the labour force engaged in providing services to consumers, and that the producer-consumer is obsolete. This may still be the path of social evolution, but it may be possible that we have reached a peak in the growth of services, and that in fact the post-industrial era will be characterised by a new balance between large-scale industrialised modes of production—of goods and services—and small-scale household production. If the pattern of social change is seen as an evolutionary spiral or pendulum—instead of an arrow, or an S-curve—then those who are dedicated to the observation, with a reasonable degree of objectivity, of human affairs, will have to develop a more sophisticated set of conceptual tools.

The two visions contrasted

At this point, it is useful to summarise some of the key differences between the two visions of post-industrial society, keeping in mind that the liberal "limits-to-growth" position lies somewhere in between, employing much of the ecological, post-materialist rhetoric of the decentralists while maintaining the assumptions of the service society.

- *Who holds what position?* Advocates of the service society are virtually all social scientists (particularly those who are successful in conventional terms), and a few Marxist historians and social reformers. Those favouring decentralisation often have an intellectual background in the humanities, although, increasingly, they are joined by ecologists. There are no survey data, but there would probably be little correlation with social class and income, and a strong correlation with location in urban or rural areas and with the degree of affiliation with large institutions.
- *Methods employed.* Service society advocates promulgate their views as objective forecasts and often use various quantitative methodologies; decentralists speak openly of their values and stress "alternatives" or "alternative futures".
- *Key concepts.* Service society advocates claim general progress in recent years involving more affluence, leisure, urbanisation, state intervention, effective use of intellectual technology, and growth of the new class of professional elites. Decentralists regard further industrialism as unworkable, GNP as an obsolete and misleading measure, the economy as on the brink of collapse, state intervention as inept or onerous, technocrats as ignorant of the real world, and self-sufficiency as the good life.
- *Attitude toward technology.* Service society advocates view technological growth as inevitable; if it has caused problems, only new technology can solve them, and technology assessment can prohibit or restrict undesirable developments. Decentralists hail intermediate, small, appropriate or convivial technologies which cost less and can be used and understood by most people.
- *Ultimate future.* Service society advocates see the inevitability of bureaucracy, growing interdependence in the national and global community, and the impossibility of returning to a more agrarian society. Decentralists stress self-help and independence in small local communities, and the necessity and desirability of returning, to some degree, to an agrarian life.
- *View of opposing position.* Service society advocates ignore decentralists or see them as nihilistic, romantic, anti-science, anti-progress, ineffective, utopian, and moralistic. Decentralists view their opponents as amoral technocrats, elitist experts, reductionists, middle-class welfare careerists, and the tools of big government, big business, and big labour.

In an unguarded moment, Alvin Toffler described the contrast as "people of the future" versus "people of the present" and "people of the past".[70] On the other side, E. F. Schumacher distinguishes between "people of the forward stampede" and "the homecomers" who seek "to return to certain basic truths about man and his world".[71] *The Mother Earth News* hints at an even simpler pair of labels: the difference between "Playboy" and "Plowboy".[72]

There is little problem in viewing the decentralist or eco-agrarian view as an ideology, a system of beliefs, or, as described by Daniel Bell, a "secular religion".[73] But Bell's definition of ideology insists that it must be accompanied by passion, a definition that comfortably shields the covert ideology of the proponents of the scientific service society.

The ideological bias of the post-industrial service society view is exposed by three French critics, in a 1976 essay in *Futuribles*, who argue that the notion is a naive and optimistic vision of progress favouring the American way of life.[74] In an earlier book, Benjamin Kleinberg argued that such thinking is technocratic social theory.[75]

A careful reading of Bell's cumbersome opus, *The Coming of Post-Industrial Society: A Venture in Social Forecasting* (which is more accurately seen as a venture in welfare-state ideology), will reveal a great number of statements that promote science, technology, and professionalism in their present forms. For example, the emerging ethos of post-industrial society is seen as the ethos of science;[76] the technocratic mode is seen as the mode of efficiency—of getting things done;[77] it is predicted that there will be more social-mindedness in the professions;[78] and the norms of professionalism are described as the norms of the new intelligentsia, departing from the prevailing norms of economic self-interest.[79]

Professionalism flourishes in a welfare state of abundant services, and new concepts of property prevail, the most pervasive manifestation being a new definition of social rights, as claims on the community to ensure equality of treatment (the most important right being that of full access to education).[80] Bell sees the politics of the future as a concern of the communal society;[81] the argument advanced in the present article is that the predominant characteristic of the politics of the future will be the conflict of views surrounding the very notion of a communal society.

Finally, Bell fires a broadside at the non-scientists:

> In the social structure of the knowledge society, there is, for example, the deep and growing split between the technical intelligentsia who are committed to functional rationality and technocratic modes of operation, and the literary intellectuals, who have become increasingly apocalyptic, hedonistic, and nihilistic.[82]

This division is no doubt aggravated by such a characterisation, and by the recurring tacit suggestion that the knowledge of science and technology is the only knowledge that matters.

The future of the two visions

At present, the vision of the service society is still the dominant vision of post-industrial society.[83] But it has been severely weakened in this decade by the environmental crisis, the energy crisis, and the economic recession. The threats of pollution have added new and unexpected costs to the production of food and material goods, aiding the arguments of those who advocate organic agriculture. The energy crisis has made us deeply aware of our finite resources and has also supported the argument for less wasteful methods of production. Finally, the unanticipated economic difficulties have made expansion of the service sector far more difficult, at least for the near future.

If the energy crisis is effectively solved by the emergence of some low-cost technology or technologies, the sense of unbounded affluence might return; there would then be ample wealth for expanding the service sector. But continuing economic difficulties would favour decentralisation and the promulgation of a greater degree of self-sufficiency.

Apart from the fortunes of the economy, another major factor in the future of decentralisation is the ineffectiveness of the decentralists in presenting their arguments. The advocates of a service society have a strong political voice, and are well established in the academic world and in think-tanks, which are seen as the key institutions of the projected society. Advocates of the decentralist view, on the other hand, tend to be involved in small organisations, not, appropriately enough, in large institutions.

The result in the USA is an unequal contest between institutional Goliaths with short names, like Brookings, Harvard, Rand, and the Urban Institute, and little Davids with long names, such as the Institute for Liberty and Community, the International Independence Institute, the Institute for Self-Reliance, and the Princeton Center for Alternative Futures. Moreover, many decentralists are apolitical, tending to work in their gardens or to organise do-it-yourself co-ops, rather than to press their demands on government or engage in policy debates. Indeed, for anyone who regards government assistance as inept or corrupting, it would be inappropriate to do so. And in that many decentralists lack the credentials and conceptual tools to debate with the technocratic elites, they are excluded from, and/or exclude themselves from, serious discussions of economic and social policy. Finally, the decentralist argument tends to be excessively romantic, with back-to-the-earth visions of the independent good life or communal experimentation proposed as the solution to many of our urban ills. The visions of the service society, however, are seldom seen as romantic because they are issued by experts, in a reasonably sober style.

Despite these severe handicaps, the decentralist position in the 1970s is gaining strength. The major battleground in the near future may well be in agriculture, where the reigning forces of high-technology, capital-intensive, chemical agriculture may be effectively challenged by the eco-agrarian forces, which advocate small-scale organic agriculture—to conserve energy, produce more wholesome food, reinvigorate rural communities, and provide jobs.[84]

The question of employment is critical. The proponents of the service society have ignored agriculture, and encouraged, in the name of humane progress, the shift of employment away from the agricultural sector. But the unemployment problem persists in contemporary society, and full employment theory—handed down by the economists—remains in the rut of considering only jobs in industry and in services; it ignores the possibilities offered by full and part-time self-employment, and by self-sufficiency. In the USA, less than 4% of the labour force was in agriculture in 1977, and the Bureau of Labor Statistics projects less than 2% in agriculture by 1985. But there is no reason why a service society could not have 10% or perhaps even 20% of the labour force in agriculture (calculated on a full-time equivalent basis). It would still be a service society, where the majority of the labour force would be engaged in services, but a very different notion of the service society from that which has been held in pre-scarcity days. Such a society would be a synthesis of the two visions of post-industrial society, and a prime example of the "good action" hinted at by C. P. Snow—if the two cultures were to come together. The two cultures and the two visions described here are somewhat different from the academic cultures described by Snow, but they share the urgent need for a dialogue. Indeed, at least in the literature surveyed here, *there is no evidence that any writer holding either of the two visions of post-industrial society has any appreciable understanding of the opposing vision.* This intellectual segregation begs for some sort of institution, such as the continuously operating surmising forum proposed by Bertrand de Jouvenel,[85] which would force productive debate between opposing positions.

There is an additional question about public preferences. In an age when there is much talk about participation, it is notable that no opinion poll has ever consulted the public about the choice between two, basically alternative, futures. Perhaps it has been assumed that there is no basic choice—that the service society is both inevitable and desirable. Rather than asking about satisfactions and dissatisfactions, or hopes and fears, it would be most instructive and democratic to ask the public which of the two visions of post-industrial society they prefer.

Notes and references

1. Sir Charles Percy Snow, *The Two Cultures and the Scientific Revolution* (New York, Cambridge University Press, 1960), page 3.
2. Sir Charles Percy Snow, *The Two Cultures: And a Second Look* (New York, Cambridge University Press, 1965), page 60.
3. Michael Marien, *Societal Directions and Alternatives: A Critical Guide to the Literature* (LaFayette, New York, Information for Policy Design, 1976).
4. Michael Marien, "The banners of Babel," *Social Policy*, 5 (5), Jan/Feb 1975.
5. Snow, *The Two Cultures: And a Second Look*, page 66.
6. Harold Lasswell, *Politics: Who Gets What, When, How* (McGraw-Hill, 1936; Meridian Books, 1968), page 31.
7. Snow, *The Two Cultures: And a Second Look*, page 65.
8. Daniel Bell, *The Coming of Post-Industrial Society: A Venture in Social Forecasting* (New York, Basic Books, 1973), page 39; A. J. Penty, *Old Worlds for New* (London, George Allen and Unwin, 1917).
9. Hilaire Belloc, *The Servile State* (Boston, LeRoy Phillips, 1913). LeRoy Phillips was the purported publisher for the anthology by Coomaraswamy and Penty.
10. Arthur J. Penty, *Post-Industrialism*, preface by G. K. Chesterton (London, George Allen & Unwin, 1922), page 14.
11. Raymond Williams, *Keywords: A Vocabulary of Culture and Society* (New York, Oxford University Press, 1976), page 137.
12. Daniel Bell, "Notes on the post-industrial society", *The Public Interest*, 6 (Winter 1967) and 7 (Spring 1967).
13. Herbert Spencer, *The Principles of Sociology*, volume 1 (New York, D. Appleton, 1882), page 596.
14. Thorstein Veblen, *The Theory of the Leisure Class* (New York, Macmillan, 1899).
15. Charles A. Conant, "The growth of public expenditure", *The Atlantic Monthly*, 87, January 1901, page 49.
16. R. H. Tawney, *The Acquisitive Society* (New York, Harcourt, Brace, 1920).

17. Stuart Chase, *The Economy of Abundance* (New York, Macmillan, 1934), page 315.
18. George Soule, *The Coming American Revolution* (New York, Macmillan, 1934), page 148.
19. Colin Clark, *The Conditions of Economic Progress* (London, Macmillan, 1940), pages 176–219.
20. Roy Glenday, *The Future of Economic Society* (London, Macmillan, 1944), page 242.
21. *Ibid*, page 247.
22. Roscoe Pound, "The rise of the service state and its consequences", in Sheldon Glueck, ed, *The Welfare State and National Welfare: A Symposium on Some of the Threatening Tendencies of our Time* (Cambridge, Mass, Addison-Wesley, 1952), pages 211 and 215.
23. John Kenneth Galbraith, *The Affluent Society* (Boston, Houghton Mifflin, 1958), page 268.
24. W. W. Rostow, *The Stages of Economic Growth: A Non-Communist Manifesto* (New York, Cambridge University Press, 1960).
25. Stuart Chase, *Live and Let Live: A Program for Americans* (New York, Harper, 1960).
26. Victor R. Fuchs, "The growing importance of the service industries", *The Journal of Business*, October 1965. This was later expanded into a book, *The Service Economy* (New York, National Bureau of Economic Research, 1968).
27. Herman Kahn and Anthony J. Wiener, *The Year 2000: A Framework for Speculation on the Next Thirty-Three Years*, introduction by Daniel Bell (New York, Macmillan, 1967), page xxvii.
28. William A. Faunce, *Problems of an Industrial Society* (New York, McGraw-Hill, 1968).
29. Dubois S. Morris, ed, *Perspectives for the '70s and '80s: Tomorrow's Problems Confronting Today's Management* (New York, National Industrial Conference Board, 1970). The Delphi survey approached 118 persons, of which 66 "distinguished experts" took part.
30. François Duchêne, ed, *The Endless Crisis: America in the Seventies* (New York, Simon and Schuster, 1970).
31. Zbigniew Brzezinski, "The American transition", *The New Republic*, 23 December 1967; *Between Two Ages: America's Role in the Technetronic Era* (New York, Viking, 1970).
32. Peter F. Drucker, *The Age of Discontinuity: Guidelines to Our Changing Society* (New York, Harper & Row, 1969).
33. Alvin Toffler, *Future Shock* (New York, Random House, 1970).
34. Paul Meadows, *The Many Faces of Change: Explorations in the Theory of Social Change* (Cambridge, Mass, Schenkman, 1971).
35. Heinz Eulau, "Skill revolution and consultative commonwealth", *American Political Science Review*, **67** (1), March, 1973.
36. Frederick L. Bates, "Alternative models for the future of society: from the invisible to the visible hand", *Social Forces*, **53** (1), September 1974.
37. Alan Gartner and Frank Riessman, *The Service Society and the Consumer Vanguard* (New York, Harper and Row, 1974).
38. Carl Gersuny and William R. Rosengren, *The Service Society* (Cambridge, Mass, Schenkman, 1973).
39. Advisory Committee on National Growth Policy Processes to the National Commission on Supplies and Shortages, *Forging America's Future: Strategies for National Growth and Development* (Washington, US Government Printing Office, December 1976).

40. Herman Kahn, William Brown and Leon Martel, *The Next 200 Years: A Scenario for America and the World* (New York, William Morrow, 1976), page 1.
41. *Ibid*, page 210.
42. Jacques Ellul, *The Technological Society* (New York, Knopf, 1964). First published in France in 1954.
43. Jean Meynaud, *Technocracy* (New York, Free Press, 1969). First published in France in 1964.
44. Bertram M. Gross, "Planning in an era of social revolution", *Public Administration Review*, *31* (2), May–June, 1971.
45. W. Warren Wagar, *Building the City of Man: Outlines of a World Civilization* (New York, Grossman, 1971).
46. Christopher Lasch, "Toward a theory of post-industrial society", in M. Donald Hancock and Gideon Sjoberg, eds, *Politics in the Post-Welfare State* (New York, Columbia University Press, 1972).
47. Albert Fried, ed, *The Jeffersonian and Hamiltonian Traditions in American Politics: A Documentary History* (New York, Doubleday Anchor, 1968).
48. James Robertson, *Power, Money & Sex: Towards a New Social Balance* (London, Marion Boyars, 1976), Figure 1, page 25.
49. Decentralist League of Vermont, "Statement of principles", 23 March 1977. Available from John McClaughry, Institute for Liberty and Community, Concord, Vermont 05824, USA.
50. See Andrew A. Spekke, ed, *The Next 25 Years: Crisis & Opportunity* (Washington, World Future Society, June 1975), for juxtaposed articles by Harman and Kahn.
51. Willis W. Harman, "The coming transformation", *The Futurist*, *9* (1), February 1977.
52. Donella H. Meadows *et al*, *The Limits to Growth: A Report for the Club of Rome's Project on the Predicament of Mankind* (New York, Universe Books, 1972). Edward Goldsmith *et al*, *A Blueprint for Survival* (Boston, Houghton Mifflin, 1972). The "Blueprint" included a statement of support by 37 leading scholars and scientists in Great Britain, but was never accorded even a fraction of the attention given to the Club of Rome report. The "Limits to Growth" argument, incidentally, was stated by a lawyer nearly twenty years earlier: Samuel H. Ordway Jr, *Resources and the American Dream: Including a Theory of the Limit of Growth* (New York, Ronald Press, 1953).
53. W. Harman, *op cit* (reference 51).
54. Hilaire Belloc, *The Servile State* (London, T. N. Foulis, 1912; Boston, LeRoy Phillips, 1913), page 112.
55. Arthur J. Penty, *Old Worlds for New: A Study of the Post-Industrial State* (London, George Allen and Unwin, 1917).
56. G. K. Chesterton, *The Outline of Sanity* (New York, Dodd, Mead, 1927), page 5.
57. Ralph Borsodi, *This Ugly Civilization* (New York, Simon and Schuster, 1929; second edition, with foreword by Harry Elmer Barnes, New York, Harper, 1933). Borsodi is best known for his popular *Flight From the City* (New York, Harper, 1933; Harper Colophon edition, 1972) which describes his personal homesteading experiences. Borsodi's *Prosperity and Security* (New York, Harper, 1938) offers a valuable foundation for a holistic economics that accounts for production in the household sector.
58. Twelve Southerners, *I'll Take My Stand: The South and the Agrarian Tradition* (New York, Harper, 1930; Torchback edition, 1962).
59. Herbert Agar, *Land of the Free* (Boston, Houghton Mifflin, 1935).
60. Herbert Agar and Allen Tate, eds, *Who Owns America? A New Declaration of*

Independence (Boston, Houghton Mifflin, 1936). Authors of the 21 essays included eight of the "Twelve Southerners".

61. Theodore Roszak, *Where the Wasteland Ends: Politics and Transcendence in Post-industrial Society* (New York, Doubleday, 1972), page xxii.
62. Ivan Illich, *Tools for Conviviality* (New York, Harper and Row, 1973).
63. Paul Goodman, *New Reformation: Notes of a Neolithic Conservative* (New York, Random House, 1970).
64. Robert L. Heilbroner, *An Inquiry Into the Human Prospect* (New York, Norton, 1974).
65. Richard Merrill, ed, *Radical Agriculture* (New York, Harper Colophon Books, 1976).
66. Alexander Solzhenitsyn, "Repentance and self-limitation in the life of nations", in Solzhenitsyn, ed, *From Under the Rubble* (Boston, Little Brown, 1975), page 106.
67. William N. Ellis, "The new ruralism: the post-industrial age is upon us", *The Futurist*, 9 (4), August 1975.
68. Scott Burns, *The Household Economy: Its Shape, Origins, and Future* (Boston, Beacon Press, 1977), page 14. Originally published by Doubleday in 1975 as *Home, Inc.* See also Borsodi's *Prosperity and Security* (reference 57) to further appreciate this basic concept.
69. *Ibid*, page 246.
70. Alvin Toffler, *Future Shock* (New York, Random House, 1970), pages 36–40.
71. E. F. Schumacher, *Small is Beautiful: Economics as if People Mattered* (New York, Harper and Row, 1973), page 146.
72. The monthly "Plowboy" interviews in *The Mother Earth News* are styled after the monthly "Playboy" interviews in *Playboy* magazine.
73. Daniel Bell, *The End of Ideology: On the Exhaustion of Political Ideas in the Fifties* (New York, Free Press, 1960; 1962), page 400.
74. Pierre-André Julien, Pierre Lamonde and Daniel Latouche, "La Société post-industrielle: Un concept vague et dangereux", *Futuribles*, 7, Summer 1976.
75. Benjamin S. Kleinberg, *American Society in the Postindustrial Age: Technocracy, Power, and the End of Ideology* (Columbus, Ohio, Charles E. Merrill, 1973).
76. Bell, *The Coming of Post-Industrial Society*, page 386.
77. *Ibid*, page 354.
78. *Ibid*, page 154.
79. *Ibid*, page 362.
80. *Ibid*, page 363.
81. *Ibid*, page 366.
82. *Ibid*, page 214.
83. For a recent nondecentralist critique see J. I. Gershuny, "Post-industrial society: the myth of the service economy", *Futures*, April 1977, 9 (2), pages 103–114.
84. New books making this point include Nicholas Georgescu-Roegen, *Agrarian Economics* (New York, Universe, March 1977); Joe Belden, *Toward a National Food Policy* (Washington, Exploratory Project for Economic Alternatives, 1977); William Ophuls, *Ecology and the Politics of Scarcity* (San Francisco, Freeman, April 1977), Michael Perelman, *The Myth of Agricultural Efficiency* (New York, Universe, March 1977), and Wendell Berry, *The Unsettling of America: Culture and Agriculture* (Totawa, NJ, Sierra Club Books, July 1977).
85. Bertrand de Jouvenel, *The Art of Conjecture* (New York, Basic Books, 1967). First published in France in 1964.

ASPECTS

The international debate about the economic and social options for tomorrow, to which the present-day problems add a sense of emergency, continues with an important contribution by Robert Heilbroner in his *Inquiry into the Human Prospect*.[1] Shortly after it appeared earlier this year, his thesis was discussed by members of the Science Policy Research Unit at the University of Sussex, UK, whose collective critique of the MIT global models was published for the first time in *Futures*.[2] The following reply to Robert Heilbroner, for which Professor C. Freeman, Head of the Unit, is personally responsible, is intended to stimulate the discussion which we hope will be as wide-ranging as that which followed *The Limits to Growth*.   Editor

THE LUXURY OF DESPAIR:
A reply to Robert Heilbroner's
Human Prospect

Christopher Freeman

Professor Freeman diagnoses Heilbroner's *Human Prospect* as a neo-Malthusian interpretation of world trends. He focuses on the possibility of hope for mankind and the responsibility of intelligentsia in this debate. First he challenges Heilbroner's projections of population growth, particularly in the Third World, which he finds unjustified both factually and logically; second, he argues with the presentation of socio-economic and environmental global futures. From this stance he questions the political prospects, viewed by Heilbroner as a future of conflict and totalitarian regimes.

HEILBRONER's *Human Prospect* is a well-written and powerful advocacy of the case for extreme pessimism in relation to the human race. Even though its message is in many essential respects the same as in *The Limits to Growth*, it is important because it includes dimensions which were lacking in the MIT models, and especially the political and social framework which was so largely absent from that work. For this reason it represents a major contribution to

Professor Christopher Freeman is Head of the Science Policy Research Unit, University of Sussex, Mantell Building, Falmer, Brighton, Sussex, BN1 9RF. He wishes to state that many of his colleagues at the Unit provided helpful comments in the preparation of this article.

the international debate which has been the positive achievement of the Club of Rome and the MIT models.

Since much of what I have to say is critical of Heilbroner's thesis, I should emphasise at the outset that there is also much in his analysis which I admire, and with which I agree. In particular I accept his view that the issue of relationships between rich and poor nations, and the problem of income redistribution within nations are likely to be at the centre of the world political stage over the next century. But I am not so pessimistic as he is about the utter hopelessness of a quest for paths by which inequalities between nations and within nations might be reduced. Nor do I share his view that human ideas, ideals and foresight have so little influence on the course of events. Indeed, it is a consciousness of the extent to which ideas *do* influence the course of events which led us to involvement in this debate.

The responsibility of intelligentsia

Heilbroner starts his book by asking the question *"Is there hope for mankind?"* and up to the last section, it was certainly my impression that he was going to follow through the logic of his argument quite ruthlessly, and end up by answering his own question with a clear and unequivocal "No". However he formally disclaims the Doomsday label. In the final section of his book, apparently himself slightly appalled at the utterly dark and dismal prospect which he has conjured up earlier in the first four sections, he has a curiously lame backtracking conclusion:

Let me therefore put these last words somewhat more "positively" offsetting to some degree the bleakness of our prospect, without violating the facts or spirit of our inquiry. Here I must begin by stressing for one last time an essential fact. The human prospect is not an irrevocable death sentence. It is not apocalypse or Doomsday toward which we are headed, although the risk of enormous catastrophes exists.[3]

If most of his readers have nevertheless concluded that he has been arguing that catastrophes "of fearful dimensions" are virtually inevitable, he has only himself to blame. For he has emphasised that imaginative anticipation or well-meaning exhortations and warnings have little or no effect and that it is catastrophes which bring about the major changes in behaviour essential for human survival. He has also argued forcefully that the Malthusian checks which will be effective are not those of foresight and planning, but those of famine and war: that there is an "ultimate certitude" about global environmental pollution; that authoritarian regimes are virtually inevitable, even in some curious way desirable, and that whether they are capitalist or socialist they are going to be involved in wars of redistribution arising from dwindling physical resources, which will make it impossible to sustain manufacturing industry and urban life. Finally, he has argued that there are fundamental traits in the human character, as well as acute social problems and physical shortages, which will favour authoritarian forms of government indefinitely.

Nevertheless one must accept his technical disclaimer, however unconvincingly it reads, and describe his prospect not as a model of doom but as a prospect of despair. Whereas some of the MIT modellers made it clear that their model was not a prediction, but a warning of what might happen if present trends continued, Heilbroner makes no such distinction, and from his final section it seems that he does not intend his piece as a warning of what might be avoided, but as a statement of what is largely inevitable to which we must all succumb and adapt. This is apparent from the extraordinary section in which he discusses the responsibility of the intelligentsia:

It is their task not only to prepare their fellow citizens for the sacrifices that will be required of them but to take the lead in seeking to redefine the legitimate boundaries of power and the permissible sanctuaries of freedom for a future in which the exercise of power must inevitably increase and many present areas of freedom, especially in economic life, be curtailed.[4]

This must be taken in the context of his prediction of the universal spread of authoritarian regimes, his despairing comments on the decline of intellectual freedom, and the abandonment of the industrial mode of production.

Certainly, I would accept (and who could not?) that individually and collectively we are often impelled to change our behaviour by "catastrophes", but I believe too that foresight, imagination and understanding can enable us both individually and collectively to avoid some catastrophes which might otherwise engulf us. We do not need a famine every other year to be reminded of the importance of the harvest. On a global scale it is just conceivable that intelligent policies could enable us to augment it sufficiently to avert the worst disasters. However, as we shall see, a curious feature of Heilbroner's variant of pessimistic determinism is that, like the Malthusians before him, he regards an increase of food production as a "danger".

This perverse doctrine may have all the greater impact by virtue of Heilbroner's reputation, at any rate on this side of the Atlantic, as one of the outstanding radical critics among American social scientists. As he himself remarks, his piece is likely to give aid and comfort to those whom he has always regarded as his enemies, and I agree with him. According to his own account, intellectual honesty compelled him to come to conclusions which he himself found unpalatable and unwelcome. I agree that there is no point in wishful thinking or self-deception about issues which are clearly so important for all of us. But equally it would be dangerous if a social doctrine based on fundamental intellectual fallacies, however sincerely conceived, were to gain wide acceptance. This would be particularly true if such a fashion were to give a cloak of respectability to economic and social policies which would otherwise be abhorrent. It is my belief that this is what occurred with the doctrines of Malthus in the first half of the 19th century, and the neo-Malthusian doctrines of our day could have similar consequences.

Malthus once again

I am aware of course that some of those who find the MIT doom models a plausible scenario resent the epithet "Malthusian" or "neo-Malthusian". It may be the case that Heilbroner too dislikes being described as a Malthusian, although this seems highly improbable. In his opening section he places the issue of population and resources right at the forefront, and in considering what he regards as the sombre prospect of world population growth he writes:

These Malthusian checks will exert even stronger braking effects as burgeoning populations in the poor nations press ever harder against food supplies that cannot keep abreast of successive doublings. At the same time the fact that population control in these countries is likely to be achieved in the next generations mainly by premature deaths rather than by the general adoption of contraception or a rapid spontaneous decline in fertility brings an added "danger" to the demographic outlook. This is the danger that the Malthusian check will be offset by large increases in food production that will enable additional hundreds of millions to reach child-bearing age.[5]

The implications of this statement seem to me to come perilously close to the type of advice which was given to the British government at the time of the Irish famine: let the "Malthusian checks" take their course, otherwise the problem will get worse. This is the straight anti-"humanitarian" message of Forrester; and it is indeed as unpalatable to me as it is totally unacceptable to the affected populations in the Third World.

Again, in his concluding section Heilbroner returns to this theme:

Therefore the outlook is for convulsive change—change forced upon us by external events rather than by conscious choice, by catastrophe rather than by calculation. As with Malthus's much derided but all too prescient forecasts, nature will provide the checks, if foresight and "morality" do not. One such check could be the outbreak of wars arising from the explosive tensions of the coming period, which might reduce the growth rates of the surviving nation-states and thereby defer the danger of industrial asphyxiation for a period.[6]

It is not merely in the repeated invocation of Malthusian terminology, but in the central intellectual assumptions, that Heilbroner's *Human Prospect* is essentially and obviously a neo-Malthusian prospect.

The fact that a doctrine was misused or is used to justify reactionary social policies would not of course be sufficient to refute it. What matters is whether the Malthusian analysis represents such a true picture of the behaviour of human social systems that it can be reliably used to forecast future trends. The predictive power of the theory is the main point at issue. Heilbroner is asking us to believe in a scenario for the Third World of which the central feature is four successive doublings of populations over very short periods. This tendency he believes is so powerful, and so unlikely to be affected by acts of individual and collective foresight that only the sterner checks of famine and war on a hitherto unimaginable scale are likely to redress it.

It is true that he does consider the possibility that population growth rates in the Third World *could* slow down well before 2070, but the main thrust of his argument is based on the view that they are unlikely to do so, except as a result of famine, disease and war. He recognises that population growth in Europe, North America, the USSR and Japan is likely to be much slower and the figure he estimates for these areas is well under 2000 million by 2070, whereas he plays with the figures of 40 000 million for the Third World by 2070 or 20 000 million by 2050. In other words he is arguing that the countries of the Third World will be unable to accomplish in the 21st century what the richer countries have accomplished in the 19th and 20th centuries. Why should this be so impossible?

Population trends in the Third World

Heilbroner's arithmetic is correct. Four successive doublings, each over a 25-year period would indeed bring the population of the Third World from 2500 million in 1970 to 40 000 million in 2070. But a similar projection made for Britain in 1801 would have predicted a population of 168 million a century later in 1901, and a projection for Europe (including USSR) in 1850 would have given a 1950 population of over 4000 million, compared with the actual 1950 population of 576 million. There are several reasons for supposing that Heilbroner's projections are similarly over-estimating the probable future trend.

In the original version of his essay, as it appeared in the *New York Review of Books*, he ignored the small but definite indications of a fall in birth-rate and major changes of attitude in the two most populous countries in the world: India and China. He mentioned only Taiwan and South Korea as countries where there had been "limited success" in introducing birth control programmes and concluded:

Thus in the underdeveloped world as a whole, population growth proceeds unhindered along its fatal course.[7]

Evidently, it has been pointed out to him that he might be making a serious error at least in relation to mainland China. There are very few changes in the paperback book version compared with the original in the *New York Review of Books*. All of them are extremely revealing, but the new paragraph on China is the most interesting of all:

In fact, the only underdeveloped nation for which some cautious optimism may be voiced seems to be mainland China, where population-control programs, reportedly aimed at a zero growth rate by the year 2000, have been introduced with all the persuasive capability of a totalitarian, educational and propaganda system.[8]

Leaving aside his introduction of the expression "totalitarian" to describe this aspect of Chinese policy, this would seem to call for some revision of the rest of his argument, since China accounts for a quarter of the entire world population, and a third of that in the developing countries. But no such revision has been made.

However, it is not only in relation to China that his argument can be faulted; he ignores much other evidence in relation to population trends both in Asia and in Latin America. The World Bank report on the MIT models pointed out that of 66 countries for which reasonably reliable data were available, 56 showed falling fertility rates.[9] His statement that "in those Latin American countries where growth rates are highest, population control programmes are not as yet even advocated"[10], is only a half-truth. In Mexico, which has a very high growth rate, and which is the second most populous country in Latin America, not only are such programmes widely "advocated", but the government has at last begun to take the issue seriously. Birth rates are already falling in several other Central American countries with very different social systems, such as Costa Rica, Cuba, and Puerto Rico. The birth-rate has been falling slowly for some time under a variety of different regimes in Chile, and it has been relatively low for some time in Uruguay.[11]

One of the most significant developments in the past 20 years has been the break-up of the previously monolithic opposition to birth control from two of the strongest ideologies in the world: Roman Catholicism and official Marxism. Indeed, one interesting feature of the widespread trend to falling birth-rates is that these are reducing simultaneously in countries with differing socio-cultural backgrounds, and very diverse political systems. This trend provides no evidence for Heilbroner's suggestion that only "authoritarian" regimes are likely to be competent in stabilising population growth rates. The birth-rate is falling rapidly in Hong Kong and Singapore as well as in China and Taiwan. Is this really due to "totalitarian" pressures? So far as Europe is concerned fertility rates are falling below replacement level in a range of countries, with a variety of political regimes. Ironically, in some cases "authoritarian" regimes are attempting (with little success) to increase the birth-rate.

In considering the position in the Third World from 1970 to 2070, by comparison with Europe from 1870 to 1970, it is of course perfectly legitimate to point out that the fall in death rates in Third World countries has sometimes been much more rapid, and the population "explosion" is consequently more severe. But equally there is now a variety of much more efficient forms of birth control, far more widely available, whose use is persistently advocated by many private organisations as well as national and international agencies. Malthusians and neo-Malthusians are entitled to take some of the credit for the very wide-spread international public concern with population growth rates and for the change in attitudes. But if they do so, then they are hardly entitled also to claim that persuasion, imagination, individual and collective choice and planning have little or no role in human affairs. Presumably still less would they wish to claim that this persuasion has come most effectively from "totalitarian" or "authoritarian" sources.

It is true that such factors are probably less important than a general rise in living standards. The possibilities of achieving a stable world population depend largely upon social mechanisms which are the very opposite of the "Malthusian check" which Heilbroner describes with such gloomy enthusiasm.

This is of course only one side of the picture. The other important aspect of the problem is the possibility of increasing agricultural productivity and here the Malthusians have a slightly stronger case.

It would be foolish to be complacent about ensuring an adequate food supply for a rapidly growing population especially in view of the present low level of stocks, the possibility of adverse climatic changes, and the difficulties experienced in many parts of the world in achieving sustained increases in yields. Nevertheless, the evidence is fairly strong that on a world scale supply has been constrained less by purely physical factors than by low effective demand because of the poverty of most consumers. The potentialities for increasing output are considerable throughout the Third World as well as in countries such as Canada, USA and Australia. Even with existing technology it would be physically possible to feed the size of world population which Heilbroner envisages. Plant and animal geneticists, entomologists, ecologists and agronomists are working hard and with considerable success throughout the world to make available to cultivators new varieties and new techniques which would facilitate sustained agricultural improvements.

Surely, in these circumstances, the responsibility of social scientists is to help their colleagues in the natural sciences and the affected populations to devise social arrangements which will make these techniques more rapidly effective, and will ensure conditions for their application which reduce inequalities of wealth and income, and which do not cause social and environmental disruption. It is more difficult to do this than to make models of doom but it might be a lot more useful. Whilst the target of increasing world food production steadily by 3 or 4% per annum, and distributing it more equitably, is difficult to achieve, it is also not beyond our capabilities.

The conflict over resources

The distinctive feature of Heilbroner's version of neo-Malthusian ideology, in common with the MIT modellers, is singling out the problem of industrial materials and the associated pollution as the most intractable global problem and the main cause of the wars of redistribution which he foresees. Heilbroner differs from them and from most other doom modellers in assigning a *qualitatively* different significance to the problem of industrial materials and the associated pollution:

Here we come to a crucial stage of our inquiry. For unlike the threats posed by population growth or war, there is a certitude about the problem of environmental deterioration that places it in a different category from the dangers we have previously examined. Nuclear attacks may be indefinitely avoided; population growth may be stabilised; but ultimately there is a limit to the ability of the earth to support or tolerate the process of industrial activity, and there is reason to believe that we are now moving toward that limit very rapidly.[12]

He then goes on to project a growth rate of 7% per annum for industrial output and consumption of materials. This of course shows that "a volume of resource extraction 32 times larger than today's" would be needed in 50 years' time and "looking ahead over the ten doublings of a century, the amount of annual resource requirements would have increased by over a thousand times". He then asks: "Do we have the resources to permit us to attain—or sustain—such gargantuan increases in output?"

The answer to his question may be "No" but neither is there any need for us to attempt it. The basis for his 7% projection is unclear but if we take it to apply to the world as a whole, and we take his upper population estimate of 42 000 million, then this would imply an annual per capita consumption about 10 times as high as the present per capita consumption in the USA. If we take a lower population estimate—say 21 000 million—then per capita consumption of materials would be about twenty times as high as the present US level. This goes beyond even the wildest fantasies of a submarine and a helicopter in everyone's back garden.

Doom models are often based on the implicit assumption that the North American use of energy and materials represents the pattern of the future towards which all nations must converge if they aspire to raise their living standards. This assumption is fallacious. A number of European countries already have what many would regard as a much higher quality of life than that of the USA, with a lower materials intensity and a lower energy intensity. The rest of the world is not obliged to follow the USA in its profligate use of oil and other natural resources, or in its pattern of conspicuous waste of packaging materials and advertising. Nor is it obliged to follow the European or Japanese pattern. It is even unlikely that the Americans themselves will continue to expand their per capita consumption of materials for another century at the rate of 7% per annum. This would imply that the so-called "post-industrial society" not only has not arrived but will never arrive. One does not have to believe in the "post-industrial society" to recognise that the scenario of an indefinite 7% increase in consumption of industrial materials is absurd. Almost all economists and sociologists are agreed that services are likely to grow much more than manufacturing in industrialised societies over the next century. It is also quite obvious that many such service activities have a much lower materials intensity than manufacturing. A possible exception is the capital investment in construction required for some services, but there are scarcely any of those concerned with potential materials shortages who are predicting a shortage of *construction* materials.

Like all the Malthusian scenarios, these projections of materials' scarcity ignore one of the most important and characteristic features of human societies, and especially of industrialised societies: their capacity for technical and social change and substitution. If the world were confronted with critical shortages of particular industrial and construction materials, then all kinds of substitution mechanisms would come into play. One of them, as Heilbroner himself says, would be the recycling of industrial materials which is already important for ferrous and non-ferrous metals, as well as for rubber and paper. Another would be the design and use of more durable products and greater economy in the use of materials. A third would be the invention and development of new materials and combinations of materials which are in more abundant supply. To be sure all of these require deliberate research, investment and economic policies but most of those who have gone deeply into the question of physical availability of materials, since the MIT models brought this question to the forefront, are agreed that sheer physical shortage of materials is rather unlikely to bring the world to a grinding halt.

Politically induced shortages are quite another matter. But although there are passages where Heilbroner himself appears to recognise the implausibility of his scenario in relation to future materials shortages, this does not stop him making it the foundation of his long-term projections, or assuming without any justification that there will be a world of *falling* physical output due to physical shortage of materials. Indeed, he goes even further and assumes a "post-industrial" society which is apparently a non-industrial society, since he talks of "dismantling" the industrial mode of production.

It is perhaps legitimate to talk about a "post-industrial" society in the same sense as one can speak of a "post-agricultural" society. Although agricultural productivity has risen so much over the past century that it is no longer necessary for more than a small fraction of the employed population to work in agriculture in Europe and North America, this is still an activity which is absolutely critical for human survival. Industrial productivity too has been rising so fast that manufacturing employment may also need only to be a small fraction of the total. This creates quite new possibilities both for employment and for leisure, but it does not mean that industry will cease to be an essential activity for the survival of the vast majority of human beings on this planet.

What has been said does not at all exclude the possibility of serious political and social conflict, including violent conflict, over such questions as access to reserves, or sources of particular critical materials, or over the terms of trade between primary commodities and manufactures. These conflicts have been with us for a long time and may well become more acute, but they do not justify the view of an inexorable worsening of the human situation as a result of acute physical shortages. Nor can we exclude the possibility that nationalistic ideologies will exploit the supposed future physical shortages of materials to provide a spurious justification for aggressive, pre-emptive, militaristic behaviour. Indeed, we know only too well that the Nazi movement used the false geo-political scenario of resource shortages and unequal access to materials, as well as the false Malthusian population scenario of *"Volk ohne Raum"*, as one of the main strands in the ideological preparations for the Second World War. One of the most "mischievous" consequences of Heilbroner's perspective may well be to provide future militaristic nationalist movements with an equally spurious, but superficially plausible, ideological smokescreen for their otherwise utterly unjustifiable and repugnant behaviour. We already know that the question of military intervention was seriously considered in the recent oil crisis and, with the experience of Suez, it would be foolish to ignore the possibility of military responses to resource problems, whether from parliamentary regimes or more authoritarian ones.

The uncertainty of environmental collapse

During the course of his exposition Heilbroner gradually moves over from warnings of the huge *increases* in materials requirements, to assuming a *decline* in physical output. Like the MIT doom modellers, he seems determined to have a black scenario. The massive increase brings the environmental disruption of the planet, and the decline justifies his scenario of the war of all against all for scarce resources. The MIT modellers at least discussed the possibility that the growth curve could asymptote gradually towards limits or that there could be non-catastrophic "hunting behaviour" as limits were approached. One reason that the MIT global modellers regarded catastrophic outcomes as more probable, although not quite inevitable, was that they assumed an inevitable association between industrial production and environmental pollution. Heilbroner takes over this crucial but unjustified assumption. Hence apparently his use of the word "certitude" with respect to environmental catastrophe. This is all the more strange, as in his own review of *The Limits to Growth*, he pointed out the fallacy in the MIT argument:

A very important conclusion follows. As the MIT models themselves show, it is not "growth" that is the mortal enemy, but pollution. The programme of the ecologically-minded scientist, therefore, should not be aimed against growth, but only against pollution-generating growth. Any technological change that will increase output without further damaging the air or water or soil, any technological change that will enable us to increase output by shifting from a less to a more abundant resource (again without an increase in pollution), represents perfectly safe growth, and should be welcomed with open arms.[13]

There is nothing "certain" or "inevitable" about pollution. As a result of a relatively small effort in the industrialised countries, important though still quite inadequate results have already been achieved in relation to both air and water pollution and in conservation of amenity. It is essential to press on with far greater vigour to ensure that environmental standards for industry are steadily improved throughout the world and that large areas of wilderness and parklands are conserved. This is a very difficult objective, especially in the USA, but it is not an impossible one.

At the time of the Stockholm Conference it was widely believed that the Third World would not take environmental problems seriously, but the experience of the United Nations Environmental Programme since Stockholm belies this pessimistic view. The peculiarly narrow and backward-looking view of the authoritarian Brazilian regime is now increasingly seen to be the exception and not the rule. The UNEP was the first UN agency in which China participated, and many Third World countries are now actively involved. Not only are most Third World governments ready to take environmental questions seriously, but the Science Councils and other scientific organisations in those countries are taking up these problems with enthusiasm, in seeking solutions to the local environmental problems which they confront. This constructive approach to the use of science and technology is in striking contrast to the fashionable malaise which attributes the ills of civilisation to science.

I was particularly encouraged to see that one of the passages which Heilbroner has substantially revised for the paperback edition concerns science: he now fully recognises that it is not "science" but social systems and human behaviour which are the problems.

Political prospects and "authoritarianism"

The most persuasive part of Heilbroner's *Human Prospect* is his discussion of political and social systems. However ill-conceived his uncritical adoption of neo-Malthusian ideas in relation to population and resources, there is nevertheless a ring of truth in some of his observations about current and future political systems. As Harold Laski never tired of pointing out, daily experience confirms the validity of one of the few major generalisations in political science: Lord Acton's dictum that "power corrupts and absolute power corrupts absolutely". Every newspaper also furnishes new evidence of the continuing realism of Machiavelli's cynical analysis of the behaviour of sovereign nation-states. No-one who has lived through the wars in Korea and Vietnam, the Sino-Soviet conflict, the Arab-Israeli wars, Ulster and Watergate, can possibly be complacent about the difficulties of averting corruption in government, brutality and torture in the treatment of political opponents, wars, terrorism, assassination and civil wars in the conduct of nation-states and political movements. Heilbroner apparently shared with me the hope of a fusion of the striving for social justice and for civil liberty, a hope which was so cruelly crushed alike in Chile and in Czechoslovakia. In all of this it is difficult to deny that Heilbroner has genuine grounds for pessimism, which stand in no need of an additional Malthusian booster-injection to put us in a black mood.

However, sobering though these considerations are, they are not essentially new. What *is* new since the Second World War, as he rightly points out, is the enormous increase in destructive power of modern weapons. But does this render our situation entirely without hope? I do not believe so, but I do agree with him that it does mean a gloomy prospect unless or until a more effective international security system is established. To this extent his warnings (and those of many others) are fully justified. But the logical conclusion from these considerations is to place even greater emphasis on the importance of international institutions, and the importance of devising "positive-sum games" for the resolution of international conflicts. It is also to press forward with worldwide efforts to reduce poverty as a major source of violent conflicts. In both these directions, although it must be conceded that the picture is black, it is not hopeless and indeed I would maintain that the US–Soviet and US–Chinese détente render the situation slightly more hopeful than it was, say in 1938 or in 1950.

The gist of Heilbroner's argument is that international conflicts are likely to become more acute because of the struggle for control over resources, which will be reinforced by a strong trend towards authoritarian regimes in capitalist and socialist countries alike. Whilst I would concede that there are good reasons for alarm on both these counts, once the neo-Malthusian prop is knocked away, then these tendencies appear a little less dangerous and all-pervasive, and by no means as inevitable future trends. I would maintain that post-war developments in both parts of Germany and in the USSR give substantial grounds for hope, by comparison with the 1930s or the 1940s. Material prosperity has been an important factor in these more hopeful developments. Even if we grant for the sake of argument the Machiavellian view that politics is mainly a matter of the expedient and cynical pursuit of self-interest by individuals, groups and nation-states, then this does not at all rule out effective international agreements based on mutual toleration and even civil liberty. Nor indeed does a more generous view of human behaviour. Only if we follow Koestler, and the more pessimistic theologians in postulating a fundamental "design-fault" in human beings must we give way to complete despair.

Like some faint-hearted liberals in the 1930s, Heilbroner is inclined to write off the purely practical advantages of democracy far too quickly, and to concede far too much to the supposed psychological advantages and other attractions of militaristic and authoritarian regimes. Even before Watergate the supporters of parliamentary democracy were very well aware of its many failings as a system of government. The only thing they maintained pretty strongly, following the principle of a well-known upholder of parliament, was that the other systems were much worse. Heilbroner has said nothing to persuade me to revise this view, and many Greek, Spanish and Portuguese people, after considerable practical experience, appear to share my scepticism.

Of course, one must have some regard to the historical circumstances in developing countries such as China and to the desirable diversity of socio-political systems, but there are several fundamental reasons for believing that capitalist or socialist democracies are *more* likely to provide effective solutions to contemporary social, economic and political problems than supposedly more "natural" and efficient authoritarian regimes. The first reason is that nobody yet knows all the answers to these problems and consequently any social system which permits an open debate on alternative solutions and proceeds to some extent by trial and error, is inherently far more likely to find and implement practical solutions. The second reason is closely related to the first: very few of the contemporary problems of agriculture, industry, the environment, and society can be solved without science. In the long run science flourishes only in an environment which permits, even encourages, an icono-clastic critical approach to established orthodoxy. Even if Heilbroner were right in his vision of an unending series of wars and conflicts, this would confer a very great evolutionary survival advantage on those nation-states which are capable of fostering and using science. Their incapacity to tolerate the unorthodox, whether in art or in science or in politics, is one of the many Achilles' heels of the authoritarian regimes.

Another is the powerful tendency of such regimes to foster extreme inequali-ties in distribution of wealth, power and privilege. Once the constraint of open criticism is removed, then the Actonian mechanism comes fully into play. Indeed it is hard to understand why one who is rightly so concerned about problems of the environment, population, industrial working conditions, and the danger of nuclear war, should accept so easily some supposed advantages of authoritarian regimes. The concentration of political power, the removal of the constraints of public debate and criticism, the suppression and victimi-sation of unwelcome critics, and many other similar characteristics of authori-tarian regimes are far more likely to exacerbate these problems than to diminish or resolve them.

The human determinants

The conclusion, therefore, which I draw from the admittedly discouraging political and social prospects confronting us, is the very opposite of that which he draws. Whereas he speaks of the responsibility of intellectuals to prepare the population for the reduction of freedoms, I would maintain that the respon-sibility of intellectuals now more than ever is to uphold those freedoms, which we know from very hard-won experience are vital to prevent the arbitrary abuse of power. It is important of course to retain a sense of history and of the diversity of cultures, to distinguish those freedoms which really are fundamental to the future of human civilisation, from the "freedom" of large corporations to pollute the environment or manipulate the political process. If this is what Heilbroner means when he speaks of curtailing "many present areas of freedom, especially in economic life", then I would be happy to concur. I would indeed maintain, like him, that this is the logic of the democratic process.

I do not at all under-rate the dangers of authoritarian regimes and attempted military solutions. Just as Orwell's *1984* was an invaluable reminder of these dangers, so too the work of the doom modellers may often provide us with useful warnings. Both the "dystopias" of science fiction and the models of doom have their essential place in that imaginary visualisation of future possibilities which helps us to try and avoid such outcomes. To this extent I have no quarrel with them. As part of a range of forecasting techniques they are unexceptionable, and I accept Jantsch's observation that good forecasting and planning probably requires the combination and confrontation of extrapolative techniques with goal-setting techniques.[14] My objection is to an *exclusive* preoccupation with models of gloom and doom and the tendency to assign to them a deterministic quality which is unwarranted. I object to this both on scientific grounds and on ethical and political grounds. Human beings are not moved only by fear but also by hope. All of us need to be to some degree both pessimists and optimists. We both need and deserve models of hope as well as models of doom.

Certainly, there are grounds for Heilbroner's mood of black pessimism. Many artists obviously share his mood. There are tragedies and problems in the world sufficient to daunt the bravest spirit and the most ardent reformers. But whatever faults Heilbroner may ascribe to the human spirit, he himself invokes the image of Atlas and he surely cannot deny that there is a certain magnificent indestructibility about human hopes and aspirations and especially about the aspirations for liberty, social justice and material progress. These hopes are themselves a part of our future and help to determine its features. If today we are not already living in a wholly totalitarian world or a Nazi-occupied poverty-stricken Europe, it is because men and women had the courage to hope and struggle against the odds of what at one time appeared almost inevitable.

Even in the most heart-breaking circumstances humans have found the courage to confirm the truth of Schiller's ode to hope. Condorcet wrote his glowing Utopian vision of the human future in the shadow of the guillotine; Gabriel Peri in the shadow of the Nazi execution squad. Hope was never entirely extinguished even in the ghettoes of Warsaw or in the Gulag Archipelago. If a young girl hiding in a cupboard in Amsterdam in 1944 or Dr Edith Bone imprisoned in Hungary by those whom she had supposed to be her friends, could nevertheless find the courage to hope, then can we as comfortably placed intellectuals in New York or in London in 1974 abdicate responsibility for models of hope and for the effort to sustain the uncertain, painful and desperately difficult progress to a better future?

References
1. R. L. Heilbroner, "The Human Prospect", *New York Review of Books*, January 24, 1974, pages 21–34; and (revised) *An Inquiry into the Human Prospect*, New York, W. W. Norton, 1974
2. Science Policy Research Unit, "World Dynamics Challenged: The Limits to Growth Controversy", special issue of *Futures*, Vol 5, No 1, 1973, pages 1–134
3. R. L. Heilbroner, *op cit*, *New York Review of Books* edition, page 33. Further references are to this original version unless explicitly stated
4. R. L. Heilbroner, *op cit*, page 33
5. R. L. Heilbroner, *op cit*, page 23
6. R. L. Heilbroner, *op cit*, page 33
7. R. L. Heilbroner, *op cit*, page 22
8. R. L. Heilbroner, *op cit*, W. W. Norton edition, page 33
9. World Bank (International Bank for Reconstruction and Development), *Report on the Limits to Growth*, 1972, page 5
10. R. L. Heilbroner, *op cit*, page 22
11. *World Bank Atlas*, International Bank for Reconstruction and Development, 1973, and *op cit*
12. R. L. Heilbroner, *op cit*, page 24
13. R. L. Heilbroner, "Growth and Survival", *Foreign Affairs*, Vol 51, No 1, October, 1972, pages 139–153
14. E. Jantsch, *Technological Planning and Social Futures*, London, Cassell, 1972

POST-INDUSTRIAL SOCIETY
The myth of the service economy

J. I. Gershuny

There is a popular view of the current pattern of change in developed societies, a view typified by Daniel Bell's *The Coming of Post-Industrial Society*, that recent economic growth has been increasingly concentrated in the collective provision of services rather than in individual consumption of material goods, and that this change of economic focus from goods to services is a trend which will continue into the future. The author argues, using UK data, that the trend is in fact away from the expenditure on services and towards expenditure on goods. The growing employment in the tertiary sector, previously used as an indicator of the growth of the service economy, emerges here as a manifestation of the division of labour—a process which increases the efficiency of production of material goods—while the final production of services, using automatic machinery and "direct labour", will increasingly take place in the home.

THE essence of Bell's post-industrial argument is to be found in his reference to Engel's theorem.[1] As societies get richer, in Bell's words, "peoples' horizons expand and new wants and tastes develop"; they move on from exclusive concern with their immediate material needs—these are largely satisfied—to the more abstract requirements associated with wealth and leisure. These "post-industrial needs" are more difficult to satisfy on an individual basis, they are more readily met on the basis of the collective provision of services; so, according to Bell, the leading indicator of the emergence of the post-industrial society is the emergence of tertiary, "service" employees, catering for these new needs, as a majority in the workforce; and indeed, such a majority is to be found in many developed states.[2]

This article is based on work carried out by the author at the Science Policy Research Unit, Sussex University, Brighton, UK on behalf of the Programmes Analysis Unit of the Department of Industry and the UKAE. This topic is covered in greater depth in J. I. Gershuny, *After Industrial Society?* (London, Macmillan, forthcoming 1978).

Objections to the service-economy thesis

There is no adequate definition of "services". Two separate ideas seem to be involved. In some cases, the concept refers to the nature of a product, and in others, to the characteristics of a job. Thus we have one word with two meanings, which we should try to separate.

The definition based on the nature of the product is easy to establish.

A "good" is material, it is manufactured or otherwise procured, and it maintains its existence after this production process; its final consumers acquire it at one point in time and may subsequently use it at their whim.

Services, by contrast, are immaterial, evanescent, often only consumable at the instant of production, always consumed "once and for all".

At the moment of its acquisition by the consumer, a good is a *thing* whereas a service is a *state* or an *activity* or a *sensation*. Why is it necessary to qualify this statement by confining it to the moment of acquisition? Simply, both goods and services supply similar functions—they both answer needs, and needs may be met either by goods or by services. If I want my shirts cleaned, I can either hire the services of a laundry, or I can invest in a washing machine. Services are distinct from goods only as alternative social arrangements, alternative commodities with different combinations of capital and labour, for meeting needs.[3]

So *service employment* can be defined as employment in an industry whose final product is a "service" in this first sense of a *non-material consumption item*. But this clearly does not exhaust the possibilities of the term, since engineers and industrial managers are often included (eg by Bell) as members of service occupations, even though their final product—the benefit to the final consumer from their employment—comes in the form of goods and not services. What differs between service occupations and other occupations here is not the nature of their product, but of their job. This second sense of "service" has to do with relative distance from material production. A *"service occupation"*, in this second sense, is one relatively *removed from the physical manipulation of material*, whether the final product of the employment is a good, or a service.

There is some overlap in the employment categories identified by these two concepts; workers who produce services for final consumption will also tend to be service workers in the sense of being relatively distant from material production[4]—but generally speaking we must take care to keep the two categories separate.

The service-economy thesis rests on this simple model: the new abstract and sophisticated "post-industrial needs" *require* increased provision of services, and this *leads to* growth in tertiary employment. And we have evidence of vastly increasing tertiary "service" employment so, goes the argument, we are indeed moving into the post-industrial era. (The argument is not normally stated this baldly, but nevertheless this does seem to be the underlying logical structure.) There are two objections to this argument.

First, needs, I have asserted, do not determine specific means for their satisfaction; I shall present evidence which suggests that services which had previously satisfied the "post-industrial needs" have been substituted for by goods over the past 20 years in the UK—so that the first step of the model, needs *requiring* services, is inappropriate. So, if the consumption of services has not risen, how do we explain the growth in service employment? I shall show that more than half of those in service occupations in the UK only qualify as such through the second of my two criteria—the nature of their jobs—and are engaged more or less directly in the production of *material goods*.

My second objection is then that the thesis embodies faulty logic; though service workers may constitute a majority of the workforce, this does not imply that the final consumption of services predominates over that of goods. There are grounds for suspecting that the substitution of goods for services may be accompanied by growing service employment (in the second sense) resulting from the division of labour in the production of goods.

The trend from services to goods

Does Engel's Law apply to modern consumption patterns? If we consider the expenditure patterns of UK households with various weekly budgets in 1953–1954—the first in which this data was collected in the UK—we do see what appears to be corroboration (Figure 1).[5,6]

The proportion of expenditure on food falls continuously throughout almost the whole range of budgets, expenditure on durables at first rises, then holds constant and finally falls—while expenditure on services rises steeply with increasing budget.[7]

This does not, however, prove Engel's Law; we need to move from a cross-sectional observation at one point in time, to a longitudinal observation of

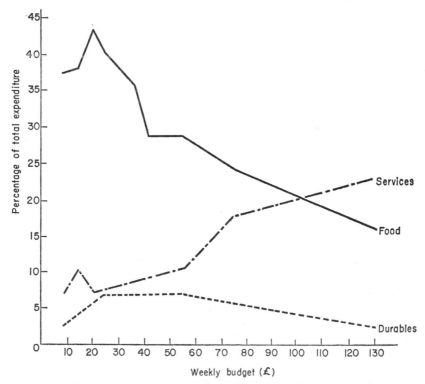

Figure 1. Weekly household expenditure[6] on three consumption categories in the UK in 1954 (in 1974 £)

change over time. Now if we were to base an estimate for 1974 on the 1954 cross-section we would certainly expect that, given the increase in national income over 20 years, the proportion of the budget spent on service would show a sizeable increase. The data however show no such change (Table 1).

TABLE 1. PERCENTAGE OF HOUSEHOLD EXPENDITURE, UK[6]

| | Share of household expenditure | | | | |
Category	1954 (%)	1961 (%)	1966 (%)	1971 (%)	1974 (%)
House and heating	14·1	15·4	17·5	18·8	19·0
Food	33·4	30·4	28·2	2509	24·5
Alcohol and tobacco	10·2	9·5	9·4	8·9	8·4
Durables and clothing	25·8	24·5	23·8	23·0	24·6
Transport	7·1	10·3	11·8	13·7	13·4
Services	9·5	9·5	9·4	9·4	9·6

Why may we not generalise from the cross-sectional to the longitudinal? We can go some way towards an answer by considering various categories of expenditure (Table 2).

TABLE 2. SELECTED EXPENDITURE ON CATEGORIES IN UK (percentage of total budget)

| | Share of total budget | | | | |
Category	1954 (%)	1961 (%)	1966 (%)	1971 (%)	1974 (%)
Cinemas, theatres, etc	2·0	1·0	1·0	0·6	0·8
Television: buy and rent	1·4	2·1	2·1	2·1	3·0
Domestic help and laundry	1·6	1·2	1·1	0·6	0·8
Domestic appliances	0·8	1·5	1·4	1·6	1·7
Transport services	3·5	3·1	3·2	2·6	2·4
Transport goods	3·5	7·2	8·6	11·3	11·1
Budget share (and *relative ratios*)					
Selected services	7·1 (*55·5*)	5·3 (*32·7*)	5·3 (*30·5*)	3·8 (*20·2*)	4·0 (*20·2*)
Selected goods	5·7 (*44·5*)	10·9 (*67·3*)	12·1 (*69·5*)	15·0 (*79·8*)	15·8 (*79·8*)
Total	12·8 (*100*)	16·2 (*100*)	17·4 (*100*)	18·8 (*100*)	19·8 (*100*)

The pattern is one of substitution. Entertainment needs which were met by cinemas and theatres are progressively replaced by television, domestic help by domestic appliances, the use of public transport by the use of the private car. In each case, a *good* substitutes for a *service*. Engel's Law does not apply over time because the technical and social systems for supplying and supporting the various consumption items change—as new products and new production processes emerge, so do altered patterns of consumption. When we compare Figure 1 with the equivalent for 1974 (in Figure 2), we see that the curves have shifted—for each "real money" budgetary category, expenditure on services falls and on consumer durables rises—thus the changes expected with increasing real income on the basis of the cross-sectional data do not occur.

This only compares *expenditures* over time. By considering budgetary proportions for each period we are implicitly assuming that a given "real money" expenditure at any point in time will give the same choice among various items of consumption—that the prices of goods and services rise at the same rate. This is misleading. In the period 1954 to 1974, the retail price index in the UK rose by a factor of 2·68, the price of consumer durables rose by a factor of only 1·72, the price of services rose nearly twice as fast, by a factor of 3·21.[8] Expenditure on services in 1974 would have brought hardly more than half the actual *con-*

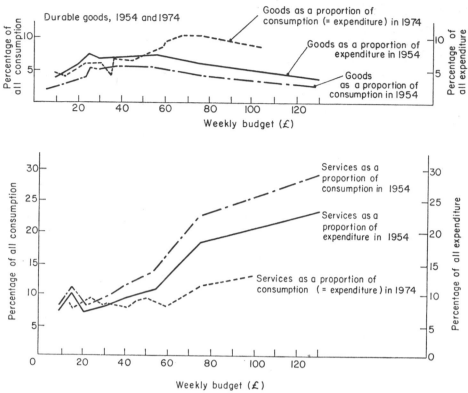

Figure 2. Real UK consumption of durables and services. "Real consumption" is estimated by inflating 1954 expenditure by the price index for the individual commodity; "expenditure proportion" is estimated by inflating 1954 expenditure with overall consumer price index. " Weekly budget" in 1974£.

sumption that a similar expenditure would have brought in 1954. The estimates can be corrected to give some idea of the real change in consumption by deflating the expenditure categories in 1954 by the price rises in each category. So we have two alternative views of the shifts in the Engel curves over time, one based on expenditure proportions, the other on estimated real consumption (Figure 2).

The shifts in these curves provide reasonably strong grounds for the assumption that there has been a considerable substitution of goods for services over the 20-year period.

So, as far as personal expenditure goes,

• the period from 1954 to 1974 in the UK did not show the increase in service expenditure we would have expected from Engel's Law
• it is obvious from the rise in the price of services relative to goods that the real consumption of services has actually fallen quite considerably; and
• it appears that this contradiction of Engel's Law may be explained by the substitution of goods consumption for services.

We must, however, be careful about the use of the word "consumption" here. When we consume services, the state or condition we pay for disappears after a short period; clothes cleaned by a laundry become dirty—and a service has been *literally* consumed, vanished away, not to return. But when we buy a washing machine, we do not expect our purchase to vanish after first use, indeed, we buy it on the assumption that it will linger for some years. Were it not that the benefit from the domestic washing machine goes in kind entirely to the household that possesses it, so that its product is not accounted for in the national product, we would certainly consider the householder's purchase, not as consumption, but as investment.

This growth in consumption of goods represents a fundamental change in the nature of economic activity. Instead of capital investment taking place exclusively in industry, and industry providing services for individuals and households, increasingly, investment is transferred from service industries into households, leaving industry engaged in what is essentially intermediate production—making the capital goods (the cookers, freezers, televisions, motorcars) used in the home production of final product. This is the trend towards the self-service economy, the do-it-yourself economy; almost the antithesis of Bell's service economy. Certainly up to now I have ignored the two areas of service consumption which have grown over the past two decades: medicine and education; indeed, when we include these two areas, the service expenditure proportion as a whole has risen. But—and this the crux of my difference with Bell—why should we assume that consumption of these two items will necessarily continue to rise? Can we not see pressures for education and medicine to go the same way as other "post-industrial" household expenditure, can we not imagine the replacement of social investment in educational and medical plant by household investment in educational and medical machines? I shall return to this observation later.

Services have certainly risen as a proportion of government expenditure; they accounted for 33·6% of the UK's government expenditure in 1954 and 59·4% of expenditure in 1974. But public expenditure is still only approximately one-third of the size of personal expenditure, so (in Table 3) we see that total UK

TABLE 3. SERVICES AS PERCENTAGE OF UK EXPENDITURE[9]

Expenditure category	Share of services in expenditure				
	1954 (%)	1961 (%)	1966 (%)	1971 (%)	1974 (%)
Consumer expenditure	11·85	11·53	11·33	10·53	10·64
Public expenditure	33·8	44·21	50·33	56·73	59·5
Total current expenditure	16·4	18·2	19·64	21·06	22·54

current expenditure on services has risen from 16·4% to 22·5% during 1954–1974. There is no price index for the public services—but if we assume that price of a unit of public provision of services has risen at the same rate relative to goods as a unit of personally provided services has over the 20-year period, then this represents a net fall in the total real consumption of services in the UK between 1954 and 1974.[10]

Service employment and material product

This leaves us with a problem. As we would expect from the foregoing argument, the level of tertiary employment is not adequately explained by the level of

TABLE 4. COMPARISON OF UK SERVICE EXPENDITURE WITH TERTIARY EMPLOYMENT[11]

	1954 (%)	1961 (%)	1966 (%)	1971 (%)	1974 (%)
Service employment[a]	34·5	38·7	41·3	43·9	48·1
Service expenditure[b]	16·4	18·2	19·6	21·1	22·5
Employment in medicine and education[a]	6·2	7·8	9·3		12·7
Expenditure on medicine and education[b]	7·1	8·4	8·7	9·2	11·1
Employment in other service industries	28·3	30·9	32·0	32·7	35·4
Expenditure on other services[b]	9·3	9·8	10·9	11·9	11·4

Notes: [a] as a percentage of total employment; [b] as a percentage of total expenditure.

consumption of services (Table 4). The proportion of service expenditure (in final expenditure) is considerably less than the proportion of service employees (compared to total employment). Furthermore, when we leave out education and medicine as categories of employment and consumption, we see that the remaining categories of service employment are even more disproportionate to the consumption of services.

The conclusion is inescapable: though the growth in demand for some services may be sufficient to explain the growth of some individual categories of service employed, in general, we must look elsewhere for such explanations. The relatively small total of service consumption, and the uncertainty and frequent reverses in the trends of individual service items, make growth in such consumption an unconvincing explanation for the steady and sizeable growth in employment in service occupations. Presumably, 35% of the working population is not engaged in supplying 11% of final consumption. What are they doing?

The argument put forward here is that this problem is no more than the confusion which results from the use of the word "services" in two different senses. The growth in "service" employment is not related simply to the consumption of "services", but is, to a major degree, a manifestation of the process of the division of labour. Put simply, as societies develop, the planning, forecasting, and organisational functions are removed from the individual artisans and passed on to other workers, who are not then directly involved in the physical manipulation of materials; hence the growth of "white collar" clerical, administrative, management occupations. The pattern of commerce becomes more geographically diffuse, the volume of international trade grows, the time span of the productive process from initial investment to final sales lengthens, so banking, insurance and other financial institutions account for a growing proportion of employment. The physical process of production becomes more technical, and so more dependent on those with technological expertise—and indirectly on the educational system which promotes this expertise.

A large proportion of those employed in tertiary industry or occupations contribute, not to the provision of services for final consumption, but to the production of goods. For example, in the UK (in 1971), tertiary industry accounted for around 47% of the industrial workforce. But the important thing to note about tertiary industry is that though it does not directly produce material goods, a large proportion of it is closely connected with the process of production in the slightly wider sense. The distribution industry, for instance, does not itself make any material object, and yet is an integral part of the process of making things—if products cannot be sold then they will not be produced. Similarly, the major part of finance and insurance is taken up with facilitating the production or purchase of goods. Among the professional and scientific employment sector, though a majority are educational, medical, or social workers still, a minority—eg those in engineering or other technological consultancy for example—are really involved in the production of material goods rather than immaterial services. It is more difficult to categorise public administration; for the purposes of the rough calculation in Table 5, half of its employment is attributed to goods production and half to services. Table 5 shows us that though, in 1971, nearly half of the working population were employed in tertiary industry, less than a quarter of it—23·1%—was involved in providing for the final consumption of services.

TABLE 5. TERTIARY INDUSTRY IN THE UK—GOODS OR SERVICES?[12]

Tertiary industry	Employment[a]	
	1961 (%)	1971 (%)
Goods-related		
Distribution, financial, part of professional and scientific plus half of public administration	18·2 } 20·2 2·0 }	19·0 } 21·5 2·5 }
Service-related		
Miscellaneous services, part of professional and scientific plus half of public administration	17·7 } 19·7 2·0 }	20·6 } 23·1 2·5 }
Total	39·9	46·6

Note: [a] as a percentage of total employment.

This only gets us part of the way to an answer: we are really interested, not in this industrial classification, but in the occupational classification—not in who employs people, but in the job they do. The argument rests specifically on the final product of people employed in tertiary occupations (in the sense of occupations relatively distant from the physical transformation of material). In 1971, 51·8% of the UK working population was employed in a clerical, sales, personal services, administrative, professional or technical capacity. What proportions of these groups were engaged in the production of goods and of services? The 1961 and 1971 UK Censuses give cross-tabulations relating members of different occupations to the industries which employ them, so we have the data to answer this question.

Even the estimate shown in Table 6—that though 51·8% (23·9% + 27·9%)

TABLE 6. THE EMPLOYMENT OF TERTIARY OCCUPATIONAL GROUPS, UK

	Employment in industry (% of working population)							
	Manufacturing[a]		Goods-related[b]		Manufacturing and Goods-related		Service-related[c]	
Occupations	1961	1971	1961	1971	1961	1971	1961	1971
Clerical	6·0	6·0	3·4	4·2	9·4	10·2	3·9	4·7
Sales	0·9	0·9	8·4	7·9	9·3	8·8	0·5	0·5
Personal Services	0·2	1·3	1·6	0·8	1·8	2·1	8·7	10·1
Administration	1·9	2·5	0·3	0·6	2·2	3·1	0·6	0·8
Professional and technical	2·5	3·2	0·5	0·5	3·0	3·7	6·0	7·8
All services	11·5	13·9	14·2	14·0	25·7	27·9	19·7	23·9

Notes: [a] includes transportation, utilities and construction; [b] distribution, banking, insurance and finance; [c] professional and scientific, miscellaneous services, and public administration.

of the working population are in tertiary occupations, only 23·9% are engaged in the final production of services—is excessive.[13] So, all in all, hardly more than two-fifths of those in tertiary occupations—around 22% of the working population—are involved in the provision of services. And this estimate compares quite well with that based on the industrial employment data—and with the estimate in the previous section of the proportion of national expenditure on services.[14]

Goods or services?

So where does this leave us in relation to the service-economy thesis? The answer takes us back to the fundamental nature of services. Their essence is their personal nature—at the simplest a one-to-one relationship between servant and served—for Bell, services are "a game between people", unmediated by "things".

Now, in an economy with considerable disparities of income, we find two things: first, a disparity of needs, the rich having, at the margin, needs for complicated and abstract luxuries, the poor for basic necessities; second, the rich are able to buy the full-time services of the poor. In such a situation, we would predict the luxury needs of the rich would be met by services—they would employ full-time servants to supply them. But as a society becomes richer, and as incomes and wealth become evenly distributed, two things will happen:

• fewer people will be willing to undertake menial tasks—to be literally at someone's beck and call;
• marginal needs will become more similar, and more and more people will be demanding these complicated and abstract luxuries.

New technical means and social organisations develop to supply these needs.[15] Though my cultural requirements may approximate those of a Prince Esterhazy, I am more likely than he to possess a stereophonic record player, and less likely to employ a Haydn and a full orchestra. In general, the changes in consumption patterns that we have observed follow this pattern—the replacement of services by goods.

Education and medicine

The main exceptions to this pattern are health and education. Historically speaking, these have been the only services to have grown over the last two decades; can we, as Bell tells us, expect them to continue to grow? Now, certainly as we get richer, we are more concerned about our health and our education—but this is not the issue. Rather, we should be asking whether these newly dominant needs will be met by goods or by services. Of course, the provision for these complicated needs by goods is not yet possible—but in education at least it is not very far off. It would only take some relatively minor technological developments (cheaper video machines and image storage media) to convert the UK Open University into a complete university education which could be bought, once and for all, over the counter of some educational emporium.

The characteristics of an open-learning system are that the learning opportunity is available to any person, at any level, at any time, in any place, and in any subject . . . you should be able to do Chinese at three o'clock in the morning in a Welsh mountain village . . . an open learning system must be built on materials—print, tape, kits—and the student must be able to control his use of them. The teacher of course is still there. He is needed to man the base where the resources are, to run classes for those who want them, to run tutorials, to mark correspondence assignments, to make up courses from material banks and to provide a diagnostic and advisory service.[16]

This is, all things considered, a much more likely picture of future "lifelong, continuing education", than Bell's image of the ramifying University, the coming of the predominant don; an emphasis on educational "material", with the teacher as a sort of maintenance engineer, and the system achieving, not just high productivity from trained manpower, but also, however repugnant to the values of those in more traditional education, a high degree of flexibility to the needs of the user. Such a development would require a fundamental change in educational philosophy—but it is a *possible* development, and it does follow the trend we have observed in household consumption. It must be seen as a viable alternative to Bell's forecast for at least part of the educational system.

Medicine is not technically so far advanced, but then, if there were no powerful lobbies interested in preventing it, how close might we be to the diagnostic and prescribing machine? Whatever the exact answer, it will lie within the same sort of timespan as I have considered in this article. We cannot say for certain, as Bell asks us to, that the same social forces that produced the home washing machine and the home music machine, will not in the future produce the home hospital machine or the home university.

New social relations

This does not mean that we may expect employment in tertiary industry and occupations to decrease in the future. On the contrary, I have argued that a major part of growth in tertiary employment has consisted of those service industries (distribution, banking, insurance, finance) which have to do essentially with the system of production of material goods and their ownership, and those service occupations (managers, technologists, and other professionals) whose activities improve the efficiency of this system. The growth of these sorts of employment is simply a manifestation of the division of labour. If, from the foregoing paragraphs, we expect the private consumption of material goods to grow, we may also expect this process of division of labour to continue—not merely within industries, as in the classical accounts, but also between industries, and between whole sectors of the economy.

Putting these two trends (decreasing service consumption, increasing tertiary employment) together we get a rather startling view of a change in the process of production.

- Final production takes place increasingly in the home, while work outside the home is more and more concerned with intermediate production, production of the goods ("capital goods" from this viewpoint) used for the home-based final production.

- Out-of-home employment is increasingly concerned with planning and programming production; presumably with automation the number of jobs involving the direct transformation of material will decrease.

Certainly this new form of organisation has advantages. It alters social relations; a change from a society of masters and servants (both in personal consumption and in the manner of provision for that consumption), to a society of consumers—still unequal in the quantity of consumption perhaps, but increasingly equal in the way in which the consumption is provided. But there are disadvantages as well. The trends tend towards a new sort of class structure; a technocratic elite employed in administering the system of material production and the mass population almost entirely separated from the wider economic system, being involved principally in the production of final services, by direct labour (ie by the final consumer) in their own homes.

The service-economy thesis, considered as a *prediction*, does not seem likely to come about. I have suggested grounds for suspecting a precisely contrary trend, towards more material consumption of goods. But this is only a trend, and trends may be reversed. There are usually alternative technical and social solutions to the problems of a society, there may be an alternative to the process of replacement of labour by capital goods which has been described in this article. The problem with the service-economy thesis, more important than the fact that it is a misleading description of the past, is that, when applied to the future, it distracts us from the possibility of influencing the pattern of development. If a service economy is desirable it will have to be promoted—present trends suggest that it will not come about without some encouragement.

Notes and references

1. Daniel Bell, *The Coming of Post-Industrial Society* (London, Heineman, 1974), page 128:

   ... as national incomes rise, one finds, as in the theorem of Christian Engel, a German statistician of the latter half of the nineteenth century, that the proportion of money spent on food at home begins to drop, and the marginal increments are used, first for durables (clothing, housing, automobiles) and then luxury items, recreation, and the like . . . health and education.

2. Bell, *op cit*, page 15.
3. See, for comparison, Karl Marx, *Capital* (London, Pelican, 1976), page 125:

   The commodity is, first of all, an external object, a thing which through its qualities satisfies human needs of whatever kind. The nature of these needs, whether they arise, for example from the stomach, or the imagination, makes no difference. Nor does it matter here how the thing satisfies man's needs, whether directly as a means of subsistence, ie an object of consumption, or indirectly as a means of production.

4. According to the UK's 1971 Census of Population, 84% of the workforce in tertiary industry were members of the tertiary occupational classification. For reference see: *Census 1961: England and Wales, Industry Tables* (London, HMSO) Part 1, Table 7 "Industry by occupation"; *Census 1961: Scotland, Occupation, Industry and Workplace* (London, HMSO), Part 2, Table 7 "Industry by occupation"; *Census 1971: Great Britain, Economic Activity* (London, HMSO) Part 3, Table 19 "Industry by occupation".
5. In the UK, of course, this excludes two major categories of expenditure: education and medicine. I shall discuss these later.

6. The sources for Figures 1 and 2, and for Tables 1 and 2, are the *Family Expenditure Survey* (London, HMSO) for the relevant years. The services category here includes such items as post and telecommunications, cinemas, and theatres, domestic help and laundry, hairdressing, repairs, television licence and rent, (private) medicine and education, holidays, charities, etc.

7. If anything, the data for 1954 underestimates the expenditure on services of the highest budgetary group—the service proportion of expenditure is reduced by a rather large payment in another category. To quote the rather indignant footnote appended to the entry for this group in the "women's outer clothing" category in the official statistics: "one member of a household in this group spent £1903 on one item during the period that records were being kept", *Family Expenditure Survey*, 1953–1954, page 14.

8. These estimates are based on the price series found in the Department of Employment *Gazette* (London, HMSO) and its predecessors.

9. Estimates are from *National Income and Expenditure* for each year. The estimates of consumer expenditure on services are calculated in a slightly different way to that in Table 1.

10. This argument is incomplete; limitations on space preclude an adequate discussion of the tricky issue of defining "goods" and "services" in precise operational terms. The size of the disparities between service consumption and service employment is, however, such that none of the possible objections to the definitions chosen affects the conclusions to any significant degree.

11. Expenditure data as in Table 4; the employment figures come from the annual Census of Employment published in the Department of Employment *Gazette*.

12. The sources for Table 5 are: *Census 1961: England and Wales, Industry Tables* (London, HMSO), Part 1, Table 2 "Industry and status"; *Census 1961: Scotland, Occupation, Industry and Workplace* (London, HMSO) part 1, Table 2 "Industry and status"; *Census 1971: Great Britain, Economic Activity* (London, HMSO), Part 2, Table 16 "Industry status and sex".

The sources for Table 6 are *Census 1961: England and Wales, Industry Tables* (London, HMSO), Part 1, Table 7 "Industry by occupation"; *Census 1961: Scotland, Occupation, Industry and Workplace* (London, HMSO) Part 2, Table 7 "Industry by occupation"; *Census 1971: Great Britain, Economic Activities* (London, HMSO), Part 3, Table 19, "Industry by occupation".

13. This estimate includes the various engineers, technologists and other professionals who are self-employed (or employed by consulting firms) so that, though they contribute directly to material production, they are still accounted for in the "miscellaneous services" employment category (these are about $1 \cdot 1\%$ of the working population). It also includes those public administrators whose work directly aids the productive process.

14. For consistency we should add that approximately 6% of the working population consists of workers in primary or secondary occupations employed in the tertiary industrial sector.

15. There is no suggestion of unidirectional *cause* here; technologies, patterns of social organisations and demand are interdependent and develop interactively.

16. Richard Freeman, Director National Extension College, *The Listener*, 14 October 1976.

THE NEW MATRIX OF POLITICAL ACTION

Alan Marsh

The increasing diversity of political involvement from the 1960s onwards led to an international study designed to explain the style of political action, and the protest potential in five countries: Britain, the USA, West Germany, Austria, and the Netherlands. The study identified five types of political involvement (inactives, conformists, reformists, activists, and protesters) together with their corresponding characteristics (including age, sex, education, and values). The number of reformists and activists is likely to increase, while the protesters pose a random threat to society. They appear to have a commitment to action but to little else. Their future impact depends on who mobilises them first.

By 1970, the visible changes of style in political participation during the preceding seven or so years had falsified most of the complacent assumptions of political scientists. A group of political scientists met in Geneva in 1970 to discuss the possibility of a new cross-national survey of political change. There was a lot to talk about.

Until the early 1960s, the main worry among political scientists was the apparent decline of mass political activism and political consciousness.[1] Yet by 1970, anyone monitoring political activity had amassed an impressive file of reports on demonstrations, boycotts, political strikes, occupations, riots, arson, and violence. These events had spread throughout what are still called, increasingly with more hope than certainty, Western democracies. Any new study of mass politics would have to take account of this increasing diversity of political participation.

Alan Marsh is now a Principal Social Survey Officer at the Office of Population Censuses and Surveys, 10 Kingsway, London WC2. The research reported in this article was conducted during his tenure as Research Officer at the SSRC Survey Unit and formed the basis for his book *Protest and Political Consciousness* (Beverly Hills, Sage Publications, 1977) and for chapters written jointly with Max Kaase (ZUMA, University of Mannheim) for the forthcoming volume edited by Samuel H. Barnes and Max Kaase, *Political Action* (Beverly Hills, Sage Publications, 1979). The views expressed in this article are those of the author and are in no way associated with the work of the OPCS. Dr Marsh gratefully acknowledges permission from his friend and colleague Professor Max Kaase freely to use data and ideas jointly developed in their work on this project.

The theory and measurement of political action

How would this be done? Despite the headlines, relatively few people actually get involved in unconventional forms of political action (few enough contribute personally to conventional politics) and those who do tend to be *ad hoc* minorities who have been bruised into action by the touch of an insensitive authority. Even in 1968, the majority of students failed to turn out for the revolution. Consequently the discussion of this part of the survey design centred upon a new concept which was called 'protest potential'.

The theory was that the model of effective unconventional political behaviour provided by the upheavals of the 1960s was in the process of transmission out into the political consciousness of ordinary members of the polity. What was needed was a measure of the extent to which people were developing a *readiness* to engage in direct-action politics. This readiness, even if it is not often realised in individual action, is a real political resource and one that modern authorities will have to take into account.

Technically speaking, the idea of a measure of protest potential was not a very promising one. When asked how likely it is that they might participate in, say, a demonstration, surely people would reply (very reasonably), "Well, that depends on the issues involved". However, detailed pilot research conducted in Britain indicated that the predicted "It depends" qualification was not too important.[2] People were quite prepared to indicate their readiness to protest in certain ways, in principle.

To measure protest potential, respondents were asked to say, for several examples of protest action, how much they approved the action, whether they thought the action would be effective, and whether they might use that form of action. The examples of protest action were: signing petitions, lawful demonstrations, boycotts, unofficial strikes, rent strikes, street blockades, occupying buildings, damaging property, and using personal violence.

This measure was set into the questionnaire alongside more familiar measures of conventional political participation: voting, and party support including campaigning for candidates, discussing politics, attending meetings, and so on. These two measures of unconventional and conventional political participation formed, in our theory, the two main pathways toward political redress now open to citizens in democratic countries: the choice between them would determine the character of political conduct—the *style* of political action—that will come to characterise democratic political communities. This knowledge (of political style) may have a critical role in the interpretation of any political changes which accompany the underlying structural changes in Western democracies, as their political economies move away from class-based material politics towards the uncertain future of post-industrial politics.

The countries that were finally to come under scrutiny in this way were Britain, West Germany, the Netherlands, Austria, and the USA. The survey in each country was independently funded from domestic sources; fieldwork was conducted between November 1973 and September 1974 on nationally representative random samples ranging in size from 1203 (the Netherlands) to 2307 (West Germany).[3] Surveys were later conducted in Switzerland, Italy, and Finland but their data are not dealt with in this article.

The research strategy was to explain styles of political action. The theoretical design that evolved to satisfy this aim was a very formal and complex array of antecedent variables having to do with political dissatisfaction, values, ideology, trust, efficacy, and so on. Rather than attempting to encompass the whole design in this article, I will concentrate on the structure of political action as it unfolded in each country studied; antecedent factors will be brought in where they best fit the story.

Protest potential

To a surprising extent, there was great structural consistency in people's attitudes toward the protest examples from country to country. Although each question was asked separately and in random order, people tended to place the examples along a single psychological continuum. At one end of this continuum are mild forms of protest (eg signing petitions, peaceful marches) and at the other are extreme forms (eg deliberate damage to property, physical violence). Between these extremes are ordered: demonstrations, boycotts, rent strikes, unofficial strikes, street blockades, and occupations.

So common was this cumulative model of protest in people's minds that, in each country, it proved possible to construct a very similar scale wherein one needed only to know the 'highest' example endorsed by a respondent to be able to

TABLE 1. PROTEST POTENTIAL

	Actions				
Ranking	Britain	West Germany	Netherlands	Austria	USA
1	petitions	petitions	petitions	petitions	petitions
2	demonstrations	demonstrations	demonstrations	demonstrations	demonstrations
3	boycotts	boycotts	boycotts	boycotts	boycotts
4	rent strikes	rent strikes	occupations	blockades	rent strikes
5	blockades	blockades	rent strikes	rent strikes	occupations
6	occupations	unofficial strikes	blockades	unofficial strikes	unofficial strikes
7	unofficial strikes	occupations	unofficial strikes	occupations	blockades
Guttman-scale scores[a]					
0	23	18	9	21	9
1	22	21	21	33	21
2	25	30	26	26	24
3	15	19	15	11	26
4	6	5	11	5	8
5	3	3	7	2	5
6	2	2	7	1	3
7	3	3	6	1	3
Coefficient of reproducibility					
	0·95	0·97	0·94	0·97	0·96
Nonscalable respondents (%)					
	6	5	4	20	6

Note: [a]The scores are expressed as percentages; columns may not sum to 100% because of rounding errors. The scales were constructed using the OSIRIS III program GSCORE, allowing for a maximum of three scale errors and two missing data to be corrected by the program, using the MEDIAN method. The scale ranges from 0 (no protest) to 7 (high protest).
Source: Max Kaase and Alan Marsh, "The matrix of political action", paper read to Special Meeting 22 at the Tenth World Congress of the International Political Science Association, Edinburgh, August 1976.

represent his or her views on protest with a single scale score. The power of the underlying dimension was such that it was as if we had asked: "Think about protest. How far are you prepared to go?" Through answering several questions, respondents indicated: "This far and no further", ie as far as demonstrations, or strikes, or, for a very few, as far as violence. The details of this finding are shown in Table 1.

Commitment to action

Since the scales reflect attitudes rather than behaviour and we know that few people actually 'get involved' in protest, we were at pains to *minimise* the number of positive responses unless there was strong evidence that potential protesters meant what they said. Accordingly, a respondent was given a positive score at each point on the scale only if he said that, at least, he might participate in the described act of protest *and* he approved of such behaviour. Commitment to action, we felt, was the product of positive intentions and favourable norms. This stringent procedure, including coding all 'don't knows' as negative answers, quickly eliminated 'damage' and 'violence' from consideration—virtually no-one supports these strategies in principle or in fact.

The rank order of the items is cross-nationally similar; petitions are consistently the most popular (or least offensive) protest tactic, followed by lawful demonstrations and boycotts, while rent strikes appear as fourth or fifth. Beyond this the ordering of the more extreme examples becomes idiosyncratic because the numbers endorsing them in each country are small and so subject to large sampling errors. Interestingly, unofficial strikes are least popular in Britain. The strength of the unidimensional scale in each country and the fact that, despite our stringent scoring system, more than half of each national sample will consider getting involved at least as far as demonstrations confirms our initial expectation that protest potential has indeed spread out to form part of modern political consciousness far beyond the students and militant ethnic minorities who were the main protagonists of the events of the late 1960s.

National variations

The highest levels of protest potential are found in the Netherlands, where 31% of the population will venture beyond demonstrations and boycotts into more extreme forms of protest. Whilst the Dutch have a reputation for political permissiveness it is difficult, even in the face of this evidence, to think of them as a nation of politically aggressive people. The US sample, who would be everyone's best guess as the most aggressive group in the study, has fewer people (19%) who will venture beyond boycotts and the same low percentage (9%) as the Dutch of people who will go no futher than petitions.

Germany and Britain show very similar levels of protest potential with 45% and 39% respectively inactive and 14% and 13% in the highly active categories (ie less than half the Dutch figure) while only in Austria is protest still an unfamiliar prospect with 54% inactive and only 9% highly active. Yet one should not focus too strongly on these 'highly active' minorities. A majority in every country except Austria (46%) will go as far as joining a lawful demonstration or even operating a boycott. Such behaviour is a strong act of protest for most people and the significance of its popularity should not be underestimated. Since the strongly behavioural character of the measure also tends to rule out most people over 50 years of age, the proportion of the active population in each country that it seems possible to mobilise in direct-action politics is really very impressive.

Conventional political participation

Among many popular commentators on the growth of protest movements there has been a tendency to see protest as an alternative form of political action to party (or representative) politics. For a few radical groups, an extreme commitment to direct action did imply a break with conventional party politics, but for the population as a whole it is an unlikely idea. On the contrary, the idea of an increasing diversity of style among activists seemed to us more likely and the data encourage this supposition. For now, let us concentrate on the measurement of conventional political involvement. In the questionnaire, this topic followed a similar format to the protest scale except that respondents were asked *how often* they participated in key examples of conventional politics: reading about politics in newspapers, discussing politics with friends, working on community problems, contacting bureaucrats or elected representatives, trying

TABLE 2. CONVENTIONAL POLITICAL PARTICIPATION

	Actions[a]				
	Britain	West Germany	Netherlands	Austria	USA
Ranking					
1	read	read	read	read	read
2	discuss	discuss	discuss	discuss	discuss
3	community	convince	community	campaign	community
4	contact	attend	contact	convince	campaign
5	convince	campaign	convince	community	contact
6	attend	community	campaign	campaign	convince
7	campaign	contact	attend	contact	attend
Guttman-scale scores[b]					
0	28	23	29	34	16
1	25	31	21	23	18
2	30	17	30	22	24
3	7	8	8	7	12
4	4	6	5	4	9
5	1	4	2	3	8
6	1	4	1	2	7
7	3	6	4	5	6
Coefficient of reproducibility					
	0·95	0·94	0·95	0·94	0·91
Nonscalable respondents (%)					
	2	1	1	0	0

Notes: [a]Read about politics in papers; discuss politics with friends; work on community problems; contact politicians or public officials; convince friends to vote as self; attend political meetings; participate in election campaign. [b]The scores are expressed as percentages; columns may not sum to 100% because of rounding errors. The scales were constructed using the OSIRIS III program GSCORE, allowing for a maximum of three scale errors and two missing data to be corrected by the program, using the MEDIAN method. The scale ranges from 0 (no participation) to 7 (high participation).
Source: See Table 1.

to convince others to vote their way, attending political meetings, and participating in election campaigns. All this is familiar ground for respondent and researcher alike.

Interestingly, the rates of reported participation in conventional political behaviour obeyed a cumulative structure in just the same way as the protest examples. There is apparently a similar narrow pathway of how far a person is prepared to go in conventional political involvement, although the rank ordering of the items tends to be rather different from country to country. The details are given in Table 2.

Just as the Dutch are outstandingly the most protest-prone nation, US citizens excel in their degree of involvement in conventional politics. Of Americans, 42% will go further than merely talking about politics, compared with only 16–21% in Britain, the Netherlands, or Austria, and 29% in Germany. The Dutch in fact produce an extraordinary response: they are actually more prepared to use protest methods than they are to get involved with their (admittedly complex) party system. The USA shows the most even balance between protest and parties and reflects the kind of active diversity one might expect to find there. Among the Europeans, the Germans are the most politically involved but with their balance tipped in favour of the conventional system rather than protest potential.

The political action repertory

Consistently in each country there is a modest degree of *positive* association between the two political action scales: the tendency to have a high or low score on the protest scale is associated with a correspondingly high or low score on the conventional participation scale. Thus the choice of direct-action protest strategies does not necessarily imply a departure from involvement in conventional politics. You do not have to hand in your party card to take up a protest campaign.

On the contrary, as we suspected, ordinary people will declare a willingness to engage in protest action to *augment* their political leverage beyond that available to them in the conventional sphere. The increasingly bureaucratic and professional nature of the establishment parties has made them, paradoxically perhaps, less responsive to the diverse character of modern political demand. The definition of a legitimate mass-political issue or target has widened considerably to include the sphere of personal morality, environmental change, the accountability of paid officials, the power of trade unions, and interest-group politics of many kinds. Many people find it appropriate to devise their own direct pathways of political redress as well as trying to prod harassed party luminaries into mobilising their threadbare organisations to take an interest in yet another novel and unfamiliar topic.

In survey research, it is difficult to do justice to a richly complex phenomenon such as that which we felt underlay the balance between the choice of conventional or unconventional political action. Yet we decided upon a simple step that would enable us to consider the two sides of this vital balance simultaneously as a single phenomenon. Protest potential and conventional political participation are positively related but not exactly overlapping: there are many

TABLE 3. A FIVEFOLD TYPOLOGY OF POLITICAL ACTION

| | Conventional political participation | | |
Protest potential	None, or no further than reading the newspapers	Discussing politics and working for the community	Actual participation; contacting officials, attending meetings and campaigns
None, or no further than signing petitions	inactives	conformists	conformists
Demonstrations and boycotts	protesters	reformists	reformists
Rent strikes, unofficial strikes, occupations, street blockades	protesters	activists	activists

Source: See Table 1.

exceptions, eg people who are 'high' on one scale and 'low' on the other. After considerable research, a typology of political action was developed. This is shown in Table 3.

This configuration of behaviour we have come to call the political action repertory. A great deal of experiment eventually defined five basic types of political action.

- The 'inactives' are the least difficult to describe; they will do no more than glance at political news and might sign a petition if asked (many of them do not even do this).
- The 'conformists' represent the traditional mode of political activity; they will progressively involve themselves in the business of good government, attending meetings, treating with officials, even campaigning for candidates but they will not participate at all in protest.
- The 'reformists' share the same level of involvement in conventional politics as the conformists but add to their political repertory what they would probably be careful to call 'moderate' levels of protest (lawful demonstrations and boycotts).
- The 'activists', on the other hand, are the complete political all-rounders; their action repertory is the widest, and among their number are people having the highest levels of conventional *and* unconventional tendencies.
- The least well understood group is the 'protesters', whose choice of political action is confined to protest methods: they shun entirely any conventional involvement. Are these then the alienated rebels from authority that the news commentators of the late 1960s told us to expect? In the best traditions of social science the answer is, of course, yes and no, which ought to be clearer in a moment.

The degree of constraint or freedom in the conduct of the political community in Western democracies will depend crucially on the distribution of the population among the five categories of the political action repertory. Table 4 reports the situation as we found it in the mid 1970s.

The inactives are less numerous than those who lament modern political apathy would believe, ranging from 30% and 27% in Britain and Germany, down to 18% and 17% in the Netherlands and Austria, and 12% in the USA. The Netherlands distributes its surplus of potential protesters evenly between the reformists, activists, and protesters. Elsewhere the tendency is to favour either reformists or protesters, while the even-handed versatility of the activists naturally results in this being the rarest group (between 6% in Austria and 14% in the USA). Democratic theorists of a traditional persuasion will not

TABLE 4. NATIONAL POLITICAL ACTION REPERTORIES

Type[a]	Britain	West Germany	Netherlands	Austria	USA
Inactives (%)	30·1	26·6	17·9	34·9	12·3
Conformists (%)	15·4	13·5	11·1	19·2	17·5
Reformists (%)	21·9	24·6	19·8	20·9	36·0
Activists (%)	10·2	8·0	19·3	5·9	14·4
Protesters (%)	22·4	27·3	31·9	19·1	19·8
Sample size (classified respondents)	*1389*	*2207*	*1144*	*1265*	*1613*
Nonclassified respondents	*6*	*4*	*5*	*20*	*6*
Total sample size (people)	*1483*	*2307*	*1203*	*1584*	*1719*

Note: [a]As a percentage of classified respondents.
Source: Max Kaase and Alan Marsh, "The typology of political action: distribution and social location", chapter 6 in the forthcoming book edited by Samuel H. Barnes and Max Kaase, *Political Action* (Beverly Hills, Sage Publications, 1979).

welcome the fact that in no country is the conformist category occupied by more than 20% of the total; in Britain it is as little as 15%.

It is one thing to define an empirical classification of the population into a typology but quite another to demonstrate that the types so defined actually differ from one another in predictable ways that are also theoretically interpretable and intuitively sensible. Let us start with some obvious characteristics: age, sex, and education.

Determinants of political type

As may be expected, the oldest groups are the inactives and the conformists; on average about half of them are over 50 years old and only 5% under 20. Except in Austria, by far the youngest groups are the activists and the protesters, 40–50% being under 30 (strikingly younger even than the reformists). The energy and commitment demanded by the higher reaches of the protest scale are clearly the telling factors here.

The impacts of sex and education are a little more difficult to unravel since they are interrelated: men are better educated than women. Women are over-represented among the inactives. Conversely men tend to dominate the reformist and activist groups with the conformists being evenly balanced between the sexes. All the literature on political sociology would predict such an outcome but it did not at all prepare us to find that women also dominate the protester category.

This last finding apart, the question arises: is the exclusion of women from the versatile reformist and activist groups due to their sex and the politically inhibiting social roles assigned to them, or is it due to their education being generally less than that of men? Education is certainly important in its own right. Predictably, as one moves from the inactives through the conformists and the reformists to the activists, the proportion of those having only a basic education falls sharply and those having some higher education rises equally dramatically. Again the surprise is provided by the protesters, whose education profile is quite unlike their more versatile co-protesters among the reformists and activists: it far more closely resembles the conformists or even the inactives.

Women and protest

An analysis combining the effects of sex and education shows that, among the more active categories, there is some lessening of the male dominance among the better educated. Yet by far the most interesting result is that women still outnumber men even among the rarer group of the well-educated protesters. In fact, the protester category can be partially described as a curious alliance between poorly educated young men and some well-educated young women. This suggests that the men fall into this category largely through an ill-formed but positive response to the idea of protest but lack the skills to adopt the versatile stance of the activists; while the women often get there by short-circuiting the pathway of development described by the inactive–conformist–reformist–activist route, moving directly from the inactives to the protester group. These women report low conventional participation, not because of a traditional inactivity conditioned by poorer education, but as a result of a sex-based lack of identification with conventional politics. Their idea of political mobilisation does involve shunning the grey-suited, male-dominated world of 'politics'. In an unsuspecting way, we stumbled into the repertory location of the women's liberation movement.

What evidence do we have for these speculations about the states of mind of the repertory types? First, we asked a simple question: "How interested would you say you are in politics?" Naturally, the inactives express little interest while the conformists, reformists and activists all claim an equally lively interest in politics. The protesters, however, show low levels of political interest akin to the inactives. This is strange; if they have no interest in politics, what do they want to protest about? Perhaps to them 'politics' means *conventional* politics which they find distasteful; especially, to the majority of women among them, male politics. Certainly we find that the protesters show a low level of attachment to political parties, as do the inactives, saying that they feel not very close to the party of their choice, or choosing no party at all.

The depth of political thought

Two far more sensitive measures of political cognition were developed for this study by Hans Dieter Klingemann. One measure, called 'the active use of ideological thinking', is derived from respondents' answers to open-ended questions about their likes and dislikes of the the two major parties in each country. The second, called 'the level of ideological thinking' is similarly derived from respondents' descriptions of their understanding of the terms 'left' and 'right' in politics. High levels of ideological thinking are most frequently found in Germany and are least common in Britain. The use of these ideological concepts, in each country, is strongly associated with the reformist and activist categories and is very uncommon among the inactives. Again we find that this lack of thinking is also shared by the protesters. Protest they might, but members of this group (unlike the activists and reformists) show little ability to interpret their position in relation to a more complex political framework. The same result is obtained using a measure of political efficacy (ie the feeling that one can influence and interpret political events). Conformists, reformists, and activists feel politically efficacious; inactives *and* protesters do not.

So we are faced with a puzzle. Four groups run true to type: inactives are not stirred by matters political; conformists are older traditional activists; reformists and, especially, activists are the *parvenus* of modern political man (particularly, man). Yet in the protesters we have a group of potential political activists who are remote from politics. Perhaps, despite their lower level of cognitive skill which seems to keep them out of mainstream politics, they nevertheless *feel* the same way as their more versatile brethren, the activists? Do they share a similar ideology?

The basic ideological polarity, left versus right, was dealt with in two ways: first in terms of party identification and second by respondents placing themselves on a ten-point scale running, literally, from 'left' to right'. Two clear effects emerge. Activists are young leftists; in Germany only 11% of them declare for the Christian Democrats and in Britain they are two to one in favour of the Labour Party. Conformists, on the other hand, tend toward identification with the political right. Reformists and inactives tend to reflect a balanced view and, most surprisingly, so do the protesters, though these last two groups more frequently say they identify with no party at all. So once more the protesters appear in a strangely apolitical light. More worryingly in Britain perhaps, young men in the protester category show some strong leanings to the right: it would be possible to name one emergent political party that has already capitalised on this unexpected fact. Combining the earlier measure of ideological sophistication with the left–right placement in a single analysis we found also that many right-wing ideologues tend to favour the reformist category—they accept the idea of direct action but stop short of illegality.

Political value priorities

Cutting down deeper into our respondents' political feelings, we asked them to choose among a set of value priorities, between such items as economic growth and stability, strong defences, civic order, and fighting crime on the one hand and ecological improvement, participation, freedom, and 'a society where ideas are more important than money' on the other. These and similar items form a single 'materialist versus post-materialist' measure of political values, which is said by Inglehart to underlie and explain much of the political change that the survey was designed to study.[4] The rise of post-materialist values among the young results from economic growth, which has freed the postwar generation to maximise their higher-order needs. This contrasts with the material preoccupations of their parents, and explains the severe intergenerational strain in political priorities and behaviour.

Gratifyingly for Inglehart's theory we find that post-materialist values are outstandingly an 'activist' characteristic. This is so in the Netherlands, where post-materialist views are common and also in Germany and Britain where they are not: only 14% and 22% respectively of all German and British respondents are post-materialists compared to 50% and 42% of their activists. Only the activists are motivated in this high-minded way. While the inactives and conformists tend toward a materialist orientation, it is again fascinating to see that the protesters show no greater post-materialist 'enlightenment' than the average.

Measuring dissatisfaction

There remains the possibility that the unifying factor which would provide a common source of motivation for all our active participation types—for the protesters as well as the activists and reformists—lies in a simpler idea. This is the connection between feelings of dissatisfaction and protest, or the 'relative deprivation' theory. After all, everyone recalls Daniel Cohn-Bendit's refreshingly succinct explanation of *les events*: "Yes," he agreed, "we are in revolt. We are fed up with everything". Despite his seductive simplicity, attempts to demonstrate this connection have generated a remarkably confused picture. Our study fielded several measures of dissatisfaction. Two of these were : 'personal material dissatisfaction' (PMD), which used self-placement on a 0–10 scale of satisfaction; and a composite measure of 'dissatisfaction with government performance' (DGP) over 10 important areas of responsibility.

The first measure produced a result typical of the confusion mentioned above. Britain produced twice as many materially dissatisfied people as elsewhere (so the measure appears valid, at least) yet the most protest-prone country—the Netherlands—was also the most satisfied. The relationship between PMD and the action repertory is very muted. Inactives and conformists tend a little to be more satisfied (being older, of course) and the activists a little *less* materially satisfied (strangely so given their stridently *post*-materialist values). There are still no signs of deviant dissatisfaction from the protesters; their PMD scores are only average.

Disaffected activists

The second measure—DGP—produced more interesting results. Inactives and conformists pronounce themselves largely satisfied with the performance of their national governments and the reformists venture only mild rebuke. The activists in contrast (the only significantly leftist group, remember) are virulent critics of government, except in Austria where activist criticism of their socialist government is suitably restrained. Elsewhere, particularly in the USA, activists are at least twice as likely as other groups to express dissatisfaction with their government. Yet the protesters do not echo the activists' dissent; their level of criticism is no greater than average. It surely demands only the minimum cognitive sophistication and no special ideological commitment to express the view that the government is doing a bad job, yet the protesters show not even this basic unity with their activist co-protesters.

To quote from the British study: "There seems to be a movement . . . away from a quiet and respectful participatory democracy towards a noisy and disrespectful participatory democracy".[5] Leading this movement are clearly the activists; they have a 'full house' of political cards to play—disaffected, post-materialist, leftist, highly competent, and efficacious—and have the education to play them well. The reformists follow them in many things but are more diverse, balanced, and reserved in their attitudes and behaviour. There is no evidence in the survey that either group nurtures any irreconcilable hostility towards the system as practised, only against some of its products and practitioners.

On the contrary, their new melding of conventional and unconventional strategies of political redress is likely to continue to stress bourgeois notions of democracy and freedom. With their youth and middle-class education it could hardly be otherwise and it means, of course, that this new versatility signals no end to the essentially middle-class character of radical political leadership. It arises from the ideology of the young and privileged, not from the material need of the poor and oppressed.

While we cannot rule out a life cycle interpretation (activists can grow old into inactives) it seems likely that the two versatile categories, the reformists and activists, will grow in numbers at the expense of the inactive and conformist categories, if for no more complicated reason than that this process is clearly fuelled and facilitated by improved and still improving education. This dual growth of activism may not always be comfortable for those responsible for administration and social control but it is more likely to revitalise the political community than to threaten it.

Unpredictable protesters

The jokers in our pack are the protesters. Each protester made a strong statement that he or she would participate in at least a demonstration and approved of such events, most of them going much further than this, some including illegal acts of protest in their manifesto. Yet they exhibit markedly low political interest, low political competence and efficacy, no special ideological commitment, not even any real dissatisfaction. So what are they likely to protest about?

The answer is that it will depend on who gets to them first. While in almost every political characteristic they strangely resemble the inactives more than any other group, they deviate in one special and obvious way: they are very young. They have learned in an apolitical way—through television, films and magazines—that a willingness to protest is somehow an indispensable part of their credentials as young people. Most of them do not know why, excepting probably the large cadre of disaffected well-educated young women among them, but even they have not spoken up too articulately.

While there is much in this analysis of political participation in five Western democracies that will encourage those who value their continued health and progress, the protesters appear as a kind of random threat, like a lead weight swinging free in a delicate machine. Their present trajectory is probably harmless and what excursions into political action they have made have likely been organised by activists. Converse and Pierce found them among the youth of France in the late 1960s and called them '*les marais*'—the marshy, unproductive middle-ground that can be turned to any use.[6] Yet to see a commitment to action, with a lack of commitment to anything else, provokes unease in any disinterested observer and it may be reassuring to stress again that the majority of potential protesters belong to the politically integrated reformist and activist groups. The main source of unease is the knowledge that there have been times in recent history when the protesters have been easily mobilised by groups of determined 'activists' whose intentions have been anything but democratic.

Notes and references

1. See for example Daniel Bell, *The End of Ideology* (Glencoe, Illinois, Free Press, 1960).
2. See Alan Marsh, "Explorations in unorthodox political behaviour: a scale to measure protest potential", *European Journal of Political Research*, 1974, 2 (1), pages 107–129.
3. Principal investigators in each country were: Britain, Alan Marsh and Mark Abrams; Netherlands, Philip Stouthard (Catholic University, Tilburg); USA, Sameul H. Barnes, Ronald Inglehart, and Kent Jennings (University of Michigan); West Germany, Max Kaase, Hans Dieter Klingemann and Klaus Allerbeck (University of Mannheim); Austria, Leopold Rosenmayer (University of Vienna).
4. Ronald Inglehart, "The silent revolution in Europe", *American Political Science Review*, 1971, 65 (47), pages 991–1017.
5. Alan Marsh, *Protest and Political Consciousness* (Beverly Hills, Sage Publications 1977), page 234.
6. Phillip E. Converse and Roy Pierce, "Die Mai-Unruhen in Frankreich— Ausmass und Konsequenzen", in Klaus Allerbeck and Leopold Rosenmayer, eds, *Aufstand der Jugend?* (Munich, 1971), page 122.

PROFESSIONAL MISMANAGEMENT

The skill wastage in employment

Denis Pym

Absenteeism and overmanning occur in management too, as do collusive games that give a false impression of the manager's worth and the professional's relevance. New forms of employment contract are one way to alleviate the problem.

My contribution to the multitudinous outpourings on managers and professionals has two origins.[1] The first is the establishment attitude which maintains industrial mythology while engaging in occupational feather bedding. The other more disturbing, radical posture is aptly summed up in Illich's *Disabling Professions*.[2] While sympathising with the latter my own views are based on the conviction that the villainy or service we bestow on others we do to ourselves. My focus here is the psychologically out-of-shape professional and manager.

Whatever may be said about the state of the economy and the distribution of the workforce between occupations, the numbers in professional services and the ranks of management continue to grow. I want to take a critical look at these activities and, more particularly, the relations between them. Though the UK manager and the service sector have each come in for a fair amount of stick in examinations of

The author is a professor at the London Business School, Sussex Place, Regent's Park, London NW1 4SA, UK.

the UK economic malaise, professionals, by and large, have not. This is not surprising for professionals spearhead the criticism and put themselves above it all.

Though our professional views on the economic system and what may be done about it are legion, two characteristics, one an omission and the other an attitude, stand out. The first derives from our expert role—the failure to implicate ourselves in the problems to which we address ourselves. With about one-fifth of the UK workforce now engaged in professional and allied services this is a luxury society can hardly afford. The second is the powerful current of pessimism and impotence now shaping professional views. We professionals play a major part in formulating lives and yet we are *not* joyful people with optimistic visions of the future.

The professionalisation of the workforce has been associated with substantial changes in the professional's own relationship with the economic system.

Traditionally self-employed, the professional now is typically an employee, usually of a large government agency or large private concern. He (and sometimes she) is first and foremost a spokesman for his employment. The professional thus helps to maintain our belief in institutional authority by fashioning problems and solutions in terms of what governments, trade unions, the media, and industry are or might be doing.

In the *past decade* we in Britain have been obsessed with games which embellish this belief—suspended production or services by people with grievances which only our institutional leaders can rectify, endless reports on their pronouncements of gloom or hope as though they enjoyed some superior perception of reality, all those 'full and frank' exchanges and paper agreements and so on. Could these antics be our equivalent of the Roman's bread and circuses, reflecting a fear that without such pantomimes disorder and chaos might break out? But surely this risk is slight? For all his accumulated wealth and possessions industrial man remains confused.

The anxieties the media can provoke over the breakdowns of systems, scarcity, or rising prices betray our confident manner and advertise our abdication from personal responsibility. The professional's own changed status mirrors a more general move away from personal authority to a heavy dependence on institutions.

For industrial man has turned himself into a knob/switch/tap operator who looks to authorities to pipe food, energy, housing, transport, entertainment, and thoughts into the dulling security of his routinised life. Scarcity, which man once knew as life, now threatens to shut off the institutional pipes sustaining his false identity. The threat of stoppages and shortages is not just economic, it reveals the powerlessness and impotence both of our person and the edifices we have built in the name of our god, material prosperity.

In all of this managers and professionals have much to answer for and, whatever they do in their public roles, they must suffer privately like everybody else.

But what if the game itself is changing in meaning if not in form, if the rewards no longer justify the nonsense, if changing attitudes with the help of technology are stirring our last vestiges of integrity? Then we must return to fundamentals, to the last of the unaskable questions, to our relationship with the economic system no less. In the 1980s we can change the tune if we can only muster the energy from those private reserves which have not sold out to our public roles.

Common backgrounds

My interest in professionals and managers in employment holds closely to personal experience. All social enquiry, though it is seldom acknowledged, has a powerful autobiographical element. The more objectivity is claimed in research the more it tells us about the claimant. So if our work is dull, wordy, and trivial it is but an advertisement for ourselves, a reflection of our own brand of destitution. He who dismisses the observations of another as mere subjectivity does so from a cultural base that denies man's nature and its commonalities.

Two observations from my earliest experiences in employment provided the focus for subsequent enquiries. The first was the *lack of fit between personal talent, educational experience, and occupation opportunity.*

The self-critical new entrant to employment might view the problem in terms of his unsuitability. Those looking outside themselves express the problem in terms of the misuse or underutilisation of their talents.

The second observation concerned managers—notably *their lack of vision, idealism, and confidence.* Both observations were the offspring of unrealistic expectations. Like countless other university and technical college graduates, I entered employment expecting the world—a ready need for my talents and training and, after several years as a competent professional, a range of glittering prizes in the ranks of management. I, too, had been nurtured on the myth of the managerial élite.

The discovery of managerial caution and indecision, the manager's ordinariness, came even before I saw through the implications of the new entrant's endless 'training experiences', investigation, reports and meetings which so often came to little. Of course, these were *not* the experiences of every professional but as the 1950s gave way to the 1960s and 1970s they applied to a larger and larger proportion working for big employers. Today I estimate that around four-fifths of those employed in a professional capacity would concur, at least in part, with these observations.

My first analyses explored the link between managerial indecision and professional overrecruitment in the vicious circle shown in Figure 1.[3]

The insecure manager overrecruits to bolster his confidence and satisfy his need for status and security. However, the relative inexperience of the new recruits does not help in this respect and the manager, as a result of his own condition and the professionals' inexperience, is reluctant to trust them. He supervises their work too closely and/or gives them undemanding, trite jobs. These experiences conflict with what the more competent professionals seek in employment. They move on, upwards, sideways, or out, leaving behind their mediocre colleagues whose performances justify the bosses' caution.

What prompted my curiosity as a researcher was the apparent contradiction between the need for scientists, technologists, and experts as widely broadcast by leaders of government, business, and education in the 1960s and the actual experiences of those professionals in employment.

Solutions to the kind of problem described in my vicious circle are elaborated in every textbook on the theory of organisations. The confidence of managers can be restored by training and education and, along with the use of professionals, boosted by democratic management styles and changes in the structure (flatter hierarchies, matrix organisations etc) and culture (theory Y) of the organisation.[4] I believed this to be so until the end of the 1960s when

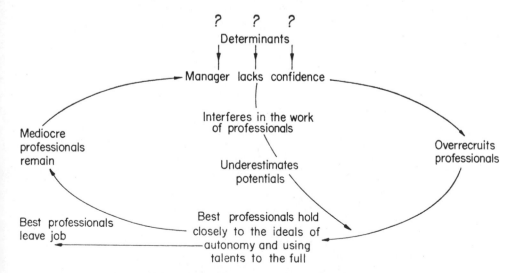

Figure 1. Managerial indecision and the misuse of professionals

it became clear that the problem was growing, indeed the solutions were adding to the tension. I concluded that little could be done by tinkering round with the internal order of the economic system.

The growth of manpower

Increases in the numbers of managers and those engaged in professional services transform the economy in well-documented ways (Table 1).

stances which apparently favour professional and managerial opportunities on the one hand but erode the power of the manager on the other.

The manager's lot

The manager's power isn't what it used to be. More experts, more cross-boundary relations to sustain, more active in-company trade unionism, more government constraints, slow growth and expansion, and larger

TABLE 1. NUMBERS OF EMPLOYEES IN MANAGEMENT AND PROFESSIONAL SERVICES IN THE UK

Year	Total workforce (M)	Managers (M)	Professional services (M)
1961	23·4	1·3	2·7
1966	24·2	1·5	3·2
1971	25·1	1·7	4·0
1976	25·8	1·9	?

Sources: Department of Employment, British Institute of Management.

Technical advances in production and communication pave the way for the steady movement of people from manufacturing to the *service sector* of employment where the proportions in professional services and managerial activities are highest. *Larger units* associated with the fashionable move to diversify in private enterprise, and economies-of-scale arguments in both private and public sectors have also provided additional opportunities for professionals and managers.

Technology too has been used to reduce the need for manpower in production (eg automation) and has increased it, so far, in service activities (eg computerisation). In all of this the role of *government* is critical, both directly through its support for higher education and indirectly through legislation which has created a vast array of new jobs many of them for those who benefited from the government's role in education.

Through the creation of new divisions of labour and the greater interdependence of those divisions, organisations have become more complex, circum-

hierarchies, all reduce the real power of the manager.

As this process has been going on for some time, it may seem surprising that the manager's declining position should not have invited attention earlier. But managerial mobility is central to industrial mythology. You must move on or get out. This makes the manager a poor student of history and of his changing circumstances. Here he contrasts with the stay-put supervisor or foreman who is only too aware of how his own influence has been eroded.

Indeed, the manager's own job involves less and less direction of his staff and more and more the managing of boundary relations (with other managers and professionals inside and outside his enterprise). This is what the growth of lateral communications is about.

A frequent complaint about bosses, among subordinates, particularly in those occupations where travel is expected, is that they are difficult to get through to and to obtain decisions from. These very circumstances also legitimise the manager's absence from the job and so conceal the extent to which he is himself withdrawing physically and/or psychologically from employment. Lack of energy, the real problem of man in employment (particularly in Britain), is not a characteristic of workers and clerks alone.

Probably the biggest deception perpetuated by social enquiry has been the emphasis given to the manager's leadership role while underplaying his status as an employee. In contrast with this bias, students of managerial behaviour—what he does on the job— have drawn attention to the manager as employee.[5] These enquirers ignored the less tangible aspects of the manager's job and demonstrate that his, like any other, is also reducible to visual symbols. In short, by ignoring the magic they prove that the manager has none.

Mintzberg's later work is even more relevant to my analysis because of his distinction between the 'facts' and 'folklore' of the manager's job.[6] In this he epitomises the researcher as industrial man by rejecting the rituals and mythology of employment and lauding the visible and literary symbol as fact. Consequently Mintzberg discards the key to a sympathetic understanding of the manager's predicament.

As an employee the manager has two areas of responsibility (see Table 2): one is his task and the other the maintenance of the system. The function of folklore (assuming people believe in it) is to legitimise activities which maintain the enterprise. If we are to take both the manager's role as employee and business mythology seriously then it may be useful to view the manager as a literate entrepreneur.

The manager's ability to organise, his capacity to examine and present issues in a linear, sequential, rational manner distinguishes him from the entrepreneur. The manager along with the professional places great store on the facts as visual literary details (words and numbers). He also believes that such data clarifies. It facilitates decision.

This is the manager as bureaucrat. The manager is clearly not an entrepreneur yet the enterprise which employs him makes much of entrepreneurial values.

An enormous amount of institutional activity is legitimised through its verbal associations with the work ethic or what McClelland calls achievement.[7] Hence the stress on goals and objectives and the need for purposeful activity. Hence also the concern with the signs of success (profit, growth, volume of sales, cost reduction) and with individual responsibility and the institutional procedures providing feedback on performance.

Now here's the problem. The very circumstances which prompt those increases in the numbers of managers and professionals also undermine the work ethic. In the corporate complex state, objectives become imprecise and even contradictory. Individual responsibility gives way to collective responsibility. Feedback, if any is useful, is likely to be negative. These are the circumstances in which the achiever's

TABLE 2. THE MANAGER'S RESPONSIBILITIES[a]

Doing the job (the facts)	Maintaining the system (the folklore)
Absorbed in brief, varied discontinuous tasks—indicating a strong orientation for action	The reflective, systematic, planner, coordinator, organiser
Problem solving through verbal, face to face, informal exchanges	Problem solving through vertical channels depending on formal meetings and written reports
High dependence on *own* information *store* and *sources* in decision[b]	Use of the company intelligence system—MIS, computers, reports from government agencies, staff departments

Notes: [a] After Mintzberg, see reference 6; [b] ie peripheral, less legitimate sources (eg the media, chance meetings, friends, rumours).

desire to succeed gives way to his fear of failure. In large organisations *the dominant achievement psychology of managers and professionals is their fear of failure.*

In this state of confusion the manager with the help of his advisers turns to literacy. Information systems, objective setting exercises, organisational development, staff appraisals, productivity meetings, cost reduction games, and dozens of new performance indices signal that words and numbers are more than mere abstractions and are substitutable for reality itself. This lifeline is a deceptive one for instead of helping to maintain the enterprise it soon begins to undermine it. Energy levels decrease as disbanded procedures and 'cure-alls' litter the enterprise like rotting hulks obstructing what little productive effort remains.

The problem with rites based on literacy rather than task is the ease with which they can be transformed from good to bad ritual, from articulating meaning, providing social cohesion and reducing anxieties to the reverse. The effect of much bad ritual which managers and professionals have generated between them is not just to their detriment, it undermines the organisation as well.[8] Overmanaged, overserviced enterprise has its own unwitting fifth column.

The professional's predicament

Those circumstances which reduce the manager do not elevate the professional, who is typically underutilised. In addition, modern employment threatens the three central tenets of professional morality: autonomy, service, and excellence.

The status of employee is contrary to the value of autonomy. The professional is expected to tackle the tasks set by his employer who also imposes limits on his method of doing work. In large organisations the professional is separated in time and space from those for whom he provides his service.

Such conditions enable, even encourage, employers and professionals to define the meaning and nature of service with little recourse to the client, who is often himself an employee. Most attempts to overcome this isolation through procedure and machinery are window dressing.

As a consequence centrally constituted charters, rules, and procedures become even more important as determinants of behaviour rather than as guides to conduct and so enable minimum standards to become the norm; standards have always been a rallying cry for the mediocre. Indeed, there are precious few fronts on which quality is not in retreat.

Once we recognise the plight of the professional in employment we begin also to understand his pessimism. It is interesting to recall that some 25 years ago W. H. Whyte was drawing our attentions to the lacklustre efforts of scientists employed in large enterprise.[9] *The professional's concern about resources and their depletion is in no small way an advertisement for his own powerlessness and resourcelessness.* Promotion into the ranks of management and the trappings of status offer a sort of way out but these are *not* elevating of the person.

Collusion courses

Contrary to the predictions of social enquirers like Gouldner conflict between the authority of hierarchy (management) and expertise (professionals) takes place only at superficial levels.[10] Collusive games designed to promote mutual protection conceal their shared plight in employment. Common backgrounds and education commend manager and professional to a host of mutually protective activities. Literacy provides both the foundation for the implicit maintenance of false worth, the manager's *consequence* and the professional's *relevance* and, as the medium of bureaucracy, legitimacy.

A prime example of such collusion is the paraphernalia associated with the computer which apparently extends and maintains the modern industrial system. I write 'apparently' because in reality the computer has also been a major instrument, rivalling the copier, in the proliferation of bad ritual in employment—at a cost which we all have to bear.

The computer upholds the concept of fact as visual/literary detail. This is not a criticism of electronics but of our use of it to extend bureaucracy. Those employed around the computer codify their information in the literary format and interpret that same format as print-out on paper or tv screen.

The exponential expansion of electronic data processing has been based on some precarious assumptions—industrial man's biased view of information, the belief that this visual/literary information clarifies and aids understanding, and its contribution to social control.

On this basis there can never be enough information or computers. The collusive underpinnings of computer mania as an extension of bureaucracy are to be found in the observation that the manager makes little use of company information systems in his decisions.[5, 11, 12] Through the act of providing the manager with information to aid his decisions, the professional conceals his own private disbelief in the authority of the manager. What the manager does with his mountains of print-out is not the professional's concern anyway.

The pressure on the enterprise to spend more on the electronic extensions of bureaucracy comes as much from managers and professionals inside the enterprise as from the manufacturers. Computer experts have only to press their demands in the languages of industrial mythology (efficiency, cost reduction, better decisions etc) and bureaucracy (more information) and victory is theirs.

Even the manager's problem solving has a repetitive element with an absence of connecting logic between means and ends. For example, organisational crises still invoke the old divide-and-rule response. But literary embroidery and clever packaging enable the decision makers to claim originality and difference. However, these are rituals only in form. By that I mean they are bad rituals. They fragment and differentiate, a characteristic of literacy, rather than connect. They do not reduce anxiety nor do they articulate meaning. They undermine rather than uphold the industrial establishment. This proliferation of undifferentiated activity has an analogy in nature. It is the scourge of modern man, cancer.

Yet another related area where the malaise born of collusion grows unchecked lies in the manager's and professional's ceaseless quest for understanding, integration, or connection. Man's difficulty in understanding 'how it all fits together' may well come from defects in the human brain.[13] Herein lies the differentiating strengths and integrating shortcomings of literacy. Rational, intelligent, industrial man is a poor connector and in so far as our organisations may be little more than a crude replica of our mental functioning, it should hardly surprise us to discover that integration is the Achilles heel of large, complex organisation.[14]

So it is that almost every innovation in organisation from computers to new divisions of labour are reckoned by professionals to *improve* systems, information, communication, and understanding while in every respect these seemingly deteriorate by the day.

The nonsense of such claims lies in the confusion they bring. Wholes, says the systems theorist in his more insightful moments, need no elaboration. He then proceeds to elaborate them to the point of absurdity.

Consider a typical interdivisional conflict like the one between marketing and production operations. The professional as consultant recommends some new division of labour or activity (called liaison, coordinator, or committee) to 'integrate' their efforts. This is pure Orwellian doubletalk. In reality our expert is recommending more differentiation but he uses the word integration to describe it.[15] The survival of the new division of labour *depends on the inability* of the old divisions, to communicate freely. As a result some of the conflict essential to relations between marketing/production operations disappears while communications and integration deteriorate still further. This in turn calls for still more divisions of labour and new kinds of experts and so on it goes. Through such 'solutions' the professional demonstrates his relevance and the manager his consequence. Thus do the collusive links between impotent manager and professional contribute to the organised chaos which is now our daily bread.

A way out

Put bluntly, the role of employee which results from an imposed contract castrates the professional.

Efforts to improve his predicament must involve changes in the employment contract itself. Undoubtedly, there can be no better test for our services or the sharpening of our ideals than self-employment. Self-employment ought also to shift the current institutionalised, centralised, one-way non-relation between professional and client towards a more personal, reciprocal kind of relationship.

However, it may be too much to encourage any but the most self-reliant and versatile to take this route. (The author is not self-employed.) A move in this direction, which every large employer and professional ought to be considering in the current need for resourcefulness and more attractive modes of living, lies in introducing changes to the employment contract which offer the professional more self-

determination and more meaningful contact with his clients.

This process is inevitably linked with decentralisation and the run down of monolithic head offices, part-time work, employment by project, and closer location in time and space of professional and client. It may just mean actively encouraging practices which have been around, albeit illegally, for some time.

There is a lot to be said for opening up negotiations with the existing professionals in the enterprise to see how many are prepared to explore some kind of change in their contract. My own enquiries show that it is the more competent who are most likely to find such an opportunity attractive, so the scope for developing such a scheme, if it proves fruitful to both employer and employee, is there.

It is the manager's task to explore these possibilities with his professional staff and more generally to tackle the serious divergence of employment from the primary task of creating wealth and providing service. It may add up to organising the retreat from employment in the interests of both man and the economic system. The manager certainly needs to take the organisational maintenance side of his job more seriously; to reduce the bad rituals and enhance the good.

A simple test is the extent to which the repetitive activities in which we now embroil ourselves are actually built upon the primary task. It is a noticeable feature of much bad ritual that it is not.

It may be asking too much of literate man and it may represent too large a threat to the industrial establishment to suggest that if we really want to improve integration and communication in complex organisations then we must also begin to make much more use of technology in providing nonliterate, less public kinds of information. The dominant view of communication and information goes hand in glove with the shift from managing people to managing situations. Both conceal the decline in convival relations which characterises life in large enterprise today.[16]

Notes and references

1. My reference to professionals is loose and broad based. The term covers all those engaging in activities for which some kind of *tertiary education* is a condition of entry. It embraces scientists, engineers, accountants, doctors, teachers social workers, architects, librarians, etc. It also includes those in marginal occupations—planners, advertisers, programmers, bankers, consultants—for which a degree or diploma affords definite occupational advantage.
2. I. Illich *et al, Disabling Professions* (London, Marion Boyars, 1977).
3. D. Pym, "The misuse of professional manpower", in *Industrial Society: the Social Sciences in Management* (Harmondsworth, Penguin, 1968).
4. V. Stanic and D. Pym, *Brains Down the Drain* (London, Anbar, 1969).
5. S. Carlson, *Executive Behaviour* (Stockholm, Stronbergs, 1951). R. Stewart, *Managers and Their Jobs* (London, Macmillian, 1967). H. Mintzberg, *The Nature of Managerial Work* (New York, Harper and Row, 1973).
6. H. Mintzberg, "The manager's job: folklore and fact", *Harvard Business Review*, August/September 1975.
7. D. McClelland, *The Achieving Society* (Princeton, NJ, Van Nostrand, 1961).
8. D. Pym, "Employment as bad ritual", *London Business School Journal, 3* (1), 1978.
9. W. H. Whyte, *The Organization Man* (Harmondsworth, Penguin, 1956).
10. A. Gouldner, "Cosmopolitans and locals: towards an analysis of latent social roles", *Administrative Science Quarterly, 1* (2), 1957.
11. V. Dearden, "MIS is a mirage", *Harvard Business Review*, January/February 1972.
12. R. I. Tricker, "Ten myths of management information", *Management Accounting, 49*, August 1971.
13. P. MacLean, "Contrasting functions of limbic and neocortical systems of the brain", *American Journal of Medicine, 25* (4), 1958.
14. D. Pym, "The demise of management and the ritual of employment", *Human Relations, 28* (8), 1975.
15. For a classic example of this confusion see P. Lawrence and J. Lorsch, *Organization and Environment* (Harvard, Harvard University Press, 1967).
16. In a recent survey among managers and professionals in a large, sophisticated process plant in north-east England, 84% of the managers were found to hold the view that industrial relations in the plant is a job for the expert.

POLITICIANS AND THE FUTURE

J. Enoch Powell

Politicians have a part to play, a part not of their own choosing. Their actions or motives are not determined by their own views of the future. Thus a gulf exists between politicians and forecasters. For the politician, a forecast that is wrong is irrelevant; and a forecast that is right is superfluous.

ALL humanity busies itself with the future, because that is all that is left. Even the historian, ostensibly busy with the past, has his eye fixed upon the publisher, the professorship, or the future student. Concern for the future resolves itself into several distinct types.

Prediction

The least common and the least important is prediction—by which I mean foreknowledge of what will actually have happened, but at a scene in which the predictor has either no part at all or a completely passive part. Old Moore wishes to know the future because the evidence or presumption that he possesses that knowledge will provide him with a source of income. He has no intention of doing anything as a consequence of the predictions he makes—least of all, anything which would frustrate them.

The next stage removed from this predictive purity is the case of the person who can benefit from correct foreknowledge but who does not regard his own action as altering what would otherwise occur. The speculator on the stock exchange wishes to know the future movement of share prices, so that he can buy or sell to advantage. He may, in assessing the future, take account of the effect of others buying and selling, but he abstracts from any effect of his own buying and selling—at the moment, at least, when it takes place.

A change in kind occurs when the object of the foreknowledge is to avoid or prevent what would otherwise take place. The soothsayer who says: "Beware the Ides of March!" may know that in fact the victim is not going to take the necessary precautions. To the victim the whole point of the foreknowledge is to enable him to do something, such as staying away from the Senate, which will render the Ides of March uneventful, ie falsify the prophecy. The future can conveniently be divided into two at the point where the recipient of the foreknowledge intervenes to prevent or alter what would otherwise have been the subsequent course of events. "If I go to the Senate, I shall be murdered" thus becomes "If I had gone to the Senate, I should have been murdered": the foreknowledge "Caesar will be murdered" turns out not to be foreknowledge at all. It was correct only up to the point when Caesar heeded the warning—and the conspirators were lined up with daggers at the ready—but after that point it was wrong.

The author has held various posts in government and opposition. From July 1960 to October 1963 he was Minister of Health in the Conservative government. In 1971 he left the Conservative party. He is now Official Ulster Unionist MP for South Down, Northern Ireland.

This commoner and more practical concern with the future I shall designate by the staff-college term 'appreciation', because it falls under that part of a military appreciation which is called enemy intentions. "I foresee", says the general to himself, "that the enemy intends to concentrate on his right flank by moving forces across my front and then to attack and envelop my left."

He does not, however, then sit back as a spectator to watch it happen, but falls with his cavalry upon the moving columns and produces an entirely different event for the historians. His interest in prediction ends at the moment when he unleashes his own attack. He would not thank you for telling him that despite his manoeuvre he will in fact lose the battle.

Almost every action is based upon some kind of appreciation. Normally the appreciation is so short term or routine as not to involve the conscious process in which the general's mind engages: all life resolves itself into continuous anticipation, viewed not as the subject matter of knowledge but as the basis of action.

A necessary distinction

The distinction between prediction and appreciation is necessary, for the typical concern of the politician with the future partakes of both categories but falls neatly into neither. Clearly his concern is not purely predictive: even the very far-sighted politician (whom Bismarck is said to have described as more dangerous than the very short-sighted politician) is not setting up to compete with Nostradamus. The politician's forbidden exclamation: "I told you so!" would not be the self-advertisement of a seller of almanacs. It implies the reproach: "If you had taken my advice earlier, this would not have happened". His concern with the future therefore is appreciative: however philosophical or Burkeian the politician, his business is with doing.

Like the general, he works with two mental pictures—the future as it would be but for him(A), and the future as he intends it shall be because of him(B). He differs, however, from the general in a number of ways which it is instructive to elucidate.

The action of the general consists in the movement and use of forces which are under his control. His two future pictures are communicated no more widely than is necessary for the purpose of conveying his intentions to those who have to carry them out—and few of those need be fully privy to the tableaux. The politician has, in this sense no resources at his command. His action consists in persuasion: he must persuade as many people as possible of the truthfulness of picture A and of the desirability and practicability of picture B. He cannot therefore, like a speculator or an entrepreneur or a military commander, keep his appreciation to himself or as nearly as possible to himself. On the contrary, he must publicly identify himself with it heart and soul, because if he does not convince, nothing—except by accident, not design—will follow.

This is why politicians both dread public forecasts and at the same time constantly make them: forecasts are as inseparable from their profession as hemp from a hangman's. Enormous authority accrues to a politician from the verification of his picture A. Although this does not logically prove his picture B to be either nice or possible, there is a certain rough-and-ready public reasoning which says: "Well, he got picture A right so far. Let us see what he can do with picture B".

Uniqueness

In order for this effect to be produced, the politician's picture A must be distinctive: it is no good to him if it is the same as everybody else's. Politicians need not only distinctive policies, but distinctive appreciations.

At this point a refinement must be introduced: it is one of the paradoxes which haunts all practical politicians. The current appreciation of the future as assumed by the majority of people is, as experimentally demonstrated a thousand times over, virtually bound to be wrong. The axioms of one decade or generation become in the next decade or generation the absurdities which excite the pity and surprise of those who are wise after the event. Yet as long as it lasts, the conventional appreciation of the vast majority is a dreadful dragon to challenge. The challenger must, by definition, place himself in a minority (which is a bad place for a politician to be in) and he must by implication be accusing his fellow beings of being less wise or percipient than himself (which is a bad thing for a politician to be thought to do). There is therefore always a difficult balance of advantage to be struck between being wrong with the herd (the ideal form of this alternative is to alter one's appreciation as nearly as possible a split second before everyone else), and being right when the herd is wrong and therefore powerless and pilloried until the herd receives practical proof of its error.

A sense of timing

Obviously the longer the time likely to elapse before the dissenting appreciation which a politician espouses can be vindicated, the less benefit his espousal of it can bring him. There is no point for a politician in being proved right when others were wrong if by the time this happens he (and they) are dead (or gone to the British political equivalent, the House of Lords). The classic case is the career of Churchill. Few politicians probably made so many bad appreciations in the course of a long political life; but Churchill made his good appreciation at just the right interval, say four or five years before the event, and just in time to be able himself to personify picture B on the strength of his belated academy award for picture A.

Not even the most astute politician, however, can pick winners so as not merely to be right but to be right the right distance ahead. That is not what happens in real life. What happens is that most politicians discard any forecast, whatever its intellectual appeal, which is too crassly at variance with public comfort and assumption, as being useless for political purposes and no proper concern of a politician. It was luck, not judgement on Churchill's part: he could not control the length of the crucial interval. As he was, for quite unconnected reasons, in a situation of political isolation, he had both the freedom and the independence of mind to live through the years of Cassandran unpopularity. But would he have painted his picture A and continued to exhibit it if the flash-point had obviously been much further ahead than 1940 (where he located it) or if the interim years of unfulfilment had drawn out?

Whatever the answer to that personalised question may be, there certainly are politicians in the business whose picture A bears a relatively distant date—eg because the outcome which they predict is the result of factors, such as generation changes or reproduction rates, which have a long minimum time span. What is *their* function? Why do these politicians nevertheless make and publish their predictions and base their whole political activity upon them? To answer that question is to elicit a further important contrast between the politician as predictor or appreciator and the military commander or indeed most others who are engaged in the futures business.

The people's voice

All nonpoliticians are essentially concerned, whatever the qualifications, with getting their view of the future right—ie with it being verified *ex post facto* by the event. The politician is not; for his profession is of a different kind altogether. I do not, of course, mean that he does not apply his best powers of intellect and imagination to forming a picture of the future, or—still less—that he deliberately perverts or distorts what he thinks he foresees. I mean that he is a part, but only a part, of a collective or social process of decision. In a way somewhat resembling that in which the players on the Athenian tragic stage dramatised and externalised the emotional experience of their audience, the politician, in what he says, and to a lesser extent in what he does, gives form, voice, and intelligibility to the predicament of the society of which he is a part. Politics is one of the methods whereby a society feels and thinks about itself. It is not the only method—music and poetry are others—but it is the method specifically appropriate to society in its manifestation as the state or nation.

The national monologue

Politics is the nation talking to itself. Politics is the nation putting its own life on the stage and then going to sit in the stalls as a spectator. The seats are often both uncomfortable and expensive; but that is no reason for dispensing with the theatre altogether. In fact, a nation cannot avoid dramatising itself, whether it likes or not: it can no more do so than an individual can at choice renounce his self-consciousness. The politician is one of the actors—leading part or chorus, no matter which—in this complex and continuing drama, on which the curtain falls only with the extinction or destruction of the society itself.

Acting in character

The significant thing about the politician is that he has a part to play. It is a part for which he was not cast by the management, nor did he choose it for himself. (Some think that they did; but they are mistaken. The cynic and the placeman have no more choice than others: they are doomed to play the parts of a cynic or a placeman.) He is cast by his own nature and destiny; and the wheel of chance is the playwright who assigns that particular part its place in the web or plot of the current section of the drama. The characters on a stage are, of course, concerned with futurity—it is not possible not to be—but their actions and their motives are not determined by their view of futurity. Unlike the investor or the commander, the politician is not the servant of the outcome: if he were in possession of an indubitably authenticated god's-eye view of the future, which informed him that his cause would fail and all that he held dear be obliterated from the face of the Earth, he would still continue to act and work as he does. He would emit the same warning or deterrent sounds, he would hold up before his fellow countrymen the same objects and ideals. He is not so much like a separate free agent as an organic part of his society which reacts instinctively to certain stimuli.

What future for forecasters

This character of the politician goes far to explain the mutual bewilderment and repulsion which is frequent between governments or political parties and those whom they encourage or employ to produce forecasts and predictions. The politician turns out not to be interested after all in the forecasts, right or wrong. They are not, after all, the stuff with which he operates. In the short run, they are useless to him unless they coincide with what he himself is engaged in projecting—and then they are superfluous. In the long run, there is no benefit in knowing, if it were possible, what the fates hold in store; for he would still be obliged to defy or ignore it as he goes about his business.

FUTURES October 1979
THE FUTURE OF MORALITY

Geoffrey Vickers

Moral criticism of human institutions is frequent: the acceptance of social constraints by the free individual is rare. This moral inversion is inconsistent with the survival of an increasingly interdependent society. Statements of human rights must be replaced by statements of human responsibility if we are to make the world viable.

THE future of morality? The question will seem to some embarrassing, to many irrelevant, to most unanswerable.

What is morality anyway? What impact does it really make on the course of human affairs? And what can be usefully said about its future development? I shall seek to show that it is not irrelevant; that its nature and impact are not obscure; and that any embarrassment which it occasions is evidence of ambivalent feelings and muddled understanding which need to be and can be cleared up.

Moral inversion

Moral imperatives are out of fashion if and in so far as they imply the acceptance of social constraints by would-be autonomus individuals. But they are not at all out of fashion if and in so far as they power criticism of human institutions and their office bearers. They are tabu in the first field but obsessional in the second. Michael Polanyi drew attention to this apparently contradictory feature of our Western culture in several papers,[1] and christened it moral inversion. Never since the religious wars has moral fervour fired so much strife, bitterness, and brutality.

Dr Johann puts it differently.[2]

... these times manage to combine an extraordinary degree of moral activism on the level of practice with an all-but-dogmatic brand of ethical nihilism on the level of theory. On the one hand all our inherited ways, traditions and institutions are being subjected to unrelenting criticism with a view to their radical transformation. Absolutely nothing is sacred. On the other, there is widespread denial of any basis in reality for judging one way of life to be morally superior to another or even for preferring the moral standpoint to some other in evaluating proposed courses of action. The situation is nothing short of absurd.

The author is a member of the *Futures* advisory board, and is the author of a series of books, of which the most recently published is *Making Institutions Work* (London, Associated Business Programmes, 1973; New York, Halsted Press, 1974).

This article is also included in a collection of his papers, *Responsibility, its sources and limits*, Intersystems Publications, Seaside, California, 1980.

The situation, if not absurd, is at least paradoxical. But I think Dr Johann oversimplifies it in presenting it as an inconsistency between theory and practice. One thing *is* sacred—the 'rights' of the autonomous, self-actualising individual. The UN has produced a Declaration of the Rights of Man and even a Declaration of the Rights of the Child, and these have been subscribed by many though not all of the world's governments. It has set up judicial machinery to determine whether these rights have been infringed. And the rights embody widespread beliefs about the optimal conditions in which men and women should live and in which children should be brought up. Many countries are under political and economic pressure from their neighbours on the grounds that they are failing to secure these rights for their subjects; and these pressures are often carried to a degree damaging to the countries which exercise them because of the vehemence of public opinion within their borders. Many other countries are equally divided internally by feuds which express themselves as the demand for 'justice'.

It is too sweeping, I think, to dismiss all these as without theoretical foundation, in that the social sciences provide abundant though not wholly consistent theories about the optimum conditions for human growth and development. However, as Dr Johann points out, these theories supply no logical reason why desirable objectives should become moral imperatives.

The freedom spiral

What has happened, I suggest, is that the Western world has come full circle, or more exactly full spiral, in the two centuries since Rousseau declared that man was born free but was everywhere in chains. To the emancipators of Rousseau's generation it seemed that nothing was needed but to strike off the chains. Men freed from tyranny, superstition, ignorance, and want would, in Condorcet's words, need "no master save reason".

Two centuries later the passion for emancipation is no less feverish but the perceived cost has hugely risen. These 'rights' can be satisfied only (if at all) by huge institutional efforts. Education, health care, nutrition, shelter (which now includes all the amenities of urban living) are not distributed freely and evenly by nature unless distorted by human institutions. Only human institutions beyond our present compass could supply them even to a proportion of those who demand them. Yet these same institutions have become as suspect, even as hated as they were in the days of the Ancien Regime. They are again widely seen as the chains which bind potentially free men.

Of course Rousseau's slogan, admirable for starting a revolution, was totally untrue. Men are not born 'free'. They are born in total dependence on other men and they perish biologically and never emerge psychologically as human persons unless they are cherished and nourished for years by men and women of the previous generation. Their debt to these they will be able to repay only by their devotion to the generation which follows. Meantime they are kept alive from day to day by the efforts of other people, most of whom they do not know and never even see. And their only possible acknowledgment of this, even where the service is made for payment, is not the money which they pay but the probably quite different contribution which they themselves (one hopes) have made. Of course there is a kind of freedom in interdependence but this is not the kind of freedom which Rousseau was talking about; and it depends on mutual trust to a degree scarcely conceived as possible today.

Ethical nihilism

Dr Johann is none the less right, I think, to emphasise the influence of what he calls ethical nihilism. Its full force can be realised perhaps only by those old enough to have experienced what preceded it. Less than a century ago in Western countries, certainly in Britain, it was widely believed that the individual was at least potentially equipped with an innate capacity, a 'conscience', which enabled him to distinguish 'right' from 'wrong' and that he had an equally inherent duty to pursue what was right. The duty had a religious origin in the will of God; but there was no lack of rationalists who were prepared to find it in the nature of man. The dimension of right and wrong, good and evil was widely accepted and human excellence was commonly assessed by reference to apparent achievement, both in the discharge of an individual's civic and occupational roles and in meeting those standards of honesty, loyalty, compassion, and so on which were held applicable to human status as such and which were comprehended in 'goodness'.

Then Freud located the conscience in the internalised voice of (primarily) the parent. He asserted the individual's need and right to review such early impositions and to confirm or replace them with criteria of his own choosing. It was a revolutionary change in so far as it threw upon the conscience the burden of proving its own authenticity. But it increased, rather than reduced, the responsibility of the ego for choosing its own standards. Freud was not very explicit about the criteria which the ego could use. He may have been unduly influenced by the pathological aspects of such internalised norms which concerned him so closely as a psychiatrist. But as I understand it, he always allowed the ego some role as an artist as well as a broker in reconciling the demands of its "three hard masters"; and his followers and deviants have spent much fruitful time in developing this aspect of the ego in a mental atmosphere less rigidly determinist than the one in which Freud wrote.

But Marx long before had insisted that this scope for self-design was limited if not negligible because the individual was too deeply conditioned by his own self-interest to make such choices with any independence. Marx confined his argument to the rich and the propertied but logic and history were bound to widen, even to universalise it. Property is not the only conditioning factor in human life. Marx's insights, propagated as a polemic on behalf of a class, contributed to the suspicion of all moral judgments as rationalised self-interest. And this was confirmed by the very culture which he was attacking. For both the market economy and representative political democracy encouraged the view that the individual knew what was best for himself and acted so as to maximise it. The concept of the self became still further narrowed to the individual (envisaged nearly always as adult and male) and altruism became an anomaly which Freudian analysis was welcome to debunk.

A further stage in the sorry story started when 'science' began to turn its attention to management and government. The evaluation of policy required an analysis of cost and benefit expressed in terms which were at least comparable and preferably quantifiable. The fact that people do constantly weigh imponderables and compare disparates, however well confirmed by experience, was not explicable in terms of any current theory of mental function except a crude dynamics which reduced them all to pushes and pulls. And this model tended to remain dominant even when it had been supplemented by the belated acknowledgment of information as an agency which produced effects otherwise than by transferring energy. We are now allowed to believe that books do not operate like bulldozers; but most of the lessons have still to be drawn.

The dynamics of moral obligation

This familiar story has its positive side. Its most precious positive contribution is, I think, the understanding that the sense of obligation associated with moral and indeed all ethical thought, feeling, and behaviour derives from expectations which people learn to expect *of themselves* as a necessary part of their identity, a term which includes their image of themselves not only as individuals but as belonging to some admired class or type.

These expectations may be imprinted in earliest childhood. Religious faith and respect for authority used to be familiar examples. They may arise, sometimes no less early, from the *rejection* of some such attempt at imprinting. The child who has been 'turned off' by efforts to 'turn him on' may long find difficulty in conceiving himself as someone who could entertain a religious faith or accept a secular authority without something approaching treason to himself.

The expectations may arise later from social pressures, as when the individual, entering a profession such as medicine, the army, or the law, absorbs the professional ethic into his image of himself. They may arise at any time by an act of conscious artistry on the part of the ego, desiring to emulate some human possibility which experience has revealed to him and which claims his commitment. Such is the response of those who fall under the influence of men whom they recognise as 'great'. However they arise, they provide in my view the source of that sense of personal obligation which is one of the components I am seeking. I will call it commitment.

It is, I think, a source of human motivation different in kind from the prudential calculation of cost and benefit which may lead a man to conform to what standards others expect of him, even though he himself feels no personal commitment to them. This is a difference which should be more familiar to us in these cybernetic days, when we are accustomed to the idea of comparing some incoming or self-generated information with some standard or norm. The 'new' information does or does not match the norm and thus a 'match' or 'mismatch' signal is generated from which flows not only information but meaning.

I have described elsewhere[3] what I think should be the impact of this thinking on theories of human motivation (which many will agree to be badly in need of some refreshing supplement). I need not develop this argument further here and need only point out that control by reference to a standard or norm is now part of our most common conceptual stock in trade.

To make the concept of commitment more precise, I emphasise the following aspects. First, commitment may be more or less intense or wholly lacking. Its presence and state can only be recognised in action or subjectively in imagined action. An individual may have no idea at all of what to expect of himself in a particular context, in which case he will act at random or assume whatever persona seems to be expected of him. He may have a standard, vaguely held in principle, which dissolves when he is faced with the actual cost of living up to it. Or he may find himself more deeply attached to it than he knew. Personalities vary in the strength, comprehensiveness, and coherence of the self-expectations which thus structure them. These are major dimensions of personality.

Second, commitment does not necessarily impel its subject to conduct regarded as moral by anyone else or even by himself. The Marquis de Sade proudly identified himself with a persona so repulsive that his name has come to stand for one of the most widely recognised vices or psychopathologies. Moreover he claimed to have made that persona deliberately by rooting out from his personality anything which could interfere with his 'enjoyment'. Confidence tricksters may take a professional pride in their success, even though it is possible only in a world where trust is sufficiently taken for granted to be betrayed. The world's Napoleons are committed to a personal destiny which neither they nor others necessarily identify with moral good. Less extreme examples are to be found in the distinguishing marks of professions or classes which are internalised by their members with a passion proportionate to their symbolic importance rather than to any imaginable scale of moral values. A breach of good manners may diminish the perpetrator far more than a failure of compassion.

This last example brings me to the third and most difficult aspect of what I am calling commitment. The dimension committed–uncommitted is by no means the same as the dimension inner directed–outer directed. All commitments are formed by accepting (or rejecting) standards with which one is invited to identify. Who can say how far the resulting commitment is due to the invitation of society and how far to the exercise of personal choice? Even where personal choice is at its highest it may owe its power to a society whose culture encouraged it from the beginning by making the individual expect of himself that he would bear the burden of assessing and accepting or rejecting the imperatives which that same culture pressed upon him. Contemporary Western culture is obsessed by the urge to claim individual credit for the shape of the personality and to deny to society anything but the power to suppress and distort it.

But in fact this inflamed distinction between the individual and society cannot be sustained. It is basically untrue that the individual must be either a mere cell in an organism or an entity free to make its own relations with its environment and entitled to ignore any which are not voluntarily assumed. Fishes are not free to live out of water.

Finally, commitment may be positive or negative. The individual may expect of himself action in some circumstances, constraint in others. He would be ashamed, for example, not to go to the help of another who was drowning or under attack and equally ashamed if he lost his temper with a subordinate. Sometimes the same commitment can be described either negatively or positively but it is convenient to distinguish the two, especially at a time when negative commitments are so out of fashion. Self-accepted constraints are commitments no less than self-accepted obligations to act.

Mutual expectations

It remains to consider the other side of the coin, the expectations which each entertains of all the others. Human societies cohere only in so far as their members can entertain reliable expectations of each other: they sustain this net of mutual expectations by means which we may fail to notice only because we take them for granted.

At their most visible, every law court in the land is busy applying to particular cases rules, usually of long standing, and defining and trying to correct deviance. Schools at all levels are seeking to transmit the culture's heritage, its approved ways of thinking, expressing, valuing, and behaving. Men in organisations take for granted that others on whom they depend will perform their roles in the ways expected of them and management is largely concerned with correcting deviance from the expected. Social relations are structured by a similar net of mutual expectations and those who violate it are made aware of their offence in culturally determined ways. The basic problem of supporting life in community is to allow variety, criticism, and innovation to an extent sufficient to permit growth and adaptation to change without so disrupting the tissue of mutual expectation as to destroy people's trust in it and each other and therewith the possibility of social order. And this is everyone's interest and everyone's business though it usually requires also the exercise of some central authority.

There has been much argument about the extent to which 'force' is needed to enforce 'order' in human societies but I question whether such general discussions are useful about subject matter so idiosyncratic and so context bound as particular human societies. In Moscow, I understand, bus passengers serve themselves with tickets and pay for them without the supervision of a conductor. An attempt to enjoy a free ride would be frustrated by the outrage of the other passengers. But so would the attempt to jump a London bus queue, though the second, unlike the first, would not be a breach of the formal law. It may be significant that the second would be an infringement of personal 'right' whilst the first would be 'only' a fraud on a public body. The consciousness of a Soviet citizen would seem to be differently structured from that of most Westerners.

The significance of mutual expectations is best seen in their simplest manifestations, such as forms of greeting and dress. In socially stratified societies these serve to assure the parties that each knows his place and concedes the place of the other. The touched cap, the raised hat, the nod, the bow all have their place. In egalitarian societies they serve equally to assert and to accord equality of status. Both can be used also to assert a claim which the other does not admit or otherwise to make a communication of an antagonistic kind. In either case they are communications and usually unambiguous. When they are ambiguous, as when a greeting is ignored, they produce disproportionate anxiety. (Am I being cut or censured or did he simply not notice?) A response so bizarre as to be outside the common repertory of both greeting and insult would be even more disturbing. What other common expectations can no longer be safely made about this particular person?

Clothes used to serve a similar purpose. At one extreme, uniform defines clearly at least one aspect of what a person is—policeman, soldier, air-force pilot—often with added details of rank and status. Within the uniformed organisation the uniform serves to make members aware of each other and of their common service. Externally it invites others to attach to any wearer of the uniform the expectations which they are accustomed to attach to members of the force and to accord whatever its members are regarded as entitled to expect. But 'uniformity' is a matter of degree. A century ago in England, the clothes a person wore and the way he spoke conveyed a great deal of information about him—largely about his occupation, his income, and his social class, each of which had an associated subculture, more or less defined. Today these indices are more blurred and this is usually welcomed as showing that these differences have decreased or are regarded as less important. But other differences can be expressed in the same media and our current subcultures often seize on them and use them as symbols. I know a young man, gifted, intelligent, and humane, who threw up his job rather than obey a company rule and wear a tie.

Mutual reassurance

Wordless communication is a huge subject, not to be pursued here. I am concerned only to make the case that a vast amount of human communication is devoted simply to *mutual reassurance*. Small talk and social ritual serves little other purpose. By such means each party assures the others that it belongs to their group (or to some other sufficiently known and trusted to be acceptable) and thereby invites the assumption that it knows and will observe the code of mutual expectations common to the group. Each member must give the others the benefit of the shared cultural assumption, to be withdrawn only if experience disproves it. And this I think explains why confidence tends to be an integrated attitude, vulnerable as a whole to evidence that even a part of it is undeserved.

Mutual reassurance is important primarily because it makes possible inter-relations *more human* than they would otherwise be. In some cultures the outer doors of houses are fitted with grilles through which a visitor may be inspected before the door is opened. In others even lone women in isolated houses feel no need to lock their doors. Obviously the mutual expectations expressed by the latter state invite far readier communication between strangers than do those of the former state. Examples can be multiplied and suggest that there is a transcultural, though not an acultural, dimension of humanity or humaneness which helps to determine how far men in society can develop their peculiarly human capacity for using communication to build relations of high 'quality' between them. There is here the nucleus of a theory not merely of commitment but of *moral* commitment. I have no space to pursue it here. But obviously if it exists—and it is widely recognised—it will need constant reinforcement even to maintain itself in a world ever more crowded with mutual strangers. The example is one of many but it is of sombre significance that 'security' is a fast-growing activity in Western countries.

Perhaps the most important assumption that anyone can extend towards another is that that other has himself internalised the responsibilities expected of him and will obey them because he expects them of himself; they are for him commitments and increasingly include constraints.

Complementary expectations

I have used the expression mutual expectations reluctantly because, although it serves to distinguish such expectations from self-expectations, it conceals the fact already mentioned that they are nearly always not mutual but complementary. Doctor and patient, teacher and taught, judge and litigant, buyer and seller, administrator and administered, husband and wife, parent and child do not entertain the same expectations of each other, except for those most general and fundamental ones such as honesty, respect, and compassion which we regard as 'obligations' due to humanity as such. This perhaps explains why role-governed relations are today so distrusted and despised. We cannot logically derive this pathology from moral inversion; for even in a world of ideally organised institutions (whatever be the ideal) role-governed relations would be not only inescapable but a major factor in life's significance and a major field for human excellence. We must attribute it to that concept of equality which, as de Tocqueville foresaw long ago, is likely to erode both sides of the complementary relations which hold any society together. In fact both kinds of mutual expectation are needed. Role-governed relations may well become rigid and inhuman unless the parties also acknowledge the truly mutual responsibilities which spring from their common humanity. But equally these, however universally shared, will not replace the huge nexus of precise role-defined responsibilities which is due from each of us and on which we all depend from day to day.

But with the appearance of such words as compassion and respect we are clearly in the realm of quality, not merely stability, in human systems.

Ethics and morals

Murder, theft, and arson are commonly regarded as more than breaches of good manners. Yet the division between manners and morals is hard to draw partly because manners are the basis of stability and stability is itself a value—if not a moral value, at least the soil in which moral values can grow. I have discussed in an earlier paper the relation between stability and quality in human systems. [4]

I seek in this article to give this distinction more precision in terms of contemporary Western culture and to consider what if anything might succeed the state of moral inversion from which we now suffer, a state manifestly unstable and not to my mind convincingly progressive in the direction of quality however defined. It would be convenient as well as logical to keep the word ethics for all those patterns of thought, concern, and behaviour which characterise a particular culture and to keep the word morals for those among them which can be commended, however controversially, on grounds of quality.

Qualitatively it does not matter whether we drive on the left of the road or the right but it does matter that we should all obey the same convention. When we refine the rule by giving priority to ambulances and fire appliances we express a value judgement that this inequality is on balance in the general interest. No doubt we shall have to ration the use of the road far more than we do now, either because of traffic congestion or because of fuel shortage. And we ration it already by requiring tested competence to drive, compulsory third party insurance, a licence fee (which as I write is under discussion) and ability to pay the price of petrol (which can be raised or lowered by taxation or subsidy) as well as by other factors. All these forms of rationing derive from conscious public decisions and express views of what is qualitatively best among the courses seen to be available.

These judgments express some degree of moral preference but they are debatable in a sense that the simplest interpersonal moral judgments are not. It is widely agreed in most cultures that it is more congenial to live in a society in which members are relatively free from the fear of violence, fraud, and other acts of malevolence by their neighbours. They vary in their standards of what is to be expected. Some enjoy standards which others do not conceive as possible. And they change with time.

Isabella Bird was free to ride alone round the Colorado Rockies in the 1870s, accepting any hospitality she was offered, exciting admiration for her horse-manship but no surprise at her trust in her fellow humans.[5] A few decades later MacMullen, an early English yachtsman, excited more surprise for his daring in sleeping alone in his boat in an English port than for his remarkable exploits at sea—and this despite the fact that unlike Isabella Bird, he was, as he put it: "not dependent on any man's forbearance". There are—or were—Bedouin tribes where stealing is unknown. A comparison of cultures discloses a wide difference in the level of their interpersonal moral expectations but a fair degree of conformity in the dimensions in which these are measured. The question: "Who is my neighbour?" admits a far wider range of answers than the question: "What are my duties to him?" however commonly neglected the duties may be.

Political morality

When we move from interpersonal duties to political morality we run into difficulties which have beset the human mind since before Plato wrote his *Republic*. Broadly they are of two kinds.

One concerns the characters of the men who are selected and preselected by the struggle for public power. The Guardians who were to run Plato's Republic were to be of a type least likely to seek power for its own sake, men who would carry for the public weal an office which was a burden to them. It is a question whether this would not have ruled out some of the world's most successful and honoured statesmen. But history records that the struggle to get and keep political power does not always lodge it in hands most likely to use it responsibly in the long-term interest of the governed. Hereditary monarchy has the merit of vesting it in those who did not seek it and who usually have had some training in using it; though this does not guarantee their competence. No doubt all countries have in their records governors who are honoured as Guardians. Englishmen need not go back a thousand years to Alfred of Wessex and Cuthbert of Lindisfarne. The long struggle to make power accountable without emasculating it has had results of which we can be moderately proud. But I doubt whether our present methods or any other methods can themselves be sufficient for the needs of the future.

The second set of difficulties concerns the nature of the political choice. The governor, individual or collective, decides for others who may themselves be divided. To satisfy the conditions which I have described as necessary for individual moral judgement there must be a collective commitment, justifiable as a move in the direction of greater humanity. This means that not the decider only but substantially all those for whom he decides must be committed to a common idea of their collective self and a common consciousness that the step which they are taking is consistent with that ideal and needed for its realisation. Such things are not impossible. The last occasion when it happened in Britain was I think the passing in 1946–1951 of the legislation giving effect to the Beveridge report. An interparty unity in and out of Parliament marked this occasion in a way seldom seen in Parliamentary activity, at least when this is devoted to internal relations. There was a widespread feeling that this was 'right'.

If this argument is right, a precondition of political morality is that the political unit shall be coherent at least in the field involved by any particular decision. This is not surprising. The individual also must be coherent, at least in the relevant area. He must have a self to which he can be true. The idea of a similar collective self is out of fashion today but only through a recent eclipse. Aneurin Bevan, architect of the National Health Service, declared that we should thank heaven for having preserved this island as an example of humanity. Statesmen of the left were as proud as statemen of the right to admit their dedication to the country which they served.

A further conclusion follows. Political units will not act morally unless nearly all the governed as well as the governors feel a profound commitment to them and identify with them. That they should do so will not of itself guarantee that they will act morally. But without such commitment they will have no chance of acting morally at all. For commitment is of the essence of morality and collective commitment is of the essence of collective morality. The quality of their actions will of course depend on the quality of their shared commitment. In what collective character do they take pride? What does their sense of collective identity most impel them to guard? These are moral questions; but they can only be posed in a society sufficiently coherent to have a collective ideal. "Lords and Commons of England consider what manner of man it is whereof ye are and whereof ye are the governors." We may give a new answer to Milton's question but the question itself needs to be asked anew not only by Lords and by Commons but by every man in the street. It is not out of date. Its answer determines what impact these 56 million people will have, not only on each other but on the billions beyond their shores.

The moral frontier

Thus we come to what is undoubtedly the most difficult field of political morality. From the dawn of time human culture, and with it all ethics and morality, has grown within specific populations. The relation of these populations to each other has been generally one of mutual hostility unqualified by any moral constraints or commitments. When they have collided, in pursuit of land or resources or slaves, or mere adventure, the weaker has suffered accordingly; and where the incursion has been permanent these have been driven out or exterminated or subordinated or absorbed. The cultured Athenians in democratic debate decided to slaughter all the males in the neighbouring Greek-speaking island of Melos and enslave the women and children in the service of an Athenian colony to be planted there. Constraint and commitment stopped at the frontier.

Cultural provision for the succour of strangers and trade, supported by trust based on treaty or custom, barely qualified this pattern of mutual hostility. J. H. Seeley, a well informed historian writing in 1865, counted it a major achievement (which he attributed to Christian morality) to have outgrown endemic hostility between all nations not bound by a specific treaty. [6] A specific declaration of war was needed to terminate the relations of peace. Even this applied only to 'civilised' nations and was to be eroded in the 100 years following his death. Yet each of these peoples which raided and destroyed each other so mercilessly in the human colonisation of the planet had an internal code of mutual obligation and a net of shared commitment and constraint often far more effective and accepted than our own.

Since statecraft is much concerned with external relations, it faces in this area moral problems far greater than in any but the most bitterly divided internal relations. And these problems are likely to grow much worse. The quest for resources and living space is no longer eased by the existence of huge land areas sparsely occupied by people ill equipped to resist the colonising West. The West itself begins to feel the limitations generated by its own expansion, and it can no longer count on the rest of the world to supply its raw materials. Much of the rest of the world and part of the Western world has already outgrown its indigenous food supplies. Already more people are starving than ever before. Pressure for immigration mounts and so, predictably, does well founded resistance to it. The surface of the planet is not everywhere equally supportive of human life and those peoples who still enjoy a viable relation between population and resources have everything to fear from those who do not.

Yet the dimensions of political morality, even of international morality, are the same as those of personal morality.

What future for morality?

Faced with this awesome prospect, few would dare to forecast the probable future structure of morality, whether interpersonal, intranational, or international, or the extent of its influence on the course of human affairs. But it is possible to make some statements about what is needed even with no assurance whether or how far the need will be met.

First, moral inversion is inconsistent with social survival and must be corrected. Its existence is explicable as a by-product of the last two centuries in the West but it is none the less a lethal danger. It is significant that it has been a central target in every major revolution of this century.

Second, ethical nihilism is an absurdity which needs to be stamped out. Moral standards are cultural artifacts without which no society can survive in the stresses of social life, especially those which await us now. Cultural artifacts are facts just as real as any other facts and even more important for a social species now dependent on a net of interdependent relations which it has no other means of sustaining.

Third, the problems of intercultural stress have to be faced in full recognition of the relation between political coherence and effective political action, whether intranational or international. Opinions doubtless differ as to the extent to which the populations of the world today show any cultural convergence, but the question is less important than the question of what culture they share.

Most important of all, perhaps, statements of human rights need to be replaced by statements of human responsibility, defining as clearly as possible on whom these responsibilities rest. They will be found to rest not only, often not chiefly, on governments. They will often be found to be unattainable and never to be attainable except at the cost of some prized alternative 'right'.

The world of the future, if viable at all, will be a world in which people know when to say "no" and when to take "no" for an answer. But it will not on that account be a less moral world. On the contrary it will be a world in which both personal and collective commitments and constraints will be developed to a level known to only a few societies today and least of all to the pampered West. It may even be a world nearer than today's to Aneurin Bevan's aspiration.

References

1. Notably in Michael Polanyi, "Beyond nihilism", Eddington Lecture 1960 (Cambridge, Cambridge University Press, 1960); and in M. Polanyi, "History and hope", *Virginia Quarterly Review*, Spring 1962, *30*(2).
2. Robert O. Johann, "Person, community and commitment", in Robert J. Roth, ed, *Person and Community* (New York, Fordham University Press, 1975).
3. Geoffrey Vickers, "Motivation theory: a cybernetic contribution", *Behavioral Science*, July 1973, *18*(3).
4. Geoffrey Vickers, "Stability and quality in human systems", a paper prepared for an Open University summer school, publication pending.
5. Isabella Bird, *An English Lady's Life in the Rocky Mountains* (Norman, OK, University of Oklahoma Press, 1960).
6. J. H. Seeley, *Ecce Homo*, originally published 1865 (London, Everyman's Library, J. M. Dent, 1970).

METHODS

RISK ASSESSMENT

Harry J. Otway and Philip D. Pahner

Many countries are experiencing a period in which traditional values are being questioned; plans for further technological development are being met by a variety of demands for a closer examination of the benefits and risks of large-scale technologies. The authors outline a conceptual framework for risk-assessment studies which includes, in addition to the consideration of physical risks, the perception of risk situations and the resulting psychological and sociological levels of risk.

STANDARDS of living have improved considerably during this century, largely due to the benefits made possible through the development of new technologies. As technological systems have grown larger, and more complex, they have offered increasingly attractive benefits which have created demands for more progress. This process of reinforcement has led to increasingly complex, and therefore fragile, systems which have become fundamental to sustaining the social fabric.

As technological systems became larger their disadvantages began to receive more attention. Some of these side-effects, such as new safety hazards, have been rather obvious, while others have been more subtle and, therefore, more difficult to predict and detect; eg new health hazards, complicated environmental interactions, technological unemployment, mental-health problems, and changes in basic social institutions.

Consequently there appears to be a growing awareness that increased consumption of goods and services has not brought a commensurate increase in "happiness". The resulting social response can been seen in the emergence of attitudes which regard much that is new as being potentially harmful; the fundamental value of science to society is also being questioned. A variety of individuals and groups have demanded closer examination of the benefits and risks of technological innovations. Indeed, many such advances are encountering difficulties in gaining public acceptance.

Harry Otway is Project Leader, Joint IAEA/IIASA Research Project, International Atomic Energy Agency, PO Box 590, A-1011 Vienna, Austria. Philip Pahner is a psychiatrist working with the International Institute for Applied Systems Analysis on the same project.

This has resulted in conflict; one segment of society may sponsor a proposal intended to fulfil a perceived social need while other groups, with different perceptions of society's needs, may be working actively in opposition.

Nuclear energy presents an excellent case study in risk assessment[1] because the public response to these risks is, in many cases, limiting the development of nuclear power. Further, the nuclear field provides many risk situations that are of research interest, eg the assessment of cost-effectiveness where operational risks may be reduced by expenditure on control equipment; the possibility of disastrous, but infrequent, accidents; accident probabilities which can only be theoretically estimated and which are thus highly uncertain; the non-random distribution of risks and benefits to different groups of people; concerns about possible future (genetic) risks weighed against present benefits. In addition, nuclear energy is an esoteric science and technology, difficult for the layman to conceptualise and understand.

The research to be presented here is oriented to understanding how societies judge the acceptability of new technologies and how information on risks, and the expected responses to them, may be considered in decision making. Such information could be useful in decisions on the selection and siting of alternative energy systems, the setting of regulatory standards, the design of control and safety systems, and the development of operating procedures.

The levels of risk

The most obvious risks, and the most extensively researched, are those directly affecting man's health and environment; that is, the risks most easily observed and measured. However, one may think of risk situations as being characterised by several levels:

- physical, biological risks to man and the environment;
- the perception of these risks by individuals;
- the potential risk to the psychological well-being of individuals based upon these perceptions; and
- the risks to social structures and cultural values as influenced by the collective psychological states of individuals.

The individual's perception of physical and biological risks is seldom considered. A number of psychological factors, conscious and unconscious, influence how people perceive situations. That is, the individual may, or may not, be aware of the determinants of his perceptions.

Psychological well-being may be affected if a situation is perceived as potentially threatening. A statistically minimal risk, if perceived as being threatening, may generate anxieties that are no less real than if the situation actually were threatening. Behavioural responses are based upon perceptions.

The final level is the potential risks to social structures and cultural values resulting from the cumulative effects of these psychological risks. If there are a number of individuals in a society who are anxious about a situation which they perceive as threatening, they will seek to express their concerns, eg through identifying and interacting with others sharing these concerns. This results in the formation of interest groups which may actively influence technological development. These interest groups themselves represent new social structures with their own value systems; this potential conflict of values may pose a risk to existing social and cultural systems. At the same time, however, this conflict may represent an adaptive effort to confront potentially threatening situations.

Examples of these four levels of risk may be seen in the controversy surrounding nuclear energy. A great deal of effort has been made to estimate the physical and biological risks of one type of nuclear power plant.[2] These estimates were then compared to other risks existing in society, with the implication that the nuclear risks should be "acceptable". However, this controversy is characterised by interest groups whose perceptions of the risks differ from these formal estimates. Their actions create the potential for social and cultural changes.

The general structure of risk assessment

Risk assessment has been suggested as a general term for the incorporation of risk concepts into decision making, and has been defined as occurring in two stages;[3] risk estimation and risk evaluation, which will be discussed in detail in this section. A general structure of risk assessment is shown in Figure 1.

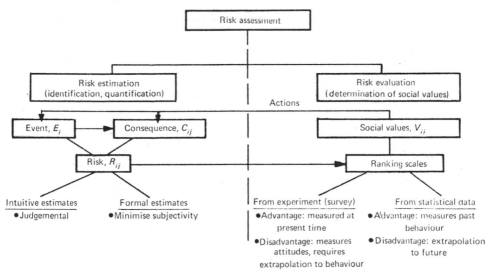

Figure 1. The general structure of risk assessment

Risk estimation

This is the identification of the side-effects of a decision, estimation of their probabilities, and the magnitude of the associated consequences. Some of the earliest formal risk assessments were made in the nuclear-energy field, the most recent and comprehensive estimates being those of the US reactor safety study[2] which treated risks from accidents in light-water-cooled nuclear power plants.

In everyday usage, risk is usually thought of as the probability of an undesired occurrence, eg an automobile accident. In this article risk is thought of as a combination of the event probability, the uncertainty of the probability, the probability of a specific consequence given the fact that the event has occurred, and the uncertainty of this probability. This is shown in Figure 1 by the combination of event, E_i, and its consequence, C_{ij}, to form risk, R_{ij}.

Probability is an important variable in speaking of risk. The measurement of probability has a long history of academic debate.[4] Definitions range from the classical notion that probability is the ratio of favourable occurrence to the total number of equally likely cases (eg the roll of a die or toss of a coin) to the subjective or judgemental view, which holds that probability measures one's degree of belief as measured by behaviour. Risk estimates might be considered as ranging from objective to subjective; however, the technological risks which are of interest to us can never be estimated in a completely objective manner because the necessary data base does not exist. As pointed out by Fishburn,[5] "all measurements of probability rely upon human judgement to some extent". What we would like to think of as objective estimates of risk, because they are the product of careful calculation, are only attempts to minimise subjective aspects through a more formal approach. The estimate of the layman that a particular risk is too high is the result of an intuitive approach to the same problem. The point is, that these two extremes differ only in the degree of subjectivity involved and, therefore, have been identified in Figure 1 as formal and intuitive estimates rather than objective and subjective.

Risk evaluation

Risk evaluation is the complex process of determining the meaning, or value, of the estimated risks to those affected. This has been referred to by Häfele as the "embedding" of risks into the "sociosphere".[6] Evaluation may be thought of as a process of ranking, or ordering, risks so that their total effects, both objective and subjective, may be compared. This process essentially defines the "acceptability" of risk. This "embedding" process is shown in Figure 1 as a mapping of risk into ranking scales that reflect social attitudes towards risks. By using the definition of risk proposed earlier we take into account the fact that man is not indifferent to the nature of the event which results in a given consequence.

A feedback path is shown which allows actions reflecting social values to affect events or consequences, eg the design of safety systems intended to prevent accidents or to limit their effects.

Two basic methods of obtaining ranking scales are outlined in Figure 1. The first is based upon the analysis of statistical data to determine the past preferences that society has shown towards existing risks. The second is experiments (eg psychometric surveys) to measure attitudes toward risks. The former yields information on past behaviour, the latter on present attitudes.

The most elementary approach to obtaining rankings is to simply compile a table of accident statistics. A new risk is placed in perspective by comparing it with existing, and therefore accepted, risks. A limitation of this method is that many variables determine risk acceptance and they cannot be reflected in such comparisons. The various risks may have no common dimension in which they may be compared.

Rankings determined by the analysis of statistical data have the advantage of being based upon actual behaviour. However, they are limited by the assumption that past is prologue, that preferences revealed in the past will be valid in the future. This would not be expected to hold for technological risks because social values are changing with time—primarily because of changes introduced by technology. Further, behaviour with respect to risk acceptance is multiply determined, ie many factors influence the response to risks and not all of these determinants are known, let alone clearly identified in the data base. Risk perception is important since the response to risk depends upon how situations are perceived; statistical data report things as they were, eg accident rates or demographic variables. Some limitations of rankings based upon revealed preferences have been summarised elsewhere.[7] At this point we may observe that evaluations of nuclear-power risks made by this method have indicated that nuclear power should be acceptable. However, experience has shown that this is not always the case. Thus revealed preferences could be useful in helping decide the risk levels that might be ethically acceptable, but they may tell us little about what the public finds acceptable.

A distinction must be made between attitudes and behaviour. The former represent what people say their views are about a given situation. Behaviour is the action they take when this situation is encountered. Rankings based upon psychometric surveys provide information on attitudes rather than behaviour, but it is attitudes which are measured at the present time.

In summary, we have two methods for risk evaluation available to us: revealed preferences and controlled experiments. The former measures past behaviour; it is difficult, though, to anticipate future behaviour based upon observations of past behaviour. The latter provides information on attitudes at the present moment; the problem here is how to anticipate behaviour from measurements of attitude.

The risk assessment of technological systems

Figure 2 introduces social dynamics into the structure of risk assessment developed in the last section. This process includes the contributions of three social groups: the sponsor who proposes a technological development, the public for whom the benefit is intended, and the regulator who has the responsibility of balancing the needs of both groups.[8] In the following discussion the numbers in parentheses refer to the respective boxes in Figure 2.

The sponsor
The process starts with a social need which may be satisfied by some proposed application of technology; eg by the construction of a power plant. The sponsor may perceive the proposal (1) as a design problem (12). In his design he must ensure that the required benefit is provided and that any potential side-effects fall within the regulating standards. These side-effects are characterised by events, E (such as accidents) and their consequences, C, which must be considered in the design.

Figure 2 also introduces the concept of an unknown set, ϕ, of potential events or consequences which could actually occur but cannot be included in the design because their existence has not yet been discovered. An additional "inverse", unknown set, ϕ', has also been postulated to represent those events and consequences which have been imagined by the designer but would, in fact, be impossible if natural laws were perfectly known. Regulations may require situations to be considered in design which are unrealistic; this is done in order to provide safety margins. These also form part of the inverse unknown set.

The sponsor's design (13) may proceed in the traditional, deterministic manner in which design base limits are assumed for E and C. Safety systems are engineered which will allow adherence to the set standards should the design base situation occur. An alternative design method is the probabilistic approach, which does not employ artificial design limits. There are no limits to the events and consequences considered; however, they are weighted by their probabilities,

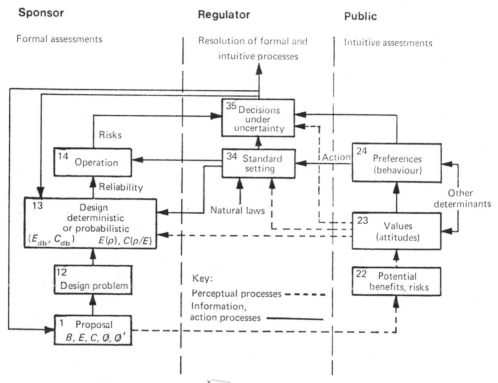

Figure 2. The process of risk assessment for technological systems

and risks are kept to acceptable levels through reliability design. Whichever design method is chosen, the reliability of systems is fixed, either directly or indirectly. Reliability combined with operational philosophy (14) determines the risks to which the public are exposed. The designer's perception of the relevant social values are also considered in the design process.

The public

The public perceive the proposal (1) as a potential source of social benefits and risks (22). Their intuitive estimations of risk can include allowances for the unknown set, ϕ, possibilities not considered in the design. These allowances are not based upon superior technical knowledge, but may be expressed simply as a lack of confidence in the designers, operators, or the regulating authorities. The inverse unknown set, ϕ', may also be considered. An example of this might be the fear that a nuclear-power plant can explode like an atomic bomb.

Unrealistic as such concerns might be, they still influence the perception of risk. The public and the designer consider different inverse unknown sets; this reflects their different conceptual frameworks.

This difference in conceptual framework initiates the process of social controversy, one manifestation of which is the interest group. The interest group may be viewed as a confluence of social systems which includes: the individual and his repertoire of psychological responses; the influence of the scientific community; the availability and communication of information; various economic and political considerations; social and cultural determinants; and the historical moment. The interest group thus represents the focal point of the interaction of these various systems.

For an individual the response to a fear-provoking stimulus (eg a new technology) is distributed along a continuum, that can be thought of simply as "flight or fight". There may be an apathetic physical and emotional withdrawal from the perceived threat. In some cases there is an attempt to deny the existence of risk. At the other extreme there may be a readiness to confront, and a struggle to understand, the nature of the risk, and a willingness to deal with it effectively. In any case these may be understood as expected human responses to anxiety-provoking, external situations. In addition to external threats, internal fears and anxieties may be be projected onto a symbolic external object. As these fears are expressed, the individual encounters others who think and feel and act similarly.

An interest group reflects, to varying degrees, elements of its members' individual responses, characteristics of its social-cultural environment, and the information available. An interest group, however, has its own intrinsic characteristics. Observations and research on interest groups support the following generalisations:

- they tend to form around social and environmental concerns that have wide-ranging effects;
- they tend to be solution-oriented rather than problem-oriented, inclined to a dialectic, adversary position rather than to collaborative exchange;
- the constituency and cohesiveness of the group is related to the degree members share similar values and attitudes;
- communication patterns are often distorted, especially in groups with a vertical status and power hierarchy;
- new information may be accepted or rejected contingent upon the support it provides for group values and beliefs; and
- the members' behaviour is influenced by the group, so the strength and integrity of individual values may be weakened or strengthened.

Thus the interest group tends to be a body of persons emotionally committed to their position and screening information according to the utility it has for their position.[9]

It must be realised that such generalisations fail to consider the more adaptive, positive aspects of interest groups. They may serve an important alerting, activating function. The interest group may counteract a tendency to withdraw from, or to deny, potential risks, and thereby promote a better understanding of technological proposals.[10]

Values or attitudes toward risks (23) are multiply determined. The perceived risks are intuitively incorporated into this system of values which can be measured by means of the ranking scales referred to earlier. Preferences related to risk acceptance (24) exist only when revealed by behaviour. Thus lines of action in Figure 2 lead from box 24 into the regulating sector.

The regulator

Regulators occur on several levels. First there is the agency responsible for setting standards (34). Standards take into account the effects on the environment as predicted by natural laws and the perception of the relevant social values (23). If standards (34) are incompatible with social preferences (24) then a change in standards may be demanded.

Second, the decision on the proposal (35) will be taken in conditions of uncertainty. This decision might require changes in the proposal, design or operation and could be influenced by social action (24). The final regulator which, depending upon the political process, might include the judiciary, is the resolution of the formal risk assessment of the sponsor and the intuitive risk assessment of the public. For simplicity, these two functions have been shown as one step (35).

Summary

Reports such as the US reactor safety study are useful in formalising the estimation of risks to which the public is exposed.[2] Such work would also allow the determination of the system reliabilities necessary to satisfy standards based upon risk consideration. The emphasis here is upon formal risk estimates (13 and 14).

Conclusion

The intent of this article was to outline a conceptual framework for risk assessment studies which includes, not only consideration of physical risks to man and environment, but also pays attention to factors influencing how risk situations are perceived and the resulting psychological and sociological levels of risk. Most risk-assessment research to date has concentrated upon estimating the risks from technological activities and comparing these estimates with other, but different, risks existing in society. These comparisons, however, cannot take account of the factors which determine both how risks are perceived and the response to them.

Preliminary results of recent research suggest that the siting of nuclear-power plants may be far from being cost effective. In fact, expenditure on nuclear safety appears, in some cases, to be several orders of magnitude higher than would be justified if biological risks alone were a sufficient criterion. The fact that these expenditures are being made, and that, even then, many facilities cannot gain broad-based public approval, underlines the practical importance of a better understanding of the sociological and psychological levels of risk. Observations indicate that anxiety generated by concern about the perceived risks of technological development pose risks to the psychological well-being of the individual. These individual concerns are then aggregated in the form of new social groups which may play an active role in trying to influence policies affecting technological development. These interest groups themselves represent new social structures with their own value system. Thus they have an impact upon the existing social and cultural values; this conflict of values poses a potential risk to social and cultural systems.

References and notes

1. It has been suggested that concerns regarding nuclear energy represent a general, and perhaps even symbolic, example of social concerns about technological development. See Pahner, Philip D. "The psychological displacement of anxiety: an application to nuclear energy", IIASA RM-76-XX (Laxenburg, Austria, International Institute for Applied Systems Analysis, 1976), in press.
2. "Reactor safety study: an assessment of accident risks in US commercial nuclear power plants", USNRC, WASH-1400, October 1975.
3. Harry J. Otway, "Risk assessment and societal choices", IIASA RM-75-2 (Laxenburg, Austria, International Institute for Applied Systems Analysis, February 1975); Harry J. Otway, "Risk estimation and evaluation", Proceedings of the International Institute for Applied Systems Analysis Planning Conference on Energy Systems, IIASA-PC-3, 1973.
4. Howard Raiffa, *Decision Analysis: Introductory Lectures on Choices Under Uncertainty* (New York, Addison-Wesley, 1968).
5. Peter C. Fishburn, *Decision and Value Theory* (New York, John Wiley, 1964).
6. Wolf Häfele, "A systems approach to energy", *American Scientist*, July/August 1974, *62* (4), pages 438–447.
7. Harry J. Otway and J. J. Cohen, "Revealed preferences: comments on the Starr benefit–risk relationships", IIASA RM-75-5 (Laxenburg, Austria, International Institute for Applied Systems Analysis, April 1975).
8. Figure 2 closely parallels the structural hypothesis of mental mechanisms proposed in Sigmund Freud, *Das Ich und das Es*, Gesammelte Schriften, 6. Band (Vienna, Internationaler Psychoanalytischer Verlag, 1925).
9. Clovis R. Shepherd, *Small Groups: Some Sociological Perspective* (Scranton, PN, Chandler Publishing, 1964).
10. Philip D. Pahner, "Some thoughts on the behavioural aspects of interest groups". internal paper, International Institute for Applied Systems Analysis, Laxenburg, Austria, 1974.

THE ECONOMIC EVALUATION OF LONG-RUN UNCERTAINTIES

Robert H. Haveman

This article looks at the question of uncertainty, as a factor in assessing future costs or benefits, and reviews its treatment in the economics literature. The importance of making an adjustment for uncertainty in the anticipation of the results of an action having long-term effects—in this case environmental damages—is emphasised. Particular attention is focused upon the attitudes toward risk displayed by individuals, and upon the social evaluation of long-term, uncertain, and irreversible actions, particularly where the effect to be evaluated is a stream of adverse consequences. Despite some disagreement in the literature, the author argues that the questions of uncertainty and risk aversion are not relevant solely at the microlevel: the expected social value of proposed activities must also reflect the uncertainty of future effects—and future tastes.

WITH economic change increasingly dominated by technological developments, the decisions of both private-sector households and firms and the public sector have consequences which extend into the distant future. Given imperfect foresight, knowledge of these consequences will be partial and hence uncertain. Moreover, many of these consequences are "public" in nature, in the sense that they are not confined solely to those responsible for the decision. If such decisions are to be purposive, that is designed to achieve some defined goal or set of objectives, evaluation of their impact must be based on a firm theoretical underpinning.

At the present time, there are two fundamental issues which dominate discussions of the proper evaluation of long-term and uncertain events. These two issues are:

● Assuming no change in tastes from one generation to the next, how should one evaluate uncertainty regarding future effects when framing a social decision?

Robert H. Haveman is Professor of Economics at the University of Wisconsin-Madison, Social Science Building, 1180 Observatory Drive, Madison, Wisconsin 53706, USA. This paper is based on a report prepared for the Organisation for Economic Co-operation and Development (OECD).

- How should the evaluation be done if the tastes of the current generation are not likely to persist into the future?

A good deal of work on the first of these questions has been done in recent years, primarily because of concern with the long-term and persistent effects associated with environmental decisions. Perhaps more than any other policy area, environmental policy is confronted with the problems of uncertainty and risk, and the role of future generations and their tastes.

This article describes the evolution of the economics literature concerned with the evaluation of uncertain, long-term environmental damages, summarises its current status, and examines the implications of the currently accepted analysis of that evaluation problem.

While the issue of uncertainty also relates to the matter of intergenerational preferences in evaluating impacts which extend over several decades, this problem will only be explicitly considered in one brief section—dealing with intergenerational taste changes. The justification for this neglect of the question of future generations' preferences is that the issue is far from resolved in the economics literature. The bulk of the discussion in *this* article will assume that future generations have tastes which are similar to those of people living today. In the discussion, it will also be assumed that the standard economic treatment of time is appropriate for effects expected to extend for hundreds of years, as well as for those which will occur within a single generation.

Uncertain long-term effects and private risk aversion

To provide the discussion with an empirical focus, I will cast the problem of the evaluation of long-term and uncertain effects as one of evaluating decisions creating persistent and adverse impacts on the environment. This is convenient, given that most of the literature on this problem has been related to the environmental issue.

In order to isolate the issue of uncertainty and long-term effects, it is helpful to lay down a few general ground rules to guide the discussion:

- Any action taken, whether accidental or deliberate, which leads to the emission of residuals into the environment or to the destruction of some environmental amenity will create environmental costs, and these costs may or may not be accompanied by benefits associated with the action.
- Costs and benefits of an activity are to be calculated according to standard economic efficiency criteria. Individual tastes and preferences, as reflected in the willingness to pay for goods and services obtained and foregone, are the basis for such a calculation. The distribution of benefits and costs is ignored.
- As far as possible, the expression of benefits and costs is to be in terms of a monetary unit.
- Although they are technically distinguishable, the terms risk and uncertainty will be used interchangeably in this discussion.[1] Both will be taken to refer to the existence of a distribution of alternative outcomes for any particular action.
- The attitudes toward risk and uncertainty are crucial to the treatment of those factors. Two attitudes are often considered in discussions of risk and

uncertainty: *risk neutrality* (in which uncertainty attached to an event does not affect how an individual appraises the event—he will simply accept its mathematical expectation as its value) and *risk aversion* (in which uncertainty attached to an event leads an individual to appraise its worth at less than its mathematical expectation. The value attached to the event by such an individual is known as the *certainty equivalent* of the event.) Allusions to both attitudes will be made in this discussion.

Let us presume that some activity leads to environmental damages which persist for each of a known number of years into the future; that the value of these damages (the willingness to pay to forego them) is known with certainty for each year in which damages will occur; and that individuals have a preference for present rather than future consumption, which preference is called their *time preference*. If there exist smoothly functioning capital markets, the decisions taken by consumers in allocating their consumption over time, and the decisions taken by producers in undertaking investment activities, will lead to the establishment of a *market rate of interest* which reflects this time preference.

If this time preference interest rate is known, along with the time stream of certain environmental damages, the present value of these damages can be calculated by a procedure known as *discounting*. Stated symbolically, the present value of these damages (P) is:

$$P = \frac{D_i}{(1 + r)^i}$$

in which

D_i is the certain damages expected in year i, and
r is the time preference interest rate.

This present value of damages must be compared with the present value of the benefits of an activity to determine if the implementation of the activity increases the economic welfare of the community.

The approach to risk
If the environmental damages of an activity are uncertain in their value, the calculation of the present value of damages becomes more difficult. Assuming that people are *risk neutral*, the uncertain nature of damages in any given year could be transformed into its mathematical expectation, and then a present value could be calculated, as above. If probabilities can be attached to the range of possible values in any year, the mathematical expectation is easily calculated. Indeed, even if only *subjective probabilities* can be attached to these possible events, a mathematical expectation can be determined, and the present value calculated.

On the other hand, if people are *risk averse* rather than risk neutral, the simple calculation of the mathematical expectation will be inadequate. Risk aversion implies that the value of an uncertain phenomenon will differ from its mathematical expectation because the very existence of uncertainty is a cost. Suppose one is risk averse and one's $20 000 home is on fire. If $10 000 of damages could be averted if a fire truck comes within five minutes, and no damages would be averted if it doesn't, and if there is a 0·5 probability that a truck will come, the mathematical expectation of the value of the fire truck's appearance would be $5000. However, if one is risk averse, one would be willing to trade this possible appearance of a fire truck with the certain appearance of a torrential rain shower that would avert, say, only $4000 of damages. The $4000, then, is the certainty equivalent of the mathematical expectation of $5000, and the existence of uncertainty has created a cost of $1000.[2]

Because it is generally accepted that risk or uncertainty aversion exists, people require a premium on purchases which have uncertain values. Thus, a risky bond will have to offer a higher interest rate than a risk-free bond. There is a structure of interest rates, with higher rates associated with instruments having high variability in outcome, and lower rates associated with low variability instruments.

If we presume the existence of risk or uncertainty aversion, the question arises: "How is risk or uncertainty to be accounted for in evaluating decisions with enduring and uncertain consequences?" This question has occupied economists for some time, and a number of rules of thumb have been suggested for adjusting the benefits of such decisions to reflect the cost of uncertainty. The primary suggestions are:[3]

- Observe every year's expected value (mathematical expectation) of benefits, and make a judgement on the degree of uncertainty which surrounds this value; then, on the basis of the degree of risk aversion which is felt, substitute a lower certain equivalent value for the expected but uncertain value.
- Place a limit on the length of time over which the benefits are expected to occur which is shorter than the expected length. This technique ignores uncertainty in early years, and uncertainty in years beyond the limit is implied to have a cost at least as great as the expected value of benefits in those years.
- Add a premium to the interest rate used for discounting benefits, with the size of this added premium reflecting a judgement of the cost of the uncertainty involved in the benefit stream. If a single premium is added to the discount rate used for discounting all future years' consequences, the effect is to reduce benefits in distant years by more than benefits in proximate years. This is a reasonable approach if the degree of uncertainty is positively related to the delay in the experiencing of benefits.

If risk aversion is relevant, each of these procedures will lead to a reduction in the present value of benefits attributable to an activity. The gap between the present value without the adjustment and that with the adjustment reflects the cost of uncertainty.

These procedures are also relevant for evaluating the adverse and uncertain consequences stemming from any decision. In this case, however, it must be emphasised that the stream of effects which is being evaluated is a cost stream rather than a benefit stream. Hence, the cost of bearing uncertainty must be added to the stream of effects and must result in a *higher* present value, if risk or uncertainty aversion is relevant. Thus, the three rules of thumb mentioned earlier must be altered in evaluating a stream of adverse consequences. In particular, the mathematical sign of the adjustment must be reversed:

- A *higher* certainty equivalent value can be substituted for the expected but uncertain value.

- The length of time over which the damages are expected to accrue can be *lengthened*.
- A discount can be *subtracted* from the interest rate used to calculate the present value.

This alteration, it must be noted, is fundamental and yet it is often not recognised in the literature. Because nearly all analysis has presumed the existence of positive net benefits, limits on length of life, reductions of expected value, and risk premiums have almost exclusively been considered. All of these adjustments are in precisely the wrong direction for evaluating an uncertain stream of costs or damages.[4]

The social evaluation of long-term uncertain effects

Few would deny that individual decision makers are averse to risk and uncertainty and should therefore apply adjustments of the sort discussed in the previous section to uncertain events;[5] but from the point of society as a whole it is not clear that an activity's uncertain future effects convey the same sort of cost. While private risk aversion exists, social risk aversion may not.

In the economics literature, two reasons for neglecting uncertainty in social evaluations have been suggested. They are the pooling argument, and the Arrow-Lind theorem.

The pooling argument

According to this argument,[6] individuals experience a cost associated with uncertain returns because they have limited resources and, hence, are unable to pool their risky events. For society as a whole, however, the uncertainty attached to the effects of one activity is pooled with the uncertainty attached to the effects of numerous other activities. If these activities are independent (ie uncorrelated), the pooled effect of the individual uncertainties has zero impact on the total uncertainty of real national income and, hence, can be ignored (see Arrow[7]).

Even the proponents of this position, however, recognise that pooling only has this effect if there is no relationship between the variability (uncertainty) in the outcome of a particular activity and the variability in the performance of the economy as a whole. If there is such a relationship, the pooling argument breaks down.

The Arrow–Lind theorem

In a recent paper, Arrow and Lind have demonstrated that as the effects (costs or benefits) of an activity are shared by an increasing number of individuals, the cost of uncertainty to any one representative individual decreases until, at the limit, this cost vanishes.[8] If the number of individuals sharing the effects is large enough, then only the expected value of the effects should be taken into account, even though each of the individuals is risk averse.

In addition, Arrow and Lind have demonstrated that the aggregate costs of this uncertainty—added up over all individuals—also approaches zero. The implication of this in the evaluation of costs and benefits (including environmental damages) is that, from the social point of view, risk neutrality is the correct position.

However, it should be noted that the Arrow–Lind theorem requires that the effects (benefits and costs) be spread over a very large number of individuals—indeed, an infinite number—if social risk neutrality is to be presumed. In a comment on the Arrow–Lind paper, McKean and Moore suggest that not even a total of 80 million US taxpayers is a sufficiently large number to permit uncertainty to be neglected.[9] In those cases in which effects or costs are distributed among a limited number of individuals, risk aversion is still to be presumed and a cost for uncertain effects is to be subtracted from expected benefit estimates and added to expected cost estimates.

And a further reservation to the Arrow–Lind theorem has been expressed. It has been pointed out that Arrow and Lind have implicitly assumed that the effects of private and public activities are uncorrelated. However, if for any particular effect generated by a public activity (and spread over a large number of individuals), there is an equivalent and correlated effect in the private sector, the risk aversion of the small number of individuals affected by that influence from the private sector should be applied in evaluating the former. Therefore, individual risk aversion should be a guide for social evaluation.[10]

In the literature, then, the existence of social risk aversion is an unsettled matter. Under certain conditions, the Arrow–Lind risk neutrality appears to hold; under others, social risk aversion exists and should be accounted for in evaluating the consequences of activities, whether private or public. In spite of the Arrow–Lind theorem, numerous economists consider that social risk aversion is relevant in evaluating uncertain activities.[11]

Evaluating uncertainty in special cases

Even if it is presumed that the conditions required for the Arrow–Lind theorem do prevail, it may be the case that some kinds of effects have characteristics such that social evaluation should presume risk aversion. Within the last few years, several papers have appeared which indicate that such characteristics do exist.

Long-term, uncertain, "public good" effects
Fisher[12] considers the example of an activity which generates a stream of benefits or damages which are spread across risk-averse individuals in such a way that what is incurred by one does not diminish what is received by others. Such effects are public goods (or, perhaps, public "bads"). Employing a model similar to the Arrow–Lind model, Fisher demonstrates that, in addition to the expected value of the benefit or cost stream, the evaluation must also consider "the amount that would be required to compensate those who bear the risk" or uncertainty associated with the future uncertain stream. That is, an "adjustment for risk should be made".

For this reintroduction of social risk aversion to hold, Fisher notes that the benefit or cost must represent a non-negligible fraction of the real income of those affected, and that the risk or uncertainty is not (or cannot be) costlessly transferred from the affected individuals to the larger community.

Long-term, uncertain, irreversible effects
Many activities are accompanied by environmental damages which significantly and permanently—or merely for a long period—reduce the variety of

future choices. An example of such irreversible damage would be the destruction, by the erection of a hydro-electricity dam, of a natural gorge.

Recent literature, concentrating on environmental damages, has demonstrated that when individuals are uncertain about their future use of a facility (or when the supply of the facility is uncertain), if an adverse impact on the facility is irreversible, and if the individuals are risk averse, an extra cost—called *option value*—must be added to the expected value of future damages.[13]

The existence of this option value—a sort of risk or uncertainty cost—is now accepted in the literature—although it may be that, applying the Arrow–Lind theorem, the cost is irrelevant from the social point of view. However, in a very recent paper, Arrow and Fisher have argued that if such effects (for example, environmental damages) are irreversible, *and* if information about these effects results in a *change* in their expected value in a later period, an addition to the expected value of damages—similar to an uncertainty adjustment—must be made.[14] Hence, even though risk neutrality is assumed for the social evaluation of uncertain future effects, if the impact is irreversible and if further information is expected, there exists "a quasi-option value having an effect in the same direction as risk aversion". The value of irreversible expected damages should be adjusted upward to reflect the resulting loss of options, and, similarly, the value of irreversible expected benefits should be adjusted downward. This same result, it should be pointed out, was obtained by Henry, employing a quite different approach.[15] Simulating the extent of the required adjustment for uncertainty using reasonable values for the discount rate and levels of uncertainty, he concludes that "13% seems to give a good idea of the degree of magnitude of the irreversibility effect".

Long-term uncertain effects with shifting evaluations
Finally, a recent contribution to the question of evaluating uncertain future effects has considered the issue of intertemporal taste instability. This contribution by Fisher and Krutilla[16] was the first to allow the tastes of future generations for environmental services and for risk and uncertainty to deviate from those of the present generation. The issue raised in their paper concerned the evaluation of environmental damages when tastes toward the environment may be shifting over time. Where there is such uncertainty regarding future tastes, Fisher and Krutilla argue that an additional cost must be added to the expected value of damages. If, for example, it is possible that future generations will place a higher value on environmental damages than present citizens, and if an activity is generating irreversible (or at least long-term) environmental damages, *ex post facto* evaluation of the damages would exceed the current evaluation. To reflect these changing tastes—and to avoid the approval of activities generating environmental damages which, from "tomorrow's" perspective, should have been disapproved—an additional cost should be added to the expected level of the damages. This is true even when uncertainty is irrelevant, from a social point of view, according to the Lind–Arrow theorem.[17]

Summary

The literature reviewed in this article indicates that there are numerous cases in which the presence of uncertainty requires an adjustment to the expected value of anticipated future costs or benefits. In spite of the Arrow–Lind theorem—implying that *social* risk aversion is irrelevant—numerous circumstances exist which require that a premium be added to the expected value of future damages (and a discount subtracted from the expected value of future benefits) in calculating the social value of proposed activities. The circumstances which are relevant in determining the need for and extent of such an uncertainty adjustment are:

- the presence and degree of *risk aversion* among the population affected by a proposed activity;
- the extent to which the effects of the activity are *irreversible*, in which case an *option value* is created;
- the economic attributes of the expected effects, in terms of their public- or private-good character and, in the latter case, the number of people affected;
- the extent to which the expected effects are *correlated* with other economic activities;
- the extent to which information on the effect of activities is expected to improve over time because of *learning from experience*; and
- the extent to which it is anticipated that *tastes* with regard to environmental questions will be altered over time.

In Table 1, combinations of these characteristics are shown and the need for uncertainty adjustment in each combination is indicated. Where more than one

TABLE 1. EVALUATIONS OF BENEFITS OR COSTS
REQUIRING UNCERTAINTY ADJUSTMENTS

	Individuals assumed to be risk neutral		Individuals assumed to be risk averse	
	effect irreversible	effect reversible	effect irreversible	effect reversible
The effect is correlated with other economic activities			✕	✕
Economic characteristic of effect: public good			✕	✕
private good affecting few individuals			✕	✕
private good affecting many individuals			✕	✕
Change in tastes with regard to effects	✕		✕	
Improvement in information expected	✕		✕	

source of adjustment is indicated in a column, the aggregate adjustment required is the cumulative effect of all of the sources. All of these adjustments can be translated into a reduction (or increase) in the discount rate used to estimate the present value of future damages (benefits) and, hence, an increase (decrease) in the social valuation of these effects from that indicated by their expected value.

Looking at the table, it is apparent that many prominent issues awaiting public resolution fall into categories which require an aggregate adjustment for uncertainty, reflecting several sources. Many of the major technological developments—for example, nuclear power—appear to carry with them irreversible negative effects, often having the character of a public good. Assuming that individuals are risk averse, evaluation of those activities would be guided by column three of the table. The cumulated adjustment for uncertainty in these cases implies a need for substantial caution in appraising requests for the commitment of additional social resources to these activities.

Notes and references

1. The distinction between them is set out most clearly in F. H. Knight, *Risk, Uncertainty and Profit* (New York, Harper and Row, 1965).
2. This statement overstates the simplicity of evaluating many decisions creating long-term uncertain consequences. As Conrad has pointed out, in evaluating the damages of acts which disturb the environment (such as oil spills): "the number of extenuating factors is so complex that no true or ideal set of states which exhaustively describes the future could be constructed. In this case the uncertainty prevailing in the mind of the decision maker would not appear to be capable of being synthesised or reduced to the single elementary level required for formulation in the standard decision making problem under uncertainty.

   The dilemma is particularly real for most of the contemporary environmental problems . . . because (1) . . . the combination of circumstances may be so unique as to preclude formation of frequency estimates based on past (objective) observations; that is, only subjective probability statements can be made and (2) many of these . . . consequences [are produced] only after sufficient lags or cumulation of past discharges so that . . . knowing what state of nature has occurred or obtained is not a trivial exercise". Jon Conrad, *Uncertain Externality: The Case of Oil Pollution*, unpublished PhD dissertation, University of Wisconsin–Madison, 1973.
3. For a more detailed discussion of these techniques and their implications, see R. Dorfman, "Basic economic and technologic concepts: a general statement" in A. Maass, M. Hufschmidt, R. Dorfman, H. A. Thomas Jr, S. A. Marglin, and G. M. Fair, *Design of Water Resource Systems* (Cambridge, Mass, Harvard University Press, 1962).
4. See R. Haveman, *Water Resource Investment and the Public Interest* (Nashville, Vanderbilt University Press, 1965) for a discussion of this. See also J. Hirshleifer and D. Shapiro, "The treatment of risk and uncertainty", in R. Haveman and J. Margolis, *Public Expenditure and Policy Analysis*, second edition (Skokie, Illinois, Rand-McNally, 1977).
5. See J. Hirshleifer and D. Shapiro, *op cit* (reference 3).
6. This position is defended in W. Vickrey, "Principles of efficiency—discussion", *American Economic Review*, 54 (Papers and Proceedings), May 1964.
7. K. J. Arrow, "Discounting and public investment criteria", in A. V. Kneese and S. C. Smith, eds, *Water Resources Research* (Baltimore, John Hopkins Press, 1966).
8. K. J. Arrow and R. C. Lind, "Uncertainty and the evaluation of public investment decisions", *American Economic Review*, 40, June 1970.
9. R. N. McKean and J. H. Moore, "Uncertainty and the evaluation of public investment decisions: comment", *American Economic Review*, 42, January 1972.
10. See A. Sandmo, "Discount rates for public investment under uncertainty", *International Economic Review*, June 1972.
11. See O. Eckstein, *Water Resource Development* (Cambridge, Mass, Harvard University Press, 1958); J. Hirshleifer, "Investment decision under uncertainty: applications of the State-preference approach", *Quarterly Journal of Economics*,

80, May 1966; J. Hirshleifer, "Préférence sociale à l'égard du temps", *Recherches Economiques de Louvain*, *34*, 1968; J. Hirshleifer, J. C. de Haven, and J. W. Milliman, *Water Supply: Economics, Technology, and Policy* (Chicago, University of Chicago Press, 1960); and J. S. Bain, R. E. Caves, and J. Margolis, *Northern California's Water Industry* (Baltimore, John Hopkins Press, 1966).

12. A. C. Fisher, "Environmental externalities and the Arrow–Lind public investment theorem", *American Economic Review*, 1974.
13. See C. Cicchetti and A. M. Freeman, "Option demand and consumer surplus: further comments", *Quarterly Journal of Economics*, *85*, October 1971.
14. K. J. Arrow and A. C. Fisher, "Environmental preservation, uncertainty, and irreversibility", *Quarterly Journal of Economics*, May 1974.
15. C. Henry, "Irreversible decisions under uncertainty", *American Economic Review*, *64*, December 1974.
16. A. C. Fisher and J. V. Krutilla, "Valuing long-run ecological consequences and irreversibilities", in H. Peskin and E. Seskin, *Cost Benefit Analysis and Water Pollution Policy* (Washington DC, The Urban Institute, 1975).
17. An example of the evaluation of uncertain environmental damages of this sort is found in A. C. Fisher, J. V. Krutilla, and C. J. Cicchetti, "The economics of environmental preservation: a theoretical and empirical analysis", *American Economic Review*, *57*, September 1972. For additional discussions regarding the role of future generations in appraising uncertain events, see S. A. Marglin, "The social rate of discount and the optimal rate of investment", *Quarterly Journal of Economics*, *78*, May 1964. The current status of this intergenerational issue was described by US National Academy of Sciences, *Decision Making for Regulating Chemicals in the Environment* (Washington DC, 1976) as follows: "There is as yet no generally accepted method for weighing the intergenerational incidence of benefits and costs".

PREDICTION AND SOCIAL CHANGE
The need for a basis in theory

Gordon Rattray Taylor

The author argues that social changes cause personality changes, and that personality changes cause social changes. This mutual feedback effect lies at the heart of the problems of social forecasting. Any valid system of forecasting requires a study of social changes; but such a study itself necessitates an investigation of personality structures and individual values. The weak links in the causal chain of social change are the source of changes in values and the effect of values upon social goals. The author describes the limited evidence that research into values has provided, and examines critically the methodology employed. He suggests an alternative—but potentially complementary— approach and describes specific problem areas; finally he reasserts his ultimate goal of a theory of social change.

OVER the past decade or two, professional forecasters have not achieved many successes, even when dealing with the simplest trends. At the moment British educators are in a stew because the expected flattening of the curve of demand for school places, predicted only five years ago, has failed to materialise. To take a different kind of example, in 1970 the US Cabinet Task Force on Oil announced: "We do not predict a substantial price rise in world oil markets over the coming decade".

Not only have many predictions proved erroneous, it is also the case that forecasters have failed to foresee or even discuss many changes of the greatest importance which have in fact taken place, although many of them were foretold by amateurs. Here, off the cuff, are a dozen examples:

- the emergence of extreme sexual permissiveness;
- the reaction against technology and the growth society;

Gordon Rattray Taylor is a member of *Futures* Advisory Board. His most recent book is *How to Avoid the Future* (London, Secker and Warburg, 1975).

- the rise in crime rates;
- the demand for political devolution;
- dominance of unions in the political field;
- Third-world cartellisation: rise in oil prices;
- use of terrorism to achieve political or criminal ends, eg taking hostages;
- emergence of large-scale addictive drug problem and alcoholism;
- major movements against nuclear power stations, fuel reprocessing, etc;
- emergence of women's liberation movement and equal-rights demands;
- emergence of interest in mysticism, the occult, Zen Buddhism, etc.

The above are all matters of political and economic importance and fore-knowledge of them would have made it possible to avoid costly errors;[1] but futurologists missed them, and politicians failed to allow for them. In short, futurologists not only fail to provide the right answers, they even fail to ask the right questions.

Structural constraints

This poor record is due, I suggest, to the curious way that futures research is structured. On the one hand there are the extrapolators. Many of the concerns which finance forecasting, or contract for it to be done, are only interested in very specific matters—how many school places will be required in five years time, how many bags of cement in 20 years time? Broadly speaking, they try to arrive at answers by extrapolating trends which seem immediately to affect their problem. They regard research into broad social changes as a luxury, or, if not a luxury, at any rate something somebody else should pay for. But in point of fact all specific trends depend eventually on general ones and in particular on changes in the goals and values of individuals.

It is not enough to forecast the demand for cement on the basis of expected road-building programmes and the like, for these are affected by a general shift of values—which may put the environment higher, and rapid transport lower, in the scheme of life. Similarly, the number of school places depends on the decisions people make about family size and spacing; and these in turn may be affected by broad aims like zero population growth. So the clients of forecasters would do well to encourage such general studies.

On the other hand there are the scenario writers, who do attempt to consider social trends but who appear to rely almost entirely on their prejudices.[2] My minor thesis in this article is that the detailed study of social changes—and in particular the scientific investigation of the goals and values of individuals—is a *sine qua non* of any valid system of forecasting. We need to know the relative importance of rival goals as they appear to different subgroups, and how their distribution is changing with time. How (if at all) do men differ from women, the young from the old, the rich from the poor? How do regional, professional or ethnic groups differ from each other? And so on.

Given this information, I believe we can discover *why* values change. If so, we can hope to arrive at some general theory or model of patterns of social change. If, and only if, we do this, can forecasting be transformed from a hit-and-miss affair into a discipline. This is my major thesis.

The questions I now wish to consider are: How can the values of a given society be studied objectively? What clues do we have to their origins? Is a theory of social change possible? What is the state of play?

Values defined

To those unfamiliar with the subject, talk of value analysis may seem impractical. Many people, it is true, talk about values in a sweeping way, as if the concept were quite woolly and imprecise. In point of fact, however, there is a taxonomy of values and it is possible to discuss them in a scientific manner. This is not the place for a disquisition on the subject, but one or two distinctions will clarify the discussion. The word "value" is sometimes used (usually by economists) to mean simply any object or service which is valued. Thus a motor vehicle is sometimes said to be "a value". In the sociological sense, however, values refer to end-states—to ways of life and patterns of behaviour, to things like security, honesty, freedom, piety, and justice. This is how the word is used here.[3]

A useful distinction can be made between lifestyles (sometimes called terminal values) and behavioural ideals (sometimes called instrumental values, a term I find misleading). Examples of the first are: comfort, excitement, wisdom, security, salvation, freedom, and prestige. Therefore, one can prefer a comfortable life, an exciting life, etc. Examples of the second are: neatness, cheerfulness, honesty, self-control, courage, imagination, and so on. After eliminating duplication, and ignoring negative counterparts (dishonesty, cowardice, etc), there seem to be about 20 in each class.

Values differ from and determine *attitudes*, which can be defined as collections of beliefs focused on a specific object: there are hundreds if not thousands of possible attitudes. Curiously enough a great deal of social research has been done and is being done on attitudes (as Professor Milton Rokeach has pointed out)[4] but very little on the values which determine them. The very popularity of attitude research may be just what has caused value research to be neglected.

There is an important difference between terminal and instrumental values. Lifestyles are, in essence, mutually exclusive. One cannot logically demand *both* security and adventure, although one can certainly desire a mixture of the two. In contrast, one can desire to be completely honest, extremely hardworking, consistently cheerful, and invariably logical. It follows that a person's terminal values can be internally inconsistent in a way in which his instrumental values cannot.

Value distribution

Currently, we do not even have any accurate information about value distribution in Britain, the USA, or anywhere else. We do not know who holds what values and how strongly. We therefore do not know how value distributions are changing, and the very first step towards forming some validatable social theory would be to gather such information. It would be desirable, as a start, to gather value data analysable by class, sex, age group, and geographical distribution. Later, in place of conventional class and geographical information we might hope to define culture groups, and chart how the relationship between such groups is changing. (In a reasonable world, of course, this would have been done first.)

From such an enquiry we might hope to gain an idea of how homogeneous the value systems of the country as a whole are; a similar study of other countries could show how far larger areas (say, Europe, or the Western world, or indeed the world itself) are in agreement. Even this crude material might provide clues to possible conflict, since conflicts seem to occur predominantly where values differ, and not (*pace* Marx) for economic reasons.

If such surveys were repeated at intervals, we could hope to see whether groups were converging or diverging; also whether they are suffering internal strain from holding inconsistent value systems. It is not difficult to think of conflicts, actual or potential, which are based on value-differences in the world today. In addition to the great political and national conflicts, there are differing views of the status of women, of homosexuals, of blacks, and so on; also of economic growth versus conservation, of activity versus quietism, etc.

In 1968, during the US election campaign, Rokeach (whose methods I shall describe more fully in a moment) applied his schema to the speeches of American politicians, and also of Lenin, in addition to polling a sample of voters. The results were enlightening. Lenin put equality top of the list but freedom 17th out of 18 items; in contrast, Barry Goldwater put both freedom and equality at the bottom of his list! The voting public put peace and security at the top of their lists, with freedom third, while all candidates rated pleasure very low.[5]

It is obvious that in recent years there have been enormous shifts in values: social equality has become, at least in Britain, a much more strongly desired goal. Spontaneity is now more widely valued than self-restraint: there has been almost a complete reversal of the position here in less than half a century. Other values are in the course of changing and we do not know how far the trend will go.[6] Thus many people now reject the acquisition of wealth as a dominant end and assert the need, not much talked of earlier in the century, of living in harmony with nature. Although at the end of the 19th century William Morris advocated a return to simplicity, the vogue for his ideas was brief; is the present movement merely a flash in the pan (as Herman Kahn maintains) or was Morris ahead of his time?

Nowhere have value shifts been more marked than in Japan, where a survey of youth conducted by the Prime Minister's office in 1969 revealed that only 40% of those questioned believed in respecting the rights and freedom of others. Only 39% thought the laws should be obeyed without question, and four out of five said they would not give up their seat in a bus or a train to an older person. Clearly the Confucian rules of respect for elders and obedience to the law, long cherished in Japan, are no longer accepted by youth.[7]

On the other hand, in Britain and the USA there is apparently a reaction against the protest and nihilism of the 1960s. It would be helpful to know how far it has gone and how general it is.

Research into values

Possibly the first person to attempt the scientific exploration of values was Charles Morris, who concluded in the 1920s that a scientific theory of value was the prerequisite of an adequate theory of human behaviour.[8] He evolved a schedule of 13 "Ways of life" or, as we now say, lifestyles, and validated it by questionnaires to students in the USA, China, Japan, India and some European countries (but not France or Germany).

Morris had strong ethical-religious preoccupations and a serious defect of his work was his deliberate exclusion of lifestyles which he regarded as destructive or evil. Another was his concentration on conceived values—on what people claimed to admire rather than how they actually lived. A third defect was the fact that his data came almost entirely from students, and even they were not sampled in any balanced manner. But what I think chiefly condemned his work to neglect was his failure to make use of the tool he spent so long forging and sharpening. If he had reported (say) that values of men differed from those of women, the young from the old, the rich from the poor, the West from the East, in their preferences, his findings would have had some news value and also perhaps some practical value.

The few efforts he did make to apply his scheme were somewhat eccentric. Having been influenced by Sheldon as a young man, he sought to show that a person's values are influenced by their body type. Even more oddly, he spent a lot of time demonstrating that one's taste in painting reflects one's value scheme. While I don't doubt that it does, it is hardly the most useful application of the tool.

More recently, Professor Milton Rokeach of Michigan State University has reopened the issue.[9] His system postulates 18 terminal values or goals of existence and 18 instrumental values or modes of behaviour. Respondents are required to rank each set of 18 values in order of desirability—a task which usually takes about 15 minutes, but which most people find quite difficult. On retest after some months, quite high test/retest correlations are obtained, around 0·75. It should be noted that Rokeach has not been applying his test in the way I am now suggesting, but has explored such matters as how an individual's value system relates to his educational choices, the difference in values between the police and the policed, and the connection between religious values and bigotry—all subjects of social importance and interest.

Rokeach's schedules are, I am bound to say, open to some criticism. They omit some obviously important values (for instance, power or possessions as terminal values) and allow no room for those who regard toughness and aggressiveness as virtues. Many people value an ordered world, which does not appear as a distinct item; others value a life of service, which does not appear at all.

But a more serious defect, I believe, is his requirement that respondents arrange preferred values in rank order. As already noted, most instrumental values are by no means mutually exclusive: one can wish to be cheerful and honest and logical and hardworking. Some values are held strongly, others weakly, while others may be denied altogether. To require respondents to assign marks to each would have revealed how values are grouped and have avoided some fictitious discriminations. The difficulty many people found in completing his schedules was a consequence, I suspect, of being required to make unreal distinctions. However, he is to be congratulated on reopening the subject, and it is disappointing that his lead has not been followed more widely.

Of course, all such questionnaries have the disadvantage of eliciting only what people are prepared to say, or think they believe, as distinct from what their behaviour reveals. Enquiries into behaviour are needed to reveal the level of validity of the questionnaire approach. However, questionnaires need not naively ask direct questions about values or even behaviour. By asking about apparently neutral matters, about preferences in music, about hobbies, about the choice of newspaper, much light can be thrown on personality structure, and thus on preferences.

The *ad hoc* lists of values produced by people like Rokeach provide useful starting points but throw no light on how values are formed or how they are interrelated. Presumably preferred lifestyles must reflect preferred behaviour; and behavioural traits must have their origin in brain structure, life experience, and so forth. There must be an internal logic of values arising from the way in which the elements of personality are integrated. In this spirit other workers have sought to identify major contrasts in approved patterns of behaviour. For instance, there seems to be a major dichotomy between ideas of order, control, and stability, and ideas of informality, spontaneity and change. The first group looks towards the past and believes in tradition and the imitation of approved models; the second looks towards the future and respects originality and progress. These groups correspond roughly to the political terms conservative and radical, but the behaviour involved extends beyond the political field, into art, religion, and sexual mores, particularly.

Goals and personality structure

It is evident that a person's goals and preferences reflect, in some degree, his personality structure. A person who is psychologically insecure will probably aim for security rather than risk. One person will prefer an active outgoing existence, another a passive or contemplative one. Hence a more modest and perhaps wider approach to the analysis of values is to start by distinguishing some clear-cut personality variables. In this way it is possible to identify one or two useful elements and gradually to add to them, instead of trying to produce an all-embracing scheme at one blow.

Personality constructs

Proceeding in this way, Professor Eysenck, in the early 1950s, distinguished the two axes, tough–tender and radical–conservative. He was able to plot the positions of various political and other groups against these two parameters. Thus communists appear as tough radicals, hippies as tender radicals, many businessmen and military officers as tough conservatives while many clergymen are tender conservatives. Obviously there are intermediate positions; I only summarise this work to illustrate the kind of approach I have in mind.[10]

About the same time, using a more Freudian approach, I argued the existence of father-identified and mother-identified patterns (termed *patrist* and *matrist*).[11] Broadly speaking, the patrist believes in discipline, effort, and the status quo, the matrist in spontaneity, altruism, and progress. There appears to be a high degree of coherence in these alternative value clusters when examined over time.

Subsequently I introduced a second dichotomy concerned with the ego—with much in common with Eysenck's tough–tender dichotomy—but which had a wider area of reference and which suggested a causal mechanism.[12]

In the 1960s, Professor Mary Douglas evolved a slightly different pair of dichotomies which she named *group* and *grid*; she applied them to several contemporary groups, including the hippies and the bog Irish, with promising results.[13] This scheme, I believe, was digging out the same underlying variables as Eysenck's and my own, though I shall not analyse their inter-relationships here. Such personality factors can be seen to influence or even determine the scheme of values preferred.

Applications

Even with this relatively unsophisticated approach it was possible to predict (as I in fact did in 1954) the trend towards unisex, the change in attitudes to property, the growth of interest in mysticism and other matters of considerable social interest. In the meantime, we have learned a good deal more about personality, and the opportunity to elaborate this type of analysis is wide open.

At the same time, we can hope to carry the investigation to a deeper level, since we now know a good deal about the factors—the influences on the infant and child—which lead to the formation of tough or tender, patrist or matrist, personality structures. To take a single and rather thoroughly researched example, it is now beyond doubt that the absence of the father, especially when this is coupled with the presence of a dominating mother, has a definite effect on personality, pushing it in the direction I have called matrist. I mention this not because I wish to explore the point but in order to proceed to a more general proposition, namely that there are social changes which bring about changes in the mean of personality structure of the individuals in that society, and hence in social goals. Thus industrialism, by taking the father away from home when children are at an early age (father introjection occurs between $1\frac{1}{2}$ and $2\frac{1}{2}$ years), may have served to bring about the matrist attitude of casual spontaneity which is one of the factors in industrial and social problems today.[14]

Whether or not this particular example is thought to be valid, there can be little doubt that social change is the product of a system of mutual feedback. Social changes cause personality changes, and personality changes cause social changes. This interplay I have named the *psychosocial nexus*.[15] Accordingly, to evolve a theory of social change which can be used to support a science of forecasting, we have to explore, on the one hand, how technological, economic, political, social, and cultural changes are affecting the nature and distribution of personality structure, and on the other, how changed personality structure is changing social goals, and behaviour patterns, and thus contributing to further changes in rearing patterns . . . and so to further changes in personality.

Methods

The first step towards clarifying the details of this nexus would be the wide administration of questionnaires (or, better, psychological tests) designed to identify how the main personality elements are distributed in society, ie by age, sex, class, region, race, etc. If we confine ourselves, in the beginning, to simple pairs of dichotomies such as those noted above, such questionnaires need not be long or difficult to administer. To have a chart, however rough, of the personality distribution of a modern society (something on these lines has been done for some preliterate societies)[16] would not only be a milestone in social research but might also yield data of practical value.

To make my line of thought clear, I have simplified and avoided side-issues. I am not attempting to provide a cast-iron theory, only to indicate what I believe to be the proper method of approach to such a theory.

It may justifiably be objected that the Eysenck–Taylor–Douglas approach (if I may call it that) produces a schedule of values which is also not exhaustive, though in a different way from Rokeach's. Eventually the two approaches must be reconciled and an attempt to do this might prove very fruitful. A multi-disciplinary attack, incorporating psychological, anthropological and sociological material is required.

Value changes

Let us now turn to the question of why or how such changes in value distribution occur. Conventional wisdom says that we acquire our values from society—we are gradually acculturated, to use the anthropologists' term. Recently it has been a common complaint of the young that they are "indoctrinated" or "brainwashed" into acceptance of the values of bourgeois society. If this were really true (and the fact that the aforesaid students are protesting shows it is not) the values of society would never change. Each generation would learn faithfully from its forebears what to hold dear.[17] Indeed, one might go towards the other extreme and say that much of the turmoil in society today is due precisely to the widespread rejection of received values.

Today there are many reasons for the failure of acculturation, notably extensive travel and migration, as well as the transmission of ideas by the media —itself a topic worthy of study. But long before modern technology began to exert its influence social values shifted for reasons which were often less obvious. Thus Roman society changed in a few generations from a disciplined, family-centred society to a disorganised and self-indulgent one.

A similar change took place in Britain between the 18th and 19th centuries. Evidently there are forces which predispose people to accept—even to intensify —the values which society proposes to them; and there are others which pre-dispose people to rejecting or modifying them. Thus the educator Mrs Sherwood, herself brought up quite severely, was even more severe to her own children. (Whereas she, as a girl, was allowed to go occasionally to a ball, her own children were never allowed to, and she thanked God this was so.)[18] Yet in our own day we often see parents treating their children more permissively than they were themselves treated as children.

I suggest that it is the structure of personality which effects such shifts. If a person's early experience renders him insecure, for instance, he will probably place a high value on security and eagerly absorb the words of those who advocate it, when he becomes an adult. Mrs Sherwood's books were read in tens of thousands because people were already disposed to favour such recommendations. Earlier, similar works had been ignored.

The child brought up in an ordered environment will probably value an ordered society, except when the pressure becomes so great that a reaction occurs.

In short, it is by studying the earliest family environment, and the lessons taught—usually unwittingly—as well as subsequent kinds of conditioning, that we shall find the clues to value changes. Moving then one step further back along the causal chain, we have to identify the social changes which contribute to the changes in the early learning environment. Thus if the needs of industry or commerce isolate children from their fathers, the absence of an authority model will favour the production of anti-authoritarian children—to say nothing of other effects.

Some sociologists, particularly Marxists, have maintained that value changes are the result of social changes, and hence that values can be predicted by studying social changes.[19] This is almost the reverse of my position: I would agree that certain rather specific social changes affect values—for instance changes which affect the family and early experience of children—but more broadly I see social changes as the consequence, not the cause, of value changes. Do people now dress informally because they value informality, or do they value informality because they dress informally? Without denying the influence of fashion, or of feedback between the two parameters, it is surely more reasonable to think that changing attitudes (attitudes are rooted in values), cause a change in actions, rather than the reverse. But the truth is, each influences the other.

Discontinuities

While there is undoubtedly a central process in society, modifying values by a feedback mechanism, it is also true that external factors, often of an unpredictable kind, distort the process. The emergence of a charismatic leader may shift the goals of a society quite abruptly. The conscious efforts of governments or pressure groups to re-educate *may* have some effect. External influences also include such unpredictables as climate changes, inflation, war, epidemics, and conceivably the arrival of little green men from outer space. I do not mean to underrate the importance of such discontinuities but I defer consideration of them to a later article, in which I shall try to show what allowance can be made for them.

In advocating value studies I restrict myself entirely to the short run. I doubt if it is possible to make accurate detailed predictions of the kind required for planning more than a few years ahead; there are too many intervening variables. But there is a lead time between value change and social change, so that to know how values are moving now may tell us something useful about the world one generation ahead.

Theories of society

Nevertheless, what might emerge from such studies is a body of theory about social change. Even if it had only short-term predictive value, it might still illuminate social change in a longer perspective, when applied retrospectively. As my own work, *inter alia*, has shown, there are certain broad similarities in the value systems of different periods, however different they may have been in technological or other respects. Asceticism remains asceticism, aggression remains aggression, traditionalism remains traditionalism, regardless of the economic, technical, or cultural level.

At the moment, the construction of social theories is somewhat in disrepute, as a result of over-ambitious attempts to do too much, too fast. In particular, the attempt to demonstrate theories of social *evolution*—inspired originally by the success of Darwin's theories—has been subjected to severe criticism. But the pendulum may have swung too far the other way. As Lao-Tzu observed, "In the affairs of men there is a system". We should not be discouraged by a false start from trying, by slower and more careful methods, and with more modest aims, to assemble something better. (The popularity of the Marxist interpretation of social change in terms of a transfer of power from one class to another, owes something to the absence of any plausible alternative account.)

To summarise: if social and economic change is rooted in value change, we are wasting our time attempting to forecast the future unless we give a high priority to the study of value changes. Methods of value study are available but they are still unsophisticated. Ideas for developing them are not lacking. The cost would be trivial when set against the waste caused by inaccurate prediction, and even a 2% improvement in performance would justify the effort.

But the exercise may have a more valuable pay-off than merely providing planners with a powerful tool. As Jerome Bruner has emphasised, we are entering an age where the analysis of purpose is becoming powerful and subtle.[20] We seek to construct models and simulations of what we wish to do. So maybe we ought to render our values clear by defining them in terms of the acts which we wish to perform. In so doing we might achieve a clearer social purpose and, in some sense, improve the quality of our society itself. The kind of research here proposed might help to do that.

Notes and references

1. For instance, if the rise in crime had been foreseen, building layouts which facilitate theft and violence would have been avoided. If public concern for the environment had been foreseen, the nuclear, airport, and motorway programmes would have been conceived and presented differently. If the establishment of Third-world cartels had been foreseen, alternative energy sources would have been developed sooner.

2. Perhaps one should add that there is a third group, of which the British Social Survey is an example, which does meticulous work in recording changes as they occur but which is highly cautious about making predictions.

3. To be more exact, there is a hierarchy, from value-orientations to beliefs. For a full discussion, see: Jay Meddin, "Attitudes, values, and related concepts: a system of classification", *Social Science Quarterly*, 55 (4), 1975, pages 889–900. It is value-orientations (sometimes known as "core-values", "world view", "culture themes", or "basic personality structure") to which I refer here. In this connection, see Florence Kluckhohn and Fred Strodtbeck, *Variations in Value Orientations* (Evanston, Illinois, Row-Peterson, 1961), a most valuable work.

4. C. Abcarian and J. W. Soule, *Social Psychology and Political Behavior* (Chicago, Merrill, 1971). Contribution of M. Rokeach, Chapter 21. There have been, of course, studies of particular values and of particular subgroups (eg university students). It is comprehensive surveys which we are lacking.

5. M. Rokeach, *op cit*.

6. In the absence of social research repeated on similar samples at, say, 20 year intervals, it is impossible to support these impressions scientifically. This is precisely my complaint. Ronald Inglehart has claimed that the younger generation in Britain is more liberal than its elders, and infers a "transformation" in political priorities. But the young are often more liberal than their elders. One

must compare like with like . . . the young of today with the young of 30 years ago, or the old with the old. Inglehart's thesis appeared in *American Political Science*, *65*, 1971, pages 991–1017; Alan Marsh's demolition of that thesis appeared in *American Political Science*, *69*, 1975, pages 21–30.

7. *Time* Magazine, 12 December 1969.
8. C. Morris, *Varieties of Human Value* (Chicago, University of Chicago Press, 1956).
9. M. Rokeach, *Beliefs, Attitudes, Values* (San Francisco, Jossey–Bass, 1968).
10. H. J. Eysenck, *The Psychology of Politics* (London, Routledge and Kegan Paul, 1954).
11. G. Rattray Taylor, *Sex in History* (London, Thames and Hudson, 1954).
12. G. Rattray Taylor, *The Angel Makers* (London, Heinemann, 1958). I was con-concerned here with the boundaries of the ego: I called the dichotomy the hard ego versus the soft ego. The former feels isolated from others, the latter feels identified with them.
13. M. Douglas, *Natural Symbols: Exploration in Cosmology* (London, Cresset, 1970).
14. H. B. Biller, *Paternal Deprivation* (Farnborough, Hampshire, D. C. Heath, 1974).
15. G. Rattray Taylor, *Conditions of Happiness* (London, Bodley Head, 1949).
16. See for instance D. G. Haring, ed, *Personal Character and Cultural Milieu* (Syracuse NY, Syracuse University Press, 1949). This approach originated with Abram Kardiner; see especially *The Individual and His Society* (New York, Columbia University Press, 1939), by Abram Kardiner and Ralph Linton.
17. In a recent *Futures* article, Jib Fowles stressed the danger of assuming the continuance of current values when legislating for the future. While several of his examples were, in my use of the term, attitudes rather than values, his argument reinforces the case for a better monitoring of value-shifts and the need to understand the mechanisms behind such swings. As he also points out, few current value studies are really comparable, owing to the lack of a sound theoretical basis for such studies. Even in the USA, where most of the work has been done, the approach is unbalanced and piecemeal, as well as being descriptive rather than analytic. See J. Fowles, "The problem of values in futures research", *Futures*, August 1977, *9* (4), pages 303–314.
18. F. J. H. Darton, *The Life and Times of Mrs Sherwood* (Horsham, Sussex, Wells Gardner Darton, 1910).
19. Compare I. Taviss, "Futurology and the problem of values", *International Social Science Journal*, 1969, pages 574–584.
20. A. Tiselius and S. Nilsson, eds, *The Place of Value in a World of Facts:* Nobel Symposium 1969 (Chichester, Sussex, John Wiley, 1970). Contribution by J. Bruner.

STABILISATION IN SYSTEMS
Chreods and epigenetic landscapes

C. H. Waddington

This article is abstracted from a forthcoming book, *Tools for Thought*. The author, C. H. Waddington, died in September 1975 shortly after completing his revision of the book. It was written as a popular guide to the new ways of perceiving and thinking about the world.

THE scale of very many of the impacts of mankind on the world surrounding him is now so great that they go right below the surface of things. At the deeper level, we find that most aspects of life and its interactions with its surroundings are interconnected into complexes. No powerful action can be expected to have only one consequence, confined to the thing it was primarily directed at. It is almost bound to effect lots of other things as well. Our old-fashioned common sense has not has to face such situations before, and is not well adapted to doing so. We need nowadays to be able to think not just about simple processes but about complex systems. Many suggestions have been made, particularly in the last years when the problems have become more pressing, of different ways of trying to do this.

The book is an attempt to bring together most of these proposed "tools of thought". Many of them were originally put forward accompanied by a lavish decoration of technical jargon. Part of this may have been due to the genuine difficulty of finding ways of formulating new ideas; part perhaps for the less excusable reason that it might make the ideas look more profound and novel than they really were. However, any idea that is going to be really useful in this connection can, after adequate time to digest it, be put into reasonably simple language.

Chreods and epigenetic landscapes

A natural living system has usually acquired some degree of stability by natural selection (it would have fallen apart and died out if it wasn't stable enough); in artificial systems man commonly designs a series of checks and counter-checks

Professor C. H. Waddington FRS (1905–1975) was Buchanan Professor of Animal Genetics at the University of Edinburgh, UK. *Tools for Thought* will be published by Jonathan Cape, London in April 1977.

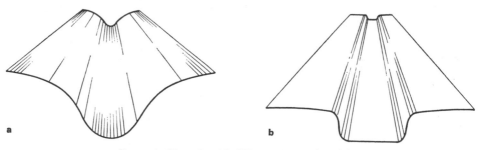

Figure 1. Chreods with different types of stability

to ensure stability. An important point to note, however, is that the stability may not be concerned to preserve the measure of some component of the system at a constant value, as in the homeostatic systems. The stabilisation of a progressive system acts to ensure that the system goes on altering in the same sort of way that it has been altering in the past. Whereas the process of keeping something at a stable, or stationary, value is called *homeostasis*, ensuring the continuation of a given type of change it is called *homeorhesis*, a word which means preserving a flow.

A phrase used to describe such systems, is to say that the pathway of change is canalised. For the pathway itself one can use the name *chreod*, a word derived from Greek, which means "necessary path". Many types of change going on in society have a more or less well-developed chreodic character; once they have got well started in a certain direction, it is very difficult to divert them.

Different canalised pathways or chreods may have rather different types of stability built into them. These can be pictured in terms of the cross-section of the valley. You may, for instance, have a valley with a very narrow chasm running along the bottom, while the farther up the hillside you go, the less steep the slope; with such a configuration of the attractor surface, it needs a very strong push of some kind to divert a stream away from the bottom of the chasm (Figure 1a). If the system is acted on by only rather minor disturbances, it is likely always to stay very close to the bottom of the valley. If one can compare several examples of such a system, there will be very little difference between them, and they will look very invariable. In contrast, we have a valley which has a very flat bottom, and the hillside gets steeper and steeper as you go away from the central stream (Figure 1b). Then, minor disturbances can easily shunt the stream from one side of the flat valley bottom to the other; it would be rather a matter of chance where in the water-meadows in the valley bottom it flows. If one looks at a number of examples of a system with this type of stability, there will be a lot of small-scale variation between them.

As an example of what the idea of chreods, or canalisation, means in an everyday context, consider the accumulation of wealth in a community. Any individual receives some income and has some outgoings; his wealth grows or diminished according to the difference between these. In the well-known words of Dickens' (pre-decimalisation) character Mr Micawber: "Annual income £20, annual expenditure £19 19s 6d, result happiness. Annual income £20, annual expenditure £20 0s 6d, result misery".

We can draw a diagram with wealth measured upwards from the base-line, and time flowing from left to right. An individual at any given time has a certain wealth, and this is represented by a corresponding point; but his current bank balance is affected by his income and his outgoings, and as time passes it will move along a line, horizontally if he keeps them exactly in balance, upwards if he is getting richer, downwards if he is getting poorer. Such lines are known as *vectors*, and the whole area of the diagram is a *vector field* (Figure 2a).

It is unfortunately common experience that in our society, and in many like it, the rich tend to get richer, and the poor poorer. So if we start with a population of people with varied incomes, the vector field tends to look like Figure 2b.

A tendency towards canalisation, or the formation of chreods in such a system, would occur if there were forces at work tending to limit the steepest increases, or the most drastic reductions, in the wealth of individuals. In practice we do have such forces in Britain, eg steeply rising surtax of large incomes and welfare benefits added to low ones. In their simplest form, such forces might act to produce a "rich, but not too rich" chreod and a "poor, but not too poor" one. Actually, the controlling forces are more complex, and tend to result in several rather than only two wealth classes. We would like, of course, to put into operation forces acting within the vector field in such a way that no one actually

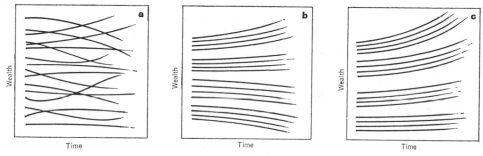

Figure 2. Vector fields showing wealth over time

ever gets any poorer (Figure 2c). And then, a further step, provisions that make it reasonably easy for individuals to move over from one chreod to another, preferably stepping up rather than down. Or, of course, we might try to set up a non-chreodic system, which did not tend to produce distinct classes at all, but at the same time prevented gross differences in wealth, and an overall upward trend.

In progressive biological systems, such as developing embryos or plants, one is usally confronted with a system which cannot be fully described in terms of a single chreod, or even collections of roughly parallel chreods, as is seen in the wealth diagrams. When an egg is developing, different parts of it will follow different courses of development, and eventually finish up forming parts of the final animal: some parts becoming muscle, some becoming nerve and so on. This can be pictured in terms of an "epigenetic landscape", in which when the process starts there is a single valley, but this later branches into two or more, and these branches split up again and agin, until they have formed a number of separate valleys corresponding to the separate parts of the adult animal.

Many progressive systems in fields other than biology behave in a similar way. For instance, when a town is beginning to grow into a city, at first it is likely that it will all be following one and the same path of change, related to a single city centre. Later on some sub-centres will develop, or suburbs will be founded, and the single pathway of change will have become diversified into a number of subsidiary paths.

Again, consider the historical development of some type of thinking, such as Christianity or Marxism. It starts with a single line of development, and later splits up into a number of more or less divergent paths of change, such as the Orthodox and Catholic churches, or Leninism, Stalinism and Maoism. Each of these not only goes on developing as time passes, but may in its turn split up into further sub-divisions. And each division has quite a lot of canalisation, or chreodic character, in the sense that someone who starts off trying to be a heretic, standing midway between Maoism and Leninism perhaps, finds that there are strong pulls trying to drag him into one or other of the orthodoxies.

In such an epigenetic landscape, there are branching points at which a valley splits up into two or possibly more branches. What can one say about them? And what can one say about the question of whether the system as a whole goes down one branch or the other, or breaks up and part goes down each? Take the second question first. Sometimes one knows that there is a branch point ahead of the system, and that if one can give the system a push at the right time, it can be diverted into one or other of the alternatives in front of it. The point to notice here is that it is in general no use giving the push too early: if you do, the system will have got back to the middle of the valley again before it reaches the fork, and the effect of the push will have been dissipated.

The period just before the branching point, during which a push will be effective in diverting the system into one or other path, is known in biology as the period of "competence". It is no use trying to act on the system to divert it into a particular branch until it has become competent to respond, by going down the valley towards which you have pushed it. Equally, of course, it is not advisable to leave the push until too late. Once the system has started to go down one of the branch valleys, if you still want to divert it into the other you have to push it right over the hill between them. Effective revolutionaries, like Lenin, have been brilliant in choosing just the right time to give a push to a society coming up to a branch point in its stability system.

The question of how the branch points come to be there at all is a difficult one. Remember that the shape of the valley (the slope of the hillsides) represents the net result of a whole lot of controlling actions, each of which is brought about by network effects, or feedbacks. Now the strength of these feedbacks and controls would depend on the amounts of the various components present in the system. Therefore, as the system progressively changes as time passes, the strengths of the controls will also alter. As some components of the system increase in magnitude and others contract, controlling interactions which were at first of minor importance may become much more significant, and vice versa. Eventually the system has altered so much that its controls can no longer ensure the stability of the former pathway. It may then break down into a general chaotic turmoil, or it may undergo a branching into two alternative new paths, each with their own stability. It is perhaps rather surprising that so many systems we come across seem to behave in the second way, rather than the first; and I do not know that there is any good explanation yet why this should be so. The theory of such breakdowns of stability is in rather an early stage of development. It is known as catastrophe theory. It seems likely to be one of the most interesting —and quite likely the most important—types of mathematical thought in the near future.

One can again use the idea of an attractor surface to help visualise what is going on. To simplify the model let us forget about providing sloping sides to a valley to represent the canalisation of a chreod, but instead indicate this by drawing arrows on the attractor surface, indicating that things get pushed in towards the line representing the pathway of change. We can start with a more or less flat attractor surface, with a line on it, and arrows pointing towards the line. The changes that are going on in the control systems as time passes can be represented by bending the attractor surface. A branch point, or catastrophe, occurs as soon as this bending results in there being a fold which brings one part of the attractor surface vertically under some other part (Figure 3). Consider

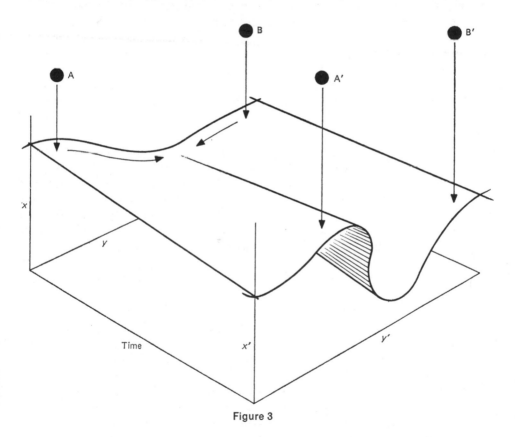

Figure 3

then what will happen if a disturbance pushes the system into an abnormal position such as those shown in A or B. The displaced point will first fall back on the attractor surface and then run along the surface to the attractor line. If, at a later time, it gets displaced to A' or B', it all depends whether it falls on the top surface of the fold, when the arrows will push it back into the top chreod; but if it has been displaced to B′ it will fall down on to the lower surface, and the arrows on that will bring it into the lower chreod.

Perhaps the visual model gives one some intuitive understanding why systems which reach the limit of their initial stability are often split up into two stable pathways rather than resulting in complete turmoil. The formation of such folds in a surface is the kind of thing one could reasonably expect if the surface had a certain solidarity or strength. Complete breakdown into chaos would have to be represented by total disruption of the attractor surface, which one might guess was less likely to happen.

Exploring a landscape

An important question about the epigenetic landscape and branching pathways is this: When we are confronted with an unknown system, how do we find out what the shape of the landscape is? In such parts of biology as the study of embryonic development, we can study a large number of individual eggs of the same species, do a lot of experiments on them, and explore their stability by seeing how far they can get back to normality after various sorts of disturbance. In many more important systems, such as those we meet in human and social life, there is only one example of the system, and we cannot use this way of exploring it.

One suggestion, due to the Russian mathematicians Gel'fand and Tsetlin, is to proceed as follows. We find ourselves doing something to a system which we believe has certain stability characteristics, which could be described by an epigenetic landscape; but we have no idea where we are on the landscape when we first start trying to affect the system. So what we should try to do is to try to alter it, slightly, in as many ways as possible, and observe its reactions. We will find that the system resists some types of change more than others, or restores itself more quickly after changes in some directions than in others. We can think of our actions as going out into the landscape for the same distance in every direction from where we stand, thus describing a circle. But the reactions of the system will be different in different directions, since it will be harder to push the system "uphill" than "downhill". Thus its response will be a distorted circle. From the directions of these distortions, we can deduce the main slope of the part of the epigenetic landscape where we have found ourselves. We then move down this slope—operating in the direction in which the system is most easily altered—taking quite small steps, until we begin to find a mounting resistance: then we immediately withdraw a bit, and are presumably on, or at least very near, the bottom of a valley.

We then remember where we started and from that point take quite a large jump—much bigger than the steps by which we descended the slope—not in the direction of downhill or uphill, or along the contour, where the reactions of the system were equal in response to thrusts of opposite direction, but in some direction intermediate between this contour and the downhill direction. This large jump may perhaps be expected to carry us on to the opposite hillside lower down the valley, and a local exploration around that spot may show us the slope going in the opposite direction. We can again descend this to the valley bottom, and thus trace the course of the valley we are in. That in itself will be quite useful information, but at some point, we have to make another big step, large enough to carry us out of the first valley, over a watershed into one of the other valleys of the landscape, which again we have to explore in the same sort of way.

As Gelf'fand and Tsetlin put it, we need by trial and error to fix the length of the long steps so that we "skirt high hills and step over small watersheds". One can't, of course, give any general rules for doing this. It has got to be largely a method of "suck it and see". A point of general principle is that in exploring such a landscape it would take too long to walk all over it step by step with paces of even length. It is better to alternate between

- local exploration followed by exploiting the direction of the easiest change, until the change begins to get difficult (ie opportunist reformism); and
- a jump in the dark to try to change some quite different aspect of the situation followed by another period of opportunist reform around that subject, and keeping in mind a readiness to abandon this attempt if it turns out to be a flop.

The procedure is, the Russians suggest, a judicious mixture of mild reforms in one area, followed by letting that area lie, when it ceases to respond, and starting another programme of mild reforms in a quite different context. This, they argue is the best way to get an idea of how the behaviour of the whole system is organised, which is an essential preliminary before one can deal with the whole thing in an effective way.

The epigenetic landscape of human society

What could one sensibly mean by "stabilising" or "controlling" the human situation in the world of today or tomorrow? The type of behaviour of progressive systems which we have just been discussing—a tendency to lead rather firmly in a smallish number of alternative directions—is found not only in material systems, but in psychological and cultural ones. Christopher Zeeman has used this terminology to describe the way in which many animals seem to switch suddenly between two different types of behaviour, say aggression or fear; it is often some minor factor which decides whether a dog behaves in the "attack chreod", and bites you, or in the "frightened chreod", and runs away. Many other students of animal behaviour have described similar phenomena, when it is touch and go whether a male and female fight or mate; though they mostly do not yet use the language of chreods and catastrophes which has been described here, but speak in more particular and less general terms.

In the world of today, many people fear that the situation may be getting out of hand, and soon may run away with itself, and us, into some sort of chaos. Most conventional discussions of "stabilisation" or "control" of human situations are in terms of simple quantitative measures. For instance, it is pointed out that population numbers, consumption of power, etc, are increasing exponentially so that plotted against time they give a J-shaped curve. It is argued that we need to introduce some negative feedback which will convert the J-shaped curve into an S-shaped curve.

The first point to note is that at present we are faced with J-shaped curves if we plot against time not just population numbers, power consumption, etc, but their rate of change. We have to deal not with exponential velocities, but with accelerated exponential. We are concerned with the stabilisation/control not of things but of processes; with homeorhesis, not homeostasis.

We are also in a phase of increasing diversification or differentiation. Whereas a few decades ago mankind could be classified into blue-collared workers, white-collared workers, professionals and aristocracy or plutocracy, there is now an enormously richer diversity of lifestyles and class identifications (if we still use the concept of class). Both these points have been extensively documented by Alvin Toffler in his book, *Future Shock*.

Toffler seems to contemplate both these tendencies continuing more or less unchecked—everything going faster and faster at an accelerating rate, and differentiation between social roles and lifestyles becoming ever more diversified, to the point that any one individual will switch styles (including marriage partners, friends, etc) every few years.

Merely to try to bring these processes to a halt would, in the first place, probably be impossible; and secondly would produce a condition of stagnation and ultimately deterioration. On the other hand, I confess to some sort of (perhaps old-fashioned) intuition that if uncontrolled, they would lead to a situation of total incoherence or turbulence. But what sort of stabilisation/control is conceivable? It is not good enough to talk about improving homeorhesis or buffering of particular chreods, since this would eliminate further diversification. It could amount to the authoritarian imposition of uniformity, even if this was imposed by impersonal social forces rather than by an individual dictator like Hitler or Stalin. Diversification demands that the branching of chreods, catastrophes in the sense we discussed above, be allowed to continue. I think what we are concerned with can be loosely put by saying we want to design a system in which the catastrophes are little ones, not big ones. That is to say, when we make a switch in lifestyle (from a junior advertising executive to a pop group/ lyric writer, or from an experimental biologist to a futurologist, philosopher or art critic), people do want the styles to be really *different*, genuinely alternative choices, not just the mixture as before with a trifle more or a trifle less bitters in the cocktail; but surely what we want to aim at is a "system" which allows us to do this without too much danger of our whole personality being torn into shreds in the process of transition.

One illustration would be the very final edge between the land and the sea in a great river delta like those of the Mississippi and the Nile—there are almost innumerable little separate rivulets of the fresh water running down to the sea, separated quite definitely but only by low banks of mud. This would be an "epigenetic landscape" of low profile. Or one might suggest a musical analogy. We do not want to listen to the confrontation of markedly different themes as in a Wagnerian opera, but to the running through of a gamut of slight variations on one or a few allied themes, as in much of Bach or boogie-woogie.

Or we could put it another way. Using the model of a chreod as an attractor surface in a multi-dimensional space, a catastrophe corresponds to an over-lapping fold in this surface. The stabilisation/control we are looking for corres-ponds to one in which there are many overlapping folds; but the top and bottom surfaces of the folds are not widely separated; a crumpled surface with many little scrumplings, rather than a few large impressive folds.

Q-ANALYSIS

A hard language for the soft sciences

R. H. Atkin

The relevant data sets in a 'soft' science can be manipulated and analysed using topology, an exercise which also reveals the 'backcloth' which limits or modifies such interrelationships. The method is currently being used in many fields: eg industrial relations, medicine, and architecture. An example of a university's committee structure is used to show how the underlying, and often unnoticed, geometry can frustrate the aims of an organisation.

SOFT SCIENCE requires mathematical refurbishing. Almost all of our daily lives falls under the spell of soft science: eg such disciplines (if that is not too strong a word) as social science, politics, economics, industrial relations, community studies, planning (by governments and other bodies), organisational analysis, decision making, and general systems analysis.

Hard science constitutes the highly mathematicised disciplines of mechanics and physics—and their 19th-century spin-offs to be found in chemistry, biology, and all the engineering fields. It is hard science which has taken man to the moon, and which has created the technological world we are trying to live in: it is soft science which is grappling with all those difficult problems which arise on the social scene—problems which seem to have become more acute as the technological advances shrink both the space and the time of our world. This shrinking is no mere illusion either, but a reality expressed by our experiences of the objects which generate our sense of space and of the events which generate our sense of time.

It is not surprising that some 'hard' scientists (and others) find it irresistible to sneer at the soft sciences, on the grounds that they are 'not science', and this criticism is sound (as a conclusion). But there was a time (the 12th century) when mechanics was just as soft as sociology is today. It is now time for us to transform our soft science into hard science—and the sooner the better. But how is this to be done?

The role of mathematics

It is certainly not just a matter of introducing some mathematical symbolism into the subject—although this is an illusion commonly, but often unconsciously, accepted

The author is with the Department of Mathematics, University of Essex, Wivenhoe Park, Colchester CO4 3SQ, UK.

by many academics working in this field. For after all mathematics is only an esoteric language, even though it is the best we have for carrying and expressing the notions of logical deduction. Behind mathematics, preceding it in the development of any hard science, lies a scientific *method* which enables us to marshal facts into disciplined sets of data—sets which are *relevant* to the study in hand. And this idea of relevance, seeming to beg the question, is quite unavoidable in any research enterprise.

No scientist worth his salt ever confuses data relevant to measuring masses with data relevant to observing electric charges, and this distinction precedes any description of these entities in an esoteric mathematical language. In the end there has to be a common ground among scientists about this very point of relevance, and this ground is an expression of the human sensibilities to external phenomena—sensibilities which appear to be tuned to intuition rather than to rational discourse.

We cannot hope to make soft science hard merely by transporting the concepts and words of (say) physics into some new area like social studies. The assumption, in general systems theory, that any system (however soft) must be modelled by a collection of differential equations is a case in point. Such systems (of differential equations) refer to a backcloth of data sets which might well have been acceptable in some field of mechanics—where 'particles' constitute the objects and 'vector fields' provide the dynamics—but in a multidimensional company manufacturing various products via the exploitation of a thousand different skills we are likely to need concepts which are more complex than that of 'particle', and relations which are more relevant and awkward than the convenient mathematical functions contained in such a model. Furthermore, when these functions are taken as probability functions (when the description becomes the so-called stochastic model) we seem to be abandoning any hope of a deterministic scientific theory.

Nor should we assume that, in making social science into a hard discipline, we shall find physics-type laws of nature—indeed the search for them could well be an intellectual straitjacket which inhibits discovery. It might be truer to expect *meta-laws*, in the sense of 'laws which tell us how the (apparent) laws are allowed to change' —or even meta-meta-laws?

This would be like finding that the law of gravity is not some fixed distance function (as we believe it to be in physics) but rather some algorithm which tells us how and when to find just one such distance function, among many. So in this sense we would expect the current model-building in the soft sciences to be replaced by *meta-modelling*—a do-it-yourself kit for building relevant models and the relations between them as they change. This point of view also emphasises that the beginnings of this whole process must be with the study of mathematical *relations* between sets of relevant data.

Such relations have their own geometrical structures which are far removed from the usual metrical and euclidean geometries of the school textbooks. Indeed there is no necessity, in the structures we have in mind, for the introduction of distance (or of angle)—those entities which mathematicians refer to as metrical—for these concepts are often an obstructive imposition on that underlying geometrical structure which is naturally defined by a relation. And the strange connectivities of these structures lift them into multidimensional spaces where only a well-programmed computer can find its way about.

The method of *Q*-analysis, which I have developed over recent years, concerns itself with this central problem of finding, analysing and interpreting the *structures* of relations in those areas of our experience we are describing as 'soft'. The whole field can in a certain sense be treated as that of decision making—for that encompasses organisations (of workforces, of committees, of assembly lines, of management, and unions), planning (by taking cognisance of structural changes and by monitoring hypothetical or actual policies), and social and political affairs (which depend upon the choice of relations between people and institutions, and on what the resulting geometry can carry in the way of traffic). In any event the claim is that we are dealing with a structure which is capable of being defined in precise mathematical terms (it is technically known as a *simplicial complex*), and in any particular study, there is a structure which acts the part of a (relatively) static *backcloth* (say, S) which replaces the conventional three-space of the physical scientist. This backcloth, S, must carry the 'traffic' of whatever kind—just as the euclidean space of the engineer must carry the traffic of 'motion particles'. By 'carry' I mean only that the connectivities of the geometry, at any appropriate dimensional level (and the letter Q in the theory merely serves as a parameter for these dimensions), must be the determining features (the so-called *topology*) for allowed flow of traffic (or changes in that flow).

Structure and traffic

For example, there might be 250 skills (job types) needed to manufacture a range of products in 150 locations (factories or parts of factories), in some large company. The distribution of these skills (whose names, we suppose, form a set Y) among the locations (whose names form a set X) defines a mathematical relation, and this identifies two geometrical structures (simplicial complexes) which we denote by KY(X) and KX(Y).

In KY(X) the skills are represented by convex polyhedra (in a suitable multi-dimensional space) whose vertices are various selections from the locations—so if skill Y_1 is employed at four locations it is represented by a tetrahedron (a 3-dimensional entity with four vertices), and so on. The connectivity between different skills is now expressed by the polyhedra (or faces thereof) they share—that is to say, by the locations they share.

In KX(Y) we get a conjugate situation, where the locations (the X's) are represented by polyhedra whose vertices are various selections of the skills. So, for example, the factory X_1 might be a 30-dimensional polyhedron (or simplex) if there are 31 skills located there. If one is primarily interested in the skills (or the people who possess them), as the trades unions might well be, then the relevant backcloth S is the structure KY(X). If one is primarily interested in the locations, as the company directors might well be, then the relevant backcloth S is the structure KX(Y)—and these are not mutually exclusive but then they are unlikely to be identical.

What is the traffic which can be observed on this kind of backcloth?

When KY(X) is the backcloth geometry we can have for example the distribution of employees per skill throughout all the locations, as possible traffic (which possibly changes over a period of time); or the wages bill per job types; or the fringe benefits, or other working conditions, per job types throughout the company. Such traffic might well be the dynamics generated by trades unions: indeed a particular trade union might well be regarded mathematically as being defined by such traffic on KY(X).

When KX(Y) is the backcloth, we need traffic to be defined on the locations (in their relation to the skills). So recurrent costs per factory could be traffic in this case; or the goods produced in each location; or the productivity per factory; or the costs of raw materials per factory; and so on. Whenever any of these things *change*, either in fact or hypothetically by way of policy proposals, the changes must adjust themselves so as to be compatible with the underlying connectivities of the backcloth, S. So, for example, production of some goods at a certain factory might fall, due to three kinds of workers staging a go-slow action. The goods affected are naturally those which constitute traffic on those polyhedra, in KX(Y), which have the three skills as vertices, and the *spread* of such changes throughout the company depends exactly on the connectivity between the locations (the X's) *vis-à-vis* these particular skills.

Such *changes* in traffic constitute the presence of *structural forces* throughout the backcloth—and such forces will be felt as keenly by the traffic (production of goods) as gravity is felt by falling bodies. Controlling such forces obviously involves being able to control the topology of these backcloth structures—and this can only be done by first discovering what they are.

Notice too that there is often a confusion between traffic on the two conjugate complexes $KY(X)$ and $KX(Y)$. For in labour relations we can find a trade union being described by forces on $KY(X)$, via its interest in job rewards throughout all locations, although the shop steward (sited at one location) is described by forces on $KX(Y)$, via some specific factory and its various skills. And when management is accused of being indifferent to the fate of the workers it is an expression of the apparent conflict between those who see only the backcloth $KY(X)$ and those who see only $KX(Y)$.

In the latter case we can understand how the workers (who represent the skills in the set Y) become 'only vertices' (or identical units) subordinate to the locations (the set X), whilst in the former case we get the exact opposite (people count more than factories). But the truth is that both backcloths are generated by the *same relation*; the real backcloth is the union of both $KY(X)$ and $KX(Y)$; traffic on one part is subtly dependent on traffic on the other. Salvation in industrial relations lies entirely within our grasps if we can only understand this interplay of traffic on the two conjugate backcloth structures. A study currently underway with a large British company has demonstrated that a new insight can be gained into that total structure on which manufacture is actually based—and the roles of unions and management can be discussed in a common language (and understanding) which augurs well for bringing the two sides together.

Although the relations which we examine in finding a backcloth must be between relevant and fundamental data sets, there are other relations (with similarly defined structures) which naturally arise via the need to avoid logical difficulties connected with the properties of mathematical sets. These are logical difficulties which centre around well-known paradoxes and which are avoided by appealing to the Russell theory of types. Essentially this means that we must be careful to distinguish between elements or members of a set X and subsets of those elements. All the subsets of a set X constitute another logically distinct set, which mathematicians call the power set, $P(X)$, of X. In this language of structure these distinctions are maintained by regarding the data sets as forming a *hierarchical* scheme, say H, in which the levels are referred to as $\mathcal{N}, (\mathcal{N} \pm 1), (\mathcal{N} \pm 2)$, etc.

Table 1 illustrates some areas where the method has been (or currently is being) applied, and indicates some of the sets (hard data) and relations which help to define the relevant backcloths.

The point is that data sets at, for example, the $(\mathcal{N} + 1)$ level consist of elements which represent subsets (or collections) of the elements at the $\mathcal{N}$ level; and so on. But such an arrangement means, once more, that the whole of H is represented by a collection of relations—with their consequent geometrical structures. For example, P might be a set of individual people and this set could be regarded as being at the $\mathcal{N}$ level in the hierarchy H of data. Then at the $(\mathcal{N} + 1)$ level we could have a set $\overline{P}$ whose members are the names of groups of these people (eg societies they belong to, or committees they sit on, or clubs they join, or area they live in). Any person, P_1, in the set P is then clearly related to some of the group-names in $\overline{P}$; the resulting relation naturally defines the simplicial complex structures $KP(\overline{P})$ and $K\overline{P}(P)$, as above. Such a sort-out of the relevant data sets into a number of hierarchical levels

TABLE 1. CURRENT APPLICATIONS OF Q-ANALYSIS

Area of study	Data sets	Relation between sets	Area of study	Data sets	Relation between sets
Urban planning	City streets, commercial activities	Defined by locating activities in streets	Design problems	Available hardware, functional requirements	Defined by dependence of one on the other
Regional planning	Towns and villages, land-use activities	Defined by locating activities in towns etc	Architecture	Visual features of hardware, portions of buildings	Defined by association of features and structure
Clinical psychology	Individual people, list of psychological conditions	Defined by associating conditions with the individuals	Medical diagnosis	Medical symptoms, patients	Defined by patients exhibiting symptoms
Industrial relations	Manufacturing sites, list of job types	Defined by locating jobs in factory sites	Politics	Political proposals, political parties, political groups	Defined by associating proposals with groups
Large organisations	Functional activities, executive employees	Defined by responsibilities of executives			
International flow of television programmes	Programme descriptors, television productions	Defined by describing the programmes	Transport	Traffic routes between towns, list of roads/streets	Defined by routes containing streets

plays a major role in any application of *Q*-analysis—and seems to constitute a novel obstacle at the beginning of any specific study. Now the backcloth, S, needs to be described at each of these levels—and is consequently denoted by $S(\mathcal{N})$ or $S(\mathcal{N} + 1)$ etc. Furthermore the traffic on that backcloth will be describable in a similar way.

What shape is an organisation in?

Using this method we can set about analysing any complex organisation—whether it be British Leyland, the civil service, or some specific community. For example, in a recently published study of the University of Essex it was argued that a minimum of five hierarchical levels were needed for the backcloth and associated traffic.[1] These were conveniently referred to as the $(\mathcal{N} - 2)$ level, $(\mathcal{N} - 1)$ level, $\mathcal{N}$ level, $(\mathcal{N} + 1)$ level and $(\mathcal{N} + 2)$ level. The level at $(\mathcal{N} - 2)$ was taken as the one at which the individual (eg person, room, lecture topic, or restaurant menu item) ceases to act as a cover for anything else. The highest level, $(\mathcal{N} + 2)$, was the level of the university senate (in the set of committees) and this acted as a cover of $(\mathcal{N} + 1)$-level committees (school boards and other subcommittees or senate). At the $\mathcal{N}$ level we were able to place departments and various other entities of an administrative nature, whilst at $(\mathcal{N} - 1)$ we would find research units/groups—being collections of individuals in the department.

A major task was to find a mutually compatible hierarchical placing of all the university's activities, either as backcloth or as traffic, but the result was a genuine view and analysis of the university as a community. It was a community study which is relevant to any large organisation. Any individual in that community presumably experiences all these hierarchical levels; when a chairman of a department attends a meeting and wears his departmental hat then he is operating in the structure as an

N-level entity. In a similar way the items of business or scholarship which circulate around the community and through its committees and bars will be expressible in this hierarchical scheme, constituting traffic on $S(N-2)$, $S(N-1)$, etc.

One of the interesting features of the university was its committee structure (in 1974) and the analysis of the traffic and backcloth found a characteristic near-complete disconnection between the structures $S(N+1)$ and $S(N+2)$, on the one hand, and $S(N)$, $S(N-1)$ and $S(N-2)$ on the other.

By disconnection I mean that there was an almost total blockage of traffic flow between these two parts of $S(H)$, and by traffic flow is here meant all the official and formal flow of business through the committee structure (commonly called the 'official channels'). There was then a strong analogy with the notion of a medieval citadel—formed by $S(N+1)$ and $S(N+2)$ in the total geometry of $S(H)$. This had far-reaching effects for the personal experience in the democratic process, for the sense (or lack of it) of participation in the decision making scheme—which at the time of the study was much occupying the thoughts and emotions of the more revolutionary of the young scholars.

Another intriguing feature of this committee structure was the discovery of what came to be called local q-holes (where the q is the dimension parameter) or *loops* formed by a few committees, in the structure $KC(P)$—here C denotes the set of committees and P is the set of people sitting on them. An example was the 4-hole with the following members: the academic planning committee, the committees on chairs, the board of maths studies, the committee on computing, and the senate, in that order, looping round to the academic planning committee again. This meant that the academic planning committee and the committee on chairs shared a 4-face (five people in common as members of their separate committees). Similarly there were at least five people common to the other neighbouring pairs in this 4-hole. Now this hole must provide a certain kind of boundary to the traffic which can move on the backcloth $KC(P)$.

Thus an item of business which interests (not less than) five people on two committees on opposite sides of the loop (eg the academic planning committee and the board of maths studies) cannot find a *single* home (committee) in which it can be discussed (for decision making)—because the local geometry does not offer a place for it. This item of business must exist in at least two places round the loop, and the class of such items of business can therefore only find their 'place' in a geometry which consists of the *whole loop*. Thus this class of business becomes identified with traffic which *circulates around the 4-hole*. So this kind of traffic must 'bounce off' any such q-hole it encounters in the structure—because it cannot go through it—and so it 'sees' the q-hole as an opaque, solid object. This is why it is also legitimate to describe a q-hole as a q-*object*: it is a q-hole when viewed as a property of the local geometry of the backcloth, but a q-object when encountered by dynamic traffic which is moving on that backcloth.

In this particular context one would suppose that the q-objects for higher q-values would be relevant to the more significant traffic in the community—in so far as it refers to business items which are of interest and concern to a larger number of people. So the filling of a q-hole (if that is possible) is likely to be appreciated by more people if q is large than if q is small. And this filling is highly relevant to the question of making decisions on university business items. For such a process involves a considerable rearrangement of priorities or rankings over many matters of policy (what is often unkindly known as horse-trading) and this requires all the relevant traffic to be accommodated in *one place* in the geometry (that is to say, in *one* committee). If the traffic is constantly having to move around a q-hole then decision making becomes impossible in that geometry.

For example, here, the 4-hole was located in $S(\mathcal{N} + 1)$ (subcommittees of senate) and so any $(\mathcal{N} + 2)$ traffic (referring to $(\mathcal{N} + 2)$ business items) will make a contribution to this category of business which is circulating around. After all, the so-called policy matters are usually at a higher hierarchical level, and so $(\mathcal{N} + 1)$ committees discussing $(\mathcal{N} + 1)$ business items will often find themselves invoking $(\mathcal{N} + 2)$ policy in their quest for decision. But these $(\mathcal{N} + 2)$ matters usually *cover* many items of $(\mathcal{N} + 1)$ business: they therefore appear (disguised) in more than one of the members of our 4-hole. This is why there is a great deal of 'circulating traffic' around the q-holes in a structure such as the one of this context. Because of this I have called such traffic merely *noise*—since it gets in the way of the 'signal', or decision making. Noise can be recognised as traffic on the structure which is (often) obviously trying to avoid the decision-making net: passing the buck is what noise is all about. And noise must be expensive; it needs a lot of energy and resources to keep it going.

Of course, all noise is not going to be consciously buck passing. Some of it will arise out of simple ignorance of the local geometrical structure (accident rather than design); and then there is the problem of how decisions are made in practice—when they relate to traffic which is circulating because of the mere presence of various q-holes in the backcloth. This is when it is necessary to 'fill' in the q-hole. In our committee example this will require either an official or an unofficial committee with suitable q-connections to join up the sides of the 4-hole. If it cannot be done officially (which requires a meta-hierarchy from which the structure of the hierarchy can be modified) then it is done unofficially by creating a *pseudocommittee* (Figure 1). This

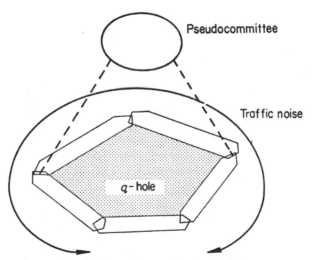

Figure 1. Pseudocommittee and q-hole

often turns out to be the vice-chancellor, in an English university, or the president, in an American university, . . . and so on for other kinds of organisations.

Of course the pseudocommittee is naturally blamed for pulling strings and wielding undemocratic power—and I think this charge must be true. However, it requires a re-examination of what is democratic (or what is regarded as virtuous in the context) in this light—because we can hardly 'blame' the traffic for circulating around q-holes if that is what the backcloth contains.

The essential point about this lies in the fact that in any complex organisation (whether political, economic, or social) the underlying structure of the backcloth is an unavoidable determining factor in the behaviour of those people (traffic) who are trying to run it. So even though the 'authorities' have the best will in the world, are full of the best of intentions, when they invite people to take an active part in decision making, yet they are powerless to transcend the topological connections of the back-cloth—connections which subtly control the effectiveness of that participation. Transcending those constraints can only begin after we have unearthed them and laid them bare.

Democracy in the sense that 'all men are equal' goes out of the window when the structure of the backcloth gets punched full of q-holes!

References

1. R. H. Atkin, *Combinatorial Connectivities in Social Systems* (Basel, Birkhäuser, 1977).
2. R. H. Atkin, *Multidimensional Man* (Harmondsworth, Penguin 1979).

MODELS

BUSINESS STRUCTURE, ECONOMIC CYCLES, AND NATIONAL POLICY

Jay W. Forrester

A system dynamics model of the national economy is now being assembled. Preliminary studies show that the production sectors can generate three different modes of fluctuation in the economy similar to the 3-to-7-year business cycle, the 15-to-25-year Kuznets cycle, and the 45-to-60-year Kondratieff cycle. These several modes arise from the basic physical processes of production and the managerial policies governing inventory, employment, and capital investment. The three modes of economic fluctuation are easily confused, and have tended to be interpreted as if they belonged only to the business cycle, perhaps leading to inappropriate policies. The work is still in progress, but results to date have important implications for many areas, including capital investment and its effect on the business cycle, monetary policy, fine tuning the economy, the severity of future recessions, the Phillips curve, factors affecting unemployment, and the trade-off between unemployment and inflation.

In the complexity of an economic structure, many different dynamic modes of fluctuating activity can exist simultaneously. Much puzzling economic behaviour can arise from the superposition of multiple modes. If the separate identities of the different modes are not recognised, inappropriate or counter-productive policies may be adopted.

An extensive literature exists on each of three different modes of periodic fluctuation in the economy—the business cycle, the Kuznets cycle, and the Kondratieff cycle.[1]

The *business cycle* is the well known short-term fluctuation of business activity. It appears as varying production rates and employment with peaks of activity

Professor Forrester is Germeshausen Professor, Alfred P. Sloan School of Management, Massachusetts Institute of Technology, Cambridge, Mass. 02139, USA. This article is based on a paper originally prepared for the National Association of Business Economists 17th Annual Meeting, Boca Raton, Florida, USA, held on 7 October 1975.

separated by some three to seven years. The business cycle lies within the experience of most persons and is the focus of attention in the press and in government policy debates.

The *Kuznets cycle* is much less generally recognised. It exists as a statistical observation that many time series in the economy seem to fluctuate with a periodicity of some 15 to 25 years. The cause of the Kuznets cycle has been a subject of debate. Other cyclic modes in the economy are of sufficient magnitude to mask the Kuznets cycle from popular awareness.

The *Kondratieff cycle* (also known as the "long-wave") was forcefully presented in the literature by Nikolai Kondratieff in the 1920s. Kondratieff was a Russian economist who made extensive studies of long-term behaviour of the Western capitalist economies. His statistical analyses of economic activity showed that many variables in the Western economies had fluctuated with peaks about 45 to 60 years apart. Such peaks of economic activity have been placed around 1810, 1860, and 1920. Kondratieff believed that the 50-year cycle was caused by internal structural dynamics of the economic system, but he did not propose a sharply defined set of mechanisms. Most other economists took the position that the long-term fluctuation had occurred, but that it was caused by events external to the economy, such as gold discoveries, wars, major technical innovations, and fluctuations in population growth.

Simulation studies with the new system dynamics national model of the economy, now being developed at MIT, have shown that realistically modelled physical and policy relationships in the production of consumer durables and capital equipment can generate simultaneously all three major cycles. The short-term business cycle can result from interactions between backlogs, inventories, production, and employment without requiring involvement of capital investment. The Kuznets cycle is consistent with policies governing production and the acquisition of capital equipment. The 50-year Kondratieff cycle can arise from the structural setting of the capital equipment sector, which supplies capital to the consumer goods sectors but also at the same time must procure its own input capital equipment from its own output.

The system dynamics national model

The system dynamics group at the MIT Sloan School of Management has been developing a system dynamics model of the national economy. A system dynamics model is very different from the more common econometric models by being drawn from a much broader information base, by representing more generally the nonlinear character of real life, by containing a deeper internal substructure of policies, by including social and psychological variables as well as the strictly economic variables, and by having the objective of choosing between alternative policies for achieving long-term improvement of the system rather than the objective of short-term forecasting as a basis for current decisions. The model contains some 15 industrial sectors, worker mobility networks between sectors for both labour and professionals, and household, demographic, financial, and government sectors (See the Appendix for a brief description of the system dynamics national model). The model-building principles include the following four points.

Decision-making within each sector is modelled on widely observed business and government practice. (It is not based on a theory of "optimal economic equilibrium".)

Special attention is given to accumulations—reservoirs or buffers—such as inventories of inputs and finished stock, employee pools, bank balances, accounts payable, and order backlogs. Such accumulations decouple rates of flow from one another and thereby make it possible to model changes that occur in economic activity when rates of flow are out of equilibrium.

Highly nonlinear relationships that exist in reality are incorporated. Such nonlinearities have a profound effect on behaviour and must be incorporated if a model is to be realistic.

Quantitative computer simulation is used to derive the qualitative behaviour of the system, that is to discern the various possible modes of behaviour and how they can be influenced by changes in policies at various decision points within the system.

Model development is still underway. But already, most sectors have been individually formulated and are under test. Sub-assemblies with various arrangements of multiple sectors have been examined. Even at the present partial assembly stage, the results raise important questions about current economic policy. The discussion in this article focuses on economic fluctuations that are implicit in the structure of the production sectors of the economy.

The production sector

Production sectors are the heart of a national economy. In the system dynamics national model, production sectors are created by replicating a set of master equations that represent a standard production sector. The standard sector can then be specialised to represent each different kind of production sector by providing the appropriate initial conditions and parameter values. The standard sector will be replicated with suitable sets of coefficients to represent consumer durables, heavy capital equipment, agriculture, education etc (see Appendix).

The standard production sector reflects the internal structure and policies of a typical industrial firm. It contains a full accounting system, order backlog, in-process and finished inventories, a production level that depends on several input factors, inventories and backlogs for each factor of production, and ordering functions that procure the various factors of production. Ordering functions exist in each production sector for each of some ten factors used in production.

The ordering functions are the primary generators of dynamic behaviour. An ordering function creates orders for its input factor by reacting to the demand for the finished product, the condition of the sector, and the supply of the factor. It does so by recognising the order backlog and the inventory of the sector output, the price of the output, the average shipping rate, the marginal productivities of the factors of production, the inventory and backlog of the input factor, the price of the input factor, the delivery delay of the input factor, the financial condition and profitability of the sector, the interest rates, and the short-term and long-term expectations.

Figure 1 shows a much simplified diagram of the production sector as used

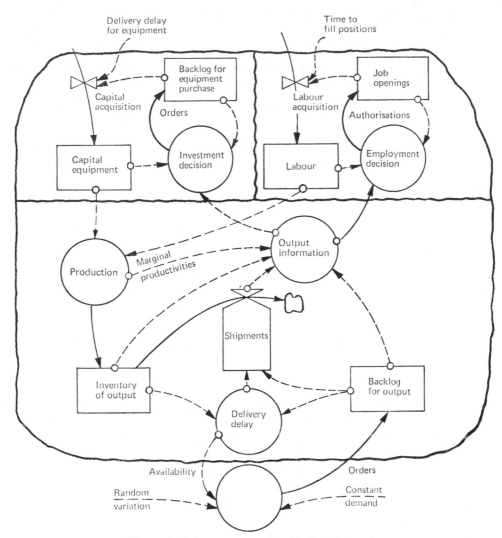

Figure 1. Major components of industrial sector

in the national model. For the behaviour discussed here, the financial and pricing parts of the sector are not active; the focus is on physical changes in inventory and backlog of output, and in the stocks of the input factors to production. Figure 1 shows a very simplified output section of the model and two abbreviated ordering functions, one for capital equipment and the other for labour.

In the output section of Figure 1, orders enter a backlog, and the relationship between the backlog and the available inventory of output determines the ability to ship product (delivery delay). The inventory is increased by production and decreased by shipments. Output information includes the condition of inventory, backlog, shipments, and marginal productivities of the factors of production.

In the two ordering functions for capital and labour in Figure 1, the decision to acquire more of either factor of production is based on multiple inputs. Shown here symbolically are the information streams from the sector output, the inventory of the factor, and the backlog of unfilled orders for the factor. In addition, the ordering function uses financial variables, the changing availabilities of the factors, expectations, and prices.

Three periodic modes in the production sector

The structure of a production sector and of the interconnecting relationships is complex enough to cause many different modes of dynamic behaviour. In other words, several different cycles originate from the interactions of inventories, production rate, acquisition of labour and capital, and the supply interconnections between different sectors. The internal dynamics of typical production sectors seem sufficiently diverse to simultaneously generate the business cycle, the Kuznets cycle, and the Kondratieff cycle.

The several modes of behaviour discussed here are internal to the production sectors themselves and are not induced by broader aspects of the economy such as changes in consumer income, prices, or interest rates. To observe the inherent characteristics of first one sector and then a combination of two production sectors, the tests described here use a constant demand for sector output modulated by the availability of the product, as would occur in an actual market. In the short run, as delivery delay increases, the demand generator orders further ahead in anticipation of need and causes the order backlog to rise. In the longer run, as delivery delay increases, the unavailability of product discourages demand and causes some decrease in orders.

The behaviour of the model will be examined in three stages: first with one sector using only labour as a variable factor of production to exhibit the business cycle, second with one sector varying both labour and capital to exhibit the Kuznets cycle, and third with two sectors both varying labour and capital to exhibit the Kondratieff cycle.

The business cycle
Figure 2 shows behaviour of a single production sector (consumer durables) when capital equipment is held constant and production rate is changed by variations in employment only. A monthly 5% random variation is superimposed on the incoming order rate to induce the sector to respond according to its inherent dynamic periodicities.

In Figure 2 the production sector is generating a sequence of fluctuations typical of the normal business cycle. Intervals between peaks vary around five years. The relative timings of the backlog, the production rate (as shown by labour), and the inventory are typical of industrial behaviour in the real world.

The significance of Figure 2 lies in its generation of the business cycle without variation in consumer income or capital investment. Prices are not changing, demand is constant on the average, money and interest rates are not active, and capital investment is not involved. The cyclic fluctuation in Figure 2 has the major characteristics of the business cycle and arises from the interaction of backlog, inventory, production, and employment. This is not to suggest that the business cycle operates without influencing other activities in the economy. But Figure 2 does raise the question of whether consumer income, investment, and monetary changes are central to the generation and control of the business cycle or are merely induced by variation arising from employment and inventories.

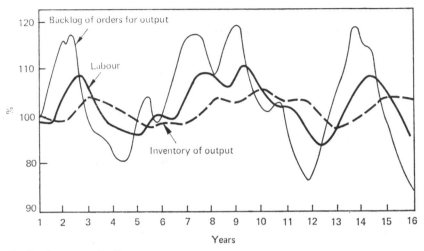

Figure 2. Business-cycle fluctuation appearing in labour, inventory, and backlog for a single production sector

The fluctuating, business-cycle-like behaviour in Figure 2 arises from the policies that control employment in response to inventories and backlogs. Such policies tend to amplify disturbances and to convert short-term random disturbances into an irregular wave that reflects the natural oscillatory character of the system structure.

The reason for amplification and overshoot of employment and production can be seen by tracing an increase in demand through the structure of Figure 1. Assume that a constant demand has existed for consumer goods and that this suddenly increases slightly. The first consequence is that orders, in the backlog for output, and shipments all increase, and the inventory of output is reduced. The increase in backlog and depetion of inventory continue until the management has confidence that the new higher level of business is not an aberration, and until additional factors of production (labour in this example) can be acquired to increase production.

Between the increase in demand and the rise in production to equal the new demand, three things occur. First, the backlog for output increases to an undesirably high level; second, the output inventory is depleted below its initial, desired level; and third, because demand is now higher, the desired inventory (not shown in Figure 1) also increases. As a consequence when production has risen to equal demand, the system is out of equilibrium. Backlog for output is too high, and inventory is too low. With production equal to demand, the new state of disequilibrium could be sustained but cannot be brought back into balance. Production must be pushed higher than the new demand to reduce the backlog for output, and to increase inventory not only back to its old value but up to the new higher desired level. When inventory and backlog reach the desired levels, production is apt to be too high so that inventory continues to rise and further corrections are necessary.

It is from many such kinds of stock depletions and recoveries that fluctuating modes of the economic system arise. Disturbances propogate through the system by changing a stock from a desired level, setting up a discrepancy between the actual and the desired conditions, activating a policy to start a corrective sequence, and progressively working through a cascade of stages. Time lags in the system delay action and eventually induce corrections greater than the initiating disturbance.

This preliminary examination of industrial structure suggests that the business cycle primarily involves inventories and employment. Capital investment, although it will show fluctuation induced by the business cycle, need not be a necessary participant in creating the short-term business cycle. Furthermore, the business cycle can exist without inputs from money supply, interest rates, or changes in consumer income. Therefore, monetary policies aimed at diminishing the business cycle through affecting investment may be coupled only very loosely to the primary causes of business-cycle fluctuation, and, therefore, provide little leverage for influence.

The Kuznets cycle

When realistic parameters for procurement of capital equipment are inserted in the simulation model of an industrial sector, dynamic behaviour suggests that investment is primarily a part of the Kuznets cycle, not the short-term business cycle. The processes of investment are too slow to interact effectively in a cycle of only a few years duration.[2] The conservatism and therefore delay in committing capital funds, the long planning time for new plant and machinery, the substantial delays in procuring new physical assets, and the 10 to 60 year life of equipment and buildings, all describe managerial and

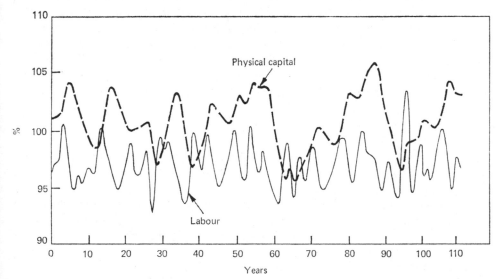

Figure 3. The Kuznets and business cycles exhibited by capital and labour respectively as factors of production

physical relationships suitable for creating fluctuation of 15-year to 30-year periodicity. Furthermore, the basic processes of production, procurement, and accumulation of capital plant are capable of creating the intermediate cycle without changes in monetary policy, interest, or consumption.

Figure 3 shows the behaviour of the structure in Figure 1 when both capital equipment and labour are varied as factors of production. Capital equipment differs from labour in having longer times for planning and procurement, and in having a depreciation time much longer than the average length of employment of labour. As before, the sector is supplying to a constant demand that is influenced by availability of the product and perturbed by a random disturbance. Two curves are shown in the figure, one for labour as a factor of production, the other for physical capital as a factor of production.

The labour curve in Figure 3 again exhibits a periodicity typical of the business cycle. The curve appears more compressed than in Figure 2 because of the changed time scale.

The curve in Figure 3 for physical capital existing in the sector also shows fluctuating behaviour, but the interval between peaks is clearly longer than for labour.

The consequence of adding capital equipment procurement is to produce an additional periodicity of some 15 to 25 years duration. In Figure 3 the internal dynamics of capital equipment procurement in a single production sector show a periodicity in the range of the Kuznets cycle. In this example there is no active capital-producing sector, so capital is assumed available at a constant typical procurement delay. Both the business-cycle-like mode and the Kuznets-cycle-like mode coexist simultaneously. Both modes of behaviour arise from the physical structure of the industrial process and the management policies followed in adjusting factors of production to an uncertain demand.

To the extent that interest rates affect investment, they should relate to the Kuznets cycle more than to the business cycle. But many businessmen would agree that demand, availability, existing plant, and shortage of labour have, over the last 30 years, been much more influential in investment decisions than have interest rates. If interest-rate fluctuations are not necessary for creating the Kuznets cycle, and if physical variables have more influence, one is left with the possibility that monetary policy may be inadequate for influencing the capital investment (Kuznets) cycle.

The Kondratieff cycle

The Kondratieff cycle is a fluctuation in the economy of some 50 years between peaks. In shape it is characterised by sharp peaks in economic activity separated by long valleys of stagnation.

The Kondratieff wave has not been taken very seriously because of a lack of a convincing theory of how it could be caused. After the peak in economic activity around 1920, the great depression of the 1930s represented a typical low point in such a cycle. Now, some 50 years after the preceding peak, economic activity has again risen to a high level, but with many signs of faltering. The question arises, is the Kondratieff wave of underlying structural origin, and does it have significance for current policy?

Recent computer simulations suggest that a long-period cyclic behaviour can arise from the physical structure connecting consumer goods sectors and the capital sectors. A sufficient cause for a 50-year fluctuation lies in the movement of people between sectors, the long timespan to change the production capacity of the capital sectors, the way capital sectors provide their own input capital as a factor of production, the need to develop excess capacity to catch up on deferred demand, and the psychological and speculative forces of expectations that can cause overexpansion in the capital sectors.

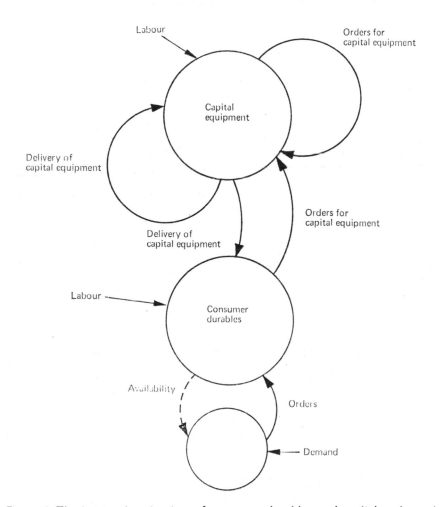

Figure 4. The two-sector structure of consumer durables and capital equipment

Figure 4 shows two interconnected production sectors. One sector has parameters, for inventories and for the time required to change production, typical of a consumer durables sector. The other is a typical capital equipment sector. The consumer durables sector orders capital equipment from the capital equipment sector and has labour freely available (the labour mobility network for interconnecting labour flows between sectors is not active). The capital equipment sector also has labour freely available but orders its capital equipment as a factor of production from its own output. This reentrant structure implies that an increase in demand for consumer durables would cause the consumer sector to try to increase both of its factors of production. It can obtain labour, but when it wants more capital equipment, the capital sector must expand. But if the capital sector is to expand in balanced manner, it needs both labour and capital as inputs. A "bootstrap" operation is involved in which the capital sector must withhold output from its customer (the consumer sector) so it can expand first in order to later meet the needs of the consumer sector. Such an interrelationship of sectors can create a mode of behaviour not seen in either sector separately.

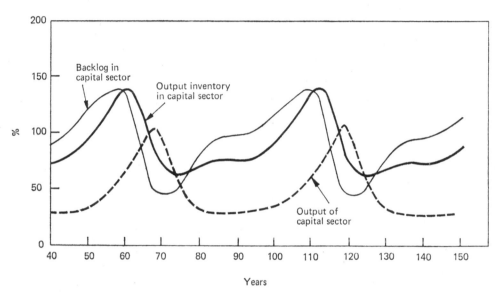

Figure 5. The Kondratieff cycle appearing in the capital sector

In Figure 5 the two-sector industrial structure shows a long fluctuation in the capital sector of some 50 years duration. The shape has similarities to the classical description of the Kondratieff wave in which steep peaks in economic activity are separated by broad valleys of depression. The model and its behaviour in Figure 5 constitutes a theory of how the Kondratieff cycle can be caused.

Although the behaviour behind Figure 5 is not yet completely understood and does not occur in all two-sector configurations, it seems reasonably certain that the processes of production and capital equipment procurement, and the relationship between consumer and capital sectors have the potential for producing a Kondratieff cycle. The mode of fluctuation in Figure 5 is strongly determined internally and is unstable for small variations and bounded by non-linearities for large amplitude. Such a mode grows quickly from any triggering disturbance and tends to sustain itself. It is especially persistent and not easy to influence unless its nature is well enough understood to discover any available points of leverage. If such a mode exists in real life, it is probable that changes over the 50-year interval in psychological attitudes, propensity to take risks, and efforts to sustain the upward growth phase by monetary expansion will all tend to accentuate the fluctuation.

The most basic cause of the 50-year fluctuation in Figure 5 is similar to the mode in Figure 2 that involved depletion of inventory and then an amplified production rate to reestablish internal balance. To illustrate the counterpart in Figure 5, consider the US economy at the end of World War 2. After the depression and the war, the capital plant of the country was depleted both at the manufacturing and at the consumer level. The physical capital stock of the country was at low ebb. But to refill the depleted pool of physical capital in a reasonable time (say 20 years) required a production rate greater than would be necessary to sustain the capital stock once the pool was filled. In other words, the production rate required to replenish the depleted physical capital in an acceptable period of time was higher than could be sustained. The capital sectors would overexpand and then be forced to retrench.

In more detail, the sequences in the long-wave mode, starting from the depression years at the bottom of the cycle, seem to be: the slow growth of the capital sector of the economy; the gradual decay of the entire capital plant of the economy below the amount required, while the capital sector is unable to supply even replacement needs; the initial recirculation of output of the capital sector to its own input; the progressive increase in wages and the development of a labour shortage in the consumer sectors that encourage capital-intensive production and still higher demands for capital equipment; the overexpansion of the capital sector to a capacity greater than that required for replacement in order to catch up on deferred needs; the excess accumulation of physical capital by consumers (housing and durables) and by durable manufacturers (plant and equipment); the developing failure of capital equipment users to absorb the output of the overexpanded capital sectors; the sudden appearance of unemployment in the capital sectors; the relative reduction of labour cost compared to capital which further diminishes the need for new plant; the rapid collapse of the capital sector in the face of demand below the long-term average needed by the economy; and the slow decline of the excess capital stock through physical depreciation.

Although investigation of this long-wave mode is incomplete, it is of sufficient potential importance to be worth serious consideration. Present symptoms in the economy seem consistent with the top of a Kondratieff wave, when the top is viewed as a time of excess capital expansion. New tankers are leaving the shipyards and going directly to anchorage. Aircraft are going into storage. For the first time since the late 1920s, many cities have an excess of office space. The US interstate highway system is nearly complete and another is not needed soon. The condition of the car industry only partly results from the oil shortage and is partly due to the consumer stock of cars having been filled. The financial plight of the US real-estate investment trusts and the decline in home construction suggest that we already have more housing than the US economy can support. Most municipalities have built sufficient schools and hospitals.

If we in the USA are indeed in a condition of excess capital stock both at the industrial and at the consumer level, the implications for business and economic policy are substantial. Under conditions of excess of capital plant, increasing the money supply will give little incentive to purchasing physical capital and instead may only feed speculative and inflationary forces.

Policy misinterpretations from multiple modes

As already shown, many different modes of behaviour should be expected in the economy. For example, the business, Kuznets, and Kondratieff cycles each seem associated with different economic structures, so they can exist simultaneously and can superimpose their consequences. Such simultaneous modes can present confusing symptoms, especially if all are erroneously attributed to a single cause. Often, all economic behaviour has been interpreted as belonging to the short-term business cycle. As a result, the longer-term modes go unrecognised, and their consequences are not forseen.

The three modes of economic fluctuation discussed here and the structures from which they come suggest two possible misinterpretations in current economic thinking. First, monetary policy since World War 2 has often been given credit for reducing the severity of recessions, whereas, the strong expansions and the weak recessions may merely reflect the way the three modes of cyclic fluctuation superimpose. Second, the so-called Phillips curve relationship seems to arise from the inventory–employment–wage substructure in the industrial sectors, and, as such, would give little guidance for how unemployment would respond to monetary policy which exists in a rather different substructure of the economic system and relates primarily to other dynamic modes.

Business-cycle stabilisation

Interaction between the Kondratieff cycle and the business cycle may have led to erroneous explanations of recessions and depressions, and to inappropriate policies for economic stabilisation. Recessions since World War 2 have been less severe than those in the immediately preceding decades. Anti-cyclic monetary policy and fine tuning of the economy have often been given credit for reducing business downturns between 1945 and 1970. But another explanation grows out of considering how different kinds of economic fluctuations can combine.

Figure 6 shows three sinusoids as stylised representations of the business, Kuznets, and Kondratieff cycles. Figure 7 and Figure 8 are on an expanded time scale and show the simple sinusoids added together and the duration of economic expansions and contractions. Figure 7 covers the rising segment of the long wave and Figure 8 the falling segment. Note that the upward thrust of the long wave in Figure 7 gives business cycles the appearance of having strong and long expansions with weak and short recessions; in Figure 8 the decline of the long wave weakens and shortens the expansions of the business cycle and deepens and lengthens the recessions. With no other influences, the superposition of business cycles on a long-term fluctuation would produce the milder recessions since World War 2, without relying on post-war monetary policy as an explanation.

Much concern has been expressed about the failure of monetary policy to cope with the current recession. But, the explanation may be simply that

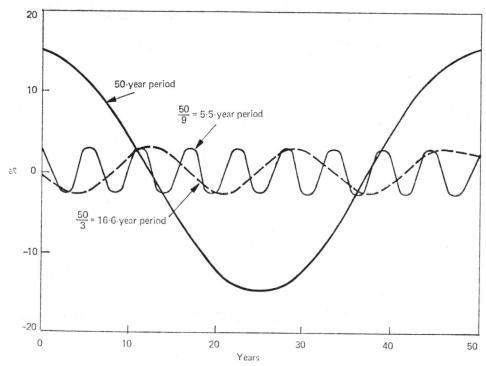

Figure 6. Three sinusoidal curves representing the business, Kuznets, and Kondratieff cycles

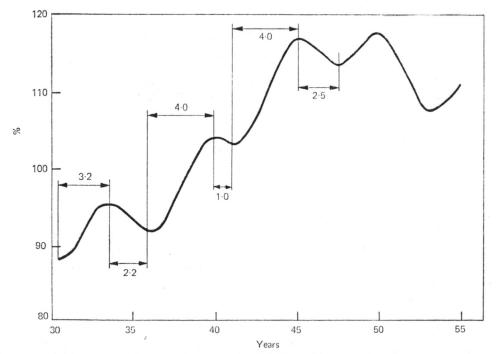

Figure 7. Addition of sinusoids during rising part of the long wave

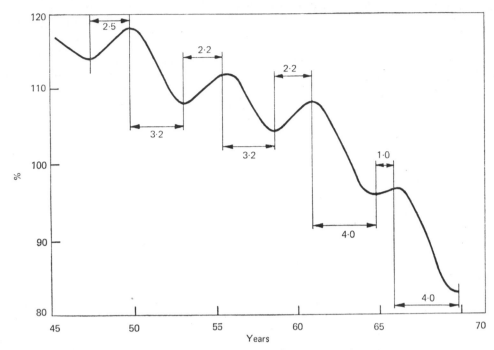

Figure 8. Addition of sinusoids during falling part of the long wave

monetary policy has at all times had little leverage over employment and the level of economic activity.

The great depression of the 1930s is sometimes attributed to an unfortunate choice of monetary policy by the Federal Reserve. Such an explanation assumes monetary policy to be crucial to economic change. But, if a long wave exists and arises primarily from internal structural dynamics of the economy that lead to overproduction of physical capital, then monetary policy may have only a weak influence on either the cause or cure of major depressions. To the extent that monetary policy has any influence on the long wave in the economy, the principal effect may be to encourage upward overshoot at peaks with a corresponding steeper decline, as a consequence of expansionary monetary policy during the late stages of the long-wave economic boom.

The existence of several different simultaneous cyclic modes in the economy would make it unnecessary to invoke monetary policy to explain the great depression, the milder recessions in the 1950s and 1960s, or the worse recession now. Instead, the three cyclic modes are all seen as arising primarily from the physical structure and managerial policies in the productive sectors of the economy. Although there could be some influence from monetary policy, the connection may be tenuous and the leverage slight. When the national model has been extended to include the banking system and the Federal Reserve, the financial structures can be examined to see how much they add to or change the behaviour modes generated in the production sectors.

Inflation versus unemployment

Many political pressures and goverment actions seem to rest on an assumption that inflation and unemployment are the inverse of one another. For example, a prevalent belief exists that by increasing money supply, with consequent inflation, unemployment can be reduced.

The presumed leverage of government in deciding the mix of inflation and unemployment in the economy may well rest on a number of fallacies and misconceptions. First, the less severe recessions since 1945 may be simply a consequence of superposition of short and long cycles. Second, capital investment has been considered a necessary link in the dynamics of the business cycle, whereas the business cycle appears possible without variations in capital stock or changes in investment in fixed capital. Third, interest rates and credit are believed to be major influences on investment decisions, whereas stronger influences probably come from fluctuating inventories, backlogs, profitability, expectations, and procurement delays. Fourth, and perhaps most seriously, the Phillips curve has been interpreted as a general relationship between all sources of inflation and all causes of unemployment. However, our work to date suggests that the balance of inflation and unemployment in the economy depends in a complex way on the many modes of behaviour in the economy as well as on the government policies being followed. For example, a simple Phillips curve relationship probably applies to wage changes, cost variations, and employment fluctuations that go on within the dynamics of the short-term business cycle. However, changes in money supply or changes in the position of the economy relative to the long-wave fluctuation will tend to cause shifts in inflation and unemployment that cannot be described in terms of simple

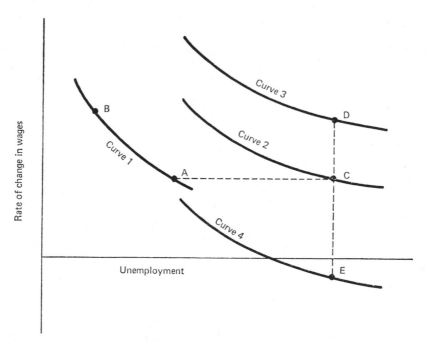

Figure 9. Phillips curves as moved by long-term unemployment and monetary policy

movements along a fixed trade-off curve. This implies, as discussed below, that the Phillips curve concept is not a reliable indicator for public policy.

The Phillips curve is a downward sloping relationship that is often interpreted as relating inflation to unemployment. Allegedly, by accepting more inflation, unemployment can be decreased. But recent experience has been disappointing. High inflation and high unemployment have coexisted. Why?

The Phillips curve, as implied by curve 1 in Figure 9, was originally measured as a relationship between rate of change in wages and unemployment. Data are drawn from many business cycles. Wage change and unemployment tended to move inversely to one another over the duration of the business cycle as along curve 1 between points A and B. The Phillips curve derives from that dynamic mode (the business cycle) that seems to relate inventory to employment fluctuations. It is the mode illustrated in Figure 2.

For a preliminary examination of the Phillips-curve relationship, the model structure of Figure 1 was extended by adding a section of the labour-mobility network consisting of an unemployment pool, hiring, quits, layoffs, and wage change. One can then record from the model two time series, one showing wage change and another unemployment rate. These are synthetic equivalents of the real-life data used by Phillips. When these values are plotted, the scatter diagram, like the data used by Phillips, suggests a downward-sloping relationship. The model (as does the real economy) shows, over the business cycle, an inverse relationship between wage change and unemployment.[3]

But a dynamic inverse relationship over the short-term business cycle, arising within the inventory–employment process, is very different from a generalised trade-off between all causes of inflation and all causes of unemployment. The observed business-cycle-related dynamic behaviour of wages and employment at the operating level can exist while saying little about the relevant policy for varying the money supply.

Potentially, three different and largely uncoupled dynamic modes may be causing shifts in unemployment and inflation. First, the business cycle appears to produce a cyclical variation in both wage change (with accompanying changes in prices) and unemployment that yields the Phillips curve relationship as shown by curve 1 of Figure 9. Second, the Kondratieff cycle may produce long-term shifts in unemployment capable of moving the short-term Phillips curve horizontally as from A to C (curve 2). Third, if money supply were increased in the hope of reducing unemployment, unemployment would not move back along curve 2 if, in fact, the money supply lies mostly outside the business-cycle structure producing the Phillips curve. Instead, a continued increase in the money supply faster than the increase in real output would produce long-term inflation by moving the Phillips curve vertically as to D (curve 3). The business cycle, deep within the economy at the inventory–employment–production level, could still cause movement along either curve 2 or curve 3, depending on which curve had been established by the long-term average rate of increase in money supply.

The relationships in Figure 9 suggest reversible price and employment changes from the business cycle, long-term unemployment from causes apart from either the business cycle or monetary policy, and monetary policy that is primarily responsible for the long-term rate of inflation. If the three aspects of behaviour are so separated, then the present increase in unemployment lies outside the reach of monetary policy. Monetary policy, however, can be used to control inflation. Such an hypothesis implies that the present level of unemployment can be accompanied by either high or low inflation, depending on how money supply is managed.

Implications

The preceding discussion is based on work still in progress. Nonetheless, preliminary observations are perhaps worth summarising for discussion and debate:

- Several simultaneous periodicities of economic fluctuation can exist in the economy at the same time.
- Basic industrial structures and management policies can generate not only the business cycle but also the Kuznets cycle of some 18 years duration and the Kondratieff cycle of some 50 years duration.
- The 3-to-7 year business cycle seems to be caused primarily by interactions between inventories and employment.
- Capital investment probably has less to do with contributing to the business cycle than it has in generating the longer Kuznets and Kondratieff cycles.
- Monetary policy, to the extent that it works through investment in plant and machinery, may have little influence on the business cycle.
- Mild recessions since World War 2 can be explained by the rising phase of the Kondratieff long wave rather than as a consequence of post-war monetary policy and fine tuning.
- The greater severity of the present recession may indicate the top of a Kondratieff long wave of capital expansion.
- Confusion between the business, Kuznets, and Kondratieff cycles may cause symptoms to be misunderstood and counter-productive national policies to be adopted.
- The Phillips curve relationship between the rate of wage change and unemployment seems to belong to the internal dynamics of the business cycle. As such it probably lies beyond the effective reach of monetary policy.
- Because the Phillips curve and monetary policy belong to different economic substructures and probably to different dynamic modes, the Phillips curve is a weak guide to either monetary policy or actions to cope with long-term unemployment.
- Recent increases in unemployment may not come from the business cycle but from the long-term Kondratieff cycle at the end of the phase of overinvestment in capital equipment.
- The belief in a trade-off between inflation and unemployment may be erroneous, with the result that increased money supply fails to relieve unemployment but does produce inflation.

The preceding observations, if correct, have major implications for government and business decisions. Even a small probability of their validity justifies further analysis. The system dynamics national model summarised here should explain the existence and the simultaneous interaction of the major modes of aggregate economic activity.

Appendix

A dynamic national model of social and economic change

The System Dynamics Group of the Sloan School at MIT is well advanced on a national model of social and economic behaviour. The structure of the socioeconomic model is intended to be general and to apply to any country having agriculture, consumption, manufacturing, and money. The structure should be rich enough in detail to represent not only industrial economies but also the underdeveloped and developing countries. Fitting the model to a particular country would require only the selection of suitable parameters and initial conditions.

The model will treat all major aspects of the socioeconomic system as internal variables to be generated by the interplay of mutual influences within the model structure. The model will contain production sectors, labour and professional mobility between sectors, a demographic sector with births and deaths and with subdivision into age categories, commercial banking to make short-term loans, a monetary authority with its controls over money and credit, government services, government fiscal operations, consumption sectors, and a foreign sector for trade and international monetary flows.

Each sector will reach down in detail to some ten factors of production, ordering and inventories for each factor of production, marginal productivities for each sector, balance sheet and profit and loss statement, output inventories, delivery delay quotation, production planning, price setting, expectations, and borrowing.

The model is being formulated for the new DYNAMO III compiler, which handles arrays of equations and makes especially easy the replication of the production sector and its parts. For example, an equation in the ordering function need be written only once with array subscripts to identify the ordering functions for each factor in each sector.

The standard production sector

A standard production sector will be replicated to form a major part of the model. By choosing suitable parameter values, the standard sector can be repeated for consumer durable goods, consumer soft goods, capital equipment, building construction, agriculture, resources, energy, services, transport, secondary manufacturing, knowledge generation, self-provided family services, military operations, and government service.

Within each production sector are inventories of some ten factors of production—capital, labour, professionals, knowledge, technological change, buildings, land, transport, and two kinds of materials. In addition, production is affected by length of work week for labour and length of work week for capital.

For each factor of production, an ordering function will create an order backlog for the factor in response to desired production rate, desired factor intensity, marginal productivity of the factor, price of the product, price of the factor, growth expectations, product inventory and backlog, profitability, interest rate, financial pressures, and delivery delay of the factor. In terms of dynamic behaviour, the ordering function will be far more influential than the production function; yet, in the economics literature, attention has been in the reverse priority.

The structure of a standard production sector is essentially the structure of a single firm in the economy with parameters and nonlinear relationships chosen to reflect the broader distributions of responses resulting from aggregating many firms within a sector. As with a firm, the sector will have an accounting section that pays for each factor of production, generates accounts receivable and payable, maintains balance sheet variables, computes profitability, saves, and borrows money. The structure should generate the full range of behaviour that arises from interactions between the real variables and the money and information variables. By carrying the model to such detail, it should communicate directly with the real system where a wealth of information is available for establishing the needed parameter values.

A production sector will generate product prices in accordance with conditions within the sector and between the sector and its customers. For testing price and wage controls, coefficients are available to inhibit price changes. The sector will distribute output among its customer sectors. Market clearing, or the balance between supply and demand, will be struck not by price alone but also on the basis of delivery delay reflecting availability, rationing, and allocation.

Labour and professional mobility
People in the production sectors are divided into two categories—labour and professional. For each category a mobility network defines the channels of movement between sectors in response to differentials in wages, availability, and need. A mobility network has a star shape with each point ending at a production sector and terminating in a level which represents the number of people working in the sector. At the centre of the star is a general unemployment pool, which is the central communication node between sectors. Between the central pool and each sector is a "captive" unemployment level of those people who are unemployed but who still consider themselves a part of the sector. They are the people searching for better work within their sector or who are temporarily laid off but expecting to be rehired. In a rising demand for more labour, those in the captive level can be rehired quickly, but longer time constants are associated with drawing people from other sectors by way of the general unemployment pool.

Demographic sector
The demographic sector generates population in the model by controlling the flows of births, deaths, immigration, and ageing. Age categories divide people into their different roles in the economy from childhood to retirement. The demographic sector divides people between the labour and professional streams in response to wages, salaries, demands of the productive sectors, capacity of the educational system, and family background. Workforce participation determines the fraction of the population working in response to historical tradition, demand for labour, and standard of living.

Household sectors
The household sectors are replicated by economic category—labour, professional, unemployed, retired, and welfare. Each household sector receives income, saves, borrows, purchases a variety of goods and services, and holds assets. Consumption demands respond to price, availability of inputs, and the marginal utilities of various goods and services for different levels of income.

Financial sector
The financial sector is divided into four parts—commercial banking, savings institutions, mortgage lending, and the monetary authority. The financial sector determines interest rates on savings and bonds, buys and sells bonds, makes long-term and short-term loans, and creates intangible variables like confidence in the banking system.

The commercial banking system receives deposits, buys and sells bonds, extends loans to households and businesses, and generates short-term interest rates. In doing so it manages reserves in response to discount rate, expected return on investment portfolio, demand for loans, and liquidity needs.

The savings institution and mortgage lending institution receive savings, extend long-term loans to households and businesses, generate long-term interest rates, buy and sell bonds, and borrow short-term from the banking system. They balance money, bonds, deposits, and loans. They allocate loans between businesses and households, and monitor the debt levels and borrowing capability of each business and household sector.

The monetary authority controls discount rate, open market bond transactions, and required reserve ratios. In doing so it responds to such variables as owned and borrowed reserves of the bank, demand deposits, the inflation rate, unemployment, and interest rates.

Notes and references

1. Arthur F. Burns and Wesley C. Mitchell, *Measuring Business Cycles* (New York, National Bureau of Economic Research, 1946); Robert A. Gordon, *Business Fluctuations* (New York, Harper & Row, 1951); Bert G. Hickman, "The postwar retardation: another long swing in the rate of growth?", *American Economic Review*, *53*, May 1963, pages 490–507; N. D. Kondratieff, "The long waves in economic life", *Review of Economic Statistics, 17* (6), November 1935, pages 105–115; George Garvy, "Kondratieff's theory of long cycles", *Review of Economic Statistics, 25* (4), November 1943, pages 203–220.

2. Of course, some earlier authors have also argued that the delays involved in movement of physical capital are too long for the dynamics of capital investment to be an essential cause of the business cycle; see Moses Abramovitz, "The nature and significance of Kuznets cycles", *Economic Development and Cultural Change, 9*, April 1961, pages 225–248.

    For a detailed discussion of an industrial sector simulation model very similar to the one used for this paper and for a detailed analysis of business cycle and Kuznets cycle behaviour, see Nathaniel J. Mass, *Economic Cycles: An Analysis of Underlying Causes* (Cambridge, Mass, Wright-Allen Press, 1975).

3. The work referred to here is being done by Dale Runge in the System Dynamics Group at the MIT Sloan School of Management.

Further reading

Jay W. Forrester, *Collected Papers of Jay W. Forrester* (Cambridge, Mass, Wright-Allen Press, 1975).

Jay W. Forrester, *Principles of Systems* (Cambridge, Mass, Wright-Allen Press, 1968).

Michael R. Goodman, *Study Notes in System Dynamics* (Cambridge, Mass, Wright-Allen Press, 1974).

Nathan B. Forrester, *The Life Cycle of Economic Development* (Cambridge, Mass, Wright-Allen Press, 1973).

POPULATION, WEALTH, AND RESOURCES UP TO THE YEAR 2000

Barry B. Hughes and Mihajlo D. Mesarovic

The authors use the second-generation Mesarovic–Pestel model to produce global scenarios. In the first (open-loop) case there is little interaction between different areas (eg agriculture, energy, or resources). The results are similar to forecasts made by other research groups. The authors show that in the long run this open-loop approach is implausible. The closed-loop approach significantly alters the scenarios. This is highlighted by the combined-problem scenario, which adopts some of the more pessimistic assumptions from the other organisations' projections while retaining the interactions between areas. The authors stress the importance of the closed-loop approach when considering global futures. They also examine the regional trends which may be masked by the global figures.

IN President Carter's environmental message 23 May 1977 he said:

I am directing the Council on Environmental Quality and . . . other appropriate agencies to make a one-year study of the probable changes in the world's population, natural resources, and environment through the end of the century. This study will serve as the foundation of our longer-term planning.

There are several important points to be made here. First, trends in population, natural resources, and the environment, are strongly interdependent. It is relatively easy to forecast population (from past data), economic development, and resource use (food, energy, raw materials) on the assumption that historical trends will continue. It is a completely different matter, however, to project the

Barry B. Hughes is Associate Professor in the Department of Political Science, and Mihajlo D. Mesarovic is Professor of Engineering and Mathematics at the Case Western Reserve University, Cleveland, Ohio, USA. The study on which this article is based was supported by the Gund Foundation, the TRW Foundation, and Holcomb Research Institute, Butler University, and it was originally prepared as input to the project Global 2000—led by Dr Gerald Barney with the assistance of Ms Jennie Robinson—established in response to President Carter's environmental directive by the Council on Environmental Quality and the State Department.

future development of the entire system. Second, while the primary interest of the study might be national or regional, it is essential to take a global view. Finally, and very important, the directive of the President indicates the growing awareness of these points among political leaders and the recognition that we need fresh approaches to establish a base for long-term planning.

This report is a preliminary analysis and suggests possible directions for longer-term planning. The analysis here was undertaken using the second-generation Mesarovic–Pestel model, called the World Integrated Model (WIM).[1] This models global development, representing the world in 12 regions: North America, Western Europe, the Pacific developed region, the rest of the developed world, Eastern Europe and the Soviet Union, Latin America, non-oil producing Arab countries, the Middle East oil-producing countries, Africa, South Asia, Southeast Asia, and China. Furthermore, each of these world regions can be subdivided using WIM into as many as five subcomponents, which can either be national or subregional units.

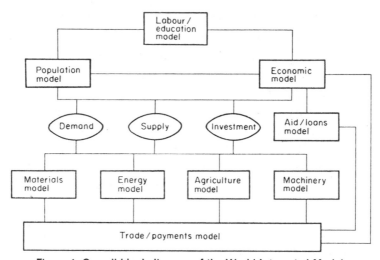

Figure 1. Overall block diagram of the World Integrated Model

As shown in Figure 1, WIM represents several areas of world development.[2] For this analysis all of the major units in Figure 1 were used except labour/education and materials.

The WIM system itself has been embedded in an assessment-of-policies tool (APT) to aid policy analysis. Though it is not possible to predict the future, the future is not unconstrained either. The real issue is how these constraints interact with assumed policies and what will be the outcome of these interactions. Our approach here will be scenario analysis using WIM within the APT system.

"Open-loop" analysis

In this section we shall report on analyses using WIM to examine trends. For this analysis we have eliminated the major linkages between the issue areas. This allows us to use WIM to analyse the projections made by other groups and governmental agencies using essentially an open-loop method, ie we will make projections without considering the relationships among the projections. No agency or group purposely makes projections without considering the connections between those projections and developments in other issue areas. Nevertheless, because they lack a method which permits a simultaneous analysis of issues, most groups and agencies must quite subjectively and tentatively assess the impact of outside developments on their projections.

First we shall look at the open-loop analysis, and compare our projections with others in each development area. Then we shall close the major linkages and re-examine the projections. Finally, we shall undertake some scenario analysis to investigate the implications of major developments.

The important model linkages

There are some linkages which are so basic to the structure that they cannot easily be broken and were not for any of the scenarios in this analysis. These include:

- *Agricultural demand as a function of income and population.* The agricultural demand function within WIM is nonlinear and takes into account the changing dietary patterns and especially the increased demand for high quality protein which accompany changes in income. Demand is determined in each of the five agricultural categories and also takes into account some regional diet differences which are not income dependent.
- *Energy demand as a function of income and population.* Again this is a nonlinear function and energy demand cannot easily be decoupled from economic growth.
- *Machinery demand as a function of investment and economic growth.*
- *Agricultural input costs as a function of energy prices.* The concern here is primarily with fertiliser.
- *Energy and agricultural prices as a function of supply and demand.* It is easy within WIM to exogenise prices. In the open-loop analysis here, the concern was with cutting loops which connect major model units and not those within submodels such as energy. Thus prices were computed in all scenarios on a market-clearing basis. Moreover, all linkages from prices back to investment and demand were left intact.

The linkages which were severed for the open-loop analysis connect major units. These include:

- *Import volume changes as a result of chronic payments deficits.* Imports by regions with chronic balance-of-payments deficits are limited by foreign exchange and credit restrictions. When this loop is closed, import demand within each of the 12 categories of trade is reduced below the physical demand. The model structure allows for the setting of priorities by regions or import categories, eg energy or food. For this analysis no priorities were set. Note that closing this loop will affect much more than import volumes. For instance, restricting imports of machinery into less-developed countries will have a direct impact on economic growth; restricting imports of food will reduce food supplies.

● *Economic growth changes as a result of energy deficits.* Energy deficits cause reduced productivity roughly proportional to the magnitude of the shortage. It is possible, of course, to have reduced economic output because of shortages in one energy type even while adequate supplies or surpluses are available in another.

● *Fertility as a function of income.* This linkage, when intact, changes the shape of the fertility distribution within each region towards that of the distribution characterising the OECD countries. The speed of the change in fertility when income increases differs somewhat among regions to represent cultural differences.

● *Mortality changes with calorie and protein availability.* In the model, calories and protein shortages threaten predominantly the oldest and youngest. Moreover, the effect is nonlinear.

Two other loops within the model were left open in all scenarios: the linkage between starvation and reduced economic growth and the effect of environmental degradation on agricultural production, mortality, and economic growth. Both these loops were left open because of the large amount of uncertainty. Presumably, closing them would result in somewhat more pessimistic projections than those presented here.

TABLE 1. OPEN-LOOP DEMOGRAPHIC AND ECONOMIC PROJECTIONS

	GWP ($10⁹)[a]	GWP growth rate (%)	GWP per capita ($)[a]	GWP per capita growth rate (%)	Population (10⁶)	Population growth rate (%)
1975	6 080	3·5	1520	1·4	4000	1·9
1978	6 830	3·8	1610	1·8	4230	1·9
1979	7 080	3·8	1640	1·9	4310	1·9
1982	7 910	3·7	1740	1·9	4550	1·8
1985	8 820	3·7	1840	1·9	4800	1·8
1990	10 530	3·6	2010	1·8	5230	1·7
1995	12 500	3·4	2200	1·8	5680	1·7
2000	14 770	3·4	2400	1·7	6160	1·6

Note:[a] US $ at 1975 values. GWP is gross world product.

Economic projections

Table 1 presents results for global population and economy in the open-loop analysis (1975–2000). In the first column we can see that the global economy grows from $6 trillion in 1975 to $14·8 trillion in 2000.[3] The growth rate for the global economy averages approximately 3·5%, slightly below the average for the 1960s, but roughly equal to the long-run global economic growth rate.

We can compare Table 1 with the projections made by the World Bank uing their SIMLINK model.[4] In their high, medium and low projections the global economy grows to $17·4, $14·7, and $12·4 trillion respectively in the year 2000.

Population projections

The global population grows to 6·2 thousand million people and the growth rate declines from 1·9% to 1·6% by the year 2000. These projections can be compared with those prepared by the US Bureau of Census. Their three projections for global population in 2000 are 6·8, 6·4, and 5·9 billion.

GWP per capital grows from $1500 in 1975 to $2400 in the year 2000. The growth rate averages approximately 1·8%.

Both the World Bank and the US Bureau of Census projections appear to be largely open-loop extrapolations. This is particularly true of the US Bureau of Census projections. Their projections are relatively high, since other projections suggest an impact of higher global income on already decreasing fertility.

TABLE 2. OPEN-LOOP AGRICULTURAL PROJECTIONS

	Cumulative starvation deaths (10⁶)	Malnourished population (10⁶)	Per capita calorie consumption (10⁹)	Per capita protein consumption (kg)
1975	0[b]	438	0·865	24·8
1978	0	523	0·847	24·3
1979	0	502	0·854	24·5
1982	0	452	0·870	24·9
1985	0	446	0·876	25·1
1990	0	452	0·879	25·2
1995	0	545	0·870	25·1
2000	0	531	0·883	25·5
	Grain production (10⁶ metric tons)	Investment in agriculture ($10⁹)[a]	Fertiliser use (10⁶ metric tons)	Grain price ($ per metric ton)[9]
1975	1280	143	89	120
1978	1500	163	105	158
1979	1560	165	110	164
1982	1670	177	123	161
1985	1780	190	135	152
1990	1980	218	156	145
1995	2250	274	182	181
2000	2650	357	227	240

Notes: [a] US $ at 1975 prices; [b] Starvation deaths are zero because the open-loop scenario severs the link between nutrition and starvation.

Agriculture projections

Table 2 gives the open-loop projections for agriculture. Projected world production of grain grows from 1280 million metric tons to 2650 in the year 2000, an increase of 107%. The US Department of Agriculture using the GOL model made three projections. In the middle or base line case, which is based on historical yield increases, grain production increases from 1109 to 2175 million metric tons in the year 2000, an increase of 96%. Our initial values differ because we have relied upon FAO calculations of 1975 production. However, the growth rates are very similar.

The USDA also calculated the inputs required. So have we (see Table 2). Many studies have noted that the principal constraints are not physical but financial. Table 2 shows that annual investment in agriculture would have to increase by 150% before the turn of the century to obtain the desired yields.

World fertiliser use would have to grow from 89 million metric tons in 1975 to 227 million metric tons in the year 2000. The USDA project an increase in global fertiliser use from 80 to 199 million metric tons.

What does this scenario mean for global nutrition? In Table 2 the cumulative total of global starvation deaths is shown as zero, because the open-loop scenario severs the link between nutrition and starvation. The second column, however, indicates the extent of global malnutrition. In the open-loop scenario this stays roughly stable at 440 to 550 million people per year malnourished. In spite of the considerable increase in agricultural production, malnourishment continues at a high level because the average diet scarcely improves. The average global consumption of calories per capita hardly changes; neither does the average global per capita consumption of protein.

Grain prices grow from \$120 to \$240 per ton by the end of the century. That is, prices approximately double in real terms. Clearly, this is a high price which is being paid for the increased agricultural production. The USDA suggested food price increases by the end of the century of between 20% and 40% even without considering the increased prices of agricultural inputs. We have taken into account the impact of increased agricultural input prices. The much greater use of fertiliser will increase food prices, even if fertiliser prices remain stable. Fertiliser prices in the WIM model are tied to the price of oil, which is very likely to increase.

Energy projections

Global energy consumption (and production) grows from 46·0 thousand million barrels to 94·5 thousand million barrels oil equivalent in the year 2000. The world energy conference (WEC) projected consumption requirements at the end of the century ranging from 83 to 133 thousand million barrels oil equivalent. The Workshop on Alternative Energy Strategies (WAES) projected (for the non-Communist world only) requirements of from 60 to 72 thousand million barrels oil equivalent.[5] Both the WEC and WAES projections are consistent with Table 3.

TABLE 3. OPEN-LOOP ENERGY PROJECTIONS

	Energy consumption[a] (10^9 barrels oil or equivalent)						Nuclear output (10^9 watts)	Oil price (\$ per barrel)	Atmospheric CO_2 increase (%)[b]
	Total	Oil	Gas	Coal	Hydro-electric	Nuclear			
1975	46·0	22·3	9·1	13·3	0·995	0·33	96	11·50	11·8
1978	48·6	23·4	10·0	13·7	1·035	0·49	139	11·30	13·3
1979	50·2	24·2	10·4	14·0	1·049	0·54	155	11·80	13·8
1982	58·1	28·4	12·1	15·7	1·092	0·79	224	13·20	15·4
1985	68·1	33·5	13·7	18·6	1·137	1·12	319	13·10	17·3
1990	77·3	35·5	16·8	21·3	1·216	2·55	727	12·90	21·1
1995	85·9	33·8	20·7	25·0	1·298	5·10	1460	22·10	25·1
2000	94·5	32·5	24·9	28·0	1·388	7·73	2210	33·20	29·4

Notes: [a] Consumption.= production; [b] Atmospheric fossil-fuel-produced CO_2 as percentage of pre-industrial CO_2 level.

The table also shows that oil production will increase significantly by the end of the 1980s and then decline. This is consistent with the WEC analysis, which suggested a peak of global oil production at 83–104 million barrels per day in 1990. We find a peak of 104 million barrels per day in 1988. Natural gas production is likely to increase more and stabilise about the end of the century. Global coal production will more than double by the end of the century.

Nuclear power (7·7 thousand million barrels of oil equivalent by the year 2000) has a high growth rate, but this is consistent with other projections. The number of nuclear plants (1000 MW each) needed to meet this projection increases from approximately 100 to 2200 (ie 2200 GW) by the year 2000. In late 1975 the OECD projected 1700 to 2100 GW in OECD countries and 300 to 400 GW in less-developed countries. More recent estimates have been lower.

Few studies have attempted to estimate oil prices up to the year 2000. The WEC study suggested a doubling; the WAES analyses looked at three price scenarios: decreasing to $7·66 per barrel, stable at $11·50 per barrel, and increasing to $17·25 per barrel. Each of these oil prices led to global oil shortages by the beginning of the 1990s. This was also projected by WEC. The implication is that the expected price increases are too small. We find in the open-loop case (see Table 3) that prices rise to $33 per barrel by 2000, moving up sharply after 1990.

By 1975 we had added an amount of CO_2 equal to about 22% of the pre-industrial level, of which about 12% remains in the atmosphere. By 2000, the additional amount in the atmosphere will more than double.

TABLE 4. OPEN-LOOP ENERGY PROJECTIONS 2005–2025

Energy consumption[a] (10⁹ barrels oil or equivalent)						Nuclear output (10⁹ watts)	Oil price ($ per barrel)	Atmospheric CO_2 increase (%)[b]
	Total	Oil	Gas	Coal	Hydro-electric	Nuclear		
2005	107·6	30·8	30·4	32·9	1·49	12·01	3 432	43·83	34·1
2015	135·8	27·4	36·5	47·0	1·71	23·16	6 618	59·69	44·9
2025	178·3	23·2	35·3	73·3	2·00	44·51	12 719	63·25	58·2

Notes: [a] Consumption = production; [b] Atmospheric fossil-fuel-produced CO_2 as percentage of pre-industrial CO_2 level.

Table 4 shows why open-loop projections are unsatisfactory; it extends Table 3 up to 2025. Energy demand growth rate drops, mainly in response to higher energy prices, since in the open-loop analysis economic growth is quite regular. Oil production declines to very near 1975 levels by 2025. Natural gas production peaks near the end of the run. Coal and nuclear both accelerate.

By 2025, there is a nearly impossible situation. Nuclear capacity reaches 12 700 GW, a figure few would accept, and the atmospheric CO_2 levels could result in disastrous climatic changes.

Something must change these extrapolations, and it cannot be a shift from reliance on fossil fuels to nuclear energy or vice versa. It must be either a slackening of energy demand growth (and therefore of economic growth) and/or a large growth in other energy production, such as solar, which will not increase CO_2 levels. *These decisions must be made well before the problem reaches the levels shown for 2025.*

Closed-loop analysis

Here we look at projections in the four development areas using a closed-loop analysis. Among the major interactions not considered in the previous section are the impact of income increases on fertility, of food shortages on mortality, of energy deficits on economic growth, and of major balance-of-payments deficits on the ability to import all categories of goods, including food and capital equipment.

TABLE 5. CLOSED-LOOP ECONOMIC AND DEMOGRAPHIC PROJECTIONS

	GWP ($10⁹)ᵃ	GWP growth rate (%)	GWP per capita ($)ᵃ	GWP per capita growth rate (%)	Population (10⁶)	Population growth rate (%)
1975	6 080	3·5	1520	1·4	4000	1·9
1978	6 670	2·7	1580	0·9	4230	1·8
1979	6 860	2·8	1590	1·0	4300	1·8
1982	7 440	2·8	1640	1·1	4530	1·7
1985	8 200	3·6	1730	2·0	4750	1·6
1990	9 430	2·5	1840	1·0	5130	1·5
1995	10 900	2·6	1980	1·2	5510	1·4
2000	11 730	2·1	1990	0·8	5910	1·4

Note: ᵃ US $ at 1975 values.

Economic projections

Table 5 shows economic and demographic projections. Here global economic product grows to $11·7 thousand million dollars as against $14·8 thousand million—a difference of 21%. The growth rate declines. The World Bank used different growth rates before and after 1985. Our projections indicate lower growth rates until 1985 and considerably lower growth rates after 1990 relative to their study.

This is for two reasons. First, the energy shortages projected by the WEC and WAES studies do materialise in our model by the late 1980s and early 1990s. Energy consumption is reduced and energy prices rise; these consequences reduce economic growth in several regions of the world. Second, foreign debt increases, particularly in the less-developed countries. In the open-loop analysis, debt had no effect on economic growth. The combined foreign indebtedness of Africa, Asia, and Latin America increases by $288 thousand million above 1975 levels by the year 2000. This takes into account current patterns of capital

TABLE 6. CLOSED-LOOP AGRICULTURAL PROJECTIONS

	Cumulative starvation deaths (10⁶)	Malnourished population (10⁶)	Per capita calorie consumption (10⁹)	Per capita protein consumption (kg)
1975	0	438	0·865	24·8
1978	6	556	0·842	24·2
1979	9	535	0·849	24·4
1982	23	525	0·858	24·6
1985	43	545	0·858	24·7
1990	82	592	0·854	24·6
1995	122	649	0·850	24·6
2000	160	669	0·852	24·6

	Grain production (10⁶ metric tons)	Investment in agriculture ($10⁹)ᵃ	Fertiliser use (10⁶ metric tons)	Grain price ($ per metric ton)ᵃ
1975	1280	143	89	120
1978	1500	159	105	154
1979	1540	160	109	155
1982	1620	168	119	141
1985	1700	179	128	131
1990	1890	203	145	138
1995	2110	230	166	178
2000	2370	268	190	246

Note: ᵃ US $ at 1975 prices.

transfers and improvements in trade terms, and thus is in addition to the debt we would expect to be supportable. In the closed-loop analysis, the unavailability of such capital transfers (private and public) leads to a reduction in imports. The total additional indebtedness of the regions grows only to $75 thousand million at the end of the century. The model assumes that the less-developed countries can minimise their dependence upon foreign capital through increased exports.

Population projections
Global population grows only to 5·9 thousand million at the end of the century. The population growth rate declines considerably relative to the open-loop analysis, dropping just below 1·4% at the end of the century. Two important reasons for this are the impact of increased income on fertility, and the impact of starvation on mortality.

Gross world product per capita increases to just short of $2000 by the end of the century. Growth in per capita income is reduced to near zero in the last five years of the century.

A cumulative total of 160 million starvation deaths is indicated by the closed-loop analysis (Table 6). Moreover, the malnourished global population grows from 440 million to 670 million.

Agricultural projections
The world average per capita calorie and protein consumption are basically stable. This corresponds to a total global agriculture production which increases by 85% through the rest of the century (ie the grain production column). The USDA projects a 96% increase and our open-loop case projected 107%. In the closed-loop case there is less money available for investment and fertiliser. Interestingly, there is no faster growth in food prices (because fewer people buy it and incomes are lower).

How can average diets deteriorate when grain production outstrips population growth? The answer is in global meat production which increases by 57% over the 25 years, with many of the animals being fed grain.

Energy projections
Global energy production and consumption of primary fuels grows considerably slower than in the open-loop case. This now falls at the very low end of the range

TABLE 7. CLOSED-LOOP ENERGY PROJECTIONS

	Energy consumption[a] (10^9 barrels oil or equivalent)						Nuclear output (10^9 watts)	Oil price ($ per barrel)	Atmospheric CO_2 increase (%)[b]
	Total	Oil	Gas	Coal	Hydro-electric	Nuclear			
1975	46·0	22·3	9·1	13·3	0·995	0·33	96	11·50	11·8
1978	48·4	23·2	10·0	13·7	1·035	0·49	139	11·17	13·3
1979	49·9	23·8	10·4	14·0	1·049	0·54	155	11·50	13·8
1982	57·3	27·7	12·0	15·7	1·092	0·78	223	12·24	15·4
1985	63·9	30·8	13·1	17·8	1·137	1·10	315	11·43	17·2
1990	73·7	35·4	15·1	19·5	1·215	2·51	717	11·25	20·7
1995	81·1	35·3	18·1	21·7	1·295	4·80	1372	12·68	24·6
2000	86·4	33·3	21·0	23·9	1·378	6·94	1983	19·64	28·6

Notes: [a] Consumption = production; [b] Atmospheric fossil-fuel-produced CO_2 as percentage of pre-industrial CO_2 level.

set by WEC. Production of all energy types is somewhat reduced, and nuclear output is slightly less than 2000 GW by the end of the century. In this scenario the price of oil is relatively stable until about 1990 and then it increases quickly to a level just short of $20 per barrel by the year 2000 (Table 7).

The effect of closing loops

Generally, those making projections in, say, agriculture or energy try to account for demographic and economic changes. Thus we find that the results of our closed-loop analysis still fall near the low end of the range of the projections made for agriculture and energy. In economics, however, relatively few projections take into account developments in resources, demography, or agriculture. Our closed-loop projections fall well short of even the least rapid growth scenario of the World Bank. Similarly, our population projections fall well short of all the projections made by the US Bureau of Census.

In the latter case, the reasons are combinations of starvation and reduced fertility. The Community and Family Planning Center (CFPC) Study attempted to account for the impact of income on fertility. They made three projections of the global population at the end of the century (5·6, 5·5, and 5·3 thousand million). All these values fall below even low projections of the US Bureau of Census. In the closed-loop case our projection is relatively close to the high projection of the CFPC group. However, the closed-loop case reduces income and hence it does not result in a dramatic reduction in fertility.

In fact, the CFPC projections require major fertility changes: *all* regions would need to reach equilibrium levels within 25 years; and global population growth would need to drop from 1·9% to 0·8% by 1990. These projections seem unlikely.

The importance of interactions

It should be clear that it is completely inadequate to base projections solely on expected developments within an issue area. *It is necessary to close the loops because when there are problems or crises in one issue area, those problems dramatically affect other areas.* When the systems are operating relatively well, they can be treated as relatively independent, eg as long as economic growth has been adequate, agricultural planners have not needed to worry about the availability of investment for agriculture.

The closed-loop analysis here has been *nearly* problem-free. We made more optimistic assumptions than the WAES study about energy availability; we allowed the less-developed countries' debt to grow faster than capital transfers have been growing; we allowed production of grain to grow by 85% with an increase in agricultural investment of only 87%, essentially ignoring increased costs of land development and decreasing returns. In spite of these optimistic assumptions, the closed-loop projections significantly differed from the open-loop projections.

Global problems *must* be studied in a comprehensive global framework. In the next section we analyse, using a closed-loop model, some major global problem areas.

Problem area analysis

At least three major problems can be identified: the availability and the price of energy resources (and, by implication of other resources); the continued ability of agriculture to increase yields at or above historical rates, even in the face of potentially deteriorating climatic conditions; and the indebtedness of the less developed countries. In this section we will spell out more conservative assumptions for each of these problem areas than were made in either the open-loop or closed-loop analyses. We will then look at a scenario combining these conservative assumptions—the worst-case scenario.[6]

In our closed-loop analysis we made optimistic energy assumptions: continued rapid growth in petroleum and natural gas production. The assumptions were more optimistic than those made in most of the WAES scenarios. We shall examine here the consequences of a slightly less optimistic scenario. We had assumed before that annual global oil discoveries would grow until the early 1990s and reach a peak approximately 50% higher than the annual discoveries of the early 1970s. The WEC and WAES studies projected near stable annual discoveries of oil resources. We will use the stable-discovery assumption in our combined-problem scenario.

For the combined-problem scenario, we have introduced a return to more irregular weather and the use of marginal land, resulting in a decrease in agricultural productivity of approximately 20% relative to the current period, ie given equivalent inputs of agriculture yields are reduced by roughly 20% by the year 2000.

Higher food and energy prices will intensify the problems of indebtedness for the less-developed countries. In the combined-problem scenario we assume practically no increase in indebtedness.

The simultaneous occurrence of these three problems cannot be ruled out. Thus we have developed a scenario in which the problems develop simultaneously (Tables 8–10). Economic growth is considerably reduced, gross world product reaches only to $10·4 trillion at the turn of the century.[3] Average per capita income grows in 25 years only by 18% (to $1800 by the year 2000).

Agricultural production falls and prices rise by 69% relative to the closed-loop case. Increased prices spur increases in agricultural investment, so that overall grain production falls by only 14% relative to the reference case.

TABLE 8. COMBINED-PROBLEM SCENARIO: DEMOGRAPHIC AND ECONOMIC PROJECTIONS

	GWP ($10⁹)[a]	GWP growth rate (%)	GWP per capita ($)[a]	GWP per capita growth rate (%)	Population (10⁶)	Population growth rate (%)
1975	6 080	3·5	1520	1·4	4000	1·9
1978	6 530	1·7	1550	0·1	4220	1·7
1979	6 670	2·2	1560	0·4	4290	1·7
1982	7 120	2·5	1580	0·9	4500	1·6
1985	7 860	3·7	1670	2·3	4700	1·4
1990	8 890	2·2	1760	0·9	5040	1·4
1995	9 590	1·0	1780	0·3	5390	1·3
2000	10 380	2·2	1810	0·9	5740	1·2

Note: [a] US $ at 1975 values.

TABLE 9. COMBINED-PROBLEM SCENARIO: AGRICULTURAL PROJECTIONS

	Cumulative starvation deaths (10⁶)	Malnourished population (10⁶)	Per capita calorie consumption (10⁹)	Per capita protein consumption (kg)
1975	0	438	0·865	24·8
1978	19	602	0·832	24·0
1979	26	593	0·837	24·1
1982	59	620	0·837	24·1
1985	99	663	0·833	24·1
1990	166	719	0·827	24·0
1995	227	761	0·827	24·0
2000	292	784	0·833	24·1

	Grain production (10⁶ metric tons)	Investment in agriculture ($10⁹)ᵃ	Fertiliser use (10⁶ metric tons)	Grain price ($ per metric ton)⁹
1975	1280	143	89	120
1978	1460	159	105	155
1979	1500	160	110	159
1982	1550	169	122	162
1985	1620	182	134	177
1990	1770	202	159	245
1995	1880	232	185	333
2000	2030	320	228	415

Note: ᵃ US $ at 1975 prices.

TABLE 10. COMBINED-PROBLEM SCENARIO: AGRICULTURAL PROJECTIONS

	Energy consumption ᵃ (10⁹ barrels oil or equivalent)						Nuclear output (10⁹ watts)	Oil price ($ per barrel)	Atmospheric CO₂ increase (%)ᵇ
	Total	Oil	Gas	Coal	Hydro-electric	Nuclear			
1975	46·0	22·3	9·1	13·3	0·995	0·33	96	11·50	11·8
1978	48·1	22·9	10·0	13·7	1·035	0·49	139	10·99	13·3
1979	49·4	23·4	10·3	14·0	1·049	0·54	155	11·11	13·8
1982	55·9	26·8	11·7	15·5	1·092	0·78	222	11·25	15·4
1985	61·1	29·1	12·6	17·2	1·137	1·09	311	10·54	17·1
1990	69·1	32·2	14·6	18·6	1·215	2·47	705	10·53	20·5
1995	71·3	28·1	17·0	20·5	1·297	4·46	1276	15·39	23·9
2000	74·1	24·2	19·9	22·3	1·381	6·25	1787	27·79	27·4

Notes: ᵃ Consumption = production; ᵇ Atmospheric fossil-fuel-produced CO_2 as percentage of pre-industrial CO_2 level.

Nevertheless, the lower agriculture production and higher prices lead to an increase in starvation deaths (by 83%) and a considerable increase in world malnutrition.

Energy production and consumption grow less rapidly (see Table 10) than in earlier scenarios, reaching 74 thousand million barrels oil equivalent at the end of the century. This is below the WAES and WEC projections and raises question about the consistency of their supply and demand projections. The price of oil increases more rapidly near the end of the century, reaching $28 per barrel in the year 2000.[7] Oil production peaks at a slightly lower level (92 million barrels per day), still quite high in the range of WEC projections. The growth in other energy forms is also reduced—nuclear output is "only" 1787 GW in this scenario.

This is a worst-case scenario, yet none of the assumptions is unreasonable.

Extending the time horizon

Many of the systems are very slow to change, especially population. Our projections (open loop, closed loop, and combined) differ only by 7% in the year 2000. Yet global population growth rates in the three scenarios range from 1·6% down to 1·2%, implying much greater differences after the turn of the century (see Figure 2). The open-loop, closed-loop, and combined-problem scenarios lead to populations in 2025 of 8·70, 7·95 and 7·59 thousand million, respectively, a difference of 15%.

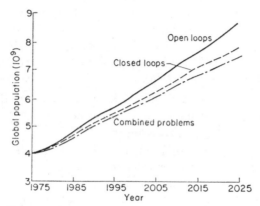

Figure 2. Global population in the three scenarios

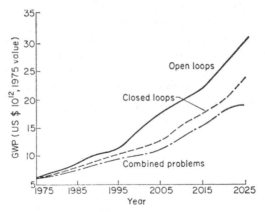

Figure 3. GWP in the three scenarios

By 2025 the global world product reaches $31·3, $24·9 and $19·6 trillion dollars. The gap between the scenarios grows from 47% in 2000 to 60% in 2025 (see Figure 3).

Other variables also diverge. Global grain production ranges from 5·2 to 3·7 thousand million metric tons (interestingly, the closed-loop scenario is only 4·1 thousand million metric tons). Global primary energy demand ranges from 178 to 116 thousand million barrels of oil equivalent.

It clearly matters a great deal whether those attempting to plan for the 21st century use an open-loop or closed-loop analysis.

Regional implications

Although GWP increases by 75% even in the combined-problem scenario, and GWP per capita increases in each of the scenarios, the global totals obscure severe problems at the regional level.

Obviously, some of the regions can cope better (eg North America, see Figure 4). In each scenario, per capita GNP grows to over $10 000 by the end of the century, and the final levels differ by only 10%.

Latin America and other less-developed regions are much less able to cope with agricultural yield decreases, energy shortages, or restrictions on capital (Figure 5). In the open-loop scenario the growth of GNP in Latin America is faster than the growth in North America. Population growth, however, reduces the per capita increases to about the same level as North America. In the other scenarios Latin America fares less well, and the gap between the scenarios is approximately 30% by the year 2000.

Slower economic growth has severe implications for the less-developed regions. In the combined-problem scenario, grain consumption per capita in Africa actually declines (Figure 6).

Average per capita incomes in 1975 were $370 in the less-developed world. In the open-loop case these incomes grow to $590 per capita. In the closed-loop scenario and the combined-problems scenario the per capita income in the less-developed countries only grows to $500, or to $410, respectively (Figure 7).[8]

The economies of the less-developed countries grow *more rapidly* than those of the developed countries in all scenarios and the ratio of their gross national products (excluding communist countries) is reduced from seven in 1975 to about five in the year 2000. The per capita ratio however, is currently 12·6 and it increases to 14 at the turn of the century due to unequal population growth rates. This, and the relatively slow growth of per capita income even in the open-loop scenario, underscores the importance of realistic projections and appropriate planning.

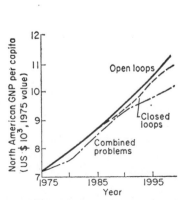

Figure 5. GNP per capita in Latin America in the three scenarios

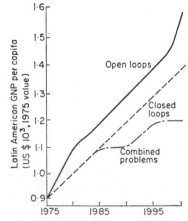

Figure 4. GNP per capita in North America in the three scenarios

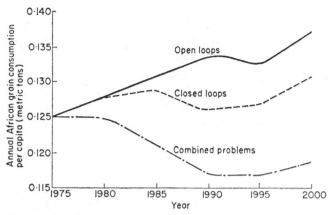

Figure 6. Annual grain consumption per capita in Africa in the three scenarios

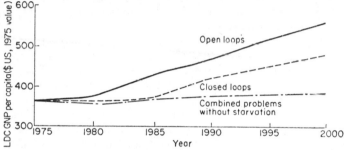

Figure 7. GNP per capita in the less-developed countries (Latin America, the non-oil producing Middle East, South and South-East Asia, and Africa) in the three scenarios

Conclusions

It is absolutely essential that major global development patterns be considered simultaneously. When we examined the open-loop economic, demographic, agriculture, and energy projections of the WIM system, we found that our projections agreed very well with those made by a variety of governmental agencies, private and public groups.

When we closed the loops, our global economic projections fell approximately 21% below those in the open-loop analysis, and were in fact lower than the lowest projection made by the World Bank. Similarly, our demographic projections had been well within the range of those made by the US Bureau of Census in the open-loop analysis, but in the closed-loop study global population projections fell by approximately 5% at the end of the century (outside of the range indicated by the Census Bureau). Similarly with agriculture and energy: energy demand, and food production and consumption (especially on a per capita basis) proved to be lower than that made by major studies in the area.

The use of an integrated methodology for long-term global projections is crucial; a problem in any one area, will have significant consequences for all the others. Problems in energy resources, agricultural production, and balance of payments highlighted the importance of the closed-loop projections. The open-loop and closed-loop analyses had made relatively optimistic assumptions in each of these areas.

Regional analysis is important. None of the scenarios led to negative consequences for all regions of the world. Higher agricultural prices do not necessarily hurt American economic growth anymore than higher oil prices hurt OPEC economies. The position of the less-developed countries is, however, extremely precarious. Economic growth closes the gap between the less-developed countries and the more-developed countries in absolute terms, but not in per capita terms. The less-developed countries are therefore particularly vulnerable to the problems, and their linkages, which we have discussed.

Notes and references

1. The first generation model was the basis for the second report to the Club of Rome, Mihajlo Mesarovic and Eduard Pestel, *Mankind at the Turning Point* (New York, Dutton, 1974).
2. WIM has, for example, a population submodel which represents the population in each region, and fertility and mortality distributions, each by 86 age categories. The economic submodel treats production and capital formation in seven economic sectors. The agricultural model handles five categories of food production: grain, non-grain, industrial crops, fish, and livestock. The energy model represents resources, production, demand, trade, and pricing for five different energy types: oil, gas, coal, hydroelectric power, and nuclear power. The materials submodel handles the same elements for iron, aluminium, and copper. The labour/education submodel divides the population into four categories by educational level: uneducated, primary education only, secondary education, university or professional training. There is also a machinery submodel within WIM, because of the great importance for the less-developed regions in particular of machinery purchases.
3. Trillion is used here in the American sense, as one million million, or 10^{12}.
4. We have drawn heavily on a wide variety of governmental and non-governmental reports; these include reports from the World Bank, the US Department of Energy, the US Bureau of Census, the US Department of Agriculture, the World Energy Conference, and The Workshop on Alternative Energy Strategies. Many of the projections are from unpublished submissions to the project Global 2000. For a discussion of SIMLINK, see World Bank, "The SIMLINK model of trade and growth for the developing world", working paper 20, October 1975.
5. We have also undertaken a more detailed analysis of the WAES scenarios, *Energy: Global Prospects* 1985–2000 (New York, McGraw-Hill, 1977), in Barry B. Hughes and Mihajlo D. Mesarovic, "Analysis of the WAES scenarios using the World Integrated Model", *Energy Policy*, June 1978, 6 (2), pages 129–139. See also World Energy Conference, Conservation Commission, *Report on World Energy Demand* (London World Energy Conference, 1977).
6. In our report to the Council on Environmental Quality we looked at the impact of problems in each area in turn. Here we have shortened the discussion by treating the problems together.
7. When the lower discovery rate alone is inserted into the closed-loop analysis, the price reaches $34 per barrel in the year 2000.
8. Many readers may believe that global starvation will be avoided. For Figure 7 we did not allow for starvation in the combined-problem scenario. When it is allowed for, the per capita income moves towards the level in the closed-loop analysis.

SARUM 76—A GLOBAL MODELLING PROJECT

P. C. Roberts

Potential world models and attitudes towards them are discussed, as the setting for development of a new model by the Systems Analysis Research Unit. The main features of this model are described and argument is presented for the choice of structure. Sensitivity analysis suggests that the two parameters having most influence on whether runs are "acceptable" or "not acceptable", are population and level of trade barriers. No clear indication has emerged to support either the doom school or the technological optimists, nor is it obvious that there are practicable policies which yield unequivocal improvement. It is proposed that the generalised character and scope for development of the new model makes it useful for wider investigations of global problems.

In the wake of Forrester's *World Dynamics*[1] and Meadows' *Limits to Growth*,[2] three schools of thought can be distinguished. I call these descriptive, normative and nihilistic.

Descriptive

Both Forrester and Meadows attempted to devise structures which represent the world system adequately enough to project decades ahead. Though it is not a view that comes readily from critics, both World 2 and World 3 are in the tradition of the natural sciences. To try to account for the changes of particular variables observed in a system by using a few simple relationships and a few parameters is a pursuit common to such diverse disciplines as astronomy, ecology, and economics. It can be objected that the models offered by the MIT Systems Dynamics School were underresearched, oversimplified and prematurely published—but these defects are not unknown in the traditional sciences. As G. K. Chesterton said—if the thing is worth doing at all it is worth doing badly.

P. C. Roberts is Head of Systems Analysis Research Unit, Department of the Environment, 2 Marsham Street, London SW1, UK. The views expressed in this paper are those of the author and do not necessarily coincide with those of the Department of the Environment. © Crown copyright 1977.

World modelling of food production (as seen by an economist) has been carried out recently by Professor Linnemann and his team at the Free University of Amsterdam in the MOIRA project.[3] This enterprise is descriptive—and more accurately descriptive—than World 2 or World 3. *SARUM 76* is also descriptive in form[4] for reasons to be explained shortly.

Normative

There is an unsavoury flavour of fatalism about the earliest world-modelling accounts. World dynamics contains runs with parameters varied, but with the runs still showing eventual collapse. While we may speculate dispassionately on the reasons for lemmings to make their headlong rush into the sea, there is a contradiction about conscious beings charting their future suicide. The normative approach to modelling entails the definition of goals to be reached and thence the adjustments and steps by which this will be achieved. Dr Herrera[5] and his team at the Fundacion Bariloche in Argentina are strong proponents of such normative modelling. The difficulty of weighting the separate, desirable objectives of adequate food, housing, health, and education has been met by subsuming them under the general goal of maximising life expectancy. Given a set of constraints applying to investment, labour mobility, etc the optimal strategy can be computed by mathematical programming methods.

The Mesarovic–Pestel work takes the form of simulations,[6] but introduces the normative element through interruptions and iterations to discover better alternative strategies.

Nihilistic

There are critics of world modelling who argue that the models are only embodiments of the particular set of prejudices held by the modeller. Hence the models tell us much about the designer, but nothing about the world.

I regard this as a form of nihilism because, if it were true, it would exclude any possibility of useful model construction. It can be reasonably supposed that critics of this sort do not hold the same opinion about the models of the natural sciences, so one wonders where the line should be drawn—are models of national economies to be rejected, or perhaps models of company operation? Allied to the extreme form of criticism which dismisses all world models, is the stressing of value-laden science. It is said that no science is "value free". If this is intended to mean that the areas chosen for investigation spring from the culture of the society which the scientist inhabits then it is obviously true, but trivial. If it is being proposed that the form and structure of scientific theories are culturally dependent then this would pose severe problems in verification of the proposition: but the worth of testing the proposition is dubious. A scientific theory is only interesting to the extent that evidence can be adduced to support it and tests devised to discriminate between it and alternative theories. Although one may be curious to know the politics, religion, and education of a scientist, the only thing that actually matters is the durability of his theory under the onslaught of testing.

Finally, among the variations of nihilism is the suggestion that exposing the results of modelling exercises only makes people miserable without serving any compensatory purpose. This is a view that merits some sympathy because if the world were indeed doomed and nothing could be done to prevent it, then apart from some religious motives ("repent, for the end is nigh") there could be no benefit in proclaiming the fact.

The Systems Analysis Research Unit

After the Stockholm conference on the environment in 1972, the momentum created gave rise to the formation of a UK Civil Service interdepartmental committee to consider the problems of resource scarcity, population growth, and environmental damage on a global scale. Concurrently with this initiative, a research unit was established to investigate the quantitative basis of the "problematique". From the Committee has come a discussion paper,[7] and from the Systems Analysis Research Unit has come a series of articles and papers on the problems of world modelling,[8] energy analysis,[9] food production in South Asia,[10] the income elasticity of demand for energy,[11] and the physical basis for metal prices.[12] More recently there has been exposure of modelling technique developed in SARU and presented at the fourth symposium on global modelling held by the International Institute of Systems Analysis.[13]

Evolution of a model

We have grown accustomed to the compilation of inventories—reserves of oil and coal, quantities of cultivable land, maximum sustainable catches of fish, areas of forest etc. Often there are stern warnings accompanying the inventory statements suggesting that rate of use divided into quantity available yields only a decade or two. Now this is a naïve use of inventory figures. Much more useful is a style commonly employed to display uranium availability: X Mt at $\$x$ kg^{-1}, Y Mt at $\$y$ kg^{-1}, and so on. The concept of "depletion functions" is applicable to almost all resources, ie one can have some more but at increased cost per unit.

Observation of human behaviour, individually and collectively indicates that if a commodity rises in price then there will result, sooner or later, a diminished rate of purchase. In the economist's terms, the price elasticity of demand is nonzero.

Two further factors affect the production–consumption equation. In many sectors of production there are ways of increasing the productivity of labour. This is often done by the effective substitution of capital equipment for workers. As well as substitution, the combined capital–labour mix improves in a variety of ways which can be subsumed within the broad category of technical progress.

There can be no useful verdict on the problem of a potential grave shortage or consequent hardship until the sums have been done to reveal the effects of depletion, elasticity of demand and progress through capital substitution and technical progress. In addition, other factors will also obtrude. If real wages are rising, then the products of any labour-intensive industry will appear more and more expensive. The provision of capital equipment depends on a continuing stream of investment and if returns on investment are falling, where is the incentive to be found? Delving deeper into these and similar questions requires a general explanation of how human societies have coped (or failed to cope) with similar sorts of problems in the past. Economists have offered verbal explanations of the feedbacks which operate to restore equilibrium to economic structures—and there is an extensive literature dealing with the mathematics of the equilibrium state. The difficulties of modelling nonequilibrium behaviour have been tackled by control engineers, ecologists, and—in a new guise—by systems dynamicists. A team comprising control engineers, biologists, economists, physicists, and operational researchers might be able to assemble a dynamic model of an economy which would be a close enough representation of real economies to allow the problems of potential shortages to be examined more realistically than by contemplating inventories.

SARUM philosophy

The models devised in the SARU contain feedback mechanisms which correspond to the verbal descriptions of classical economics. The diagraph representation which illustrates the feedback loops for a single sector of an economy is

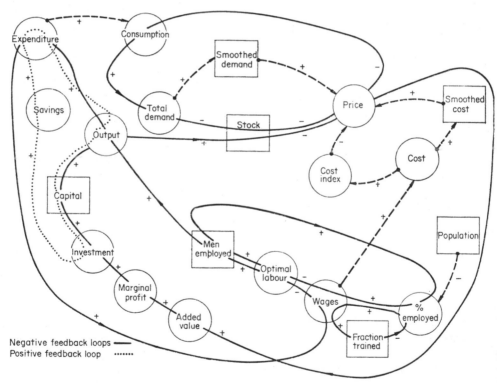

Figure 1.

shown in Figure 1. The full-line loops are negative, ie tending to restore equilisbrium, the dotted loop is positive, and the dashed lines are minor (nondominant) effects. An assembly of such modelled sectors exhibits the sort of behaviour seen in real economies (Adam Smith's "hidden hand" at work), but it is not designed to provide convincing simulations of booms and slumps. An analogy with climatology may be helpful here. Weather forecasting, ie of short term effects local in time and place, is important for many purposes but to the climate modeller this local variation is "noise" in the larger changes that he is seeking.

The assembly of sectors to yield whole economies can be followed by the linkage of economies through trade to represent a global economy. Several objections can be raised to the use of such a model and all of these have been faced:

1. There is an in-built assumption that the restorative feedback loops are always effective, and that the distortions from a free-market structure do not upset their equilibrating properties.

    The argument on distortions parallels the physicists' case for supposing frictionless pulleys or inelastic strings in the first instance and then modifying the model to mirror additional real-world effects as they are shown to be important.
2. Such a model would be difficult to calibrate and even if all the data required were available—the projections would be subject to too great an error to be useful.

    It is true that some variables and parameters can only be considered as probability-density functions, ie the "noise" background is high. However, the objective is not to predict but to discover the region of choice left when the many constraints have been taken into account. This is much less demanding.
3. Technical progress consists not only of steady improvements of productivity but also of the emergence of totally new sectors whose key features cannot be foreseen prior to their invention or development.

    The emergence of new sectors is modelled by postulating "seeds"— sectors in embryo form which can grow when the economic climate becomes favourable. This can be done for the next few decades, because the sectors coming to fruition in that time must now exist in "seed" form. Clearly the visualisation of future seeds is too speculative to be useful— hence an effective time horizon on modelling of about 50 years.
4. No account is taken of the different political regimes and their inter-ference with market operations.

    Although political regimes are very different in form, the functions of produc-tion and distribution are necessarily similar. The demands of the populace for food and other goods do not differ much. The overall objectives are manifestly similar even though the efficiency of achieving them may be noticeably different. Finally the physical constraints are no more or less pressing.
5. It is essential to be able to describe demand qualitatively, and the demand pattern is quite different between, say, the USA and China.

    A careful study of demand patterns across income variations of two orders of magnitude indicates that consumption is very closely related to the level of income. For example, Figure 2 shows the expenditure per capita on food across a range of countries spanning wide differences in income per capita. Complications arise as "inferior goods" (in the eco-nomists' jargon) are discarded—the substitution of animal products for grains in diet illustrates this. A general demand function can be specified.

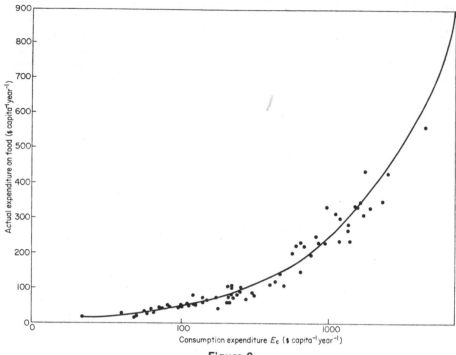

Figure 2.

6. The only outputs from the model are physical quantities, prices, and money flows. The quality of life is nowhere apparent.

   If the model is constructed to study the effect of physical constraints and the possible responses of an adaptive species to the pressure of constraints, that is in itself a useful enterprise. The fact that nothing is being said about repression, wars etc only reflects the fact that models never catch all the features of the real world.

7. Only tenuous connections link population changes with economic variables, so the structure cannot be complete.

   Causal models of fertility are not yet satisfactory enough to use confidently as a part of world models. A very convincing cross-sectional relation between crude birth rate and GNP per capita can be shown with birthrate falling: as GNP rises. However, the effect of recessions appears to be to depress the birthrate—the opposite result from that suggested by the cross-sectional data. It is therefore appropriate to run the model in an exploratory fashion to discover the consequences of a range of population scenarios.

Features of the model

The model is operated through a dynamic simulation program with a time step which can be varied, but is currently two months.[14] The relations between the values of state variables and change rates are defined by differential equations, and the integration routine can be chosen but is currently Euler. The program is written in Fortran and consists of a main central spine with successive subroutines called. Economies can be defined by any chosen number of sectors, and the current version contains 13 sectors: capital goods; minerals; primary energy; land; water; cereals and roots; fruit and vegetables; agricultural services; other crops (excluding food); vegetable processing; livestock production; livestock processing; consumer goods (excluding food).

The number of country blocs or regions can be chosen and the current version uses three strata selected by income bands as shown in Table 1. It will be ap-

TABLE 1. WORLDS OF THE MODEL

Income per capita (1968$)	Countries included
Stratum 1 > $3500	USA
Stratum 2 $650–3500	Most of Europe, Canada, Japan, Australisia
Stratum 3 < $650	Essentially the third world: India, China, Indonesia most of South America and Africa

parent from the choice of sectors that the main emphasis of the model is on food. The reason for this emphasis is that food supply as a global problem is much more severe in both the short- and long-term than the supply of minerals or energy. Ways of maintaining energy supplies are well understood and quite modest price increases will stimulate both production and extensive economies in use. In the case of mineral sources, it is only for elements of low crustal abundance that any difficulty is likely to arise. Mercury is often cited as a problem, but it is hard to find uses for which mercury has no substitute. The only "uniquely useful" elements of low abundance are helium (cryogenics), silver (high-resolution photography), and phosphorus in living systems (particularly adenosine tri- and di-phosphate). Only the phosphorus appears to set a real limit over a period of more than a millenium and there is good reason to think that, in the longer term, recycling techniques could be made sufficiently effective to avoid phosphorus starvation. In contrast, additional cultivable land and the necessary irrigation water to accompany it are in such short supply that a real physical limit could be apparent before a mere three or four doublings of population have occurred (even with a worldwide vegetarian diet). This is not meant to suggest that energy and mineral supply problems are negligible but that it will be appropriate to examine them by disaggregating sectors currently representing them.

The base year is taken as 1968 and the calibration is performed to ensure that all physical flows accord with recorded figures at that time. Labour figures are less secure and the values of capital even less so. A hierarchy of data from secure, to error-prone, to nonexistent faces the modeller. The weight given to each layer of the hierarchy is related to this security, and the dubious material is constrained by the requirements of self-consistency.

Production functions are taken as Cobb Douglas.[15] Some detailed analysis of production in cereal growing suggests a CES (constant elasticity of substitution) function with gamma equals 0·5 approximately is a better representation, but tests with varied gamma values show that the runs are not particularly sensitive to this factor. Here again the program is structured to accommodate alternative production functions. Indeed for agriculture a more elaborate function is essential because the output is constrained by the factors of land area, fertilizer application, and irrigation levels, rather than by the labour and machinery employed.

Depletion functions have been constructed using a mass of empirical evidence. The diminishing returns to increased applications of fertiliser and water, the increased cost of bringing into cultivation successive additional millions of hectares of land, the rising cost of securing the next additional million gallons per year of irrigation water have each been studied by crop, and by zone, within each stratum. One example of a depletion relation is shown in Figure 3. The increased cost of providing irrigation water rises sharply in the second stratum as the possibilities of tube wells are exhausted and interbasin transfer becomes necessary.

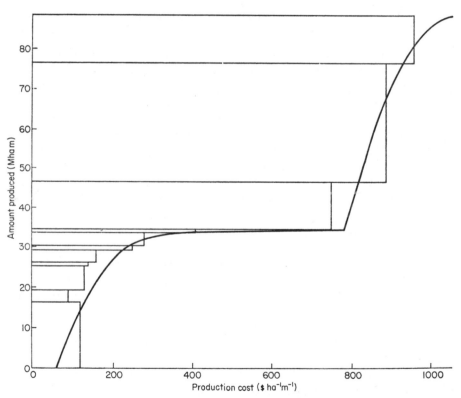

Figure 3. The cost of irrigation

Continued technical progress in food production (better cultivars, more effective use of fertilisers, etc) and a further rise in labour productivity is assumed. In addition, the emergence of a single-cell protein industry supplying alternative animal feedstuffs has been modelled as a seed sector which can grow if the economic climate becomes favourable. It is found that this potential industry becomes viable before the end of this century in the first and second strata, though not in the third.

Results

A run of the model generates a large amount of output in terms of wages, prices, income per capita, output of sectors, etc and it is practicable to refer here only to the main significant findings to date. Apart from the usual sensitivity tests to assess the effect of changing each parameter in turn, a slightly smaller version (three strata, ten sectors) was tested by sampling probability distributions for each of the parameters simultaneously (Monte Carlo) in order to discover any synergistic effects and to find the range over which a linear expression is adequate

TABLE 2. VALUES OF K^{-1} (for 40 countries during this century)

Country	K^{-1} (years)	Country	K^{-1} (years)
Denmark	93	Czechoslovakia	40
Finland	69	German Democratic Republic	32
Ireland	545	Hungary	27
Norway	123	Poland	61
Sweden	69	Romania	83
England and Wales	79	Greece	87
Austria	36	Italy	68
Belgium	55	Portugal	121
F.R. Germany	55	Spain	100
France	94	Yugoslavia	76
Netherlands	158	Ceylon	296
Switzerland	111	Chile	129
Canada	163	Taiwan	253
USA	143	Jamaica	1130
Argentina	140	W. Malaysia	477
Australia	293	Mauritius	313
NZ	455	Mexico	1690
Japan	107	Puerto Rico	168
USSR	51	Singapore	688
Bulgaria	48	Trinidad and Tobago	714

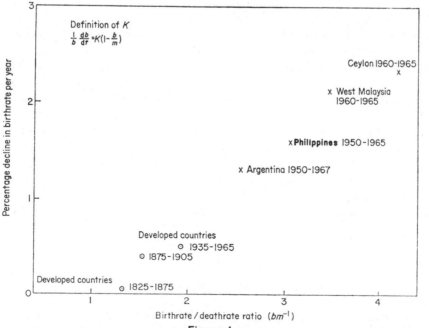

Figure 4.

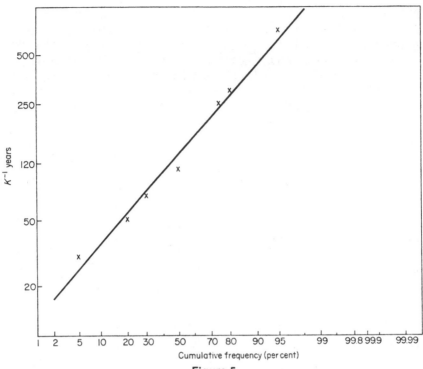

Figure 5.

for the synthesis of separate sources of uncertainty. The outcome of these several tests indicate that only a small set of the parameters has any significant effect on the variable values at given time points in a run.

The parameters which can result in striking changes to the run results are: (1) the population "control" parameter; (2) the values used for "trade barriers".

The first of these refers to the slope of the line which can be drawn through a set of points with coordinates representing the crude birthrate/crude deathrate ratio and the percentage decline in birthrate with time, as shown in Figure 4. Table 2 and Figure 5 give the parameter values and distribution. The second term relates to the degree of stiffness operating in trade. A trade barrier of unity implies completely free trade with no tariffs present, and a value of infinity implies that all economies attempt complete self-sufficiency.[16]

If: there are n trading countries or blocs and a given good has price ρ_j purchased from the jth country, then a proportion ϕ_{ij} of demand is satisfied by supply from the jth country.

A bias b_{ij} is postulated so that:

$$\phi_{ij} = \frac{f(b_{ij}\rho_j)}{\sum\limits_{k=1}^{n} f(b_{ik}\rho_k)}, \qquad (b_{ii} = 1),$$

where f is some monotonically decreasing function conveniently chosen to be $f(x) = x^{-\gamma}$.

A trade-bias matrix for values applying in recent years is shown in Table 3 and a distribution of these biases in Figure 6. Runs can be split into two classes:

TABLE 3. TRADE BIASES (based on data for 1968)

Bias of	Bias against 1	2	3	4	5	6	7	8	9	10	11
1 USA	1·00	1·61	2·27	3·24	7·02	3·01	2·76	2·32	2·62	15·52	2·62
2 Canada	2·99	1·00	3·82	4·19	8·44	4·15	4·87	4·14	4·50	8·17	4·18
3 Latin America	3·51	3·45	1·00	3·42	4·60	5·64	5·13	3·70	5·50	6·17	5·14
4 W. Europe	2·85	2·25	2·28	1·00	3·03	1·79	1·56	2·88	2·09	4·22	2·10
5 USSR + E. Europe	7·73	4·64	3·61	3·28	1·00	—	2·97	4·77	3·67	4·00	4·25
6 S. Africa	6·27	5·35	8·42	7·67	—	1·00	4·13	5·06	4·96	—	5·10
7 Less developed Africa	5·31	5·73	5·85	3·09	4·87	2·30	1·00	3·39	3·68	5·27	5·15
8 Japan	3·95	3·13	3·60	4·63	5·45	2·51	3·21	1·00	2·48	4·62	2·39
9 Less developed Asia	3·49	3·72	4·90	3·00	4·38	4·31	3·18	2·27	1·00	3·41	2·79
10 Centrally planned Asia	—	4·43	5·69	5·67	4·63	—	4·96	4·32	5·69	1·00	4·14
11 Australia + New Zealand	5·14	3·98	8·71	4·11	11·63	4·75	6·02	3·86	3·90	7·56	1·00

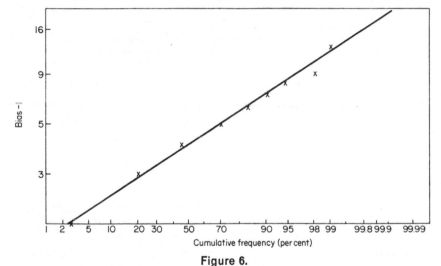

Figure 6.

those in which the food intake per capita of the third stratum turns down at some future point in time and continues downwards thereafter; and those in which this does not occur. The parameters which exert most effect in deciding the class of run are the two defined above.

The fact that these two factors are important is not surprising. A weak population control parameter results in continuing explosive population growth and the stark impossibility of carrying through all the measures required to accelerate food production at the necessary rate. Nor is it unreasonable that a stiffening of trade barriers should exacerbate the situation, because the high population-growth regions do not correlate well with the potential food-producing regions, and the transport of food between the two could ameliorate hunger.

The interest is not so much in these qualitative comments but in the quantitative relations between control parameters, trade barriers and a split between unacceptable projections in which the majority of the world's population continue to receive less food per person and the acceptable projections where this does not occur. In Figure 7 the boundary line separating these two sorts of future has been delineated by searching with repeated runs using different

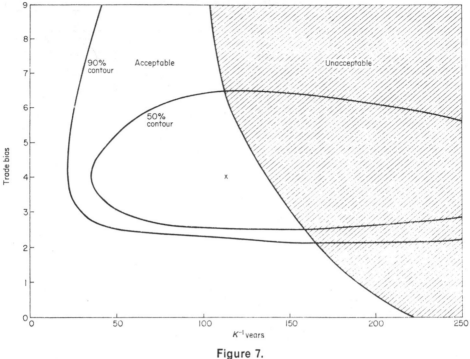

Figure 7.

values for the parameters. It is not possible to put a dot on this diagram labelled: "We are here". The situation is analogous to defining the position of an electron where the best that can be done is to draw contours showing the probability of it being in some particular part of space. Hence the contours of probability are shown in Figure 7.

This result will be of no comfort to either the doom school or the technological optimists.

Policy

The SARUM structure is designed to describe the operation of the various mechanisms which are observable, in rather the same way as an ecologist looks at the species interactions in an ecosystem. The argument about looking and describing before prescribing is the same as the ecologist would use. Not until you have some confidence that you understand the main features of the system under study should you undertake macro-changes.

It is not at all obvious what changes are desirable from a general consensus viewpoint. Some of the experiments performed with SARUM suggest that the trade-offs involve value judgements on which dispute can be expected. If, for example, the income distribution in the third stratum is brought nearer to equality then the effects, operating through demand to food production, result in improved food intake per capita. However the rate at which vulnerability is reached, in terms of closeness to the cultivable land limit, becomes accelerated.

Though higher values of the population control parameter may be considered desirable by very many people, it is not clear how this is to be brought about. The initial data show no consistent relations in respect of factors like income per capita or growth rate. One is reluctantly obliged to conclude that major prescriptive measures do not emerge clearly. This is not necessarily disheartening: we understand a great deal more about the dynamic behaviour of ecosystems than we did 50 years ago—sufficient in fact for the principles of good management to be starting to appear.

Model development

In order to facilitate the process of evolutionary model development SARUM has been cast in a very generalised form. It is a testbed for performing experiments. Large numbers of experiments have been tried on Forrester's World 2 because it is easy to set up on a computer and simple to change the relationships which are defined by look-up tables. Unfortunately World 2 is too simplified to be interesting. It lacks some of the feedback loops which are glaringly obvious in the world about us. It is too aggregated to tell you when a part of the world is suffering and the rest going scot free. Interesting and productive work is more likely to come from a structure which, though still as transparent as World 2, contains more of the texture of the real world and more scope for progressive disaggregation.

Modelling experiments should be repeatable by separate modelling groups and therefore programs should be generally available; the SARUM 76 listing is available. A range of questions come to mind of areas that should be explored with the model: eg climatic changes, pollution abatement costs, energy, seed sectors and cartel action.

Notes and references

1. J. W. Forrester, *World Dynamics* (London, Wright-Allen, 1971).
2. D. Meadows, *The Limits to Growth* (Cambridge, Mass., MIT Press, 1972).
3. H. Linnemann, *MOIRA—A Model of International Relations in Agriculture* (Amsterdam, North-Holland Publishing Company, 1976).
4. Systems Analysis Research Unit, "SARUM 76: research report", Department of the Environment, London, UK. 1977.
5. A. Herrera, *Latin American World Model* (Buenos Aires, Fundacion Bariloche, 1974).
6. M. Mesarovic and E. Pestel, "Multilevel computer model of world development system, Proceedings of IIASA Symposium, Schloss, Laxenburg, Austria, 1974.
7. Cabinet Office, *Future World Trends* (London, HMSO, 1976).
8. P. C. Roberts, "The world can yet be saved", *New Scientist*, 23 January 1975, pages 200–201.
9. D. J. Wright, "The natural resource requirements of commodities", *Applied Economics*, 1975, 7, pages 31–39.
10. D. Norse, "Development strategies and the world food problem", The Agricultural Economics Society, 1975 Conference, Aberystwyth, UK.
11. P. G. O'Neill, "The income-elasticity of demand for primary energy", Institute of Fuel/Operational Research Society Conference, April 1975.
12. W. G. B. Phillips and D. P. Edwards, "Metal prices as a function of ore grade", *Resources Policy*, September 1976, pages 167–178.

13. P. Roberts *et al.*, Proceedings of IIASA Symposium, Schloss, Laxenburg, Austria, 1976.

14. The full specification of SARUM 76 and detailed accounts of the data base, parameter determination and test runs appear in a research report published by the Department of Environment, UK (See Ref. 4).

15. Cobb Douglas $Q = K^\alpha L^\beta$ ($\alpha = 1 - \beta$ for constant returns to scale)
    Constant elasticity of substitution (CES) $Q^\gamma = K^\gamma + L^\gamma$
    where
    Q is the output; K is the capital; L is the labour.

16. K. T. Parker, "Modelling intra and inter regional activity", 2nd International Conference on Dynamic Modelling and Control of International Economies, Palais Auersperg, Vienna, Austria, 1977.

SCENARIO ANALYSIS IN INTERFUTURES

David Norse

The INTERFUTURES project used a scenario approach and focused on issues of economic development over the next 20 years. The author describes the five main stages of scenario construction and gives a summary of the six scenarios which were finally chosen. The scenarios provide possible boundaries for the world economy in the year 2000. If there are no major discontinuities, most OECD countries are likely to experience structural unemployment, protectionism, and moderate rates of growth throughout the next decade—the outlook for Third-world countries is perhaps more favourable, with growth rates generally higher than in the OECD countries.

ESTABLISHED in January 1976, to study "the future development of advanced industrial societies in harmony with that of developing countries", the INTER-FUTURES project is due to finish at the end of October 1979. It has been a study in prospective analysis carried out at the OECD headquarters by a specially recruited team with a large degree of autonomy.[1]

The existence of INTERFUTURES is partly a reflection of the doubts sown in the minds of politicians and government officials by certain futures studies. For example, *The Limits to Growth* raised a number of issues regarding resource depletion and the writings of Daniel Bell (on post-industrial society) and Ohlson (on institutional sclerosis) questioned the ability of industrial countries, particularly those belonging to the OECD, to adapt readily to some of the changes facing them.[2] Such studies confront governments with a very basic question: do they have to respond to the issues raised, and if so, how? Governmental support for the establishment of INTERFUTURES therefore arose from two related sets of concerns. The first was a feeling of uncertainty about current and potential problems. The second was a feeling that government actions ignore or pay insufficient attention to the long term.

David Norse was a head of division in the INTERFUTURES project, OECD, 2 rue André Pascal, 75775 Paris CEDEX 16, France. The views expressed in this article are those of the author and should not be attributed to any official body or organisation. The author acknowledges the contribution of colleagues past and present who, through discussion or analysis, have aided the elaboration of the INTERFUTURES approach to scenario analysis.

The first set of concerns was, and still is, about economic disequilibria—with persistent unemployment, inflation, balance-of-payments problems, low investment, and difficulties with the international monetary system. To these were added uncertainties about food-grain and energy supplies, difficulties in adjusting to changes in the pattern of world trade, and growing imbalances between developed and developing countries. The response of politicians and other policy makers to these concerns was, and still is, further complicated by the conflicting views among established economists over the reasons for the slowdown in economic growth and over some of the underlying causes of sustained high inflation rates.

The second set of concerns was more specifically longer term, and related particularly to an almost constant feature of governments. Because of the pressure of immediate problems, governments are commonly unable to pay particular attention to longer term prospects and problems, or to the implications of the long term for current policy. In many instances a government presents goals which are already defined by a crisis, and it is unable to stand back to examine problems in a balanced fashion.

The aims

These concerns had a major influence on the aims, and hence the methods, of INTERFUTURES. The general aims have been: to provide OECD-member governments with an assessment of alternative patterns of longer-term world economic development, to clarify the implications of these patterns for domestic and foreign policy, and to shed light on the interdependencies among policy issues. More specifically, the aims were:

- to provide a clearer understanding of current problems;
- to identify other problems which may appear in the future;
- to analyse possible socioeconomic developments within and between advanced industrial societies;
- to provide a better understanding of likely Third-world development strategies and the underlying reasons for those strategies;
- to identify the opportunities for more harmonious development between the North and the South;
- to clarify the overlap and interaction of short and longer-term problems; and
- to indicate how long-term issues can enter short and medium-term policy.

The year 2000 was the main time horizon but some probing was done beyond the middle of the next century for population and natural-resource questions. Although the analyses were largely of an economic nature, social and political elements were not ignored.

The approach

Through prospective analysis and not forecasting, INTERFUTURES has attempted to provide a coherent picture of certain possible or plausible futures resulting from the strategies of various actors, and from the constraints they may face. The actors of particular concern to INTERFUTURES were governments or groups of governments but multinational companies, trade unions, and social groups were also examined. The constraints included the strategies or behaviour of other actors and the institutions which represent them, the limitations of natural-resource supplies, and the availability of capital. Once inconsistencies in the strategies of the actors, potential conflicts of interest between the actors, and other problem areas had been identified, policies to overcome these problems were formulated.

The construction of global scenarios, though central to the prospective analysis, has provided insights only on certain problems and policy issues, because of the necessary aggregation of nations and industries and the simplification of some socioeconomic features. The global scenarios have been complemented by more specific long-term studies: eg on key industries and on development strategies open to Third-world countries. These specific studies were subsequently integrated into the analysis.

Each global scenario is an image of the year 2000, ie an end-state scenario. The concept of an end state is used to elaborate the sequence of socioeconomic and political transformations and events which could lead up to it. Based mainly on explicit sets of assumptions, the scenarios are also influenced by the assumptions explicit in the computer models used to form their macroeconomic framework.

Two aspects must be stressed. First, the scenarios are not, and should not be interpreted as, forecasts. They are a means of improving our understanding of the long-term global, regional, or national consequences of existing or potential trends or policies and their interaction. Second, although global, national, and regional models have been used in the construction of scenarios, the model output has been the starting point and not the end point of the scenario analysis. Whilst some of these models are complex and useful analytical tools, they all rely on a core of invariant macroeconomic, or even microeconomic, structural relationships. This structural invariance is generally not acceptable for long-term scenarios because, as the time horizon recedes, the model reveals more accounting consistency than structural consistency, necessitating the introduction of analyses exogenous to the model.

The INTERFUTURES scenarios had four main functions:

● to provide coherent macroeconomic and geopolitical frameworks of the world economy over the next quarter century;
● to assess the overlap and interaction of policy issues arising from changes in relations between OECD countries and from differing patterns of North–South relations (eg problems that could be triggered off by growing economic disparities between industrialised countries and by the growth of industrial redeployment);
● to explore the consequences of broad strategies that might be adopted by OECD governments (eg for energy or international trade); and
● to integrate the complementary studies.

Scenario construction

Figure 1 illustrates the five main stages of scenario construction, and the text that follows describes each stage in some detail.

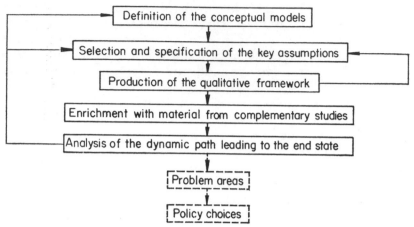

Figure 1. The stages of scenario construction

Definition of the conceptual models

These models are based on an INTERFUTURES study of the socioeconomic and sociopolitical dynamics of the advanced industrial societies since World War 2, particularly the shifts in the balance of power between OECD countries and the shifts in relations between OECD members and the Third world. The four main dimensions, each of which can be associated with contrasting assumptions of varying plausibility, are: North–North relations, North–South relations, internal dynamics of industrial societies, and internal dynamics of developing countries.

East–West relations have not been ignored but were largely beyond the terms of reference of the project. The range of possible patterns of international relationships is very wide and INTERFUTURES chose from the following subset of North–North relations:

- the USA, the EEC, and Japan hold equal status and collectively manage the OECD area (collective management);
- reemergence of US leadership of the OECD area;
- fragmentation and the growth of protectionism between North America, Europe, and Japan (fragmentation, protectionism); or
- fragmentation within Europe, possibly along North–South lines.

The choice of North–South relations was made from the following subset:

- continuous negotiation, progressive integration of the more industrialised countries (large growth of economic exchanges);
- North–South confrontation, the South becomes collectively self-reliant (confrontation, divisions widen);
- regional fragmentation in the South, as economic poles emerge and seek to establish spheres of influence; or
- the South fragments and makes regional alignments with economic poles in the North (South makes regional alignments).

The elements of these two groups can be paired in 16 ways, of varying plausibility. The three combinations of international relations, shown in Table 1, were chosen and combined with assumptions about the third dimension—the internal dynamics of industrialised societies. These assumptions are:

● The industrialised societies will establish a consensus regarding the dominant postwar values, will give priority to high economic growth, and will achieve that growth (consensus, high growth).
● Post-materialist values will be rapidly adopted and there will be a social consensus about moderate growth as an objective (rapid value changes, moderate growth).
● There will be no consensus regarding long-term objectives. Many will retain postwar values and favour aiming for high growth to achieve full employment and price stability—others will not, or will dispute their share of the national product. Conflicts will therefore arise between social groups, the necessary socioeconomic adjustments will be held up and moderate growth will result (social conflicts, moderate growth).

Table 1 illustrates the INTERFUTURES choice of scenarios, selected from combinations of the international dimensions with the assumptions on internal growth characteristics.

TABLE 1. THE DERIVATION OF INTERFUTURES SCENARIOS

Scenario	North–North relations	Relative productivities	Internal dynamics of developed countries	North–South relations
A	collective management	converge	consensus, high growth	large growth of economic exchanges
B1	collective management	converge	rapid value changes, moderate growth	large growth of economic exchanges
B2	collective management	converge	social conflicts, moderate growth	large growth of economic exchanges
B3	collective management	diverge	social conflicts, moderate growth	large growth of economic exchanges
C	collective management	diverge	social conflicts, moderate growth	confrontation, divisions widen
D	fragmentation, protectionism	diverge	social conflicts, moderate growth	South makes regional alignments

Selection and specification of the key assumptions
The qualitative and quantitative assumptions follow fairly directly from the conceptual models chosen and from preliminary studies, on particular problem areas (eg food and energy) and on specific features of the world economy (eg trade, the international monetary system, and industrial redeployment). These and other supporting studies ensure that any quantitative values (eg for trade and energy elasticities, rates of change of trade liberalisation) are soundly based.

A major assumption in the scenarios concerns the long-term evolution of relative productivities in the OECD countries. Two alternatives were examined —catching up and convergence, or further divergence. The first assumes that under an open trading system with extensive international cooperation, the differences in labour productivity will be progressively eroded and the values for the different countries will converge on the long-term trend of the country with the highest productivity, the USA. The second is based on the idea that countries vary greatly in their structural adaptability, particularly because interest groups contribute to the emergence of certain rigidities, which Olson calls institutional sclerosis. Variations in these rigidities cause the divergence. The second alternative is perhaps more plausible than the first, but both have interesting implications for North–North relations and the evolution of the world economy (see Table 1).

Production of the quantitative framework
It was initially hoped that one of the global models available in 1976 could be used directly by INTERFUTURES to transform the basic assumptions of the scenarios into a coherent quantitative framework. Nine such models were reviewed, and operational experience was gained with some of them, but none was found to be entirely satisfactory. Consequently a multiple approach was adopted:

- Calculation of the GDP growth paths of individual OECD countries was based on the recent trends for the size and composition of the labour force, and on the convergence or divergence assumptions for labour productivity.
- The results from these calculations were used to derive growth rates for various groups of developing countries, by using the figures an an input to the World Bank's SIMLINK model.[3]
- The originators of the Systems Analysis Research Unit model (SARUM)[4] modified their model at the request of the INTERFUTURES team. The main changes were further geographical disaggregation to give 12 regions and to identify major geopolitical actors, sectoral transformation to give greater stress to industry rather than agriculture, and some development of the macroeconomic mechanisms. SARUM was then used to produce the basic qualitative framework for each scenario by introducing the appropriate assumptions for such variables as GDP growth, energy elasticities, aid flows, and rates of increase or decrease in trade barriers. The output from SARUM provided estimates of the main macroeconomic variables, eg sector outputs and trade flows.
- INTERFUTURES developed a trade model which linked simple models for each of the OECD countries and each of the main developing-country regions. The model focused on balance-of-payment problems and long-run exchange movements.

The multiple approach was applied less comprehensively than it had been planned, because the various elements were not in phase: in practice, the framework was largely elaborated from INTERFUTURES GDP-growth-path calculations and the use of the modified SARUM.

Enrichment with materials from complementary studies
There were two principal sources of this complementary material. The first was a series of 21 studies completed during the early stages of INTERFUTURES: these studies covered a wide subject area and the object was to review the literature and to identify problem areas for further examination. The second

source was a series of studies, completed largely in parallel with the scenario exercise and focusing on three main areas:

- long-term prospects and problems in key industrial sectors, eg cars, capital goods, electronics, textiles, and chemicals;
- socioeconomic dynamics in the OECD countries—particularly the possible evolution of value systems and their effect on socioeconomic structures, the operation of labour markets, and long-run investment requirements; and
- alternative development strategies for Third world countries (produced by consultants from the developing countries and further elaborated in a series of seminars with those consultants—the aim was to add a Third-world perspective to the analysis of the internal dynamics of the developing countries).

Analysis of the dynamic path leading to the end state

The examination of the path from the present or the recent past to the end state also draws on both the scenarios and the complementary studies, since it requires interactive analysis between the two. At the general level, INTER-FUTURES focused on the evolution of regional shares of world gross product and of world trade in capital goods and other manufactures. This brought out the possible changes in the economic strength of different regions: changes which could have a major influence on the international behaviour of those regions and on their own internal actions.

At a more specific level it has been possible to look at the conceivable economic pathways for individual countries and then to relate these to the general picture. Likewise by drawing on the detailed sector studies, it has been possible to consider the evolution of specific industries.

Both general and particular analyses helped to indicate possible inconsistencies in the strategies of various actors, and the steps they may take in response to the challenges or changes confronting them. For example, what might be the response of multinational companies facing depressed markets in the North but growing markets, protected by trade barriers, in the South? How might Japan react to growing protectionism—will it entrench, compromise, or focus increasingly on its neighbours in South-east Asia?

The analysis of paths to the end state highlighted inconsistencies in the conceptual model of some scenarios, and in the quantitative assumptions used in the generation of the macroeconomic framework. Iterative steps back to the assumptions underlying the conceptual model or the quantitative framework were introduced to resolve these inconsistencies.

The choice of scenarios

Whilst some of the scenarios chosen by INTERFUTURES are obviously more plausible than others, particularly because of the interdependence between the dimensions, plausibility has not been the only criterion for selection. Some of the scenarios are improbable because the time horizon, the year 2000, is too short for certain social changes or for the establishment of certain developing countries as major economic forces. Such scenarios become much more probable in the longer term, but are still pertinent to the analysis of the next two decades in that they indicate the possible consequences of incipient trends. Other

TABLE 2. A SUMMARY OF THE SCENARIOS CHOSEN BY INTERFUTURES

Scenario A

Collective management of the OECD zone by the three major poles (North America, Japan, and the EEC) who attempt to sustain high and stable economic growth. Free trade increases. Relative productivities of the OECD countries converge on the long-term US trend. Value patterns change slowly, primarily as a consequence of growth itself. There is progressive integration of Third-world countries, particularly the rapidly industrialising ones. Aid flows are large, but there is growing differentiation between the economies of developing countries.

Scenario B

There are three variants: B1, B2, and B3. All have similar assumptions for North–North and South–South relations. The OECD countries experience moderate growth, but its content differs in each variant. In B1, values change rapidly and there is a consensus for slower, less market-oriented growth, together with an open attitude towards the integration of the South. The other two variants assume no significant, unanimously accepted change in values: slower growth follows from institutional rigidities and difficulties of structural adjustment. In B2, productivities converge whereas in B3 they diverge because of national differences in the acceptance of structural adjustment.

Scenario C

North–South relations deteriorate in the early 1980s. The Third-world countries break those links which they feel have maintained or increased their dependence on the North. Aid is greatly reduced. There is collective management in the North and increased trade liberalisation. Growth is moderate or slow in the North, since regions are differentially affected by the loss of markets in the South. There is no convergence of productivities and no significant value change.

Scenario D

Protectionism mounts in the early 1980s between the major poles of the OECD (North America, Japan, and the EEC). The poles establish preferential aid, capital flow, and trade links with the developing country regions along historical, cultural, or geographical lines (North America with Latin America, the EEC with Africa, and Japan with Southeast Asia). Productivities in the North diverge, with slow or moderate growth.

---

scenarios, although extreme, identify possible inconsistencies in the strategies of actors and contribute to the analysis of the more plausible scenarios.

The scenarios chosen by INTERFUTURES, already indicated in Table 1, are summarised in Table 2.

Conclusions

The conclusions from the INTERFUTURES projects may conveniently be subdivided into the operational, the methodological, and the perceptual.

Operational. Although research groups may 'stagnate' if they continue too long without changes in compostion, they must have an active life of at least three years to reap the full benefits of an exercise like INTERFUTURES. The adoption of a method with a large number of interlocking elements led to problems of scheduling. Industrial-sector studies by external consultants arrived late, external modelling groups changed their direction, internal staff and financial limitations created delays. These problems disrupted the phasing of scenario analysis—the main analysis had to be completed within six months and the supporting material has been underutilised.

Methodological. The conceptual models underlying most of the existing mathematical models, including those developed for or used by INTERFUTURES, are partially inconsistent with the conceptual models for some scenarios, eg the B scenarios. The mathematical models largely assume a prefect world, whether it is neoclassical or centrally planned. It is therefore necessary to bear this inconsistency in mind when interpreting the results of such models.

Modellers commonly introduce a number of mechanisms to keep their models running—these give the models excessive stability. Short-term price fluctuations in the real world have a major effect on the expectations of investors and workers, which in turn are closely linked both to questions of inflation and capital formation and to the evolution of relative productivities. The stabilising mechanisms tend to produce in the model rates of structural adjustment which have seldom been observed outside war-time. Yet it is impossible for modellers to bring in some of the social lags and other elements of value systems because most of the necessary social statistics do not exist.

Perceptual. The scenario-analysis approach evolved by INTERFUTURES has made it possible to isolate or examine some of the main features of the world economy, particularly those features that could be the principal driving forces over the next 25 years. Scenario analysis has helped to clarify some of the strengths and weaknesses of major countries and regions both now and in the future: it has also led to a general picture of various trends which could strengthen or emerge with harmful consequences unless adequate government policies are introduced.

By indicating the possible strategies of certain actors in defined situations, the scenarios highlight areas where there may be conflicts or convergence of interests. If the policy options open to countries in such situations are elaborated, they can be fed back into the analysis to examine their consequences (eg in terms of robustness).

To some degree, all the scenarios that have been explored are rather extreme, whether it be in terms of a level or form of regional fragmentation which is geopolitically unlikely, or in terms of an unrealistically rapid rate of change in values (compared with those observed in the real world in recent times). Transitions in the real-world economy take place slowly in the absence of major geopolitical ruptures—the dominant demographic, technological, and climatic trends tend not to change direction rapidly at the macro level.

The six scenarios chosen by INTERFUTURES therefore represent the probable boundaries within which the future state of the world economy and international relations are likely to lie. However, the scenarios do not take into account important uncertainties about the long term. They give an incomplete picture of the possible range of futures, because they are either essentially continuous or explore ruptures only at the level of major geopolitical regions. The scenarios can be used in the form I have described to examine a number of important problems, but they may also be used as the initial framework for the analysis of other problems, since the future may be a composite of the scenarios described or may be subject to reversible or irreversible discontinuities.

A plausible and undesirable mixture

The future could have components of all the INTERFUTURES scenarios. The mixture which currently seems plausible or even possible for the next decade is most undesirable, and would require major changes in policy to prevent its realisation. The elements of this mixture are:

- slow or moderate growth in most OECD countries for 10–15 years, with continuing structural unemployment;

- inadequate coordination of short-term economic policies, and continuing haphazard structural adjustment, of variable effectiveness;
- protectionism aimed at imports from other industrialised countries and from the Third world;
- the higher growth in productivity caused by the more rapid and effective adjustment of some countries, such as Japan and West Germany, generates frictions between these countries and the less successful members of the OECD; and
- governments face problems of arbitrating between the majority with traditional demands and active minorities pressing new demands.

The implications of the 'mixture' scenario for the Third world are perhaps more favourable than they are for the OECD area:

- There is increasing diversity in the aims and achievements of developing countries, but growth rates are generally higher than those of OECD countries.
- Some countries, particularly the poorer ones, attempt reformist or radical development strategies to improve basic-needs satisfaction in all social groups—the degree of success varies.
- Difficulties among OECD countries in reaching agreement on their relations with the Third world favour the latter's attempts to organise cooperation among its members and to foster collective self-reliance.
- Attempts at cooperation and self-reliance are only partially successful —when the severance of links moves beyond the rhetorical stage, some countries decide that their interests are furthered by closer integration with the North rather than with the South. Thus close links remain between specific countries or regions of the North and the South for cultural, political, military, and economic reasons.

Protectionism continues in some industrial sectors or subsectors and grows in others, mainly in the North but also in the South. In the North it is directed at other industrial countries, at the South's poor raw-material producers who wish to upgrade their exports, and at the newly industrialising countries. Nonetheless extensive industrial redeployment continues. The newly industrialising countries increase their exports to the OECD area, and to other developing countries. In the Third world, both the newly industrialising countries and other developing countries with relatively mature industrial sectors (eg India) displace imports from OECD countries.

Alternatively, the future could contain major political or socioeconomic discontinuities superimposed on, or causing substantial breaks from, the dominant trends of the six INTERFUTURES scenarios. Growing socioeconomic disparities within and between groups of developed and developing countries could cause greater social fragmentation in some countries: political rifts could lead to a partial dissolution of the EEC, revolutions in Third-world countries, and conflict between some developing countries. An energy shortage stemming from government policies which failed adequately to foster greater energy conservation and greater investment in energy 'production' could alone, or in conjunction with political rifts, lead to an inflationary recession. Any such recession would prevent the development of the type of growth paths portrayed in scenarios A and B.

The application of the scenario-analysis method has reinforced and clarified the conclusions of studies by INTERFUTURES on specific problem areas. Collectively these studies lead to the view that the major difficulties facing OECD countries do not follow solely from problems in specific fields but from the conjunction of these problems. The difficulties are unlikely to be overcome by a compartmentalised view of the issues, nor by the application of conventional macroeconomic policies of demand management wedded to the unwarranted belief of many governments that they are able to fine tune their economies. Unless governments look at the links and overlaps between problem areas, and some of the institutional questions underlying those areas, the undesirable 'mixture' scenario is unpleasantly plausible, at least for the 1980s.

Notes and references

1. For a general description of INTERFUTURES, see Daniel Malkin and Giuseppe Sacco, "INTER-FUTURES: the OECD research project", *Futures*, June 1977, *9*(3), pages 255–259; see also the final report of INTERFUTURES, "Facing the future: mastering the probable and managing the unpredictable", Paris, OECD, June 1979.
2. Donella Meadows *et al*, *The Limits to Growth: the First Report to the Club of Rome* (New York, Universe Books, 1972); Daniel Bell, *The Coming of Post-Industrial Society* (New York, Basic Books, 1973); Mansur Olson, "The political economy of comparative growth rates", in Joint Economic Committee, *Long-term Economic Growth*, volume 2 (Washington, DC, Government Printing Office, 1977).
3. World Bank, "The SIMLINK model of trade and growth for the developing world", staff working paper 220, Washington, DC, World Bank, October 1975.
4. Departments of the Environment and Transport, research report 19, *SARUM 76 Global Modelling Project* (London, HMSO, 1977).

RETROSPECTIVE

FUTURES December 1978

THE HISTORIAN AND THE FUTURE

Asa Briggs

Historians had to come to terms with the fact that there is no 'absolute' past, long before forecasters were pondering the benefits of the 'absolute' future. They have also had to come to terms with their style of presentation, their personal biases, and the fact that they are grounded in the present and are therefore influenced by present preoccupations. Historians and futures researchers have much in common. This article explores the extent of their common ground and how it might be extended.

WHEN Marc Bloch was in a German prison camp in 1944, finishing off his fascinating book *The Historian's Craft*, he contemplated concluding it with a seventh section called "The Problem of Prevision". Before he had time to complete his text, he was taken from his cell and shot in an open field near Lyons with 26 other members of the French Resistance.

Bloch's faith in the future remained unshaken until the very end of his life, but it is difficult to reconstruct what he would have chosen to write about the shape of that future on the basis either of his personal experience or of his historical scholarship. He was a brilliant analyst of past events, but there is very little detail in his work about tendencies, trends and forecasts relating to the 20th century. He believed, however, that history is not "the science of the past"—there is just "one science of men in time"—and that "the faculty of understanding the living" is "the master quality of the historian". He also called prevision "a mental necessity", suggesting as sub-headings of his seventh section "the ordinary errors of prevision" (selecting as variables economic fluctuations and military history); "the paradox of prevision in human affairs" (prevision which is destroyed by prevision); "role of conscious awareness"; "short-term prevision"; "regularities"; and "hopes and uncertainties". It is tempting to try to fill in the outline.

Most other historians have been far more chary of identifying tendencies and trends in their own life-times than Bloch was, and of making forecasts, however provisional, about the future. Increasingly, indeed, they have become

Lord Briggs is Provost of Worcester College, Oxford, UK.

specialists in short periods or highly specific problem areas of history, losing, in consequence, much of their freedom as travellers in past time. A few historians concerned with historical methodologies have turned, however, to the problem of 'predictability' (and probability) and the role of 'prediction', including what they call 'prediction in the past', and its 'uses' in professional historical scholarship.[2]

Professional historians engage in 'prediction' exercises, often without knowing it, when in their work they anticipate later sequences of events in the past and try to account for them or fill in their detail. Often, indeed, they will sort out ranges of possible outcomes, not very different from the 'possible futures' sorted out by futurologists, except that historians, unlike futurologists can benefit from hindsight.

Thus, the American historian J. H. Hexter, one of the most refreshing methodologists, has drawn the following instance from his own detailed study of the 19th century English Civil War:

> If a distinct cleavage separated war party from peace party, given the side a Member [of Parliament] took on one question involving war or peace, we should be able to predict his position in regard to any other question involving the same issue. For example, if a Member voted against a treaty of peace in February that would identify him as one of the War party. We should then expect that in July as well as February he would oppose a treaty ... Let us try the powers of prediction with which this hypothesis endows us on the stubborn facts that we find in the journals and in the diaries of the Civil War Parliament.

Hexter found that his predictive hypothesis did not stand. The subsequent pattern of voting did not conform. He demonstrated, therefore, that there was no 'war party' or 'peace party'.[3] Hexter was honest as well as sophisticated, therefore, in the testing of predictive hypotheses. Indeed, he was far more explicit than most historians in subjecting his own work to such analysis, putting 'causality' to the test as well as probabilities. Bloch had called history "une petite science conjecturale": Hexter distinguished between history with a capital H and history without it, urging 'de-escalation', coming down from capitals to lower case.[4]

This is just what the two major groups of historians who have been concerned with the future as well as the past—the historians most read by the futurologists —have refused to do. The first major group are the prophets of decline, like Oswald Spengler, who have had considerable influence. The second are the confirmed believers in 'progress', who have seen no break between past and future but merely an upward or onward linear movement. There is a third group, too. Marxists treat laws of historical motion, which cover both past and future, as scientific. Marx's own thought about society was historical: his unrest about the present and his vision led him to the future.

The prophets of decline have followed in the wake of what a recent Swiss writer, with Jakob Burkhardt and Friedrich Nietzsche in mind, has called the 19th century "tragic futurologies".[5] Spengler, like Toynbee after him, thought in cyclical rather than in linear terms and concerned himself with "cultures", not with nation states. They refused to start, as both Marx and many of the confirmed believers in progress did, with the economic sub-structure and the way it evolved. Some of their long-term prophecies, like those of Burkhardt and Nietzsche before them, look perceptive. So, too, do those of Paul Valéry, who wrote briefly on themes which Spengler and Toynbee covered at great length.[6] Valéry started not with war or empire, however, but with the acceleration of rates of technical change in his own lifetime and their human and cultural consequences—a problem which also interested Bloch and his interpreter Lucien Febvre. The relationship between economic history and cultural history seemed basic.

'Decline theories', which often echo earlier cyclical theories of history, are in a sense replies, in a sense parallel counterparts, to the earlier theories of progress. Ruins and achievements always attract different temperaments. J. B. Bury, the historian of progress, dedicated his volume to the memories of the Abbé de Saint Pierre, Condorcet, Comte and Spencer and "other optimists" he had mentioned in his text. Two of his named writers belonged to the 18th-century 'Enlightenment', which produced new vistas of the future (along with one immensely influential work on ruins—Volnay's *Les Ruines* (1791)): two belonged to the 19th century, when the idea of progress was translated into visible material expression. Yet Bury traced ideas back through Bacon and into the ancient world and gave due weight to 19th-century Darwinian theories of evolution and their influence on historians.[7] He made much of Sébastien Mercier, "the father of Historical Futurity",[8] but he did not once mention Macaulay who usually figures so prominently in the historiography of progress.

Historiography has come to be regarded as a necessary dimension to the study of history, so that writers like Macaulay have been studied in depth and in perspective as, of course, have both Bury's confirmed believers in progress and the prophets of decline. As much attention has been paid to values as to anthologies. One general theme in historiography is the debate between historians about the same topic—and why we can never have one definitive version of the past. A second theme is why particular historians range themselves on one side or the other or neither. A third theme is why particular topics are chosen for debate at particular times. This leads from biography into intellectual (and political and cultural) history.

The same kind of concerns could well guide critical studies of futurology, which already has its own history. Indeed, it may be that stronger links between historians and futurologists could be established through historiography than through history itself.[9] Futurologists have emphasised recently that they are treating 'futures', not *the* future, and that we always have to look at a range of possible futures. This is not very different (except, again, that historians enjoy the benefit of hindsight) from the historians' emphasis not on one past, but on many—with the sense of the past shifting in each generation at the same time as the sense of the future. Even the language is similar. Historians talk of 'landscapes' and 'watersheds': futurologists of 'scenarios'.

Futurologists have so far been less concerned, however, with studying the effects of the stance of the particular futurologist on his conclusions than they have with the influence on forecasting of different 'vantage points'. They have been able to distinguish sharply say between Hermann Kahn and Seymour Melman, but they have devoted little time to the way particular futurologists 'rig' scenarios. It is interesting to note, for example, that the Open University's collection of readings *Man-made Futures*, which insists that "alternative directions can and should be the subject of open debate", ends with an index of concepts but with no index of persons.[10]

It is easier, perhaps, to deal with vantage points than with individual futurologists. Inevitably, both the futurologist and the historian start from the present. What they select from the accessible past or forecast for the future is influenced directly or indirectly, therefore, by present preoccupations. Daniel Bell made this quite explicit in his account of the American *Towards 2000* project. His main interest, he said, was less in predicting the future than in making explicit the structure of his own society: for this reason Raymond Aron claimed that *Towards 2000* was merely a way of trying to secure better planning: it was less imaginatively stretching than history. Likewise, many historians have emphasised, as Herbert Butterfield has done, how difficult it is to escape from the attitudes of the present in writing about the past. People of the past are treated as if they were people of the present, and this is a restriction on imagination also.[11]

For those historians who are content to write narrative history—with occasional survey passages and summaries of events and the people who made them—links with futurology at first look unimportant or irrelevant, although it is often in relation to such historians—Ranke is a good example—that historiographers have been most illuminating when they set out to place and to interpret them.[12] Narrative historians may be mainly concerned with events and the order in which they took place, but they give themselves away both in their selection and their presentation.

Since futurologists are in no position to predict precise events or the time when they will happen, their field of interest contrasts sharply at first sight with that of such narrative historians. Nor can futurologists tap the rich resources of personal biography. Through historiography, however, the apparent contrast between the operations of historians and futurologists looks less sharp. The narrative is not definitive and historians know far less about the depths of individual personalities than they wish.

It is obvious, of course, that the more historians turn from narrative to 'problems' and 'patterns of interpretation' and that the more they show themselves prepared to examine past people and events out of their strict time sequence, the more the fields of the historian and the futurologist converge or overlap. For many social and cultural historians the 'fact' is no longer a datum in itself: it is considered in relation to structures of similar 'facts' not necessarily chronologically close. It can be argued, indeed, that both historians and futurologists are concerned with change and resistance to change—which is achieved not by simple cause and effect, but by and through elaborate networks or webs of interrelated variables. In dealing with the processes of change, and their controversial implications, both futurologists and historians have to concern themselves with secular and cyclical changes, with the relationship between planned and unplanned changes, with varying contemporaneous rates of change, with constants, and, not least, with contingencies.

Historiography is useful (again) in pointing to the choice both of themes and of methods. Of course, historians do not have to 'invent' contingencies. They have to get behind them. They start with specificities and go on to try to explain them. Naturally, they very frequently get caught up in the detail. Indeed, they may find the detail more significant to them, through the multiple meanings it conveys, than broad generalisations, particularly when generalisations are based on incomplete sets of data and inconclusive documentation. The futurologist has to proliferate his own detail, and the critical reader will be more sceptical about accepting it than he will in treating the detail provided by the historian. In both cases, particularly the latter, there may be 'anachronisms'. They are particularly prominent in science fiction about the future unless the novelist 'thins out'. Yet writers of science fiction, who often introduce historians into their novels—a theme in itself[13]—have often been ingenious in trying to deal with the 'individual' in the future. One man may be unpredictable—Asimov can envisage a Mutant—but in large numbers, people are as dependable as machines or figures. "They can be measured, examined, classified".[14] These words of Heinlein were written in 1940, when fortunately more than one man proved 'unpredictable'. The 'mass' theory, which was forecast in some of the 'tragic futurologies' of the 19th-century prophets of decline, is problematic, not proven.

Given that more historians are now concerned with 'problem history', including 'history from below' (that dealing with people whose names have long been forgotten) and with counter-factual history, the history of *ifs*, rather than with narrative history, which deals with leaders and 'great events', it might be concluded that the *rapprochement* between the historian and the futurologist will grow stronger. The computers are at work. Yet, this is not the whole story. Since the historiographical shift has been accompanied by a greater concern to probe in detail particular historical situations, microscopes are more in use than telescopes. It is not only that prophets are treated with suspicion.[15] No one would now think of writing a contemporary version of H. G. Wells's *Outline of History*.

Wells remains interesting because he wrote novels as well as articles and books about both past and future. In other words he allowed freer play for his fantasy than either analytical historians or committed futurologists usually allow themselves. Although he has often been dismissed as a somewhat crude spokesman of material progress, he was sensitive and subtle enough, too, to recognise that historical evolution might move in reverse. It was not just that late in life he tasted despair. Even when young, he felt no confidence in man's permanent ascendancy. In a fascinating article written in *The Gentleman's Magazine* in 1891, he suggested that "the Coming Beast must certainly be reckoned in any anticipatory calculations regarding the Coming Man". He ranged far wider than the 'tragic futurologists' of the 19th century into the realm of first and last things, the realm where cosmography and eschatology meet. He would have appreciated a remark of Claude Lévi-Strauss that "the world began without man and will end without him".[17]

If historiography is one field which could be profitably explored by historians and futurologists together; another with Lévi-Strauss in mind—and with Wells's novels as much as his histories and anticipations—is the relationship of both history and futurology to anthropology. The 'history of events' looks inadequate in the light of concern for 'structures' and 'myths', but so, too, do those versions of futurology which are concerned solely with extrapolation and probabilities.

The 'otherness' of both past and future needs to be felt. So also, however, does the 'otherness' of much in our present. "The virtue of anthropology consists in reminding us that we have to discover the rules of our own society just as we discover those of other societies."[18] Our task starts here and now. And our here and now are as far removed as they can be in place and time from those of the Arab historian Ibn Khaldun who was content to observe that past and future are as alike as two drops of water.

Notes and references

1. M. Bloch, *The Historian's Craft* (Manchester University Press, Manchester, 1954), Introduction by Lucien Febvre, page *xvi*.
2. 'Covering law' theories of history have treated prediction of the future and explanation of the past in terms of the same model of logic, suggesting that in both cases the analyst must deduce desired statements from a covering law that covers all the phenomena studied. See A. Grünbaum, *Philosophical Problems of Space and Time* (New York, Knopf, 1963).
   Their critics have treated explanation of the past and the prediction of the future as different operations. See M. Scriven, "Truisms as the grounds for historical explanation" in P. Gardiner, ed. *Theories of History* (Glencoe, Illinois, Free Press, 1959).
3. See J. H. Hexter, *The History Primer* (London, Allen Lane, 1972), page 46 ff.
4. *Ibid*, page 59.
5. A. Reszler, "L'Europe et le mythe du declin", in *Cadmos, 1* (2), University Institute of European Studies, Geneva, Summer 1978, page 96. Reszler starts his study of "decline as a prospective study" with Gobineau's *Essai sur l'inégalité des races humaines* commenting that "history is of interest to Gobineau only insofar as its study facilitates the anticipation of the future", *ibid*, page 94.
6. P. Valéry, *Variété I* (Paris, Gallimard, 1924).
7. J. B. Bury, *The Idea of Progress* (London, Macmillan, 1932).
8. R. C. Churchill, *A Short History of the Future* (London, Werner Laurie, 1955), page 14. Mercier's *L'An 2440* appeared anonymously in Amsterdam in 1770.
9. Nonetheless, Ernest Gellner has argued in *The Historian Between the Ethnologist and the Futurologist* (Paris and the Hague, Mouton, 1973), page 21, that "the curious and ironic role of history" is that "it helps to prejudge questions for which if we had to face them rationally we could simply have no determinate answers. All the premises would be too slippery".
10. N. Cross, D. Elliot, and R. Roy, eds, *Man-Made Futures* (London, Hutchinson Educational/Open University Press, 1974). For concern with values, see, in particular, K. Kumar, "Inventing the future in spite of futurology" (pages 129–133). Melman is quoted (pages 56–61) on "the myth of autonomous technology". There is no Kahn extract in the book.
11. H. Butterfield, *The Whig Interpretation of History* (London, Bell, 1931).
12. See P. Geyl, *Debate with Historians* (Groningen, J. B. Wolfers, 1946).
13. Note how A. C. Clarke introduces his historian in *Prelude to Space* (New York, Ballantine, 1954) and I. Asimov deals with psycho-history in *Foundation* (New York, Doubleday, 1955). Asimov has explained some of his interests in his notes on "Social science fiction", in R. Bretner, ed, *Modern Science Fiction: Its Meaning and Future* (New York, Coward, McCann and Geoghegan, 1953), page 181. For the use of Spengler in science fiction, see also R. D. Mullen, "Blish, Van Vogt and the uses of Spengler" in the *Riverside Quarterly*, 3 August 1968, pages 172–186. Some of the most sophisticated writers of science fiction have stressed that science fiction is rarely trying to predict what will happen and it should not be judged by its predictive accuracy. Rather it examines various things which might happen, and tries to imagine their consequences if they do. See R. Schimdt, "The science in science fiction" in T. D. Clareson, ed, *Many Futures, Many Worlds* (Kent, Ohio, Kent State University Press, 1976), page 29.
14. See R. A. Heinlein, "The roads must roll" in his collection, *The Past Through Tomorrow* (New York, Putnam's, 1967). Heinlein, like Asimov, has always been interested in history and sociology.

15. See W. H. Dray, *Philosophy of History* (Englewood Cliffs, New Jersey, Prentice-Hall, 1964), pages 60–66.
16. See the anthology of critical articles on Wells; B. Bergonzi, ed, *H. G. Wells: A Collection of Critical Essays* (Englewood Cliffs, New Jersey, Prentice-Hall, 1976).
17. C. Lévi-Strauss, *Tristes tropiques*, quoted in Reszler, *loc cit*, page 115.
18. E. Gellner, *loc cit*, page 33.

PROBAPOSSIBLE PROLEGOMENA TO IDEAREAL HISTORY

James Blish

In this essay (which means 'trial') I propose to do five things: define science fiction; show why it arose when it did; explain why it is becoming steadily more popular; demonstrate that just as it has thus far produced no towering literary masterworks, so no such work can be expected of it in the future; and place it as a familiar phenomenon in world history.

NOTHING so much gratifies the critical temper as criticising other critics, regardless of the subject matter they are all ostensibly examining.[1] To put my readers at their ease, then, I shall begin in this enjoyable mode.

Archaic zelotypia

As others have noted, both historians and creators of science fiction are often unusually eager to claim for it respectable ancestors, working backwards through Voltaire, Swift and Cyrano de Bergerac to Lucian of Samosata. Most recently, Peter Nicholls has carried this process probably as far as it can be made to go, by including in science fiction's family tree the epic of Gilgamesh, which seems to have been composed a considerable time before the Sumerians discovered that they could produce serviceable laundry lists by biting spoiled bricks.

It should be noted, however, that Mr Nicholls' ongoing critical history is a sophisticated one, so that his examples

William Atheling Jr died in 1975; as James Blish he wrote science fiction from the 1940s onwards. This article first appeared in *Foundation: the Review of Science Fiction*, May 1978, *13*, North East London Polytechnic, Dagenham, RM8 2AS, UK. Illness prevented the expansion of the historical references and note 10 was compiled by *Foundation*'s staff. We would like to thank the estate of the late James Blish for permission to publish the article.

are not primarily ancestor worship or fake genealogy; among other things, he is instead out to show certain traits and states of mind findable throughout literary history which, put together like puzzle pieces, unite to form works we call science fiction. (If there is any real objection to his approach, it is that we most successfully define things by their centres, not their edges, in Dr Jack Cohen's telling formulation.)

The formidable Professor Darko Suvin, the only formalist critic of science fiction known to me, is not an ancestor hunter either; but his definition of science fiction as "the literature of cognitive estrangement" eliminates family trees by permitting the inclusion of more ancestors than all the others put together (including some not intended as fiction at all), like an international convention of everybody named Smith—Smythes, Psmiths Blacksmiths, and Blacks also welcome.

The critics in apparent oppositon are equally numerous and cover as wide a spectrum. Among these we may safely pass by the group exemplified by Judith Merril, to whose members science fiction is simply the Now Thing and Where It's At. The central, general tenet of this school is that science fiction was impossible before, and coincided with, the advent and rise of science and technology.

The position is attractive and has the merit of relatively hard edges; at the very least, it does not throw into despair the prospective student who cannot read medieval Latin or Linear B. Like its converse, it has its megalomaniac extremes: for instance, I subscribe to it; and the late John. W. Campbell maintained that science fiction *is* the mainstream, of which all other kinds of fiction are only backwaters.

A more reasonable representative is Heinlein's claim that science fiction is more difficult to write than contemporary or historical fiction, and superior to them both. I disagree with every word of this, but I can see no possible argument with his immediately preceding point that no fiction, written in a technology-dominated era, which ignores technology can claim to be realistic.

Kingsley Amis, throwing out of court any form of cultural aggrandisement, and admitting—as so few critics do—that a major function of science fiction is entertainment, sees it as an exclusively 20th century form of social satire (though with the unavoidable and richly earned inclusion of H. G. Wells). This is perhaps *too* narrow, leaving out other *kinds* of science fiction, eg as thought experiment, as early warning system, as generator of paradigms, and so on. Brian Aldiss's history casts its net far wider, but also holds that science fiction cannot sensibly be said to have existed before science; his earliest allowed starter is Mary Shelley, a consistent choice and admirably founded and defended.[2]

But these two schools, despite their apparently fundamental opposition, are simply two sides of the same balloon; take the best of the first school (Nicholls), turn him inside out, and you have the best of the second (Aldiss); topologically they remain identical. (In some of the lesser possible pairs you will have to let quite a bit of gas out first.) There is an important sense in which Gilgamesh, Grendel and Co. indeed do belong in any history of theory of science fiction—though it is not a sense either advocated or rejected yet by either side. If I can establish this detail, the five theses I listed at the beginning will follow almost automatically.

The future presentation of the past

Somewhere around 90% of the central thesis of this essay—which I haven't stated yet—is not mine at all; I stole it from Oswald Spengler. This is something more than the usual acknowledgement of a debt, for the fact itself is a supporting datum for the thesis.

However, it also requires some definitions, since for the sake of brevity I shall use a few Spenglerian terms. Because these words are also in common use, considerable confusion would result without prior notice of the special senses Spengler attaches to them; hence I place a glossary here instead of in the usual place.

Culture. This word has no anthropological meaning in Spengler's hands (as for instance, we might refer to the Navajo culture, the culture of the Trobriand Islands, etc). Spengler's cultures span many centuries and many countries; for example, his Classical culture extends from pre-Homeric times to the fall of Rome. In his view, only Chinese, Indian and Egyptian histories lasted long enough to develop into independent cultures with definite geographical boundaries.

Civilisation. There are essentially only two kinds of historical philosophy, the linear (or progressive) and the cyclical.[3] Marxism and Christianity are familiar linear theories; both believe that events are marching (or zigzagging) toward some goal. The cyclical theorist believes that history repeats itself. (Toynbee tried to believe both at once, resulting in eight volumes of minutely documented bewilderment.) Spengler's theory is cyclical, on an enormous scale. For him, civilisation is but one of the phases every culture must go through unless disrupted by outside forces—and not one of its best phases, either. Since we are now living in the garbage dump of just this phase of his Western culture, I shall have more to say about this later.

Contemporary. In the ordinary sense, I am contemporary with everyone who lived through a majority of the same years I did. Spengler means nothing so trivial. In his sense, one man is contemporary with another if each plays a similar role in the corresponding phases of their cultures. For example, Sargon (Babylonian), Justinian I (Classical), and Charles V (Western) are eternal contemporaries—'late springtime' figures whose careers are similar because they had to be; the choice for each was either to play this role at this time, or be nobody. Hence the fact that I am alive during most of the same decades as Richard M. Nixon is meaningless; his true contemporaries are Lui-ti[4] and Caligula. My own, necessarily, are some Hellene one of whose lost 140 plays placed last in the Games in a bad year, and a sub-priest trying to make sense of the chaos Amenhotep IV's experiment in monotheism made of Egyptian religion.

I have drawn these examples of contemporaneity to illustrate as well another striking principle of Spenglerian history, which is that it is cyclical only at the intercultural level; history does *not* repeat itself on any smaller stage, let alone moment by moment in fine detail as in Nietzsche's 'eternal recurrence'.[5] Hence it would be futile to seek parallels between, say King Arthur and Napoleon, though some can be forced; both were Westerners in sharply different phases of that culture.

It follows from this that Spenglerian history, since it is not rigidly deterministic, allows for considerable exercise of individual free will, within the role as appropriate to the cultural phase or season.

In 1975 we live late in that era of civilisation he calls Caesarism. In such a period he would not counsel a poet to try to become an army officer or courtier instead; but he might well say, "Now it is too late to attempt writing a secondary epic; in Milton the West has already had its Vergil". The incompletion and overall structural failure of Pound's *Los Cantares* would have been predictable to him from the outset.[6]

On a broader scale, most of Spengler's predictions for the 20th century after 1921 have come to pass, and in the order in which he predicted them, a good test of any theory. He did fail to foresee that they would happen so fast; but he set the date for the utter collapse of the West at around 2200, which is just about as much time left as the Club of Rome gives us, and for the same reason—insanely runaway technology.

Gnosis of precreate determination

It now remains to place science fiction within this scheme. This requires a further short discussion of the nature of our own times in general.

Spengler's view of history is organic rather than casual, and so is his imagery; as previously implied, he compares the four major periods of each culture with the four seasons.

The onset of civilisation is the beginning of autumn. At this point, the culture has lost its growth drive, and its lifestyle is codified—most particularly in architecture, with the building of great cities or cosmopoloi which both express the culture's highest spirit and drain it away from the countryside. Here, too, law is codified and history is written (*all* history is urban history); and the arts enter upon a period of attempted conformity to older, 'standard' models, like the 18th century in Europe, when it became increasingly difficult to tell one composer or playwright from another.[7] In the West, civilisation began to set in about the time of Napoleon.

Civilisation may last for centuries and be extremely eventful; imperial

Rome is a prime example. At first, too, great creative works remain possible; I have mentioned Vergil, and in the West we have had Milton, Goethe, Joyce, Mozart, Beethoven, Wagner, Einstein. (Spengler would unabashedly add himself to such a list, I think justifiably.) But autumn ends, and a civilisation becomes a culture frozen in its brains and heart, and its finale is anything but grand. We are now far into what the Chinese called the period of contending states, and the collapse of Caesarism.

In such a period, politics becomes an arena of competing generals and pluto-crats, under a dummy ruler chosen for low intelligence and complete moral plasticity, who amuses himself and keeps the masses distracted from their troubles with bread, circuses, and brushfire wars. (This is the time of all times when a culture should unite—and the time when such a thing has become im-possible.)

Technology flourishes (the late Ro-mans were first-class engineers) but science disintegrates into a welter of competing, grandiosely trivial hypo-theses which supersede each other almost weekly and veer more and more markedly toward the occult.

Among the masses there arises a 'second religiousness' in which nobody actually believes;[8] an attempt is made to buttress this by syncretism, the wrenching out of context of religious *forms* from other cultures, such as the Indian, without the faintest hope of knowing what they mean. This process, leads inevitably toward a revival of the occult, and here science and religion overlap, to the benefit of neither.

Economic inequity, instability and wretchedness become endemic on a hitherto unprecedented scale; the high-est buildings ever erected by the Classical culture were the tenements of the imperial Roman slums, crammed to bursting point with freed and runaway slaves, bankrupts, and deposed petty kings and other political refugees. The

group name we give all this, being linearists by nature,[9] is Progress.

Given all this, it is easy to deduce the state of the arts: a period of confused individual experimentation, in which traditions and even schools have ceased to exist, having been replaced by ephemeral fads. Hence, the sole aim of all this experimentation is originality— a complete chimera, since the climate for the Great Idea is (in the West) 50 years dead; nor will nostalgia, simply an accompanying symptom, bring it back. This is not just winter now; it is the Fimbulwinter, the deep freeze which is the death of a culture.

We can now define science fiction; and against this background, see why it arose when it did, why it is becoming more popular, and why we can expect no masterpieces from it, *quod erat demon-strandum est*, in the simple act of definition.

Agnosis of postcreate determinism

Science fiction is the internal (intracultural) literary form taken by syncretism in the West. It adopts as its subject matter that occult area where a science in decay (elaborately decorated with tech-nology) overlaps the second religious-ness—hence, incidentally, its auto-matic receptivity from its emergence to such notions as time travel, ESP, dianetics, Dean Drives, faster-than-light travel, reincarnation, and parallel uni-verses. (I know of no other definition which accounts for our insistence that stories about such non-ideas be filed under the label.) It is fully con-temporary with Meng-tse (372–289 BC), the Indian Nagarjun (AD 150), the Egyptian New Empire after Amen-hotep IV, Byzantium in the time of Psellus (AD 1017–1078), and the Magian Abbassid period—we have lots of company, if it's ancestors we're looking for.[10]

It is not a utopian prospect—utopia being, anyhow, only a pure example of linearism in a cyclical world—but neither need it be an occasion for despair. I repeat, we have free will within our role and era, as long as we know what it is and *when* we are. Even without any background, or belief, in Spengler, many of us have already sensed this.

When a candidate for the presidency of the Science Fiction Writers of America made 'fighting drug abuse' part of his platform, most of us felt almost instinctively that he was making a fool of himself; and Harlan Ellison's call to turn science fiction into a 'literature of the streets' met with dead silence. Nor has there been noticeable response to the challenges of Philip José Farmer, Michel Butor, George Hay, or British Mensa to turn science fiction into fact (and the Stalinist-oriented Futurians who published exactly this challenge 35 years ago gathered no following, either). It was this situation which led me to say six years ago that if an artist insists on carrying placards, they should all be blank.

The last words must be Spengler's:

our direction, willed and obligatory at once, is set for us within narrow limits, and on any other terms life is not worth the living. We have not the freedom to reach to this or to that, but the freedom to do the necessary or to do nothing. And a task that historic necessity has set *will* be accomplished with the individual or against him.

Ducunt Fata volentem, nolentem trahunt. (The Fates lead the willing, they drag the unwilling.)

Addendum

I wrote this in hospital with no reference books to hand but the second volume of *The Decline of the West*. I now find that Spengler's 1924 speech was not his only public appearance; he also delivered a lecture in Hamburg in 1929.

The substance of the second speech, however, was exactly the same as that of the first.

Notes and references

1. V. Nabokov *vs.* Wilson, superficially about Pushkin's *Eugene Onegin*.
2. In this summary I have made everybody sound as solemn as owls, but many of these critics are witty writers; see particularly Aldiss, Amis, de Camp, and Nicholls.
3. I omit the accidental or meanwhile-back-at-the-corral accounts of most school and popular histories; since they see no pattern to events, they cannot be said to have a philosophy.
4. 'Ti' is an honorific meaning, roughly, 'the august'; and the first Chinese emperor to so style himself was, by no coincidence, contemporary in the Spenglerian sense with Caesar Augustus.
5. Nevertheless, Nietzsche was one of Spengler's two chief influences, the other being Goethe. He acknowledges them both at the outset and refers to them frequently thereafter.
6. There is a grimly interesting real example of this in Spengler's own lifetime. Hitler was contemporary with Wu-ti (AD 119–124) and Trajan, but utterly failed to sense the spirit of the time—though some of his counsellors did, most notably Hjalamar Schacht.

   At the beginnings of the Nazi movement, Spengler in his only public lecture told the cream of the Hitlerjugend that they were doing the (historically) right thing at the right time, but that their leader had it all balled up and that it would end in disaster for the entire West. The leader of a national movement, he said with grisly humour, ought to be a hero, not a heroic tenor. In 1933 he expanded the speech into a 160-page book, *The Hour of Decision*. The Nazis banned the book three months after its publication (as well as forbidding all mention of his name in the press—luckily he was too famous to shoot), but by that time it had already sold 150 000 copies.
7. A charming work called the Jena Symphony was long attributed to early Beethoven because one of the orchestral parts had his name on it, though some musicologists suspected Haydn. It turned out to be by somebody no one had ever heard of.
8. The Eisenhower religiosity: "Everyone should go to the church of his or her

own choice, I don't care which it is".

9. The characteristic spirit of the West which Spengler calls Faustian, is inherently linear.

10. (*Editor's note:* the following was compiled by Peter Nicholls.) Meng-tse, the only Chinese philosopher besides Confucius to have his name latinised—as Menicius—emphasised the ruler's duty to the people, advocated social welfare, and amplified the confucian concept of 'magnanimity'.

Nagarjuna, philosopher-monk and convert to Mahāyanā (Greater Vehicle) Buddhism, founded the 'Middle Path' school whose clarification of the concept of 'emptiness' (*śūnyatā*) is seen as a peak of intellectual and spiritual achievement in Indian thought; and wrote several critical analyses on views of the nature of reality, the means of knowledge and the origin of existence.

Amenhotep IV (better known as Akhenaton; his wife was Nefertiti) reigned from 1379–1362 BC and besides advocating new intellectual and artistic freedom of expression, was the first monotheist known to history. Abandoning the old gods of Egypt for a single god of love and switching capitals from Thebes to his new city, Akhetaton, his neglect of practical politics prevented his reforms from surviving.

Michael Psellus, philosopher and politician, headed the philosophy faculty at the new imperial university in Byzantium, initiating the renewal of classical scholarship by reversing the Aristotelian predominance in favour of Platonic thought and advocating a fusion of Platonic and Christian doctrine, thereby prefiguring the Italian Renaissance.

The Abbassids were the second great dynasty of the Muslim Empire of the Caliphate (AD 750–1258), the Magian period being the mystical decadence of this.

The *individuals* here aren't themselves villains of the piece; rather, it is the piece in which, and against which, they were historically forced to participate which is properly 'villainous'—as the following (abridged) quotation from Spengler indicates. "Contemporary with the 'positivist' Meng-tse there suddenly began a powerful movement towards alchemy, astrology, and occultism. It has long been a favourite topic of dispute whether this was something new or a recrudescence of old Chinese myth-feeling—but a glance at Hellenism supplies the answer. This syncretism appears 'simultaneously' in the Classical, in Indian and China, and in popular Islam. It starts always on rationalist doctrines—the Stoa, Lao-tse, Buddha—and carries these through with peasant and springtime and exotic motives of every conceivable sort ... The salvation-doctrine of Mahayana found its first great herald in the poet-scholar Asvagosha (c 50 BC) and its fulfilment proper in Nagarjuna. But side by side with such teaching, the whole mass of proto-Indian mythology came back into circulation ..."

"We have the same spectacle in the Egyptian New Empire, where Amen of Thebes formed the centre of a vast syncretism, and again in the Arabian world of the Abbassids, where the folk-religion, with its images of Purgatory, Hell, Last Judgement, the heavenly Kaaba, Logos-Mohammed, fairies, saints and spooks drove pristine Islam entirely into the background. There are still in such times a few high intellects like Nero's tutor Seneca and his antitype Psellus the philosopher, royal tutor and politician of Byzantium's Caesarism-phase ... like the Pharaoh Amenhotep IV (Akhenaton), whose deeply significant experiment was treated as heresy and brought to naught by the powerful Amen-priesthood." O. Spengler, *The Decline of the West*, translated by C. F. Atkinson (London, Allen & Unwin, 1971), volume 2, pages 312–313.

THE WAR THAT NEVER WAS

Correlli Barnett

BETWEEN the conclusion of the Franco–Prussian War in 1871 and the coming of the Great War in 1914, the military leaderships of Europe faced one of the most momentous problems of prediction in history, for on the accuracy of their calculations depended the fate of their countries, of Europe as a whole, and the lives of hundreds of thousands (millions, in the event) of men. It was at the same time one of the most perplexing riddles ever to confront professional predictors, because of three new factors which together totally altered the terms of reference of warfare.

The first of these factors was the technological and military revolution represented by the magazine rifle, the water-cooled and belt-fed machine gun, smokeless propellants, and quick-firing artillery. The second factor was the novel problem of supplying, deploying, and directing unprecedented numbers of troops; and this was linked with the related problems of making the right military use of the latest inventions—the telephone, wireless, the internal combustion engine, the flying machine. Practical progress in these fields was astonishingly rapid. In 1896 motor vehicles figured for the first time in French manoeuvres; by 1914 it was clear that motor transport, while still not replacing the railway,

Mr Corelli Barnett has a worldwide reputation as a military historian. His publications include *The Desert Generals, The Swordbearers, Britain and Her Army, The Collapse of British Power*, and *Marlborough*.

boots, and hooves as the primary means of moving armies, would be a significant factor. By 1914 too the most progressive armies were equipped with mobile field radio sets. Count Schlieffen, Chief of the German General Staff until 1906, had a science-fiction vision of the future commander, controlling his distant armies from a desk loaded with telephones. All armies had their air force by 1914, whether aircraft or airships. Although still without striking power, these were clearly of immense potential importance for reconnaissance and fire-direction.

There was also the question of the impact of mass technological warfare on the highly geared and, so it seemed, therefore fragile economies of the new industrial states. What would be the direct expense of keeping massive armies in the field, of equipping them and resupplying them, of feeding their men and guns? And what would be the economic effects of such a vast diversion of manpower and resources out of production into war making? How, in a word, would a future war be paid for? *Could* it be paid for?

The military leaderships had to solve all these riddles not only in general terms, but also in regard to the political and strategic situation of their countries, the plans of their allies, and the likely plans of their enemies. Diligently, and according to their intellectual lights and national traditions, they pondered and re-pondered.

The French, who came late to the

ENTRÉE A LONDRES DU MARÉCHAL JAMONT A LA TÊTE DE L'ARMÉE FRANÇAISE. — (Dessin de M. Thiriat.)

Forecasts of future wars were frequent before 1914. This issue of *Le Monde Illustré* from March 1900 described a French victory and the occupation of London

THE PEOPLE KNEW THE ANSWER OF VON HINDEN-
BURG. THEY HAD READ IT, AS HAD ALL THE WORLD
FOR MILES AROUND, IN THE CATACLYSM OF THE
PLUNGING TOWERS. NEW YORK MUST SURRENDER
OR PERISH!

By 1915 the Americans had begun to read stories
the coming German invasion of the United States

Conan Doyle's famous prediction of submar
warfare, in the July issue of the *Strand* magazine

THE SHIP LAY WITHIN TWO HUNDRED YARDS OF US AND IT WAS EASY TO
SEE THAT SHE HAD HER SEA-BOATS

DANGER!
Being the Log of
Captain John Sirius
By
A CONAN DOYLE
Illustrated by F.S.Hodgson

The Opinions of Naval Experts on this striking story appear on page 20.

IT is an amazing thing that the
English, who have the reputation of being a practical
nation, never saw the danger
to which they were exposed.
For many years they had been
spending nearly a hundred
millions a year upon their army and their

fleet. Squadrons of Dreadnoughts costing
two millions each had been launched. They
had spent enormous sums upon cruisers, and
both their torpedo and their submarine
service were exceptionally strong. They
were also by no means weak in their aerial
power, especially in the matter of hydroplanes.
Besides all this, their army was very efficient

systematic study of war, only founding their École de Guerre in 1878, adopted something of the approach of medieval thinkers—an arbitrary vision, based on faith, that disdained inconvenient fact. Moreover, they limited themselves to war in terms of armies and battlefield tactics, rather than war in all its technological, economic, and social implications. By the 1880s the memory faded of attacks stopped in slaughter by modern firepower in the Franco–Prussian War. Thereafter, under the inspirational teachings of such heads of the École de Guerre as Cardot and Foch, the French army came to believe that, in the words of the *Reglement d'Infanterie* of 1887, "Brave and energetically commanded infantry can march under the most violent fire even against well-defended trenches, and take them". This mystical faith in moral *élan* survived the development of quick-firing artillery and machine-guns, and the proof supplied by the Russo–Japanese war of 1904 of the immense strength lent to the defence by such weapons in the hands of well-entrenched troops.

In the sphere of strategy the French —great *idealogues* as a nation—fell victims to Napoleonic myth, to emotion and faith rather than to observation and analysis of fact. They came to believe fervently in the offensive— violent, immediate, and pushed to extremes. When in 1910 General Michel, then Chief of the General Staff, realistically proposed a defensive strategy in the fact of what he— rightly—believed would be a vast German wheeling movement through Belgium, it cost him his post. Under his successor, Joffre, French strategy obeyed the precepts of such advocates of the Napoleonic offensive as Colonel de Grandmaison, and this found its ultimate expression in the afterwards notorious "Plan Seventeen" of 1913.

So, according to French predictions, August and September 1914 should have gone like this: two closely con-

centrated groups of French armies attack in Lorraine on both sides of the German fortress area of Metz. To loud cheering and the blare of bugles the French infantry, supported by the fire of 75 mm field-guns, sweep over the defenders by sheer force of impetus and moral ascendancy and win a decisive victory. The pursuit is carried forward in a north-easterly and easterly direction to the Rhine, so isolating any German formations that have advanced into Belgium. Germany, faced simultaneously with a Russian conquest of East Prussia and advance on Berlin, sues for peace.

The German General Staff, for their part, though by no means free of the distortion of the judgement caused by worship of glorious military tradition, on the whole set about finding the answers to the riddle of future war by thorough analysis of technical factors and such regional conflicts as the Boer War and the Russo–Japanese War. After 1871 the elder Moltke saw little hope of repeating his decisive victories over France. In the case of a two-front war he planned for a defensive in great depth in the West and a strictly limited victory against Russia in the open ground of the Polish plain. He feared the possibility of a "people's war", like the closing phase of the Franco–Prussian war, which he saw could prove intensely difficult to bring to an end. Count Schlieffen, who became Chief of the General Staff in 1905, was no less haunted by the consequences of a prolonged struggle between modern industrial states, which he—like some civilian commentators—believed must prove economically ruinous.

The German reading of the broad evidence was therefore much more sombre and cautious than the French. German planners also had to recognise that Germany would have to fight on two fronts, against France and her ally Russia, and with only the dubious assistance of the Austrians. To Germany, therefore, a prolonged war would be doubly ruinous. It followed that a quick decisive victory was doubly vital. But how to achieve it against the firepower of the modern defence? Schlieffen ruled out a frontal offensive as bound to fail. The answer could only lie in outflanking the enemy defences. In adopting this solution Schlieffen and his successor the younger Moltke recognised that Germany's bid for a quick victory could only be a colossal gamble; and, in contrast to the romantic rhetoric of the French, they evinced a caution verging on pessimism about the chances of their gamble succeeding.

Germany's "war that never was" unrolled as follows: the conflict opens with a colossal offensive against France by seven-eighths of the German field army, while the remainder defend East Prussia against the ponderous Russians. In Lorraine and Alsace weak German forces give ground in the face of a French offensive, so drawing the bulk of the French army eastwards. Meanwhile the mass of the German forces in the West (36 corps out of 41) carry out a vast wheel through Belgium and Luxembourg (Schlieffen had included Holland, but Moltke deleted it), pivoting on Metz, and completely outflanking the powerful French frontier defences and the principal strength of the French army. The edge of the German wheel passes through Brussels and Lille, down across the Oise and the Seine. Every time the French seek to build up a defence line, to entrench, they are freshly outflanked and forced to retreat again, so that the campaign remains mobile. The German wheel passes to the westward of the fortress of Paris and then swings east, crowding the French armies away from the capital, the centre of their rail net, and back against the rear of their own frontier defences. Here, caught in a gigantic corral, a super Sedan, the French army is forced to capitulate. Leaving

behind occupation forces to supervise the armistice, Germany rails her army across Europe to launch, in conjunction with the Austrians, an encirclement battle in Poland against the Russians, who, defeated and bereft of their ally, also sue for peace.

The Russians and Austrians followed their senior partners in hoping and planning for a quick war of manoeuvre and a decisive victory: Russia for an advance on Berlin while their French ally was advancing to the Rhine; Austria hoped for the conquest of Serbia, an early success in Galicia, and a decisive victory with her German ally over Russia. The British General Staff, whose planning was necessarily circumscribed by the limitations of a small all-professional army, could not look beyond a supporting role in French strategy; a minor part in the colossal battles which British generals, as much as their European counterparts, hoped and expected would swiftly decide the war.

As we know, none of these predictions came true. Instead the early battles were indecisive; stalemate supervened. For the first time in European history the quantity of military manpower enabled a continuous front to be held from Switzerland to the sea, and (though more sketchily) in the East from the Baltic to the Black Sea; for the first time in history there were no flanks to be turned, no possibility of manoeuvre until first a breakthrough had been achieved. And for three years every attempt at breakthrough—except on the more thinly held Eastern Front—broke down in the face of barbed wire, trenches, machine-guns, and massed gunfire. The defensive became supreme. The war became a prolonged exercise in the attrition of demographical, moral, industrial, and economic resources—ruinous to victors and vanquished alike.

It is therefore easy to see why the pre-1914 general staffs of Europe have been universally condemned ever since for getting it all so wrong. By way of contrast their critics point in particular to the predictions of one I. S. Bloch, a Polish banker, and his vast work of analysis published in 1897 (*The War of the Future in its Technical, Economic and Political Relations*, of which part was published in English translation in 1900 under the title *Is War Impossible?*). Bloch predicted a stalemated war in which entrenched armies faced each other impotently across an impassable zone of fire. The outcome would eventually be decided through attrition of the entire resources of the combatant nations; economic exhaustion and disruption would bring in their train social uprisings and even revolution.

Nevertheless Bloch was not always right. He wrongly thought that the magazine-rifle would be the decisive weapon, not, as it proved, the machine-gun and artillery. He thought the range of modern rifles would put an end to close-range fighting, whereas trench warfare was to prove a matter of extremely close ranges. He believed that, because of the scale of casualties, care of the wounded would be beyond the medical services. In fact, never before had been casualties better looked after. He considered Russia to be the nation best able to sustain a long war without social collapse. In fact, she was the first to undergo revolution and the first to make peace. He also believed—writing only a few years before Japan humiliatingly defeated Russia in the Far East—that Japan posed no danger to Russia.

On the other hand not all Europe's soldiers were as lost in illusion as their critics seem to think. The French certainly were fantasists; they were terribly awakened to reality by the bloody repulse of their offensives in 1914. But the younger Moltke, for example, told the Kaiser in 1905 that the next conflict "will become a war of peoples which is not to be concluded with a single battle but which will be a long weary struggle with a country which will not acknowledge defeat until the whole strength of its people is broken". Von Bernhardi, author of the best-selling prewar book *On the War of Today*, foresaw that frontal attacks on a well-entrenched defence would almost always fail. He also grasped that industrial states had immense adaptive capacity and would be able to sustain a struggle much longer than Bloch expected.

Nevertheless this kind of sober wisdom was alloyed in Germany too with a traditional military faith in the offensive as the "virile" and victory-bringing form of war, and in the sovereign virtues of the decisive battle as practised by Frederick the Great and Napoleon, and preached by Clausewitz. This faith dovetailed all too neatly into the practical necessity of avoiding a long war.

Perhaps the real charge against the pre-1914 military leaderships is not that they failed to foresee and prepare for a long war, but that, unlike their successors in 1936–1939, they failed to warn their governments that Europe's problems could not be solved by military means, and that to resort to such means must inevitably result in catastrophe.

It would not, however, be fair for us today to sneer at the pre-1914 soldiers for planning exclusively for a single, short campaign on the grounds that a long war would be either impossible or ruinous. For this is exactly what NATO is doing today— with the full approval of its member governments—and despite the precedent of two world wars; a precedent which the military analysts before 1914 did not enjoy.

THE ACCURACY OF TECHNOLOGICAL FORECASTS, 1890–1940

George Wise

Predictions of future technological changes and the effects of those changes, made by Americans between 1890 and 1940, are compared to the actual outcomes. Overall, less than half of the predictions have been fulfilled or are in the process of fulfilment. The accuracy of predictions appears at best weakly related to general technical expertise, and unrelated to specific expertise. One expert (or non-expert) appears to be as good a predictor as another. Predictions of continuing status quo are not significantly more or less accurate than predictions of change. Predictions of the effects of technology are significantly less accurate than predictions of technological changes.

INDIVIDUALS frequently assert a need to forecast future technological changes and their likely effects.[1] Less frequently do they attempt to evaluate whether or not accurate forecasting—either of changes or of their effects—is possible.

Most modern long-range forecasting studies were done too recently to allow evaluation of their accuracy.[2] But people made forecasts long before techniques such as Delphi, cross-impact analysis, and systems dynamics were invented. Most of these forecasts were intuitive. And intuitive views about the future remain the raw material upon which modern forecasting methods operate. As a consequence, an analysis of the accuracy of such intuitive forecasts is worthwhile.

My analysis is based on a collection of 1556 predictions made publicly by Americans between 1890 and 1940. These predictions were limited to two types of statements: predictions of technological changes that were to occur (or not occur) in one of 18 specified areas of technology (Table 1); and predictions of the effects—social, economic, or political—to be expected from changes in these 18 fields.

The author is with General Electric R and D Center, K1-3A15, PO Box 8, Schenectady, NY 12301, USA.

TABLE 1. THE SUBJECT AREAS OF THE PREDICTIONS USED IN THE STUDY

Subject area	Sample prediction	Number of predictions	Batting average
Energy sources	"Oil will probably be gone in a generation or two", Stuart Chase, *The Economy of Abundance*, 1934, page 102	259	0·386
Energy conversion	"There should be a great future for the gas engine in this country", *Scientific American*, 1896, *74*, page 16	128	0·344
Energy handling	Electricity transmission by wireless may be commercially feasible, see "The future", *Scientific American*, 1920, *123*, page 322	71	0·408
Air transport	"The steamship man today is faced with the possibility of airship competition", E. P. Farley, *Merchant Airship Bill*, US House of Representatives, 10–11 March 1932, page 27	178	0·410
Communications	"The everyday application of television is . . . a probability in fifteen years", Franklin F. Stratford, "Television not yet on tape", *Literary Digest*, 27 August 1927, *90*, page 22	104	0·480
Land transport	"Not even our great-grandchildrens' children will have to seek a museum when they want to see how a steam locomotive works", *New York Times*, 10 July 1898, page 6	207	0·377
Automata	"An automaton may be contrived which will have its 'own mind' ", Nikola Tesla, "The problem of increasing human energy", *Century* July 1900, page 187	9	0·445
Computers	"There are machines that exhibit a crude sort of memory . . . it seems reasonable that they can be developed to display a certain amount of judgement, according to a predetermined pattern", C. C. Furnas, *The Next Hundred Years*, 1936, page 208	9	0·556
Factory automation	"There will be no manual labour in the factories of the future", Thomas Edison, "Inventions of the future", *Independent*, January 1960, *68*, page 16	23	0·520
Heating and cooling	Electric home heating is not likely to gain wide acceptance see *Technological Trends and National Policy*, 1937, page 266	50	0·680
Housing	Modular construction of houses will soon be developed, see Arthur D. Little, Boston *Herald*, 30 November 1930, page 16	22	0·182
Lighting	Fluorescent lighting will play "an important part in the artificial production of light for practical commercial processes", W. S. Andrews, "Fluorescent light", *Trans. AIEE*, *17*, 1913, page 970	24	0·459
Processing of materials	"A cheap industrial process for the manufacture of fresh water from the sea" can be made available soon, see Alexander Graham Bell, "Prizes for the inventor", *National Geographic*, *31*, 1917, page 141	55	0·472
New materials	Heavy hydrogen compounds will be of great industrial importance. Robert E. Wilson, in *Previews of Industrial Progress* (pamphlet, General Motors, 1934), page 11	18	0·780
Sources of materials	Artificial food will not replace agriculture. Edward Murray East, "The future of man in light of his past", *Scientific Monthly*, *32*, April 1931, page 302	31	0·290

Table 1—*continued*

Subject area	Sample prediction	Number of predictions	Batting average
Military aviation	Airplanes will be used in warfare for reconaissance. Samuel P. Langley, "Mechanical flight", *Cosmopolitan*, *13*, May 1892, page 58	139	0·504
Naval warfare	"I do not believe it [the battleship] is becoming obsolete", Henry A. Stimson, *Hearings on a Treaty on the Limitations of Naval Armaments* (Washington, 1930), page 21 US Government Printing Office	52	0·443
Other weapons	The "death ray" for destroying aircraft is a potentially valuable weapon. Lt Cmdr Fitzhugh Green, USN, *New York Times*, 29 November 1924, IV, page 3	20	0·500

The predictions was divided into four classes, based on my knowledge and judgement, as fortified by standard reference sources. The classes are:

- *Fulfilled:* the events or effects occurred substantially as predicted.
- *In progress:* the change or effect predicted was visibly evident at the time predictions were evaluated (summer 1974), but had not become solidly established.
- *Not proven:* the prediction had not been fulfilled, but had not been proven impossible.
- *Refuted:* the prediction had not come true, and was no longer capable of being fulfilled.

This classification was used to explore two general questions: how accurate were past technological predictions, and are there any properties of predictions that increase or decrease their *a priori* probability of being fulfilled?

Previous work

The present study parallels one carried out nearly 40 years ago by the sociologist S. Corum Gilfillan.[3] He concluded that predictions made before 1937 by knowledgeable predictors about technology were correct or destined to be correct about two-thirds of the time. Possible biases influencing this relatively high score (at least compared to the one reported in this article) include the use of the category "destined" (really a prediction of a prediction) and the admitted omission of certain obviously incorrect predictions from at least one of the sampled books.

Subsequent studies of predictions, consisting of multiple-choice questions given simultaneously to selected panels of predictors, are difficult to compare with Gilfillan's work.[4] They did show, however, that short-range prediction of the alternative selection type could be done with greater accuracy than that obtained by naive chance models (such as flipping a coin or rolling a die).

A recent study of the correlates of prediction compared predictive accuracy of opinion-poll respondents on political or social questions with other attributes of the same respondents.[5] Its main positive finding was that "a conservative and pessimistic attitude tends to illuminate the crystal ball, while a liberal and optimistic attitude tends to darken it". A main negative finding was a lack of evidence that schooling increases competence in forecasting.

Some of the questions left unanswered by previous studies are shown below. The conclusions from the present study are in italics. An explanation of these findings and a discussion of their implications follows.[6]

- How well do predictors fare on their longer range efforts—those stretching ten or more years into the future? (*They are right less than half the time.*)
- Do experts predict better than non-experts? (*Slightly, at best.*)
- Do some experts (non-experts) predict better than other experts (non-experts)? (*No.*)
- Are predictions of the continuation of the status quo more accurate than predictions of change? (*No.*)
- Can the effects of technological changes be predicted as accurately as can the changes themselves? (*No.*)

Findings

The total sample of 1556 predictions broke down as follows into the previously defined classes: *fulfilled:* 499 predictions (32%); *in progress:* 121 predictions (8%); *not proven:* 420 predictions (27%); and *refuted* 516 predictions (33%).

For convenience in subsequent discussion, the categories *fulfilled* and *in progress* will be lumped together to define the category of "right" predictions; the categories *not proven* and *refuted* will be lumped to define the category of "wrong" predictions. The term "batting average" of a predicator is defined as the number of right predictions divided by the total number of predictions made by that predictor. By this definition, the batting average for all predictors put together is 0·399 (620/1556).

It is meaningless to ask whether this batting average should, by itself, be considered to be either high or low. But once known, it can be used as a standard against which to judge individual batting averages. (This is similar to baseball, where the overall batting average is not meaningful by itself, but serves as the standard which allows us to say, for example, that the player who bats 0·300 is a good hitter.) Nevertheless, the data certainly indicate that even if evaluation takes place a long time (more than 40 years) after the prediction was made, the majority of predictions are still not proven or have been refuted.

To judge the effects of expertise upon prediction, the performance of experts and non-experts was compared. Fifty individuals, each of whom were represented by five or more predictions in the sample, were divided into two groups: those who were employed in professions requiring knowledge of the physical sciences, or knowledge of one of the 18 technological fields; and those in professions not requiring such knowledge. Represented in the first, or expert, group were astronomers, engineers (electrical, mechanical, and civil), physicists, chemists, and inventors. Represented in the second, or non-expert group were business analysts, writers (journalists and novelists), biologists, soldiers, sociologists, and mathematicians (Table 2).

The batting average of the experts, 0·444, was significantly better than that of the non-experts, 0·336. (Significant here means $p < 0.05$ using the chi-squared test).

TABLE 2. FIFTY FREQUENT PREDICTORS

Name	Occupation	Number of predictions	Batting average
Abbot, Charles	Astronomer	7	0·286
Babson, Roger	Business analyst	25	0·360
Baxter, William, Jr	Writer	9	0·445
Bell, Louis	Electrical engineer	14	0·642
Bellamy, Edward	Writer	14	0·358
Chase, Stuart	Writer	24	0·418
Chubb, L. Warrington	Electrical engineer, research director	9	0·556
Compton, Karl	Physicist	9	0·333
Duncan, Louis	Electrical engineer	11	0·454
East, Edward	Biologist	11	0·454
Edison, Thomas	Inventor	34	0·588
Egloff, Gustav	Chemist	12	0·417
Eliot, George	Writer	5	0·400
Fernald, Robert	Mechanical engineer	11	0·182
Fessenden, Reginald	Inventor	9	0·222
Fieldner, Arthur	Mechanical engineer	13	0·384
Ford, Henry	Inventor	6	0·000
Furnas, Clifford	Chemist	37	0·568
Hale, William	Chemist	10	0·200
Hammond, John, Jr	Inventor	10	0·300
Harrison, George	Physicist	17	0·471
Haupt, Lewis	Civil engineer	6	0·166
Hering, Carl	Electrical engineer	14	0·572
Kaempffert, Waldemar	Writer	48	0·333
Kettering, Charles	Inventor	5	0·800
Lake, Simon	Inventor	14	0·357
Lincoln, Paul	Electrical engineer	9	0·667
Little, Arthur	Chemist, research director	32	0·532
Martin, Thomas	Writer	14	0·276
Martyn, T. J. C.	Writer	7	0·428
Maxim, Hudson	Inventor	21	0·477
Midgley, Thomas, Jr	Chemist	9	0·444
Millikan, Robert	Physicist	9	0·333
Mitchell, William	Soldier	19	0·368
Muller, Hermann	Biologist	11	0·263
Ogburn, William	Sociologist	18	0·500
Parsons, Floyd	Writer	42	0·214
Pupin, Michael	Physicist	8	0·625
Rentschler, Harvey	Electrical engineer, research director	9	0·333
Shaler, Nathaniel	Geologist	10	0·500
Slosson, Edwin	Writer	10	0·500
Steinmetz, Charles	Electrical engineer	25	0·360
Suplee, Henry	Writer	14	0·428
Tesla, Nikola	Inventor	52	0·404
Thomson, Elihu	Inventor	14	0·787
Thurston, Robert	Mechanical engineer	15	0·266
Walker, John	Writer	17	0·412
Whitney, Willis	Chemist research director	15	0·333
Wiener, Norbert	Mathematician	7	0·143
Williams, Henry	Physician	6	0·333

Total. 777 predictions; 236 fulfilled; 85 in progress; 197 not proven; 269 refuted. **Overall batting average** 0·413.

A warning is needed here. The significance of this result depends strongly on the choice of a method for dividing the predictors into expert and non-expert classes. A case in point is the engineer turned journalist Floyd W. Parsons. His 42 predictions were classified as "non-expert" because of his principal profession. Had they been classified as expert, because of his engineering training, the difference between experts and non-experts would no longer have been significant.

This suggests that the difference between experts and non-experts is of questionable actual (as opposed to statistical) significance. A related test cast a doubt on the value of more specialised knowledge for prediction. This compared the predictive accuracy of technically trained predictors in their own specialties (physics, chemistry, electrical technology, or mechanical engineering) with accuracy of the same predictors in other areas. There was no significant difference between the within-specialty and outside-speciality results (Table 3).

TABLE 3. THE 2 × 2 CONTINGENCY TABLES OF THE CORRELATES OF PREDICTIVE ACCURACY

Predictions	Experts**	Non-experts**	Experts, in own field	Experts, in other fields
Good	205	106	42	55
Bad	257	209	46	68

Predictions	Status quo predictions	Change predictions	Event predictions**	Effects predictions**
Good	176	423	570	50
Bad	244	662	788	148

Notes: * significant at $p < 0.05$; ** significant at $p < 0.01$.

Two tests were conducted to see whether some experts (non-experts) predict better than other experts (non-experts). The first test tried to account for the observed distribution of "right" predictions by the 50 experts and non-experts by the following simple model: on any prediction, an expert has a 0·45 probability of being right; a non-expert has a 0·35 probaility of being right. A

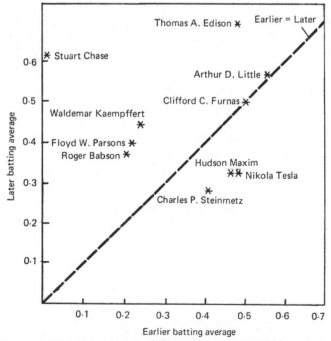

Figure 1. "Early" and "late" prediction accuracy for ten predictors

chi-squared test of the observed distribution of "right" predictions, compared to the distribution predicted by this model, fails to reject this simple model (ie the deviation of observed from predicted results is not statistically significant at $p < 0.05$).

Second, the predictions made by each of 20 predictors who individually made more than 20 predictions were divided chronologically into two classes: early and late. In each case, the dividing year was chosen as one which cut the total set for that predictor in half. The correlation between earlier and later predictions was low. In other words, the batting average scored by a predictor on his early predictions was *not* a very good indicator of how the predictor would do later.

This result shows up clearly in Figure 1, a graph plotting the early batting averages of these ten predictors against the later batting averages of the same predictors. (Incidentally, the graph also suggests that predictors improve with age. Seven out of ten had higher batting averages in the later than in the earlier period. The improvement was especially marked for the non-expert predictors.)

To test whether predictions of continuing status quo are more accurate than predictions of change, the entire sample was divided according to this criterion, and the batting averages were compared. The status quo predictions scored a slightly, but not significantly, higher batting average.

Finally, the initial sample was divided between predictions of the technological *events* expected to occur or not to occur (such as innovations, inventions, resource crises, and so on) and the predicted *effects* of those events. The batting average for the predicted events, 0.420, was significantly higher than that for the predicted effects, 0.253.

An "effect" prediction is here defined as a statement that a certain technological change will give rise to a consequent change in the political, economic and social institutions of the society undergoing the technological change, or in the habits of specified individuals in that society. Examples of effect predictions are shown in Table 4.

TABLE 4. EXAMPLES OF EFFECT PREDICTIONS

Areas affected	Effect predicted
Public taste	(After automobiles come into general use) "we shall probably find public taste changing so that many people will prefer to travel from place to place more slowly than at present", Cleveland Moffett, "Automobiles for the average man", *Review of Reviews*, June 1900, *21*, page 710
Industrial geography	"Water power may have a powerful influence in rearranging the centres of industry throughout the world", "The age of water power", editorial, *Scientific American*, 6 November 1897, *77*, page 291
Politics	"Superpower, dotting the earth with new units of production, may quite conceivably plant in each of them the kernel of a revived, self-conscious, localism", Charles Merz, "Twentieth century medievalism", *Century*, June 1923, *84*, page 234
Foreign policy	"The adoption of an oil-burning navy will prove a tremendous drain on the oil reserves of this country [the USA], and the question obtrudes whether a successful maintenance of our present naval program will not demand the control of the large oil pools of Mexico", J. E. Pogue, "Mineral resources in war", *Scientific Monthly*, August 1917, *5*, page 131
Family life	"As long as outside-home electrical powered entertainments are cheaper than home ones, the family's importance will diminish", William F. Ogburn, "The future of man in light of his past", *Scientific Monthly*, 1931, *32*, page 297

Implications

This study provides an estimate of the accuracy of public predictions of technological change which is lower than that given by Gilfillan in the only directly comparable previous study. But, as indicated earlier, this overall figure is of little value by itself. Its main value is as a baseline in measuring the correlates of predictive accuracy.

One obvious candidate for such a correlate—professional training in the field under examination—proved in fact to be statistically significant (with the reservation previously noted). However, specialised professional training did not further improve prediction. This suggests that while general expertise helps the predictor by allowing him to rule out obvious chimeras, specialised expertise does not permit him to make the further step of choosing among the reasonable alternatives.

Further, for prediction purposes, it appears that one expert (or non-expert) is just as good as another. This finding extends a result which has previously been found to be true for stock-market forecasters, economic forecasters, and weather forecasters.[7] Excessive daring or excessive caution on the part of predictors does not seem to explain this result, since predictions of continued status quo did not differ significantly in accuracy from predictions of change.

The evidence that effects of technology are harder to predict than the technological changes themselves should give pause to practitioners of technology assessment. Like forecasters, they still need to establish a track record for accuracy. Most of the incorrect predictions of effects were quite simplistic: they saw a Second World War destroying civilisation, or the use of military aviation as abolishing war altogether, or dramatic technological solutions to such problems as city slums or low farmers' incomes. In retrospect, it appears that social and economic conditions evolve in response to the entire complex of technology, rather than to a single innovation.

The results given above should be taken with reservations no doubt already evident to most readers. First, the sample of predictions was not randomly selected. Statistical calculations apply only to the results of grouping items in the sample into categories (for example, testing the association between expertise and accuracy). They cannot be assumed to apply to the universe from which the sample was drawn. Second, the judgement of whether a particular prediction is right or wrong is a highly subjective one. I regret I did not have available independent judges to confirm or refute my assessments.

Notes and references

1. For example "Future problems have their roots in today's trends. The main approach to identifying and bounding coming problems must be through forecasting the emergence or evolution of present and foreseeable trends and events", *Handbook of Forecasting Techniques*, US Army Engineer Institute for Water Resources, Contract Report 75–7, December 1975, page 5.
2. One attempt at such an evaluation is Robert H. Ament, "Comparison of Delphi forecasting studies in 1964 and 1969", *Futures*, March 1970, *2* (1), pages 35–44. He found that of 46 developments given a 50% occurrence probability by the median of a Delphi panel in 1964 (event occurrence to be by 1980), 18 had occurred by 1969; 11 had "partly" occurrred; and 17 had not occurred.

3. S. Corum Gilfillan, "The prediction of inventions", in US National Resources Committee, *Technological Trends and National Policy* (Washington, Government Printing Office, 1937), pages 15–23.
4. Douglas McGregor, "The major determinants of the prediction of social events", *Journal of Abnormal and Social Psychology*, *33*, 1938, pages 179–204; Abraham Kaplan *et al*, "The prediction of social and technological events", *Public Opinion Quarterly*, 1950, *14*, pages 93–110.
5. William R. Avison and Gwynn Nettler, "World views and crystal balls", *Futures*, February 1976, *8* (1), pages 11–21.
6. George Wise, "Technological prediction, 1890–1940", unpublished PhD thesis, Boston University, 1976.
7. Alfred Cowles III, "Can stock market forecasters forecast?", in John W. Hooper and Marc Nerlove, eds, *Selected Readings in Econometrics* (Cambridge, MIT Press, 1970), pages 1–16; "There's no more blood in the synoptic turnip", *Technology Review*, February 1974, *77*, pages 85–86; Geoffrey Moore, "What forecasters do right", *New York Times*, 3 February 1974, III, page 14.

ECONOMIC FORECASTING IN BRITAIN 1961–1975

A critique of assumptions

G. R. Chapman

ALL the forecasts considered here, which refer to periods prior to 1975, have proved to be overoptimistic: those relating to the post-1975 era, from all evidence of present trends, appear to be falling into the same trap. Of the latter type, the ones made before the present economic recession and the oil crisis are, needless to say, tending to prove particularly erroneous.

The thesis of this paper is that the predictions owe their excessive optimism—and hence their margin of error—to

- an overemphasis on quantitative assessment based, more often than not, on almost linear projections of past trends; and
- a resulting neglect of non-quantifiable political phenomena which have had, and will continue to have, an all-important bearing upon the outcome of events.

For obvious reasons the majority of forecasts have had an economic bias, being based on the assumption (which this author accepts) that the economy, more than any other element, tends to determine the social climate of a country. Unfortunately, as we hope to illustrate, scant attention has been paid

G. R. Chapman is a research officer with the Europe 2000 project, Department of Geography, University of Reading, Whiteknights, Reading, RG8 2AB, UK.

to the social and historical features which interrelate with that economy. In view of the fact that we are attempting to prove this last criticism empirically, most of the emphasis has been placed on forecasts of periods prior to 1975—the only ones which are verifiable.

Within the narrow parameters of purely economic forecasting a great deal of emphasis has, quite rightly, been placed on the gross domestic product (GDP). Without exception forecasters have consistently overestimated it for the UK, varying from predictions of 4% annual growth in the National Economic Development Council (NEDC) projection for 1966[1] down to the meagre 2·4% implied in the OECD projection for 1969–1975.[2] Predictions of the GDP made in 1975 show that the lessons of the past and the apparent continuation of downward trends have not cured forecasters of their optimism—as both the government white paper[3] of January 1975 and the Cambridge Economic Policy Group Report of 1975 illustrate.[4]

A further complication, directly related to this optimism, is provided by the inability of many forecasters to decide whether indeed they are predicting what will happen or are concerned with what they hope will occur. Due to the present economic recession this theoretical weakness is becoming an even greater source of error.

National forecasts

Let us take some of the predictions of the early 1960s as a starting point. The NEDC report for 1961–66 depends on a "no change" situation for the fulfilment of its projection for a 4% growth rate in GDP: "no change in terms of international trade" and it expected "that the rate of industrial expansion in the rest of the world will remain the same". As for its other assumptions, they are implicit: that the economy will not suffer any downswings as a result of trends (mostly social) built up in the past, but which were not yet evident in statistical (quantitative) terms; that the British economy was capable of exploiting the spin-offs from the industrial expansion in the rest of the world, and that this industrial expansion would not in the future rebound upon itself in terms of market saturation.

In doing so the NEDC report maintains the traditional assumptions of economic forecasting (in Britain at least)— assumptions which have not been challenged since in any radical way. It is equally in keeping with tradition in another way—ie, in terms of its lack of success, as Table 1 illustrates.

Nor were the projections of the national plan of 1965, although they were revised downwards, any nearer the mark (see Table 2).[6,7] The GDP was still expected to be 0·3% higher than the previous year, in direct contradiction to the underlying social and economic trends, ie the gradual strengthening of the trade unions and

TABLE 1. A COMPARISON OF HISTORICAL DATA WITH NEDC PREDICTIONS

	Annual growth rate (%)	
	predicted[a]	actual[b]
GDP	4·0	3·2
Consumer expenditure	3·5	3·1
Public consumption	3·5	2·7
Investment	5·3	6·6[c]
Productivity *per capita*	3·2	2·75

Notes: [a] 1961–1966; [b] 1960–1964; [c] the high level of investment, I suspect, is due to a high level of public investment in non-marketable produce and increasing private investment within the tertiary sector. Sutcliffe and Glynn show that industrial productivity in the period subsequent to 1965 was rapidly slowing down (2·2% for 1965–1970; 1·0% in 1971).[5] This tends to corroborate the assumption of a low level of investment in the productive sector.
Source: NEDC, *Growth of the UK Economy 1961–66* (London, HMSO, 1963).

consistent underinvestment in industry. The relative optimism of this plan, it would seem, was once more related to the buoyancy of other Western economies. Again it overestimated the capacity of the home economy; again it took the line that increased international trade would spread productivity increases. In making this latter assumption in particular, it tended not to consider the alternative possibility: that increased industrial output abroad might end up by swamping British industry. Nor did it consider fully the major long-term effect of high growth on the international scene—inflation— with all its inevitable consequences for a low-growth economy such as Britain's.

TABLE 2. A COMPARISON OF HISTORICAL DATA WITH THE NATIONAL PLAN PREDICTIONS

	Annual growth rate (%)				
	prediction[a]	1967[b]	1968[b]	1969[b]	1970[b]
GDP	3·8	1·8	3·1	2·8	2·5
Private consumption	3·2	1·6	0·0	2·5	3·0
Public expenditure	3·0	3·2	2·8	0·7	1·5
Investment	5·5	0·8	4·5	4·1	1·5
Productivity *per capita*	3·4	—	—	1·5	2·3

Notes: [a] 1965–1970; [b] actual.
Source: The National Plan 1965–70 (London, HMSO, 1965).

To what extent such an outcome was foreseeable in 1965 is impossible to say. The conclusion must be drawn, however, that the plan lacked historical and political perspective.

If the short-term government-sponsored forecasts were restricted by political necessity, the more ambitious project of Beckerman *et al* was less so.[8] However, he too commits the same error of considering the curve of supply and demand as a self-regulating mechanism, operating almost irrespective of social and political influences. Basing his assumption on a 3·8% growth rate, he too expected increased international economic activity to boost Britain's national product—or at least, this is the impression given by a table of the GNPs of other countries "at the same level of development" and from which he extrapolates his prediction for Britain. Once more, compartmentalisation of disciplines leads the author to shie away from the political factors upon which his predictions must finally rest. Ideological distaste for "politics" and a belief in the self-sufficiency of economics, limit the study to being, fundamentally, a statistical survey. Thus the only concretely expressed constraint of his projection of a steady growth rate is a purely legalistic one— that of the raising of the school-leaving age, which was foreseen for the early 1970s. To be fair, however, there is a passing comment regarding the assumption of a successful incomes policy.

A further constraint which was considered likely in Beckerman's 1965 study was the expectation that there would eventually be a shorter working week. An illustration of the degree to which Beckerman and associates are bound by an almost theological faith in the perfection of the market mechanism is revealed by their belief that shorter hours can only occur as a result of, and therefore *subsequent to*, a rise in productivity. As is now evident, a reduced working week is becoming prevalent irrespective of the rate of productivity.

Thus Beckerman provides us with a stream of highly optimistic predictions. A 3·3% annual average rise in consumption, investment moving up from 18·6 to 21·8% of GNP, *per capita* productivity increases varying from 3·5–3·8% per year, while government expenditure, which has recently declined to a growth rate of around 1·8%, is given as increasing at an annual 3·1%.

One area where Beckerman is more correct, and where he does not make a linear growth projection, is employment. He projects a workforce of 26·35 million for 1975, whereas it is currently running at around 25 million (though dropping rapidly). In accordance with the 1965 OECD national survey,[9] he too sees a rise in the level of employment up to 1967, followed by a slight decline. However, a comparison of his detailed list of sectorial employment figures and statistics issued in the Department of Employment *Gazette*[10] illustrate yet another problem of forecasting: being right (or nearly right) for the wrong reason.

The wrong reasons are again related to his excessive optimism, stemming from a lack of historical insight. The author foresees a rapidly increasing non-productive population (due to a higher level of fertility), along with an improved standard of living, provided for by capital intensification combined with a moderate shift of the labour force to his designated industrial growth sectors. As a result of increased demand, therefore, the inevitable capital intensification would not threaten (in the near future at least) present employment levels. On the other hand, it would be sufficiently widespread as to limit the eventual demands for labour. As it turned out, however, neither the growth in production, nor capital intensification occurred to the degree forecast. The drop in employment levels which one would normally have expected under such circumstances, was prevented by government policy, the reluctance of British industry to cast off labour, and absorption by the tertiary sectors. Thus we have a contradictory situation (in terms of classical economics, that is) of low productivity and a relatively high level of employment. As a consequence, the numbers employed in the productive sectors are constantly below the levels forecast by Beckerman, even though the total number of employed are comparatively similar, given the circumstances.

TABLE 3. A COMPARISON OF
HISTORICAL DATA WITH
BECKERMAN'S PREDICTIONS

Sector	Sector employment (thousands)		
	1960	1975 prediction	1975 actual
Engineering and electrical	1819	2327	1942
Textiles	906	810	525
Aircraft	294	306	202
Motor manufacturing	488	555	493
Chemicals	474	606	440
Electricity	212	298	186
Gas	128	199	103

Source: W. Beckerman *et al, The British Economy in 1975* (Cambridge, CUP, 1965).

In fact, as we can see from Table 3, except in a few areas the distribution of employment has changed little over 15 years.

Sector forecasts

If we can conclude that the economic predictions we have mentioned restricted themselves too much to their own discipline, this is all the more the case for those studies concentrating on one small area of development, such as Stone's forecast for housing in 2004,[11] Paige and Jones's (1966) predictions for the 1975 health services,[12] or A. H. Tulpule's (1969) forecast for vehicles.[13] All assume an anti-historical stance in so far as their main motive force for the growth of their sector is seen in terms of the needs of the population. Thus their measuring stick becomes demographic growth (overestimated in all three cases).

Two interpretations could be put on this: either they consider the democratic system to be so functionally perfect that there will be an even distribution of resources according to numbers (this could perhaps be feasible for cars, the production of which depends on mass consumption, but not for social necessities such as housing and health); or by projecting needs they are illustrating what they hope will be, without at the same time demonstrating what in fact could happen. In both cases there is a risk of utopian predictions and therefore irrelevancy.

Paige and Jones's growth rate for the health service is 5·0% per year, whereas the actual rate, even considering the lower level of population growth, fell far short of this—less than 2·7% per year. According to a government white paper this low level of expenditure is expected to continue.[3]

In the case of Tulpule's (1969) projections, they have been and will continue to be distorted, not so much by the lack of population growth, which so far would not have affected the vehicle sector, but rather by the economic recession, market saturation, and the oil crisis.

TABLE 4. A COMPARISON OF
HISTORICAL DATA WITH TULPULE'S
PREDICTIONS

	Number (millions)	
	1975 predicted	1975 actual[a]
Cars	16·6	14·0
Motorcycles	1·1	1·0
Public transport	0·1	0·1
Heavy goods	0·7⎫	1·6
Light vans	1·0⎭	

Notes: [a] Even these figures may be slightly reduced since they are based on projections made in 1974 by basic road statistics.
Source: A. H. Tulpule, *Forecasts of Vehicles and Traffic in Great Britain 1969* (Crowthorne, RRL, 1969).

Even so, it would be unfair to state that forecasters have completely neglected the political variables when making their predictions. In recent years especially, almost all forecasts have included the proviso that their predictions will hold good only if wage demands are moderated. That they have emphasised this one reservation in particular has, however, led to the neglect of other variables—such as the level of investment, which is equally important. Again one can retrace this tendency to an excessive faith in the curve of supply and demand. First, the rate of investment is incorporated into an economic model and is considered one of the spontaneous results of profitability: excessive wage demands— ie demands unrelated to productivity— are not; on the contrary they tend to be considered as distortions. Second, the level of fixed investment is always more difficult to assess than the wage/ productivity ratio, and its consequences for the profitability of a company are far less immediate. As a result, a certain level of productive investment is assumed, and its absence is only noted over a lengthy period of time. Wage concessions on the other hand are far more blatant and more easily taken into account. Another factor, more ideological than theoretical, also comes into play. Excessive wage rises, being "distortions" of the classical model are considered unjustifiable, while private profit is held to be perfectly legitimate.

The outcome of this is that the withdrawal of investment is seen as a *consequence* of disproportionate wage levels. Underinvestment, therefore, is tacitly assumed to be a corollary of high wages—which is not always the case.

This, I believe, is the only possible explanation for the consistent lack of attention paid by forecasters to the all-important factor of investment and its long-term effects on the performance of the British economy. Indeed it would be no exaggeration to claim that this omission is perhaps the chief explanation for their unabated optimism.

The lack of progress

However, it would appear that even more recent forecasts have failed to learn from the past. Both the Cambridge Economic Policy Group (CEPG)[4] report and the government paper[3] of January 1975 follow traditional lines, neither distinguishing between prediction and hope nor freeing themselves from the narrow parameters of purist economics. They do, however, appear to be more willing to qualify their predictions than on previous occasions. The CEPG 3·6% growth forecast, for example, depends largely on the implementation of "artificial" methods: a successful wage policy whereby planned increases in earnings are restricted to 4–5% per year, and severe import restrictions or deflation/ devaluation. This, along with government cutbacks, is expected to weaken the labour market sufficiently to enable recovery to take place. The assumptions are many, and they all appear to depend upon political decisions: the willingness of a Labour government to deflate, the acceptance of such a policy by the unions, the incapacity of unions to organise themselves in the face of unemployment and thus to pursue "excessive" wage claims, their ability to control their members, and the willingness of the OECD and the EEC to accept devaluation or import controls. If all this could be guaranteed, then the CEPG deserves to be taken seriously. In the absence of an adequate political analysis which might justify such assumptions the only reaction, however, must be one of doubt.

The government white paper,[3] although based on more self-fulfilling predictions than its CEPG counterpart, still remains dependent on socio-historical variables. Three GDP growth projections are provided, 2·5%, 3·0%, and 3·5%. The latter, to quote *The Guardian* "is in the land of make-believe". The forecasts depend on reductions in government and consumer spending and the stability of commodity prices. What the consequences of the three alternatives will be remains ill-defined. In fact even in the case of the central assumption of 3%

TABLE 5. THE PREDICTIONS MADE BY THE UK GOVERNMENT AND THE CAMBRIDGE ECONOMIC POLICY GROUP

	Predicted growth rate (%)		Actual growth rate
	HMG[a]	CEPG[b]	1973–1974 (%)
GDP	2·5, 3·0, 3·5	3·6	0·6
GDP available for domestic use	1·9, 2·3, 2·7	4·0	−0·4
Public expenditure	2·8, 2·8, 2·8	2·2	1·6
Private investment	4·8, 5·4, 6·4	9·2	−6·0
Private consumption	1·3, 1·8, 2·2	3·8	0·3

Sources: [a] *Public Expenditure to 1978–79*, Command 5879 (London, HMSO, 1975); [b] Cambridge Economic Policy Group, *Review of Britain's Economic Prospects 1975*, Dept. of Applied Economics, Cambridge.

productivity growth, the long-term effects on the economy of the proposed cutbacks in schools and housing—all part of the important infrastructure necessary for growth—tend to be glossed over. A comparison of the CEPG report and the government white paper is given in Table 5.

The long-term perspective

If the oil crisis and the recent coming to a head of long-term trends has given the utmost difficulty to short-term economic forecasters, it is all the more so for such ambitious predictions as Colin Lester's *Britain 2001*[14] or Unilever's *Forecast for Britain 1984*.[15] Both are based on the assumption that the economic structure, its mode of finance, the distribution of its surplus value, and the resources at our disposal would remain relatively stable. This has not been the case, and this change is due to highly political factors: once more we see the restricted nature of non-historical forecasting illustrated. At the same time as Glynn and Sutcliffe were historically justifying vast structural changes in the world economic system,[5] Colin Lester was making accumulative linear projections until the year 2001, based on a continuation of the trends of the previous 20 years.

Obviously Colin Lester's claims—that we will be more educated, that we will be spending more on leisure and goods, trade will be freer, that our increasing social consciousness will be paying less attention to material goods of consumption—may still prove to be

true. So may his statistical conclusions. I should, however, like to suggest that the downswing which we are now experiencing has at no stage been considered and that his predictions have been given a very bad start. Therefore any correlation between his forecasts and the world in 2001 will be no more than coincidence.

This failure is the failure of most long- (and even short-) term forecasting. It is the result of an impressionistic statistical analysis of superstructural trends and a consequential neglect of structural undercurrents which may be detected only by a historical perspective.

In relation to this latter point, the forecasts of the 1963 Unilever project are more fortunate,[15] since they were made in a period when, although the structure of the British economy was showing strain, it was by no means on the verge of radical transition. *Britain 1984* also has the advantage of being theoretically more aware of the tremendous constraints placed upon forecasting.[15]

Economic development and social change are two facets of the same phenomenon. . . . For this reason long term economic analysis must include a study of sociological aspects and in particular an analysis of interrelationships of economic, psychological and sociological factors.

To this list we must add historical factors. As a result of this lucidity, its conclusions of an average annual 3·0% growth in GNP, a consumer expenditure growth rate of 2·8%, and public authorities outlay growing at 3·1% with a slight positive trade balance are relatively realistic.

In particular, it seems to be more aware than most of the other short-term forecasts of the period, of the idiosyncratic weakness of the British economy and its relationship to the historical conditions in which Britain finds itself—that of a late-capitalist, post-imperial country with a tendency towards mass consumption rather than production. Unfortunately, as the study admits "no attempt was made to integrate psychological and sociological factors with economic analysis into a proper dynamic model". Thus the rationale behind these observations is never convincingly proved except in psychological terms, and the long-term structural effects of this propensity to consume and demand more leisure are given little attention.

Where then does this leave the forecaster at the present moment? Except in the case of a few socialist economists (Mandel, Kidron, and Glynn and Sutcliffe)[5,16] the upheavals of recent years have been for the most part unforeseen. The inability of forecasts based on classical economic models to predict accurately the structural movements of the British (world) economy and their incapacity to relate economic activity with political decision and historical trends reveals enormous theoretical gaps in their mode of analysis. In a period when new resources were constantly available and material expectations, in the West at least, did not go completely unsatisfied, a purist economic model based on steady growth and a high degree of profitability could hide its inadequacies. In a situation either of low growth or of demand in excess of the availability of resources, the question of allocating those resources immediately becomes more obviously political. How this politicism manifests itself is in turn very largely a matter of history. Any futures research which ignores such considerations is doomed to failure.

Notes and references

1. National Economic Development Council, *Growth of the United Kingdom Economy* 1961–66 (London, HMSO, 1963).
2. Organisation for Economic Cooperation and Development, *Growth in Outputs 1960–80: Retrospect, Prospect, and Problems of Policy* (Paris, OECD, 1970).
3. *Public Expenditure to 1978–79*, Cmnd 5879 (London, HMSO, 1975).
4. Cambridge Economic Policy Group, *Review of Britain·s Economic Prospects* (Cambridge, Department of Applied Economics, 1975).
5. A. Glynn and B. Sutcliffe, *British Capitalism, Workers and the Profit Squeeze* (Harmondsworth, Penguin, 1972). This study is not in the strictest sense of the word a forecast.
6. It must be remembered, however, that government reports tend to be over-optimistic for political reasons.
7. *The National Place 1965–70* (London, HMSO, 1965).
8. Wilfred Beckerman *et al.*, *The British Economy in 1975* (Cambridge, Cambridge University Press, 1965).
9. Organisation for Economic Cooperation and Development, *National Survey of OECD Economies: United Kingdom 1964–65* (Paris, OECD, 1965).
10. Department of Employment, *Gazette* (London, HMSO, January 1975).
11. P. A. Stone, *Urban Development in Britain, Standard Costs and Resources 1964–2004*, volume 1 (Cambridge, Cambridge University Press, 1970).
12. D. Paige and K. Jones, *Health and Welfare Services in Britain in 1975*, National Institute of Economic and Social Research, occasional papers 22 (Cambridge, Cambridge University Press, 1966).
13. A. H. Tulpule, *Forecasts of Vehicles and Traffic in Great Britain 1969*, Road Research Laboratory Report LR 28 (Crowthorne, Road Research Laboratory, 1969).
14. Colin Lester, *Britain 2001 A.D.* (London, HMSO, 1972).
15. R. Brech. *Britain 1984: A Unilever Report* (London, Darton, Langman & Todd, 1963).
16. M. Kidron, *Western Capitalism Since the War* (London, Weidenfeld & Nicholson, 1968); E. Mandel, *Europe versus America: Contradictions of Imperialism* (London, New Left Books, 1970).

The British Economy in 1975 revisited

C. J. F. Brown and T. D. Sheriff

Thirteen years ago a medium-term economic forecast was published, *The British Economy in 1975* by W. Beckerman *et al*. This article assesses the study, the reasons for its lack of success, and their implications for medium-term economic forecasting in general.

In 1965, the National Institute of Economic and Social Research published *The British Economy in 1975*—a view of what the British economy might look like in 1975 given certain optimistic assumptions.[1]

It was assumed in the study that the annual rate of growth of output per person for the whole economy could be raised to 3·5%, 1963–75. This was a formidable increase over the 1950–63 figure of 2·0%, although comparable with others being suggested in the mid 1960s (eg in the National Plan and by the National Economic Development Office). The corresponding forecast for annual growth of gross domestic product (GDP) was 3·8%. The higher growth rates of output and productivity were based on an assumption of improved international competitiveness through the virtuous circle of export-led growth. In fact, productivity and output growth did improve but the improvement came nowhere near the figure predicted (Table 1).

TABLE 1. THE PREDICTED AND ACTUAL GROWTH OF UK PRODUCTIVITY AND GDP

	Productivity[a] (%)		GDP[a] (%)	
	predicted	actual	predicted	actual
1960–1975	3·1	2·3[b]	3·5	2·7[b]
1963–1975	3·5	2·5[b]	3·8	2·7[b]

Notes: [a] Average annual rate of change. [b] Final year here is is taken as 1975*, not 1975 (see reference 2).
Sources: The British Economy in 1975; UK Department of Employment Gazette; Economic Trends, Annual Supplement, 1976, "Average estimate of GDP", page 5.

Over the period 1963–75*,[2] productivity grew only 2·5% per year and GDP 2·7% per year.

In the post mortem we have, where possible, adjusted Beckerman's forecasts to allow for the overall growth-rate error. This enables us to comment on detailed projections such as the patterns of output, productivity, consumption, and investment.

The authors are at the National Institute of Economic and Social Research, 2 Dean Trench Street, Smith Square, London SW1P 3HE, UK. The assistance of colleagues at the National Institute, especially F. T. Blackaby and G. F. Ray who read and commented on a draft of this article, is gratefully acknowledged.

One of the ways we have assessed the projections has been to compare them with a naive forecast to see whether the relatively sophisticated methods used in the study improved upon simple ones such as assuming past trends would continue. The post mortem relates only to the main body of the study—the forecasts of population and the patterns of output and expenditure. We have not dealt with the special chapters on housing, education, transport, energy and the social services.

The results of the post mortem

The total population projection diverges considerably from the actual outcome in a way which suggests that this area is certainly one deserving a great deal of attention (see Table 2). The main sources of error were the misforecast of net migration (the

TABLE 2. THE PREDICTED AND ACTUAL UK POPULATION CHANGES[a]

| | Population (M) | | Total natural increase (M) | Migration (M) | Total population increase (M) |
	1960	1975			
Predicted	52·5	59·2	5·9	0·7	6·7
Actual	52·5	56·0	3·9	−0·3[b]	3·6

Notes: [a] Components do not sum to totals due to rounding errors. [b] Residually determined.
Sources: The British Economy in 1975; Central Statistical Office, *Annual Abstract of Statistics,* 1974 and 1975.

study projected an inflow rather than the outflow that occurred) and the large overforecast of fertility rates—both particularly hazardous areas of population forecasting as has been noted recently by the Central Policy Review Staff.[3] The working population forecast is close to the actual figure for 1975 but this is the fortuitous result of two offsetting errors—an overforecast of the male working population and an underforecast of the female one. The sources of these two errors are to be found in the study's projections of the participation rates of men and women.

A shortage of labour does not seem to be the reason for the failure to achieve the improvement in output growth. It is quite likely that, with greater demand, participation rates and hours worked would have been higher than they were. Moreover, given the increase in unemployment over the period, it is difficult to argue the case for a general labour shortage.

The foreign sector was treated in such a way that a target surplus on visible trade was set, given an expected deficit on capital account and an invisible surplus. This was rather overtaken by events. In 1974 and 1975 there was a surplus on capital account which was making some contribution to the deficit on current account. On current account, the contribution of tourism was an unforeseen development and, within the visible balance, the increase in imports of manufactures was not accounted for. World trade grew much faster than anticipated and the UK's share was much lower than expected.

As a result of offsetting errors in the forecasts of aggregate consumption and total population, the forecast of the growth rate of real consumption per head differs only slightly from the actual figure for 1960–75* (2·5% and 2·3% respectively). This allows us to compare the forecast pattern of consumers' expenditure per head with a naive forecast (assuming the growth rates for 1950–60 would continue) to see whether the study improved upon a naive forecast using trend extrapolation. There is no evidence to suggest that it did. On the output side, the ranking of output growth by manufacturing industry was not forecast any better by Beckerman than by a naive forecast (which assumed rankings stayed the same as they were over the period 1950–60). There was only mixed success for the forecasts of the growth rate of output of nonmanufacturing sectors, even allowing for the overall growth rate error.

Productivity growth was projected by industry and employment growth calculated as a residual. The growth rates of productivity by manufacturing industry were forecast entirely with reference to the growth rates of output. Adjusting for errors in the latter growth rate gave forecasts which were reasonably accurate, although there were exceptions—notably textiles, shipbuilding, metal goods, other manufacturing, and coal and petroleum products. However, even allowing for errors in the output forecasts, the forecast of the growth of productivity of non-manufacturing sectors met with only mixed success. The growth rate of productivity of manufacturing itself was only slightly overforecast if the figure is calculated over the period, 1960–73. However, output growth and employment growth were well below forecast. There were around 1·5 million fewer workers in manufacturing in 1975* than the study predicted.

The results of projecting investment for the individual main sectors seem to be broadly satisfactory. Errors occur where the pattern and size of demand were not adequately foreseen (ie errors made elsewhere in the study) or in areas where investment depended crucially on policy assumptions which were not borne out (and which the study could not have foreseen). Total manufacturing investment was forecast correctly when adjustments are made for errors in the growth of output. However, Beckerman's method of projecting the pattern of manufacturing investment did not perform as well as a naive forecast.

The share of GNP going to public consumption was underestimated, although the absolute increase in public consumption was slightly less than forecast since GNP was overforecast. The predicted distribution between military consumption and public civil consumption was wrong: Beckerman expected a real increase in military spending (though not its GNP share) whereas there was a fall in real terms.

Relative price movements between the main categories of national expenditure were forecast with reference to relative productivity-growth rates alone. This simple (but probably unavoidable, given the length of the forecast period) method led to the forecast of the relative price of fixed investment being in the wrong direction.

Implications for medium-term forecasting

In this section, we shall draw some lessons relevant to economic forecasting exercises over a 10–15-year period. These comments are not intended as criticisms of Beckerman's approach, since we advocate changing the terms of reference. We cannot criticise his study for not doing what it did not set out to do but we do feel it might be useful to point to areas where effort may have been misdirected and where there are alternative approaches for future medium-term forecasting exercises.

Is it at all useful to make economic forecasts over a 10–15-year period? The study's forecast period was longer than the conventional medium term and, hence, has a greater degree of uncertainty attached to it. Nevertheless, economic advisers have to make assessments over a 10–15-year period, or longer, particularly where large indivisible capital expenditures are involved. In the energy field, for example, the life of a power station from conception to obsolescence is 40 years or more. An advantage of pushing the horizon of forecasts further forward than the conventional 5 years is that this avoids having to forecast the stage of the business cycle. There is also a case for taking a view of the economy when the trend in productive capacity is not given, since future changes in productive capacity will be an important determinant of the long-run performance of the economy.

Would it be necessary for a modern-day Beckerman to use relatively sophisticated econometric techniques? Generally, the study's projections did not improve upon naive forecasts. This either suggests that the level of sophistication in the study was unjustified or that it was not sophisticated enough. It can be argued that while both naive and econometric methods have the rationale that the past will continue, econometric techniques do at least attempt to *explain* past movements, whereas naive methods do not. On balance, we remain sceptical about the usefulness of sophisticated methods, given the level of uncertainty involved over such a long forecast period.

The expectation must be that some existing relationships will change and we do not feel that, given the present state of the art, the use of such techniques can reduce uncertainty to the extent that their use is justified. It is also unlikely that we should attempt such a detailed exercise as *The British Economy in 1975*. Consumption per head of dairy products, output of timber and furniture, and so on, are difficult enough to forecast over a relatively short period. Over a period of 15 years, they are probably impossible to forecast with any degree of confidence. Given that such an economic forecast is based on a macroeconomic framework, little would have been lost had a less-ambitious degree of disaggregation been used. The prospects for individual industries or markets are probably best assessed by means of particular studies at the microlevel of possible developments in those sectors and not by means of a system of macroeconomic equations.

The Beckerman study was a one-scenario approach to economic forecasting. It would probably be more useful to attempt a multiscenario approach in an exercise over this length of forecast period. This would involve presenting the forecast in three forms—optimistic, pessimistic and central. Any multiscenario approach is open to the criticism that decision makers can base their decisions only on one set of numbers—three sets of numbers merely add confusion. On the other hand, decision makers can base their decisions on one of the scenarios. Further, such an exercise can be revisited from time to time and can be developed into a rolling programme, incorporating analyses of the alternative policies designed to bring about one or other of the outcomes.

The problem with the study was that its one scenario was an optimistic one. Once it was apparent that the growth rates of output and productivity were not going to be achieved, little further use could be made of the forecasting framework that had been developed. Given that an economic forecast of the whole economy for 15 years hence is a useful thing to have, it appears sensible to update it continually and to incorporate alternative scenarios.

The setting of a productivity-growth target is not the only way to approach medium-term economic assessments. *The British Economy in 1975* assumed that the rate of growth of productivity was the major constraint on the rate of growth of output in the UK. However, others have argued that it is the balance of payments which is the fundamental constraint on UK growth. The argument is that the world-income elasticity of demand for UK exports is lower than the UK-income elasticity of demand for imports. If incomes in the UK rise at the same rate as world income, the demand for UK exports will grow less quickly than UK demand for imports. This means that although export-led growth may increase the theoretically attainable growth rate, an economy will hit a balance of payments constraint at a lower growth rate unless measures are introduced to influence both import- and export-income elasticities of demand so that the balance-of-payments-constrained attainable growth rate is increased. As Houthaker and Magee wrote as long ago as 1969:[4]

The exact contrary [to the Japanese case] is true for the United Kingdom, whose international economic problems have been making headlines for decades . . .the income elasticity of demand of British exports is only half that of British imports . . . Britain can therefore grow only half as fast as the rest of world in the long run if it wants to maintain its exchange rate.

What was true in Beckerman's time appears to be equally true for the medium-term economic forecaster today. Thirlwall shows that, for 113 UK manufacturing industries studied, the income elasticity of demand for exports was in all cases lower than the income elasticity of demand for imports.[5]

If the balance of payments constrains the growth of productivity (in the sense that deflationary cures for payments problems will stunt the growth in productivity) then there is an alternative to Beckerman's 'productivity-driven model' and that is a 'balance-of-payments-driven model'. This latter approach makes a forecast of world trade and then deduces what share of world trade can be expected for UK exports. Subsequent forecasts of the balance on invisibles and on the capital account allow a forecast of the volume of imports that can be afforded. Given that a relationship between imports and output exists, a likely growth rate will be suggested. Although this approach has certain *a priori* appealing characteristics, it depends on three specific variables which in the past have shown themselves to be particularly difficult to forecast: the growth of world trade, the UK's share and the relationship between output and imports.

In reality, it is likely that the rate of growth of productivity and the balance of payments constrain each other. The study's approach required an assumption of unemployment to obtain an assumption about the growth of GDP, whereas the balance-of-payments approach forecasts the growth of output and, together with some forecast of productivity growth, this gives a figure for unemployment. Thus the latter approach has the advantage of making unemployment endogenous.

In Beckerman's time, an assumption of full employment was reasonable, which it is not, of course, any longer. Both the study's approach and the balance-of-payments-driven model require assumptions about the income elasticities of demand for UK exports and imports. It is here that the medium-term forecaster must pay a great deal of attention.

The study assumed that because comparable economies such as France, Germany, and Italy had relatively high productivity growth rates, greater UK productivity growth and competitiveness could be achieved. This was unsatisfactory because the questions of how adverse income elasticities were to be improved and a greater growth of productivity achieved were never addressed.

There was an absence of discussion of microeconomic problems of the economy which a medium-term economic forecaster today would have to present. To start such an exercise with an improved productivity assumption one must have some notion as to how improved industrial relations, or industrial structure, or greater investment and so on are to come about. If it is believed that greater demand alone is sufficient to cure supply-side ills in the economy (and we must seriously question this today), then the economic forecaster must specify exactly how increased demand will come about. The study had export-led growth as the cornerstone of the mechanism but there was very little discussion as to how increased export competitiveness was to come about. Other than an aside about "the key role of incomes policy", policy was ignored. Devaluation was not even mentioned. *The British Economy in 1975* correctly identified that the UK was in a vicious circle of import-led relative stagnation but the forecast assumed that it would jump out of this circle on to the merry-go-round of export-led growth without telling us how this was to be done.

As stated earlier, this is not a criticism of the study. It states (page 67) "these are major problems in their own right (the construction of a workable incomes policy), and an analysis of future growth, *within the terms of reference we have set ourselves*, does not give us any special insight into the most appropriate measures for solving these basic problems" (our italics). In other words, Beckerman decided explicitly to ignore policy measures. However, the medium-term economic forecaster of today should perhaps recognise that Beckerman's efforts may have been misdirected and should therefore discuss policy problems if any improvement in performance is sought or assumed.

Finally, is it wise for medium-term economic forecasters to calculate private consumers' expenditure as a residual after other components of GNP have been subtracted from the forecast of GNP itself? This was the study's method; it argued (pages 272–273) that this reflected

a particular view of the process by which overall equilibrium is reached . . . [namely] that the authorities will take such fiscal and other action as may be necessary, given their estimates of the likely claims on resources from the other components of final expenditure, to ensure that personal disposable incomes are such that (given the assumed savings ratio) private consumption will be just about right to achieve full employment equilibrium.

The problem here for the economic forecaster is that, with an optimistic target for growth rate, wage inflation may occur if real private consumers' expenditure fails to rise in line with national product. If real consumption is increased to a larger share of the cake, then either exports or investment will have to be lower as a result and the growth rate will not be achieved, given the assumption usually made that real public consumption is fixed inflexibly.

This problem raises the point that medium-term forecasters should consider 'mixes' of expenditure which are not only economically sensible but are sensible politically as well. Exercises such as Beckerman's, which had real private consumption as the 'adjustment' variable, failed to appreciate the amount of inflationary pressure which can result. The study ignored inflation; it is a particularly difficult thing to forecast over 10–15 years. However, the possibility of inflationary pressure should be borne in mind when one is choosing the 'mix' of public and private consumption, investment and exports.

Some component of GNP has to be residually determined; to achieve the target GNP growth rate this must be real consumption. However, the forecaster should allow for some flexibility in public consumption since adjustments *are* made to public expenditure plans. Especially when one is looking 15 years ahead it is sensible to make provision for adjustment in both public and private consumption.

Conclusions

Our post mortem on *The British Economy in 1975* shows that:

- While a forecasting period of 10–15 years is useful, periodic revisiting of the forecasts (or even a rolling programme) *within* the period would be valuable.
- Relatively sophisticated econometric techniques did not significantly improve the success of the forecast or reduce uncertainty. We do not think that their use is justified.
- The level of disaggregation in *The British Economy in 1975* was overambitious given the macroeconomic forecasting framework which was used.
- Medium-term assessments based on a unitary outcome have little value if the single assumption on which they are based proves wrong. An approach based on alternative scenarios is likely to have a more lasting value, especially since the 'on-track' scenario can be updated.
- The constraining influence of the balance of payments on the UK's growth rate is particularly important and consideration of policies oriented towards tackling the UK's adverse income elasticities of demand for imports and exports should be included in any assessment of the UK's medium-term prospects.
- In a target-growth-rate approach to medium-term assessments where some component of GNP is determined residually, it is sensible to make provision for adjustment in both public and private consumption.

Notes and references

1. W. Beckerman *et al*, *The British Economy in 1975* (London, Cambridge University Press, 1965). A more detailed analysis of the individual sectoral forecasts can be found in C. J. F. Brown and T. D. Sheriff, "Approaches to medium-term assessment", *National Institute Economic Review*, *86*, November 1978; "Problems of medium-term assessments—a post mortem of *The British Economy in 1975*", National Institute of Economic and Social Research, discussion paper 11, December 1977.
2. We calculated growth rates to a terminal year of 1975*—an average of 1973, 1974, and 1975. This is because both 1974 and 1975 were recession years and so an average of these years plus a peak year, 1973, is more likely to give 'on-trend' figures.
3. Central Policy Review Staff, *Population and Social Services* (London, HMSO, 1977).
4. H. S. Houthaker and S. P. Magee, "Income and price elasticities in world trade", *Review of Economics and Statistics*, *51* (2), May 1969.
5. A. P. Thirlwall, "Britain's economic problem, a balance of payments constraint", *National Westminster Bank Review*, February 1978.

PROSPECTIVE

UK PRODUCTIVITY AND EMPLOYMENT IN 1991

G. F. Ray

Compared to prewar rates, the growth of UK productivity since 1945 has been rapid, but it has been slower than that of comparable countries. How is it likely to evolve over the next 14 years? To answer this the author makes assumptions about the population size, and the social and economic changes that will shape lifestyles in 1991. He examines productivity and employment in the UK, using four scenarios of output and productivity, presented in two versions. The four scenarios range from the continuation of past trends to the achievement of higher targets (eg EEC levels of productivity growth): each has two starting points, the 1977 level or the average 1973–75 level of output. The scenarios illustrate the trade off between unemployment, productivity, and growth, and highlight the possibilities facing the country in 1991: low productivity growth and a comparatively poor UK, or European levels of productivity growth and four million unemployed unless considerable changes take place. The results are not necessarily forecasts; they are the arithmetic consequences of given assumptions.

A CENTURY ago national output per employee was almost twice as high in the UK as in comparable European countries. Although the gap had narrowed by 1950, the UK was still top. The Macmillan election slogan around 1960, that the British had "never had it so good" was true in an absolute sense; yet it was not the whole truth because by then the UK was already sliding in the international income and productivity league. By the middle of this decade almost all European countries had outpaced the UK, some of them very considerably.

Productivity is of course a blanket word; although usually interpreted as labour productivity, its indicators reflect not just the labour input, but also

The author is senior research fellow at the National Institute of Economic and Social Research, 2 Dean Trench Street, Smith Square, London SWIP 3HE, UK. The views expressed are those of the author and are not necessarily shared by the NIESR.

more complex factors—such as the use of capital, resource endowment, educational levels, social attitudes and morals, the quality of management at all levels, and historical heritage—and the resulting output of goods and services.

Economic policy may follow a number of objectives: eg growth, full employment, stable currency, or external equilibrium. For some years to come, full employment, or more precisely the reduction of unemployment to an acceptable level, is likely to be in the forefront of UK policy. I will concentrate on this, without belittling the importance of any of the other possible main aims of economic management.

Past trends and forecasts

Output per head in the UK has roughly doubled since the war; its growth was rapid compared with the past, but slower than elsewhere, eg in the original European Community (Table 1). The gap in manufacturing productivity has become even larger, whether we compare countries or industries, whether we count in official exchange rates or in purchasing-power parities (Table 2).

TABLE 1. THE LAST 100 YEARS (relative GNP per head)[a]

	Relative GNP per head[a] (UK = 100)				
	1871–1875	1900–1904	1922	1950	1973
France	—	—	93	83	132
West Germany	59	64	68	63	129
Italy	52	37	52	44	100
Belgium	—	—	—	107	141
Netherlands	—	87	113	94	154
UK	100	100	100	100	100

Note: [a] GNP per person employed.
Source: See Jones,[6] and Paige *et al.*[7]

TABLE 2A. RELATIVE LEVELS OF VALUE ADDED [per person employed in manufacturing (1970) by country (UK = 100)]

	Value added	
Country	At PPP[a] rates	At OERs[b]
France	164	177
West Germany	155	176
Italy	105	111
Belgium	155	160
Netherlands	183	182
EEC[c]	147	160
UK	100	100

Notes: [a] Purchasing-power parities calculated on the basis of Mayer,[8] and Kravis *et al;*[22] [b] Official exchange rates; [c] EEC of the five countries listed.

TABLE 2B. RELATIVE LEVELS OF VALUE ADDED [per person employed in manufacturing (1970) by country for the EEC[a] at PPP rates [b] (UK = 100)]

Industry	Value added
Food, drink, and tobacco	160
Textiles, leather, and clothing	104
Chemicals[c]	151
Basic metals	253
Metal products	158
Other manufacturing	141

Notes: [a] EEC consisting of France, West Germany, Italy, Belgium, and the Netherlands; [b] Purchasing-power parities calculated on the basis of Mayer,[8] and Kravis *et al;*[22] [c] Including coal and petroleum products.

The more detailed analysis of output, employment, and productivity growth rates in the three cycles since 1960 (Table 3) indicates, however, a somewhat less depressing development: that the rates of growth of productivity in the UK have come nearer to those in the original EEC countries in the more recent cycles.

TABLE 3. PRODUCTIVITY AND OUTPUT[a] (average annual change in the UK and the EEC)[b]

Average annual change	UK(%)				EEC(%)				UK : EEC(%)			
	1960–1964	1964–1969	1969–1973	1960–1973	1960–1964	1964–1969	1969–1973	1960–1973	1960–1964	1964–1969	1969–1973	1960–1973
Output per employee												
Agriculture	6·0	5·7	7·1	6·2	7·4	6·1	6·3	6·6	0·8	0·9	1·1	0·9
Industry	3·1	3·5	3·9	3·5	5·0	6·1	4·7	5·3	0·6	0·6	0·8	0·7
Services	1·1	1·4	1·7	1·4	3·1	3·3	3·7	3·4	0·4	0·4	0·5	0·4
Gross domestic product	2·2	2·5	2·8	2·5	5·2	5·3	4·6	5·0	0·4	0·5	0·6	0·5
Industry												
Mining	4·4	4·2	1·8	3·5	4·6	5·8	5·2	5·3	1·0	0·7	0·3	0·7
Manufacturing	3·2	3·4	4·4	3·6	5·5	6·3	4·7	5·6	0·6	0·5	0·9	0·6
Electricity, gas, and water	3·5	5·5	9·7	6·1	6·6	9·1	9·6	8·5	0·5	0·6	1·0	0·7
Construction	1·6	2·7	0·4	1·7	3·2	4·3	2·9	3·5	0·5	0·6	0·1	0·5
Manufacturing												
Food, drink, and tobacco	2·2	2·9	3·5	2·9	5·5	4·3	4·4	4·7	0·4	0·7	0·8	0·6
Textiles, leather, and clothing	2·7	4·4	5·1	4·1	4·1	5·0	3·4	4·2	0·7	0·9	1·5	1·0
Chemicals	6·4	6·0	7·3	6·5	6·5	8·4	5·9	7·0	1·0	0·7	1·2	0·9
Base metals	1·2	1·7	3·0	1·9	0·9	6·0	2·6	3·4	1·3	0·3	1·2	0·6
Metal products	2·7	3·1	3·5	3·1	3·8	5·1	4·0	4·3	0·7	0·6	0·9	0·7
Other manufacturing	4·1	2·9	5·1	4·0	5·9	5·4	4·5	5·3	0·7	0·5	1·1	0·8
Output												
Agriculture	3·1	1·3	3·9	2·6	1·9	1·7	1·4	1·7	1·6	0·8	2·8	1·5
Industry	3·4	2·8	2·6	2·9	6·5	6·0	5·1	5·9	0·5	0·5	0·5	0·5
Services	2·9	2·3	3·3	2·8	4·9	5·0	5·5	5·1	0·6	0·5	0·6	0·5
Gross domestic product	3·1	2·5	3·0	2·8	5·4	5·3	5·0	5·2	0·6	0·5	0·6	0·5
Industry												
Mining	0·4	−3·7	−2·8	−2·2	0·9	−0·7	1·8	0·6	0·4	—	—	—
Manufacturing	3·3	3·2	2·8	3·1	6·6	6·5	5·4	6·2	0·5	0·5	0·5	0·5
Electricity, gas, and water	5·6	5·2	5·2	5·3	7·3	8·1	10·0	8·5	0·8	0·6	0·5	0·6
Construction	4·5	2·3	1·3	2·7	7·1	4·3	2·4	4·6	0·6	0·5	0·5	0·6

Notes: [a] Agriculture includes forestry and fishing. Services include transport, communication, distribution, and all services. Chemicals include coal and petroleum products; [b] EEC of five, ie France, West Germany, Italy, Belgium, and the Netherlands.
Source: The author's calculations, and Jones.[6]

Unfortunately, this is only true of productivity and not of output. Agriculture alone appears to have been successful on both counts—but it accounts for less than 3% of GDP in Britain. Productivity in some sectors (electricity and gas, textiles and clothing, base metals, chemicals, and "other" manufacturing) came up to the EEC mark in the 1969–1973 cycle, but there remained a yawning gap in services (the biggest employer),[1] construction, and mining (the latter because of geology and strikes). The advance in output was, however, generally not much more than half of that in the EEC.

There are two conflicting interpretations of the differences in productivity growth between countries (or industries):

● these differences are independent variables, implying that productivity is to be improved by better productive equipment, improved organisation, harder work; or

- productivity is a dependent variable, governed from the demand side, ie higher demand generates higher output, in a sense automatically resulting in higher productivity.

Probably no one would hold either proposition as wholly true, to the exclusion of the other. Indeed, neither an earlier investigation,[2] nor the analysis of the data presented now, provides evidence for proving or rejecting either of the two propositions. It is clear that direct measures to increase productivity may have an immediate effect on labour requirements and a lagged impact, in the longer run, on total output. It is also true that increases in demand at times when resources are not fully employed are accompanied, at least in the short term, by rising productivity.

None of these propositions can provide a consistent explanation of the UK's "failure". For example, while it is true that the level of investment has been consistently lower in the UK than in West Germany,[3] thus providing relatively reduced scope for installing improved productive equipment, the GDP growth rate achieved by the UK has been considerably less than could have been expected on the basis of actual investment (applying, for example, the West German capital/output ratio). The same is true in the long term for industrial output and investment, indicating relatively lower utilisation of industrial capacity.[4]

There is a considerable body of academic literature analysing the UK's "malaise",[5] to which an opinion poll has recently been added (see Table 4). Of course, no single reason can explain a phenomenon of such complexity.

Relatively little has been said of the part played by the UK's enormous war burdens. Ever since statistics started, the UK trade balance has always been in deficit, but invisible earnings, chiefly though not exclusively from investment

TABLE 4. THE CAUSES OF THE UK'S SLOW GROWTH[a]

	Support					Support		
	strong	fairly strong	divided	weak		strong	fairly strong	divided	weak
Insufficient investment	+				Bad government	+			
Profits too low, taxes too high			+		Delusions of grandeur		+		
Slow growth leads to more slow growth		+			Bad management		+		
Not as much scope for raising productivity as in other countries (because of the lack of a major agricultural sector)			,	+	Trouble with the trade unions	+			
					Overmanning	+			
					Antiquated social values		+		
					Too few good engineers and technologists				+
Not enough war damage				+	Others work harder			+	
Too much government spending		+							

Note: [a] The survey was conducted by the Consumers' Association,[10] early in 1976 among members of parliament, industrialists, trade union leaders, "City" personalities, and economists.

abroad, covered it. The sale during World War 2 of huge parts of the UK's portfolio investments and other properties abroad (forced on Churchill by the war debts) reduced this source of income.

Thus, while in 1935–1937 invisible incomes accounted for as much as 45% of goods exports, in 1957–1959 they were not more than 8% (and were further reduced later on). This change can be considered as one of the chief causes of the persistent UK balance of payments troubles since the war, which led to the stop–go policies; this, in turn, affected investments by creating an underlying crisis of confidence, thereby contributing to the short-term underutilisation of resources.

The difference in the rates of productivity growth was noted at an early stage, but there was a tendency to attribute the advance in continental Europe to postwar recovery. In 1961, one of the more thorough studies said that "it will be unprecedented if the rapid postwar rates (in Europe) are continued for another ten or fifteen years".[7] The unprecedented has nevertheless occurred.

Growth rate forecasts

In order to put forecasting into perspective, it seems useful to see how well or how badly earlier long-term forecasters fared.

There have been a number of medium and long-term forecasts for the UK economy. Most of them are not very helpful for our purpose (the ill-fated National Plan, for example, covered the much shorter period of 1964–1970). The one chosen for comparison was the result of considerable intellectual input in the early 1960s, attempting to forecast what the UK economy in 1975, ie 10–15 years later, would be like.[11]

The overall forecast for long-term (1960–1975) productivity growth was 3·1% per year whilst the actual annual advance (1960–1975) was only 2·5%.[12] Though this discrepancy makes quite a difference on a compound basis, one could argue that had output (GDP) been rising as fast as forecast—ie at the rate of 3·5% instead of 2·8%—the actual productivity gain would also have been larger, and come very near to the forecast. Hence the productivity forecast was not bad at all. The forecast was, however, right for the wrong reason. Productivity growth was grossly overestimated in some sectors (services, construction, metals) and underestimated in others (agriculture, electricity and gas, textiles). The more the analysis extends to the details, the more serious the deviations that emerge between forecast and actual.[13]

Other types of forecast, which are easily checked, are population forecasts, which have considerable bearing on any economic projection. These are published regularly in the UK, but have been subject to very significant revisions (this is not unique to the UK). Thus, the forecast for the total UK population changed as follows (the first figure is the date of publication, the second is the forecast population): 1964 (65½ million in 1990); 1968 (64¼ million in 1990); 1976 (57¼ million in 1991); ie the population forecast for 1991 was reduced by eight million, which is enormous.[14] Welfare provisions—dwellings and schools—for this additional mass of people could result in serious and unnecessary misallocation of resources (eg the recent oversupply of teachers in the UK).

Given the inaccuracy of long-term forecasts which were produced using the best methods available, it seems admissible to take a simpler approach. The output of any model, computerised or otherwise, depends on the quality of the input; surely the forecasters mentioned above, as well as others, did their best to maintain a high quality of input; what invalidated their forecasts were unforeseeable technological, structural, social, and other changes. Unforeseeable changes are also likely to occur over the next decades—a point which some may interpret as speaking against long-term forecasts. Actually I am advocating more frequent forecasts.

Life in 1991: guesses and assumptions

Economics is about people. The majority of people in a democratic society—and it is assumed that the UK will remain one—have considerable influence in shaping society, albeit slowly. But in what direction? There are many possibilities—only some can be considered here.

The end of acquisitiveness

It is probably not possible to go on indefinitely loading men and women with personal possessions. People would then cease demanding, and making more money. What they could buy with it would no longer be worth having and what they would love to buy would be beyond their means, or not available—eg domestic service.

Such a scenario assumes the end of poverty. However, the number of people falling below a changing subsistence level is still high, and does not seem to decrease much, even in the rich countries. Radical change is therefore unlikely in the short term—the acquisitive society will still be here in 1991.

The North–South problem

This is imminent. The bargaining position of the primary-producing countries (the South) has changed substantially. Yet it is difficult to imagine the South collectively marching against the North. A much more likely outcome is either some kind of general agreement or a string of piecemeal settlements, otherwise with "business as usual".

Primary products from the South may become more expensive in real terms to the less-well-endowed industrial countries and there may be other ways in which the transfer of resources from the North to the South is accelerated within a "new international economic order". The UK will have to accept this.

Overcrowding

As population increases, will a collective claustrophobia become a social force? If this should occur, the price of privacy—in a sailing boat, on a hilltop, and most of all at home—would soar, although probably not in the UK since the expected addition to the population by 1991 is relatively modest. Traffic congestion will be the order of the day—just as it is now.

The challenge of the computer

This stems from the vision of automated factories and computerised offices. The displaced people gradually become discontented enough in their idleness to start a Luddite group—breaking the computers before the machines break their spirits. This possibility cannot be ruled out entirely but there are strong signs of attempts to counter it. In any case we have yet to see empty corridors in offices (private or public). Parkinson's Law has definitely overshadowed the labour-saving effects of the computer in many, if not all applications. On the whole large-scale unemployment caused by the computer seems unlikely.

The leisure syndrome

It has often been asked—what will people do with their leisure time? Working time may be reduced further by 1991—but not by much. There will be no trace of the 25-hour week or of a universal annual vacation of eight weeks. At the level of about 40 hours a week most people seem satisfied and prefer more income (particularly when paid at overtime rates) to more leisure. Should working time be further reduced, they are ingenious enough to convert leisure into some do-it-yourself work and mothers would no doubt welcome help from men in reducing their 80–90 hour week. There would certainly be no trouble on this score in the UK where the majority of the population can always spend more time in their back gardens growing radishes or roses.

A total change of values and outlook

In a democratic society communism in its present form, or fascism in its past form, can be excluded by definition. But in the past 10–15 years we have been witnessing other movements aimed at a radical change in outlook. The hippies and beatniks—products of the postwar decades—are considered idiosyncratic by many and are on the way out. They have been publicly discussed quite widely, much more so than the revival of Christianity which manifested itself in the increase of churchgoing in the early 1960s in the USA and later on in the mushrooming of smaller congregations, often outside the institutionalised churches, affecting not just the youth but other age groups, and other countries, among them the UK. The spreading of such a revival and the resulting changes in attitudes would solve many problems, such as acquisitiveness, of our present-day society. However, it could not occur without a genuine miracle. And we have to stay within the realm of a surprise-free future—which excludes major wars and major miracles alike.

All in all, the likelihood is that society in 1991 will be rather similar to that in 1977. Of course there will be differences, but in the historical perspective they are likely to be minor rather than major ones.

Resources

Manpower

Human resources will increase considerably between now and 1991. On the basis of the population forecast by the UK Registrar General (which, despite the uncertainties mentioned, still remains the best available), the following changes can be expected (see Table 5).

In 1991 (the year of the official forecast) there will be about 1·4 million more people in the UK; by a curious demographic effect, however, the addition to the "working age" category will be more, about 2·2 million. The number of those over retirement age is expected to rise by 0·3 million and that

TABLE 5. UK POPULATION (1973 and 1991)

	1976(10³)			1991(10³)			Difference 1976–1991(10³)		
	all	males	females	all	males	females	all	males	females
Total population	55928	27219	28709	57288	28099	29189	1360	880	480
of which not available for work									
0–14	12838	6594	6244	11889	6111	5778	−949	−483	−466
15–19ᵃ	2126	1092	1034	1845	950	895	−281	−142	−139
20–24ᵇ	389	200	189	446	228	218	57	28	29
60–64ᶜ	1652	—	1652	1480	—	1480	−172	—	−172
65+	7927	3075	4852	8431	3299	5132	504	224	280
Total not available for work	24932	10961	13971	24091	10588	13503	−841	−373	−68
Available for work	30996	16258	14738	33197	17511	15686	2201	1253	948
Percentages									
By sex (%)	*100·0*	*48·7*	*51·3*	*100·0*	*49·0*	*51·0*	—	*0·3*	*−0·3*
Available for work (%)	*55·4*	*59·7*	*51·3*	*57·9*	*62·3*	*53·7*	*2·5*	*2·6*	*2·4*
Not available for work (%)	*44·6*	*40·3*	*48·7*	*42·1*	*37·7*	*46·3*	*−2·5*	*−2·6*	*−2·4*

Notes: ᵃ One half of those in this age group; ᵇ one tenth of those in this age group; ᶜ females only.
Source: Annual Abstracts of Statistics (London, HMSO, 1975).

of children and young people to fall by over 1·2 million, leaving a bigger share of the larger population in the "working age" category.[15]

Capital

The capital required for the scenarios described in more detail in the following section is likely to be available in view of the sophisticated services of the City of London. It is worth remembering that UK labour costs have become the lowest in Europe (Table 6). Although there is, of course, no particular aim

TABLE 6. TOTAL HOURLY LABOUR COSTSᵃ (UK = 100)

	1964	1974		1964	1974		1964	1974
EEC			*Other Europe*			*Other*		
France	103	118	Austria	80	120	USA	268	194
West Germany	119	185	Finland	102	126	Canada	192ᵇ	186
Italy	93	122	Norway	122	189	Japan	42	105
Belgium	105	175	Sweden	153	208			
Netherlands	95	184	Switzerland	110	157			
Denmark	119	188						

Notes: ᵃ Including all social charges; at official exchange rates; ᵇ 1967.
Source: Ray.[16]

in retaining this "leadership", it is a fact to be reckoned with, and may attract foreign investment if improved industrial relations can be maintained. Where investment was low in the past, the usual cause was not lack of funds but lack of confidence.

If investment capital is forthcoming, there is hope for expecting that modern technology will spread through industry rapidly enough to improve the technical level of products and processes. Several academic and government investigations have found that although research and development in the UK in aggregate compares favourably with other industrial countries, it has been concentrated on prestige projects (such as Concorde). The development of less glamorous but, in international trade, more important areas has been neglected. And whereas the UK has excelled in highly original innovations, she was slow in diffusing them through industry.[9] It is reasonable to assume that some lessons have been learnt for the future.

The UK's resource base for industrial materials is meagre; she depends on imports. In this, however, she is no different from many European industrial countries. The materials for her industry will be forthcoming either in the conventional way, ie via the market mechanism, or in some negotiated new international economic order. There is, nevertheless, one important exception which makes the UK's medium-term future significantly more hopeful, and this is the area of energy. The North Sea will supply enough oil and gas to meet all UK requirements by the early 1980s; this situation may continue to 1991 and perhaps even somewhat longer.[17]

Last, but certainly not least, good management at all levels—government, employers, and unions—is an important requisite of progress. On the whole, Britain cannot be said to have excelled on this point in the recent past (Table 4).

For the future, the assumption is made that the quality of management will improve; more precisely, that demand will be tuned to the growth rates envisaged in the scenarios; that the competitiveness of British goods and services will be raised both abroad *and* in the home market; that industrial relations will not deteriorate; and that the better organisation of production and services will help to attain those productivity goals which are set out in the next section. These may seem heroic assumptions against the isolated background of the earlier economic history of the UK, but they are attainable if viewed within an international context.

Eight scenarios

These scenarios are focused on one particular objective of economic policy: full employment. In other words, given certain output targets and productivity goals, what will employment and unemployment be by 1991? The quantified assessments are rigid and are based on present conditions, eg working time. A discussion of foreseeable or possible changes follows.

The scenarios are based on simple extrapolations of assumed trend growth rates. There is, however, one basic question to be faced at the outset: the starting point of these trends. It is tempting to take the view that past long-period growth rates reflect booms and recessions alike and therefore a start should be made from a position which is more or less "on trend". One such position could be the average of three years: 1973, 1974, and 1975, the first being a boom year, the third a recession year, and the second in between.

Attractive as this procedure may seem, there are a number of objections. Cheap energy is unlikely to return between now and 1991; inflation is world-wide and remains a major preoccupation to an extent unknown in the two previous decades (at least in most industrial countries); and the stresses on the world economic and monetary system are different in kind, let alone in degree, from those of the Bretton Woods era.

Most forecasters have taken the view that we have to resign ourselves to the prospect of slower growth in the world economy. The UK is unique among

TABLE 7. FOUR SCENARIOS FOR 1991 (output, productivity, and employment in the UK)[a]

	Agri-culture	Manufacturing						Industry				Total	Services	GDP
		Food, drink, tobacco	Textiles, leather, clothing	Chemicals	Base metals	Metal prod-ucts	Other	Manufacturing	Mining	Electricity, Gas, Water	Constr-uction			
Version A: 1977–1991														
Scenario 1: past trends[b]														
output[c]	2.6	2.6	1.8	6.0	0.5	2.9	4.2	3.2	−2.2	5.3	2.7	3.0	2.8	2.9
productivity[c]	6.2	2.9	4.1	6.5	1.9	3.1	4.0	3.7	3.5	6.1	1.7	3.4	1.4	2.2
employment[a]	0.25	0.70	0.70	0.44	0.40	3.23	1.44	6.91	0.16	0.31	1.45	8.83	15.62	24.70
Scenario 2: possible[e]														
output[c]	3.0	2.9	2.3	6.5	2.0	3.4	4.6	3.7	0.0	5.5	2.5	3.4	3.0	3.2
productivity[c]	5.0	3.1	4.3	6.8	2.6	3.3	4.4	3.9	3.0	6.0	1.5	3.5	1.9	2.6
employment[a]	0.31	0.71	0.72	0.45	0.44	3.37	1.44	7.13	0.23	0.33	1.45	9.14	14.99	24.44
Scenario 3: desirable[f]														
output[c]	3.5	3.2	2.7	6.8	3.0	3.8	5.0	4.1	0.5	5.8	3.0	3.9	3.2	3.5
productivity[c]	7.1	3.5	5.1	7.3	3.0	3.5	5.1	4.3	3.5	9.7	1.7	4.1	2.0	2.9
employment[a]	0.25	0.70	0.69	0.44	0.48	3.46	1.38	7.15	0.23	0.21	1.51	9.10	15.18	24.53
Scenario 4: EEC[g]														
output[c]	3.5	3.2	2.7	6.8	3.0	3.8	5.0	4.1	0.5	5.8	3.0	3.9	3.2	3.5
productivity[c]	6.3	4.4	3.4	5.9	2.6	4.0	4.5	4.2	5.2	9.6	2.9	4.2	3.7	4.0
employment[a]	0.28	0.62	0.86	0.53	0.51	3.23	1.50	7.25	0.18	0.21	1.28	8.92	12.05	21.25
For comparison: employment in 1977[h]	0.40	0.73	0.95	0.47	0.48	3.32	1.40	7.35	0.35	0.35	1.26	9.31	12.89	22.60
Version B: 1973–5 to 1991														
Employment in														
Scenario 1	0.23	0.71	0.71	0.43	0.40	3.36	1.54	7.15	0.14	0.31	1.58	9.18	15.80	25.21
Scenario 2	0.30	0.73	0.75	0.45	0.46	3.53	1.54	7.46	0.22	0.32	1.58	9.58	15.03	24.91
Scenario 3	0.23	0.71	0.70	0.43	0.51	3.64	1.47	7.46	0.22	0.19	1.66	9.53	15.27	25.03
Scenario 4	0.27	0.62	0.93	0.54	0.54	3.36	1.62	7.61	0.17	0.19	1.36	9.33	11.53	21.13
For comparison: employment in 1973/5	0.42	0.75	1.04	0.47	0.51	3.47	1.49	7.73	0.36	0.35	1.34	9.78	12.52	22.72

Notes: [a] No change in the working time (ie length of working week, annual leave, national holidays) has been allowed for in the estimates. Self-employed are excluded. Productivity is output per employee per year. Columns do not always add up to totals because of rounding; [b] Projection of the past(1960–1973) trends in the disaggregated sectors; these may result in output and productivity growth rates which differ from the actual past trend for the aggregates. [c] Annual average compound percentage rates; calculated at 1970 prices; [d] This is the employment required in 1991, assuming the given growth rates of output and productivity (but no change in the working time), in millions; [e] A possible development, assuming somewhat faster overall output growth (which may, however, realistically mean slower growth in some sub-sectors). Faster productivity growth is assumed, though not as fast as achieved in 1969–1973; [f] Output somewhat faster as under scenario 2, productivity as in 1969–1973, or in 1960–1973, whichever is higher, with additional improvement in the productivity of services; [g] Output as in scenario 3, productivity as in EEC in 1969–1973; [h] Millions of employees, partly estimated.

the industrial countries (except for Norway) in view of her luck in the North Sea, but her advantages did not begin to unfold before the closing months of 1977.

Between 1973 and 1977 the UK was struggling with a balance of payments deficit, a rate of inflation that was much higher than in most industrial countries, unemployment, and all sorts of allied problems. Unlike most other industrial countries, she experienced no recovery from the 1975 world recession and incurred large overseas debts. Hence, this dark period is best written off and a new and clean sheet started in 1977. This, therefore, is taken as the starting point of the trend growth rates in the first set of scenarios (version A) which are, in a way, an assumed continuation of the past, albeit after an important break (Table 7).

The first set (version A) of scenarios may be thought to be erring on the gloomy side because of this break. A countervailing factor is that even the worst scenario supposes the continuation of the trends achieved in a "better world" (ie pre 1973). But whilst the past might have been better for "the world" it was certainly not good for the UK economy, bedevilled as it was by the seesaw of stop–go. If the main cause of the stop–go policy and the chief villain of postwar years, ie the balance of payments constraint, is removed by the oil income, surely the *past* trend in the *new* circumstances cannot be considered too ambitious.

On the same grounds, another set of scenarios (version B) has also been compiled; this takes its start in 1973–1975, on the basis that "a trend is a trend" and if there are bad years they should be balanced, within the trend, by good ones. In other words, in the long run to 1991, during 17 years from 1973–1975, there is time for catching up. There may be arguments in favour of this view which, however, seems improbable to me. Therefore, the version A ("with break") will be shown in detail; exactly the same output and productivity assumptions have been applied in version B (the "uninterrupted" trend) as well but only the end results are presented.

It should be remembered that the projections are the results of simple arithmetic. They are not forecasts; they are answering a "what if" question: what will employment/unemployment be if . . .

It is almost certain that developments will differ from these simple projections; there will be technological developments leading to structural changes that are impossible to foresee with any accuracy. These and other changes will have to be accommodated within the framework of the projections which yield altogether eight scenarios (four each for versions A and B).

Within each version there are four sets of output assumptions: the first is a continuation of past (1960–1973) trends, the second ("possible") aims at modestly higher goals, and the third ("desirable") and fourth, on the whole, apply the growth rates of the 1969–1973 cycle with some adjustments. Given somewhat better conditions (eg the reduction of the balance-of-payments constraint), these rates of output growth seem attainable (Table 7).

The productivity assumptions vary more. In scenario 1 the past trend is carried forward again, whilst the other three start from the higher output assumptions mentioned above. In scenario 2 productivity growth is above the past long-term trend but not as high as it actually was in 1969–1973. Scenario

3 assumes that productivity will continue growing at the fastest rate already achieved either in the long-term past or in the recent cycle—whichever is higher—with allowance for the abnormally low productivity in mining and construction (due to extreme past conditions), and a higher productivity rate for services.[1] Finally, scenario 4 takes the productivity growth rate of the EEC in 1969–1973, and applies it to the output growth rates of scenario 3.

The higher productivity growth rates in scenario 3 appear feasible—given the low utilisation of investment, the various measures which may be taken on both the employers' and the employees' sides, and the prospect of improved economic conditions caused by the abandonment of the stop–go policy.

Scenario 4 presents problems. The EEC's productivity rate in some industries was higher than in the UK; in others, the UK rate in the recent cycle was just as high or even higher. The reorganisation of UK industry may achieve the higher productivity rates even in those sectors where the UK was lagging. However, to more than double the productivity growth rate in the services sector is impossible if the present UK system of accounting is retained (although it would not be beyond reach if the EEC method of calculation was applied).

The scenarios are given without the direct effects of oil production, except for the part played by it in 1977 in version A. The comparison with the past is clearer without oil. It is uncertain what oil production will be in 1991; it may be already declining and not very different from that in 1977 or—if the more optimistic expectations come to pass—it could also be high. In this case it would add 0·1–0·2% a year to GDP growth in 1977–1991, or about 0·3% in 1973/75–1991. But its implications for employment are marginal since fewer than 25 000 persons are likely to be directly employed in North Sea oil and gas production.

The scenarios assess the employment requirements on the different assumptions. The results are set against the forecast working population in 1991 in

TABLE 8. EMPLOYMENT: THE 1991 SCENARIOS

	1977[a]	Version A				1973/1975 average	Version B			
		1	2	3	4		1	2	3	4
Population[b]	55·9	57·3	57·3	57·3	57·3	56·0	57·3	57·3	57·3	57·3
Population in working age[b]	31·0	33·2	33·2	33·2	33·2	30·9	33·2	33·2	33·2	33·2
Population "working"[b]	26·3	28·1	28·1	28·1	28·1	25·7	27·6	27·6	27·6	27·6
Participation rate (%)	84·7	84·7	84·7	84·7	84·7	83·0	83·0	83·0	83·0	83·0
Of those "working"										
in employment[b]	22·6	24·7	24·4	24·5	21·3	22·7	25·2	24·9	25·0	21·1
employers and self-employed[b]	1·9	1·9	1·9	1·9	1·9	1·9	1·9	1·9	1·9	1·9
armed forces[b]	0·3	0·3	0·3	0·3	0·3	0·4	0·3	0·3	0·3	0·3
unemployed[b]	1·5	1·2	1·5	1·4	4·6	0·7	0·2	0·5	0·4	4·3
unemployed (%)	5·7	4·3	5·3	5·0	16·4	2·6	0·7	1·8	1·4	15·6

Note: [a] Partly estimated; [b] in millions.
Source: Tables 5 and 7; *Annual Abstract of Statistics,* August 1976, HMSO, London; *Monthly Digest of Statistics,* August 1976, HMSO, London.

Table 8. With unchanged participation rate and working time they indicate the following:

Version A

● if past trends are resumed as from 1977 unemployment would be reduced

from its high level but not by very much, leaving 4·3% of the active labour force still unemployed;[18]
- the higher output and productivity assumptions result in even higher unemployment;
- on the EEC-based scenario 4 unemployment reaches 16%. The crucial role of services employment is clearly demonstrated and will be discussed later.

Version B
- past trends would lead to overfull employment; 0·7% unemployed indicates an overheated economy;
- the higher rates of productivity in scenarios 2 and 3 would leave 1·4–1·8% unemployed;
- scenario 4 again gives unacceptably high unemployment rate (15·6%).

Scenario analysis

The difference between the two versions is partly due to the "break", and partly to the participation rate which was considerably lower in 1973–1975 than in 1977, accounting for 1·7% of the labour force. For clearer comparison this figure should either be deducted from the results of version A (making the unemployment percentages more acceptable in scenarios 1 to 3 at 2·6, 3·6, and 3·3% respectively) or added to the unemployment percentages of version B (which thus become 2·4, 3·5, and 3·1% respectively).

These estimates must be considered in the light of possible changes which may affect the working population and the length of the working year.

Retirement age: this is now 65 for males, 60 for females; it may change for three reasons. First, under pressure from the present high unemployment, the government has already announced a voluntary scheme for earlier retirement, but because of its unattractive financial provisions it is unlikely to be successful, although it may be a pointer to the future. Second, following the miners who have begun to retire earlier, there is pressure from other groups of workers as well for earlier retirement; this is likely to spread. Third, some measures may be taken in the near future in view of the Sex Discrimination Act to bring the retirement ages for the two sexes nearer to one another. The outcome of all these is difficult to foresee but the aggregate effect may be a reduction of the working population.

School-leaving age: this has recently been raised to 16 and is unlikely to change.

Participation rate: this could change—as it indeed changed significantly between 1973–1975 and 1977.

Annual leave: at present the average annual vacation is 3·7 weeks (3·2 weeks for manual and 3·9 for nonmanual workers). By 1991 it may rise to 4–4½ weeks.

Public holidays: their number has been raised, as from 1977, to eight, which is still the lowest in industrial countries.[19] One more day may be added by 1991.

However, these shortenings of working time do not influence employment requirements proportionately. Their impact is complex, so that while initially they result in more overtime, they are offset by reorganisation of the workflow (ie increased productivity). Thus, whilst the reduction in working time, on the above assumptions, may seem considerable (altogether 7–7½% or 0·5% per annum by 1991), its impact on labour requirements may be small because of the offsetting effect of higher productivity during the time actually spent in work.[20] The impact of changes in working time on productivity is included in the base data for the past periods in the calculations and is thus unlikely to have any major influence on the crude estimates concerning employment and unemployment. If the retirement age is lowered, it should reduce the working population and thereby unemployment, by perhaps 250 000.

The structure of employment

Table 9 indicates how the structure of employment would change in the various scenarios. Apart from scenario 4, which leaves an unacceptably high unemployment, the share of employment of manufacturing, or that of all industries,

TABLE 9. THE PATTERN OF EMPLOYMENT IN 1991

	1977	Version A				1973/1975	Version B			
		1	2	3	4		1	2	3	4
Agriculture[a]	1·8	1·0	1·3	1·0	1·3	1·9	0·9	1·2	0·9	1·3
Manufacturing[a]	32·5	28·0	29·2	29·1	34·1	34·0	28·3	30·0	29·8	36·0
Mining[a]	1·5	0·6	0·9	0·9	0·9	1·6	0·6	0·9	0·9	0·8
Electricity, gas[a]	1·5	1·3	1·4	0·9	1·0	1·5	1·2	1·3	0·8	0·9
Construction[a]	5·6	5·9	5·9	6·2	6·0	5·9	6·3	6·3	6·6	6·4
Industrial total[a]	41·2	35·8	37·4	37·1	42·0	43·0	36·4	38·4	38·1	44·1
Services[a]	57·0	63·2	61·3	61·9	56·7	55·1	62·7	60·4	61·0	54·6
Total employed[b]	85·9	87·9	86·9	87·2	75·8	88·5	91·3	90·2	90·6	76·4
Employers and self-employed[b]	7·2	6·7	6·7	6·7	6·7	7·5	6·9	6·9	6·9	6·9
Forces[b]	1·2	1·1	1·1	1·1	1·1	1·4	1·1	1·1	1·1	1·1
Unemployed[b]	5·7	4·3	5·3	5·0	16·4	2·6	0·7	1·8	1·4	15·6

Notes: [a] Percentage of employed labour force; [b] percentage of population "working".
Source: Table 7.

would fall considerably from the 1977 level—a level that has already been considered by many as a sign of "de-industrialisation". In parallel, employment in services would rise in scenarios 1–3 to well over 60%, from 57% in 1977.

Services employment in these scenarios would be higher by about 2 million by 1991 as compared with 1977 in version A; in version B the rise is even higher. The question naturally emerges: is it conceivable that services employment should be 2 million higher in 14 years' time? In the past 14 years, 1963 to 1977, the rise in services employment was of the same order. Will this trend continue?

There are several aspects to be considered. On the one hand, the importance of services has grown, and probably will continue to do so; the shift towards a post-industrial, service economy may gather momentum. Moreover, the 1975–1977 austerity measures reduced employment in services, and it is quite conceivable that as soon as these can be abandoned employment in some service sectors will rise (eg health); this effect, however, should not be overrated.

It should also be remembered that UK services have been, so far, more competitive internationally than manufactures; hence from this viewpoint too, exportable services may be a growing sector. Also, the shift to services is not a phenomenon unique to the UK: it happened in all EEC countries, as well as in the USA and Japan. Although the 1977 share of services in employment in the UK was among the highest, neither the relative addition to the numbers employed in services in the past 12–14 years, nor the share of labour force

TABLE 10. EMPLOYMENT IN SERVICES

	Year	Employment (million)	(%)ᵃ	Year	Employment (million)	(%)ᵃ	Number of years	Increase (million)	(%)ᵇ	Shift (%)ᶜ
Belgium	1963	1·6	46·8	1975	2·1	56·5	12	0·5	30	9·7
France	1962	7·3	39·2	1975	10·4	50·1	13	3·1	40	10·9
West Germany	1962	9·6	37·5	1976	11·5	47·0	14	1·9	20	9·5
Italy	1963	6·1	31·8	1976	7·8	41·1	13	1·7	30	9·3
Netherlands	1961	2·1	48·0	1975	2·7	58·6	14	0·6	30	10·6
USA	1963	40·2	59·0	1976	56·8	67·0	13	16·6	40	8·0
Japan	1963	18·6	40·4	1975	26·9	51·5	12	8·3	45	11·1
UK	1962	11·8	48·0	1976	13·9	56·4	14	2·1	20	8·4

Notes: ᵃ Percentage of total civilian employment; ᵇ percentage of increase in services employment, rounded; ᶜ shift of employment from other sectors into services, as percentage of total civilian employment.
Source: OECD Observer.

affected by this shift was particularly high—indeed it was lower, in these terms, than in most of the countries mentioned (Table 10).

On the other hand, there are developments favouring a decline in service employment. Some services are not competitive internationally, in terms of productivity; their labour force is likely to be reduced. If services become *the* growth area, innovative activity will be livelier there and this is also likely to reduce labour requirement, at least relatively.

Finally, much depends on the method of calculating productivity in services. This is clear when the service employment figures of scenarios 3 and 4 are compared: for the same output, employment is three–four millions higher if productivity, is reckoned on the basis of the UK system rather than by the EEC system. Even high productivity levels in some service sectors in the EEC cannot account for such a large gap: to a large extent it must be due to differences in definitions.

This is important. If the past UK productivity figures are recalculated on the EEC basis, the future rates would probably become higher, reducing labour requirements for services; but of course this "saving" would add to unemployment.

Scenario 4 (in both versions) also deserves some comments. It indicates a reduction in service employment by 1½ million. This again is due to the high-productivity assumption and is the most unlikely outcome of the arithmetic. But apart from services, the productivity targets of this scenario and the resulting employment are not basically different from those in scenarios 2 and 3, indicating that in the industrial sectors (leaving aside services, which are bedevilled by methodological puzzles) there is a good chance of catching up with the past growth rates (though not the level) of productivity in the EEC.

It is not possible to go into the productivity of services here. It is an important subject and more study is needed of this relatively obscure area.

The UK economy in 1991: productivity

The "productive potential" (ie the growth rate in the medium or long term which keeps the UK economy in reasonable equilibrium) has been estimated at around 3% or, more recently, rather lower at perhaps $2\frac{1}{2}$%. (Oil production, a new phenomenon, will raise it a little.)

This is borne out by scenario 1 (in both versions) after adjustment for the different participation rates. At this rate, however, the GNP gap between the UK and other European industrial countries will probably continue to widen. Therefore the attainment of higher productivity growth is highly desirable and according to scenarios 2 and 3 this does appear possible.

Indeed, conditions may be favourable for an even more rapid advance in productivity. If, with the help of oil revenues, the UK economy can free itself over a long period from the straitjacket of its recurring balance-of-payments restraint; if the planned reconstruction of industry is only moderately successful and a wider dissemination of "best practice" techniques is achieved; and if relatively peaceful industrial relations can be maintained, the higher rates of real productivity growth seem within reach.

Employment

The concept of full employment used to be identified with an unemployment rate of $1\frac{1}{2}$–2%, but it is arguable that, given changed conditions, perhaps $2\frac{1}{2}$%, or even 3%, may be regarded as "full employment". Special attention should be devoted to the question of employment in services. But with this *caveat*, scenario 2 already points to a higher ($3\frac{1}{2}$%) unemployment figure, and the faster Britain's productivity grows, the higher unemployment becomes, *unless* there is additional output. This is not impossible, since the output targets in the scenarios are not excessive. But it will require adjustments in attitudes: the recognition of the desirability of faster growth (which would be needed for a more rapid improvement in the partly obsolete social infrastructure as well— a factor often neglected by the champions of "zero growth"); an atmosphere of confidence as an incentive for job-creating investment; a stronger competitive position extending to non-price factors as well; and changed attitudes at all levels, including the government, business, and the public, aimed at the attainment of more ambitious goals.

These are not minor requirements, but if the UK is to emerge from her present unfortunate predicament a start must be made.

There are three ways for avoiding the higher unemployment shown in the scenarios: higher output and hence more jobs, earlier retirement, or shorter working week. The last two, however, may have social and practical disadvantages.

There may be more to the solution of the present unemployment problem, and to the prevention of its recurrence than the simple, though by no means easy, prescription of higher output. The right and the desire to work are genuine human priorities. Creating conditions which prevent the re-emergence of unemployment in a future whose shape is unknown, will require institutional and social innovations. In Tinbergen's words: "Spiritual leaders and statesmen should try to ensure that genuine human priorities are not forgotten. It is an imbalance that natural scientists and technologists have so far been much more successful inventors than social scientists or spiritual and political leaders".[21]

Notes and references

1. There is a considerable difference between the calculation of productivity in various countries. The UK method produces unduly depressed figures as compared with the procedure applied in most EEC countries. For more details, see T. P. Hill, *The Measurement of Real Product* (Paris, OECD, 1971). This, however, does no more than partially account for the difference between the UK and EEC.

2. C. T. Saunders, "International comparison of productivity growth in the 1950s", paper delivered to the productivity conference of the Royal Statistical Society, 20 February 1963.

3. The percentage share of gross fixed capital formation in GDP in 1962–1972 was 18·1% in the UK and 25·5% in West Germany.

4. OECD, *The Growth of Output 1960–1980* (Paris, OECD, 1970), especially Appendix V.

5. Among others, see R. Bacon and W. Eltis, *Britain's Economic Problem: Too Few Producers* (London, Macmillan, 1976); R. E. Caves and associates, *Britain's Economic Prospects* (London, Allen and Unwin for Brookings Institution, 1968); C. F. Pratten, "Labour productivity differentials within international companies", University of Cambridge, DAE, Occasional Paper 50 (London, Cambridge University Press, 1976); G. F. Ray, "Grundprobleme der britischen Wirtschaft," *Wirtschaftsdienst*, Hamburg, *56*, February 1976.

6. D. T. Jones, "Output, employment and productivity in Europe since 1955", *National Institute Economic Review*, *77*, August 1976.

7. D. C. Paige, F. T. Blackaby, and S. French "Economic growth: the last hundred years", *National Institute Economic Review*, *16*, July 1961.

8. J. Mayer, "Comparison réelle du produit intérieur brut des pays de la Communauté Européenne", *Analyse et Prévision*, *17* (6), June 1974.

9. L. Nabseth and G. F. Ray, eds, *The Diffusion of New Industrial Processes: An International Study* (London, Cambridge University Press, for NIESR, 1974).

10. *Which?*, Consumers' Association, June 1976, *Money Which?* section, pages 71–80.

11. W. Beckerman and associates, *The British Economy in 1975* (London, Cambridge University Press for NIESR, 1965).

12. The forecasts were for 1960–1975; the actual figures are those for 1960–1973. 1974 and 1975 have been omitted because their inclusion would have introduced serious distortions in view of the energy shortage in the former and the recession in the latter year. Their inclusion would very considerably widen the gap between forecast and actual; which is wide enough even for the "very good" 1973. A much more detailed analysis is contained in "Problems of medium-term assessment: a post-mortem on 'The British Economy in 1975' " by C. J. F. Brown and T. D. Sheriff, Discussion paper 11, National Institute of Economic and Social Research, 1978.

13. Some examples are: the decline in coalmining was not foreseen; output of the gas industry was severely underestimated because of the unforeseeable emergence of North Sea gas, although some allowance was made in the forecast for the import of natural gas; manufacturing employment fell (a rise was forecast); in construction there was an increase in employment, not a decline as expected; within manufacturing there were also gross misforecasts, eg the output of the aircraft industry was expected to grow fast (4% per year): output actually fell considerably.

14. The misforecast crudely equals the total population of New York (1970 census) or Austria.

15. The calculation is based on the present retirement age (65 for males, 60 for females); this may change—as will be discussed later.
16. G. F. Ray, "Labour costs in OECD countries, 1964–1975," *National Institute Economic Review, 78*, November 1976.
17. Research suggests that even a very sharp decline in world oil prices would leave existing fields sufficiently profitable for supplies up to 1991 not to be greatly affected—but such a sharp fall seems highly unlikely. See C. Robinson and J. Morgan "World oil prices and profitability of North Sea oil", *Petroleum Review*, April 1976. Treasury estimates suggest that the net effect of the North Sea oil programme will, for some considerable period, relieve the balance-of-payments constraints which have been a feature of British economic policy (eg stop–go) over the past two decades. See (UK) Treasury, *Economic Progress Report, 76*, July 1976, HMSO, London.
18. Unemployment rates have been calculated on the UK definition: those registered as unemployed.
19. The number of public holidays is 14 in the USA (+ 1 in New York, + 2 in San Francisco), 11–12 in West Germany, ten in France, 16 (reduced to ten) in Italy, 13 in Belgium, and eight in the Netherlands.
20. In 1960–1973 productivity in UK manufacturing per year rose by 3·6% and productivity per hour worked rose by 4·1% a year.
21. J. Tinbergen, "Economic progress: a vision", in *Plan Europe 2000: The Future is Tomorrow* (The Hague, M. Nijhoff, 1972), pages 274–310.
22. I. B. Kravis *et al*, *A System of International Comparisons of Gross Product and Purchasing Power*, United Nations International Comparison Project (Baltimore and London, Johns Hopkins University Press, 1975).

TECHNICAL INNOVATION AND INDUSTRIAL DEVELOPMENT

1. The new causality

Keith Pavitt

The author argues that the nature and importance of technical change in industry in the OECD countries began to alter in the 1970s. Statistical evidence suggests that investment activities embodying process innovations were the main motor of technical change in the 1960s. In the 1970s, however, there are signs that innovative activities (research, development, and design) resulting in product and systems innovations grew in importance. If the trend continues, countries and industries with strong capacities for industrial innovation will have higher living standards and industrial employment than those without. In this article the author discusses the nature of, and the evidence for, the changes taking place. In the next article he will discuss the policy implications.

IN A PREVIOUS article, I argued that, in the 1970s, a number of factors have resulted in the beginnings of significant changes in the rate and direction of technical innovation in manufacturing industry in the OECD countries.[1] Here, I will explore the validity and the implications of this point of view.

At one level it is an attempt to begin to build an analytical framework, and to identify related research questions. At another level, it is a set of speculations about some of the possible future effects of technical innovation on OECD firms, industries, and countries. It draws heavily on work already done at the Science Policy Research Unit, and in particular on work to be published early in 1980.[2]

Keith Pavitt is a senior research fellow at the Science Policy Research Unit, University of Sussex, UK, and a member of *Futures* editorial advisory board. He is editor of *Technical Innovation and British Economic Performance* (London, Macmillan, 1980).

The author is grateful for critical and constructive comments on an earlier draft of this article from John Clark, George Ray, Christopher Saunders, and Luc Soete.

Central to this exploration are the changing nature and importance of innovation in the industrially advanced countries. Competition from the newly industrialising countries in standard goods will continue to increase; patterns of consumers' tastes and expenditures in the industrially advanced countries will continue to change; energy and environment will continue to be scarce and expensive resources; and the opportunities for rapid technical change will remain considerable in electronics, and may become so in bio-chemistry.

Successful innovators will be those who respond to these trends. They will probably be those with a strong capacity for innovation in one or more of the following areas: capital goods, process engineering, fine materials, durable consumer goods, or automatic assembly. This capacity will probably rely increasingly on formally established activities in research, development, and design, and on the ability to mobilise and assimilate technologies from a wide range of sectors, including electronics, in response to market and production needs.[1]

My starting hypothesis is that many of these changes are already being felt, and that they will have increasingly important effects on international patterns of industrial development, and on the policies of industrial firms and governments. I shall begin by describing in more detail the prevailing, invest-ment-led view of technical change in industry and by contrasting it with the innovation-led view that I am proposing, before making some preliminary and crude statistical tests on the validity of the latter view.

The prospects of future international divergence in industrial development within the OECD region, and the related questions of national and company policy will be discussed in part 2 of this article.[3]

Technical change in the 1960s: capital-embodied process innovation

Since the 1950s, economists and other writers have increasingly recognised the importance of technical change for industrial performance and economic growth. Implicit in much of the writing are two assumptions.

- Most technical innovation is capital-embodied process innovation for the production of physically homogeneous goods; the mental image is that of bulk steel production, where increased demand leads to increased investment embodying the latest process technology.
- Advanced process technology is developed and first commercialised in the USA, before spreading internationally as a consequence of other countries' investment activities.

A recent and persuasive exploration of the validity of such assumptions can be found in the analysis by J. Cornwall of growth in the OECD countries between 1950 and 1970.[4] Drawing on the work of Schumpeter and Svennilson,[5, 6] he argues that growth involves structural change, with new products and tech-niques being developed in response to changing tastes, technology, and relative prices. Between 1950 and 1970, such change was very rapid compared to preceding periods, largely because government action maintained aggregate demand, thereby creating a favourable climate for innovation.

According to Cornwall, differences amongst countries in their rates of economic growth in this period resulted mainly from differences in the performance of manufacturing industry, which in turn resulted from differences in entrepreneurship and skills, the former being reflected in the rate of investment in manufacturing. This investment incorporated international best-practice (ie US) technology, so that poorer countries had the possibility of catching up more quickly. These assumptions were incorporated into a model which gave statistically significant results.[7]

Thus Cornwall's model (and that of many other analysts) of industrial development in the OECD area is basically a convergence model with capital-embodied technical change. Its main conceptual weakness is that it does not define or measure 'entrepreneurship' and 'skill' independently of the volume of investment. As Eltis has shown,[8] it considerably overestimates the rate of manufacturing growth in the UK: actual growth was less than two-thirds of predicted growth, which confirms that the quality and efficiency of investment should be considered as well as its volume. The model also has a related practical weakness, since it cannot explain a process of industrial divergence that began to take place in Europe in the 1960s: as D. Jones has shown,[9] British manufacturing industry then began to diverge downwards from the rest of Western Europe in terms of output per man–hour, and Italy began to do so in the 1970s.

Technical change in the 1970s: R & D-dependent product innovation?

Furthermore, the changes in tastes, technology, relative costs, and competitive pressures that have emerged in the 1970s, and that I have identified earlier, may be making Cornwall's model obsolete. Many of the manufacturing sectors that grew rapidly, or invested heavily, in the 1950s and 1960s in the OECD area were those involving the production of relatively standard goods where new technology was embodied mainly in new capital equipment: eg consumer durables and intermediate products, such as bulk chemicals, paper, glass, ferrous and nonferrous metals.

Production of such goods in the OECD area is unlikely to expand so rapidly in the 1980s, given saturation effects in the OECD countries (ie diminishing income elasticities of demand) which have often been accelerated as a consequence of the higher costs of energy and environment; and also given the spread of capital-embodied process technology—*à la* Cornwall—beyond the central OECD area to regions with more favourable cost structures and demand elasticities: Southern and Eastern Europe, and certain countries in the Middle East, Latin America and South-East Asia.

For many of the same reasons, the OECD countries are being increasingly constrained to concentrate their production and trade in sectors dominated by product and systems innovations produced by organised research, development, and design. To some extent, this is a continuation of a very long-standing trend in the OECD countries toward greater specialisation in capital goods at the expense of consumer goods. And to some extent, it reflects shifts of emphasis within sectors: towards product novelty, quality and reliability, and automated assembly in durable consumer goods; towards high-value-added materials in

chemicals and other intermediate products; and towards the growing incorporation of electronics in capital goods. As Cornwall himself points out, nonprice
factors can be critically important in the success of these products.[10]

At the same time, the distribution within the OECD area of the capacity
to create and commercialise new technology has changed considerably since
the 1950s. In 1962 the USA accounted for about 54% of all industry-financed
R & D in the OECD countries.[11] This was down to just under 50% in 1967,
and to about 45% in 1975. Between 1967 and 1975, France, West Germany,
and Japan increased their combined share from about 29% to nearly 36% of
the total.[12]

Cornwall speaks of a 'development ladder' in industrialisation with countries
moving from low-wage industries like textiles, towards investment-intensive
industries (such as chemicals, steel, consumer durables) in response to the
relatively rapid growth of domestic demand. In conditions of rapid growth, the
diffusion of the most up-to-date process technology will also be rapid, with the
possibilities of reaping static and dynamic economies of scale. At some stage, a
country will be competitive in export markets in these industries, a position
that it will be able to maintain if it continues to exploit economies of scale and
to respond to new opportunities emerging in the domestic market.

I am suggesting a further step in this 'development ladder' with the following
characteristics. Entrepreneurial activity is no longer focused on responding to
domestic demand by investing in borrowed and adapted foreign technology, nor
is it focused on competing on the basis of price. It concentrates instead on
seeking new product opportunities in all the industrially advanced markets, in
market segments where quality may take precedence over price, and on exporting equipment, technology, and skills to the newly industrialising countries. Its
main competitive advantage is not geographical proximity to a richer expanding market but its ability to respond to international threats and opportunities
emerging from changing tastes, technology, relative prices, and competition.
Essential features of this ability are capabilities in R & D and design, and the
ability to couple them to developments in world markets. The dominant
activity moves from investment in productive capacity to investment in R & D
and in the other activities necessary for product innovation and related process
changes.

In viewing technical change, this is a shift from a world inspired by Keynes,
where demand and investment policies predominate, to a world inspired by
Schumpeter, where the entrepreneurial search for new market opportunities
predominate.

The causal structure of the former (as exemplified in the work of Cornwall)
is as shown in Figure 1a. I am suggesting that the causal structure is as shown
in Figure 1b.

Any shift from the former to the latter causal structure will be reflected in a
greater correlation between direct statistical indicators of innovative activities,
on the one hand, and indicators of industrial competitiveness, on the other hand.
It may also be reflected in a diminishing capacity to explain relative competitive
performance in terms of price. All these characteristics can certainly be detected
in studies of competitive performance in specific industrial sectors.[13] But doubt
can always be expressed about the validity of generalisations based only on a

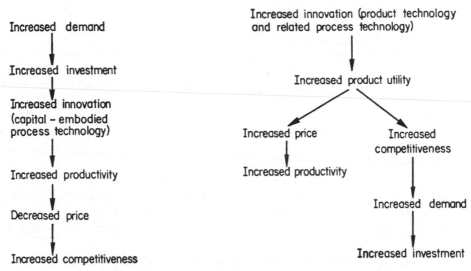

Figure 1. (a) Former and (b) suggested causal structures

few sectors. For this reason, I shall now explore briefly the degree to which the characteristics show up in broader aggregates in manufacturing industry.

Statistical analysis

The direct statistical indicators of national innovative activities that I shall use are expenditures by industry on R & D, and the number of patents granted to foreign countries in the USA;[14] the essential data for 11 OECD countries are shown in Table 1. The measures of industrial competitiveness are levels and trends in productivity and exports. The causal structure that I shall be exploring is set out in Figure 1b. At this early stage, readers will have to tolerate a certain fuzziness in the exploration.

TABLE 1. INDICATORS OF INNOVATIVE ACTIVITY IN 11 OECD COUNTRIES

	US patents per capita (UK=100)			Industry-financed R & D per capita (UK=100)		Industry-financed R & D in 1975 (% of 1967)
	1963	1969	1975	1967	1975	
Belgium	27	40	51	56	80	133
Canada	95	82	103	45	46	103
France	53	63	82	61	86	136
West Germany	125	135	180	101	148	138
Italy	20	18	24	24	36	148
Japan	12	37	106	61	113	189
Netherlands	81	76	82	103	110	104
Sweden	150	147	204	83	152	173
Switzerland	341	298	424	124	187	147
UK	100	100	100	100	100	92
USA	na	na	na	128	158	114
Total US patents (10 countries)	7833	15720	23289	na	na	na

Note: na means not applicable.
Sources: See References 12, 15, 16, 17.

Manufacturing productivity

The experience of the 1960s shows that national levels of innovative activity did not have a determining influence on national levels of industrial productivity. There is no positive and significant relationship between national levels of innovative activity in 1963, on the one hand, and manufacturing productivity levels in 1963 (*1*) and rates of increase up to 1970 (*2*), on the other. (The numbers in brackets refer to the relevant regression analysis, see Table 2.) Indeed, for the latter, the relationship is negative, which is consistent with Cornwall's model of countries catching up through closing a (production) technology gap. This was probably the case for Belgium, Italy, and Japan, all of whom had rapid rates of increase in productivity in this period. Neither does the picture change in the 1970s. The association between national innovative activities and manufacturing productivity levels in 1974–1975 remains virtually insignificant (*3*), and that between national innovative activities in

TABLE 2. SUMMARY OF CORRELATION AND REGRESSION RESULTS

Row	Variables		Countries[a]	r^2	t	Significance[b]
1	Manufacturing output per man-hour (1963)	US patents per capita (1963)	B,F,G,I,N, UK	$+0\cdot17$	$0\cdot914$	ns
2	Increase in manufacturing output per man-hour (1970/1963)	As above	C,F,G,I,J,N, UK	$-0\cdot25$	$1\cdot303$	ns
3.1	Manufacturing output per man-hour (1974)	US patents per capita (1975)	B,F,G,I,N, UK	$+0\cdot03$	$0\cdot360$	ns
3.2	As above	Industry-financed R & D per capita (1975)	As above	$-0\cdot09$	$0\cdot194$	ns
4.1	Increase in manufacturing output per man-hour (1978/1969)	US patents per capita (1969)	C,F,G,I,J, UK	$-0\cdot25$	$1\cdot163$	ns
4.2	As above	Industry-financed R & D per capita (1967)	C,F,G,I,J, UK, USA	$-0\cdot24$	$0\cdot920$	ns
5.1	Increase in US patents (1976/1963)	Increase in manufacturing output per man-hour (1976/1963)	C,F,G,I,J, UK	$+0\cdot86$	$5\cdot057$	1%
5.2	Increase in industry-financed R & D (1975/1967)	As above (1975/1967)	C,F,G,I,J, UK, USA	$+0\cdot77$	$4\cdot044$	1%
6	As above	Increase in manufacturing output (1975/1967)	B,C,F,G,I,J, N, Swe, UK, USA	$+0\cdot21$	$1\cdot475$	20%
7	As above	Increase in industry-financed R & D as a percentage of value added (1975/1967)	C,G,J,N, Swe, UK, USA	$+0\cdot63$	$2\cdot890$	5%
8.1	As above	Increase in manufacturing investment (1975/1967)	C,F,G,I,J,N, Swe, UK, USA	$+0\cdot38$	$2\cdot053$	10%
8.2	As above (1973/1967)	As above (1973/1967)	As above	$+0\cdot89$	$4\cdot377$	1%
9.1	As above (1975/1967)	Gross rate of return in manufacturing (1975/1967)	C,G,J, Swe, UK, USA	$+0\cdot05$	$0\cdot439$	ns

(continued)

TABLE 2—*continued*

Row	Variables		Countries[a]	r^2	t	Significance[b]
9.2	Increase in industry-financed R & D as a percentage of value added (1975/1967)	Gross rate of return in manufacturing (1975/1967)	C, G, J, Swe, UK, USA	−0·59	1·360	ns
10.1	Increase in industry-financed R & D (1975/1967)	Increase in manufacturing unit values (1975/1965)	B,C,F,G,I, J,N, Swe, Swi, UK, USA	+0·33	2·098	10%
10.2	As above	Increase in currency value in US $ (1975/1967)	As above	+0·11	1·039	ns
11.1	Share of world manufacturing exports (1963)	Share of US patents (1963)	B,C,F,G,I, J,N, Swe, Swi, UK	+0·85	6·802	0·2%
11.2	As above (1969)	As above (1969)	As above	+0·82	6·104	0·2%
11.3	As above (1975)	As above (1975)	As above	+0·77	5·111	0·2%
11.4	As above (1967)	Share of industry-financed R & D (1967)	As above, plus USA	+0·65	4·130	1%
11.5	As above (1975)	As above (1975)	As above	+0·58	3·536	1%
12.1	Manufacturing exports per capita (1963)	US patents per capita (1963)	B,C,F,G,I, J,N, Swe, Swi, UK	+0·32	1·935	5%
	As above	As above	As above, less B	+0·84	6·126	0·2%
12.2	As above (1969)	As above (1969)	As above, plus B	+0·19	1·358	ns
	As above	As above	As above, less B	+0·75	4·531	0·2%
12.3	As above (1975)	As above (1975)	As above, plus B	+0·20	1·434	20%
	As above	As above	As above less B	+0·64	3·552	1%
12.4	As above (1967)	Industry-financed R & D per capita (1967)	As above, plus B	+0·18	1·310	ns
	As above	As above	As above, less B	+0·52	2·731	5%
12.5	As above (1975)	As above (1975)	As above, plus B	+0·25	1·629	20%
	As above	As above	As above, less B	+0·64	3·531	1%
13	Increase in manufacturing exports (1970/1963)	US patents per capita (1963)	B,C,F,G,I, J,N, Swe, Swi, UK	−0·17	1·297	ns
14.1	As above (1977/1970)	As above (1969)	As above	−0·01	0·266	ns
14.2	As above	Industry-financed R & D per capita (1967)	As above, plus USA	−0·01	0·236	ns
15	Increase in manufacturing exports (1977/1965)	Increase in manufacturing unit values (1977/1965)	As above	0	0·062	ns
16.1	As above (1970/1963)	Increase in manufacturing productivity (1970/1963)	F.G.I.J. UK, USA	+0·88	5·408	1%
16.2	As above (1978/1970)	As above (1978/1970)	As above	+0·93	7·422	0·2%
16.3	As above (1970/1963)	Increase in manufacturing prices (1970/1963)	As above	−0·21	1·017	ns
16.4	As above (1978/1970)	As above (1978/1970)	As above	+0·17	0·914	ns

(continued)

TABLE 2—*continued*

Row	Variables		Countries[a]	r^2	t	Significance[b]
17[c]	Trends in industry-financed R & D (1967, 1969, 1971, 1973, 1975)	Trends in manufacturing investment (1967, 1969, 1971, 1973, 1975)	Canada	+0·44 (0·20)	1·534	20%
			France	+0·92 (0·47)	6·073	1%
			West Germany	+0·78 (0·55)	3·222	5%
			Italy	+0·95 (1·06)	7·529	0·2%
			Japan	+0·70 (0·87)	2·647	10%
			Netherlands	+0·52 (0·09)	1·792	20%
			Sweden	+0·95 (1·69)	7·324	0·2%
			UK	0 (0)	0·058	ns
			USA	+0·15 (0·40)	0·736	ns
18[d]	Trends in industry-financed R & D as a percentage of value added	Trends in the gross rate of return in manufacturing	Canada (1967, 1969, 1971, 1973, 1975)	−0·46	1·610	20%
			West Germany (1967, 1969, 1971, 1973, 1975)	−0·50	1·725	20%
			Japan (1967–1973)	−0·35	1·645	20%
			UK (1964, 1966–1969, 1972, 1975)	+0·23	1·237	ns
			USA (1967–1975)	−0·78	4·959	0·2%

Notes: [a] Countries: B (Belgium), C (Canada), F (France), G (West Germany), I (Italy), J (Japan), N (Netherlands), Swe (Sweden), Swi (Switzerland). [b] ns means not significant. [c] Numbers in brackets under r^2 show the percentage increase in R & D for each percentage increase in investment between 1967 and 1975. [d] Numbers in brackets after each country are years for which data are available. *Sources:* National patenting in the USA (*1–5, 11–14*);[16] industry-financed R & D (*3–6, 8–12, 14, 17*);[15] industry-financed R & D as a proportion of value added (*7, 9, 18*);[18] population;[17] growth of output per man-hour in manufacturing (*2, 4, 5, 16*);[19] growth of output in manufacturing (*6*);[19] levels of manufacturing productivity (*1, 3*);[9] investment in manufacturing (*8, 17*);[20] return on investment in manufacturing (*9, 18*);[20] trends in unit values of manufacturing exports (*10, 15*);[21] trends in currency values (*10*);[19] shares and trends in manufacturing exports (*11–15*);[21] trends in manufacturing exports (*16*);[19] and trends in manufacturing prices (*16*).[19]

the late 1960s, and the growth of manufacturing productivity in the 1970s is weakly negative (*4*).

However, there is a close association, from the mid 1960s to the mid 1970s, between the growth of national manufacturing productivity and the growth of innovative activities (*5*). This cannot be explained by the greater or lesser success of national policies to promote industrial growth. Only about a fifth of the differences amongst countries in the growth of industrial R & D can be explained in terms of increased output (*6*). Considerably more can be explained by the differences amongst countries in the way that industrialists changed the proportion of resources at their disposal that they allocated to R & D: the countries with relatively large increases in industry-financed R & D were those where the proportion of value added spent by industrialists on R & D increased most rapidly, and vice versa (*7*). This is consistent with the view that a high growth of productivity and of innovative activities are both reflections of dynamic and entrepreneurial management: relatively high productivity growth requires innovative activities for learning and improvement of borrowed technology. It results in fewer possibilities for borrowing better technology from elsewhere, which requires a greater in-house search for new and better products and processes. It is also consistent with the significant association between national rates of growth of industrial R & D and of manufacturing investment between the mid 1960s and the mid 1970s (*8*), although it has not been possible so far to explore which way the causality runs between these two variables.

In this context, it is worth noting that differences in national *trends* in profit rates[22] do not appear to have had a significant influence on differences in national trends in R & D expenditures, or in the percentage of value added devoted to R & D (*9*). However, increases in industry-financed R & D have been positively associated with increases in manufacturing export prices. But the association is weak, and the causal relationship difficult to interpret; in any event, appreciating national currencies do not appear to have been a significant stimulus to increase industrial R & D (*10*).

Manufacturing exports

The close links between innovative activities and the international competitive environment have been recognised since the 1960s in the development of theories of international trade.[23] Since the early 1960s at least, there has been a close association between national shares of innovative activities and national shares of manufacturing exports (*11*). To some extent this simply reflects the considerable variation amongst countries in their population size. However, the association between per capita innovative activities and per capita exports is also close, when Belgium (which has the highest per capita exports, but one of the lowest levels of per capita innovative activities) is excluded from the sample (*12*).

The deviance of Belgium results from its rather special industrial structure. Together with Soete, I have shown elsewhere that there is considerable variance amongst industries in the degree of association between innovative activities and export shares.[18] The coefficients of determination are not significant in most traditional sectors (nondurable consumer goods, metals), but are significant in most capital goods and chemicals, and in many consumer durable goods. Figures 2 and 3 summarise some of our results for chemicals and non-electrical machinery. Most of the large deviations from the regression lines result from the behaviour of multinational firms in relation to small countries. These are particularly active in Belgium, in addition to which Belgian-owned firms have relatively strong innovative activities in sectors with relatively low levels of R & D and patenting activity (metals and stone, clay and glass).

In spite of this strong static association between innovation and exports, the trend in the 1960s was that of the weaker countries catching up. The association between per-capita innovative activities in 1963 and the growth of manufacturing exports between 1963 and 1970 is weakly negative (*13*). The four countries with the most rapid growth of exports in this period were all countries with relatively low levels of innovative activity: Belgium, Canada, Italy, and Japan.

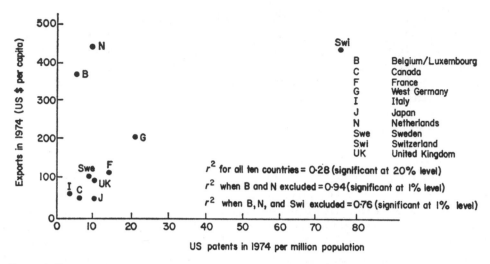

Figure 2. Export performance and US patenting: chemicals (US Standard Industrial Category 28)

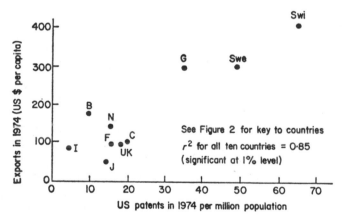

Figure 3. Export performance and US patenting: nonelectrical machinery (US Standard Industrial Category 35)

This, again, is consistent with Cornwall's model. However, the picture may be changing in the 1970s, when the weak negative relationship between per-capita innovative activities in the late 1960s, and the growth of manufacturing exports between 1970 and 1978, virtually disappears (*14*). Canada's rate of manufacturing export growth moves from the highest to the lowest of the group, those of Belgium and Italy decline relative to those of other countries, and that of Switzerland (with relatively high innovative activities) improves relative to other countries. Japan's manufacturing exports continue to expand rapidly, and so does the volume and intensity of its innovative activities.

In spite of the received wisdom, the association between relative movements in manufacturing prices and relative competitiveness has empirically been a shaky one. Houthaker and Magee found this to be the case for the period from 1951 to 1966.[24] From 1965 to 1977, differences amongst countries in the rate of increase in manufacturing prices explained virtually none of the intercountry differences in the rate of growth of manufacturing exports (*15*). The problem may be the inadequacy of export-price indices; perhaps the major inadequacy is that these indices do not sufficiently reflect differences in product quality (ie utility).

This last hypothesis has gained considerable ground recently, particularly in the UK. Stout and Saunders have shown that,[25, 26] in spite of markedly greater unit values, German and French engineering goods are more competitive than British goods. Posner and Steer have shown that British manufacturing exports have continued to decline relatively over the past ten or more years,[27] in spite of favourable price competitiveness. Hibberd and Wren-Lewis have shown that movements in relative prices cannot explain the considerable increase over the past 15 years in UK imports of manufactures.[28, 29]

Some rough correlations covering the six major OECD countries suggest that there may have been a significant change in the 1970s in the way in which the international market for manufactures works. Between 1963 and 1970, the relations amongst relative national trends in productivity, prices, and exports were what the textbooks say that they should be: relatively high growth in productivity was reflected in relatively small increases in prices, and relatively high growth of exports. However, between 1970 and 1977, relatively high growth in productivity was reflected in relatively rapid increases in exports, and relatively *high* increases in prices (*16*). Could it be that value added and competitiveness is being reflected increasingly in greater product quality rather than the lower cost of inputs?

Divergence in industrial development?

Considerably more thorough and careful statistical work will need to be done to assess the degree to which innovative activities are becoming a dominant influence on industrial performance. Evidence on the (lack of) relationship between innovative activities and productivity levels in the 1960s and the 1970s suggests that it is not yet dominant. Yet there are a number of trends that suggest that it might become so: the close association amongst trends in productivity, investment, and innovative activities; the close links between innovative activities and export performance; the importance of nonprice factors in export competitiveness.

If this trend continues, national patterns of economic growth, income per capita, and industrial employment will all be strongly influenced by capacities and performance in industrial innovation.[30] In my next article I shall explore the degree to which different OECD countries have this capacity for innovation, and what any differences might mean for the future.

Notes and references
1. K. Pavitt, "Technical change: the prospects for manufacturing industry", *Futures*, August 1978, *10* (4), pages 283–292.
2. K. Pavitt, ed, *Technical Innovation and British Economic Performance* (London, Macmillan, 1980).
3. K. Pavitt, "Technical innovation and industrial development: the dangers of divergence", *Futures*, February 1980, *12* (1).
4. J. Cornwall, *Modern Capitalism* (London, Martin Robertson, 1977).

5. J. Schumpeter, *The Theory of Economic Development* (Oxford, Oxford University Press, 1961).

6. I. Svennilson, *Growth and Stagnation in the European Economy* (Geneva, Economic Commission for Europe, 1954).

7. For example, Cornwall showed the following relationship for the six big OECD countries (France, West Germany, Italy, Japan, UK, and USA):

$$Q_m = -0 \cdot 036 + \frac{0 \cdot 953}{q_r} + 0 \cdot 229 \left(\frac{I}{Q}\right)_m,$$

where Q_m was the national rate of growth of manufacturing output, q_r was the ratio of national to US per capita income, and $(I/Q)_m$ was the ratio of investment to value added in manufacturing. The R^2 statistic was $0 \cdot 80$, significant at the 5% level.

8. W. Eltis, in a book review, *Economic Journal*, September 1978, *88* (351), page 585.

9. D. Jones, *Output, Employment and Labour Productivity in Europe since 1955, National Institute Economic Review Number 77* (London, National Institute for Economic and Social Research, 1976).

10. J. Cornwall, *op cit* Reference 4, page 173.

11. C. Freeman and A. Young, *The Research and Development Effort* (Paris, OECD, 1965).

12. OECD, *Technical Advance and Economic Policy* (Paris, OECD, 1980).

13. R. Rothwell, "Innovation in textile machinery", in K. Pavitt, *op cit* Reference 2; E. Sciberras, *Technical Change and the US Consumer Electronics Industry* (Brighton, Science Policy Research Unit, University of Sussex, 1980); and W. Walker and P. Gardiner, "Innovation and competitiveness in portable power tools", in K. Pavitt, *op cit* Reference 2.

14. For a systematic discussion of the validity, advantages, and drawbacks of these measures see K. Pavitt and L. Soete, "Innovative activities and export shares: some comparisons between industries and countries", in K. Pavitt, *op cit* Reference 2. Suffice to say here that, taken together, they give consistent results. The advantage of the patent measure is that it enables international comparisons at a relatively disaggregated level.

15. OECD, *Trends in Industrial R and D in Selected Member-Countries, 1967–1975* (Paris, OECD, 1980).

16. Office of Technology Assessment and Forecast, *Company Listing and Patent Activity Profiles;* and *US Patent Activity in Thirty-Nine Standard Industrial Classification Categories:* information supplied to the Science Policy Research Unit, University of Sussex, 1977.

17. United Nations, *Statistical Yearbook* (New York, UN, various years).

18. K. Pavitt and L. Soete, *op cit* Reference 14.

19. Various titles in the *National Institute Economic Review* series, London, National Institute for Economic and Social Research.

20. OECD, *Report on Past and Present Trends in Industrial Investment* (Paris, OECD, 1979).

21. United Nations, various issues of the *Monthly Bulletin of Statistics*, New York.

22. Defined as gross operating surplus divided by gross capital stock: see Reference 20.

23. R. Vernon, ed, *The Technology Factor in International Trade* (Irvington, NY, Columbia University Press, 1970).

24. H. Houthaker and S. Magee, "Income and price elasticities in world trade", *Review of Economics and Statistics*, May 1969, *51*, pages 111–125.

25. D. Stout *et al*, *International Price Competitiveness, Non-Price Factors and Export Performance* (London, National Economic Development Office, 1977).

26. C. Saunders, *Engineering in Britain, West Germany and France* (Brighton, Sussex European Research Centre, University of Sussex, 1979).

27. M. Posner and A. Steer, "Price Competitiveness and Performance of Manufacturing Industry", in F. Blackaby, *De-industrialisation* (London, Heinemann, 1979).

28. J. Hibberd and S. Wren-Lewis, "A study of UK imports of manufactures", Government Economic Service Working Paper Number 6, London, HM Treasury, 1978.

29. In his 1978 presidential address to the Royal Economic Society, A. J. Brown observed that "The international price mechanism does not seem to have worked very effectively to induce export-led growth . . . . Is there a continuous decline in the competitive quality of British and US goods, or in the relative effort or quality of advertising and after-sales service related to them?"

30. Reports and analyses discussing this question are now being published in a number of countries. See, for example: Science Council of Canada, *Forging the links: a Technology*

Policy for Canada, report 29 (Ottawa, SCC, 1979); C. Stoffaes, *La Grande Menace Industrielle* (Paris, Calmann-Levy, 1978); K. Oshima *et al*, *The Role of Technology in the Change of Industrial Structure* (Tokyo, Industrial Research Institute, 1977); Boston Consulting Group, *A Framework for Swedish Industrial Policy* (Boston, USA, BCG, 1978); and Royal Swedish Academy of Engineering Sciences (IVA), *Technical Capability and Industrial Competence* (Stockholm, IVA, 1979).

TECHNICAL INNOVATION AND INDUSTRIAL DEVELOPMENT
2. The dangers of divergence

Keith Pavitt

Given that innovation is playing an increasingly important role in industrial growth (see the first half of this article), one can attempt to identify the countries likely to succeed or fail in this area. The author concludes that countries may be classified into three groups—and analyses which countries will be able to make the transition into higher divisions (eg Japan). Most countries will remain outside the first division, with the result that national economies will tend to diverge rather than converge. At the micro-level firms will have to choose between developing a capacity for innovation or opting for cheaper, and less effective, strategies (eg locating operations offshore).

To WHAT degree does each of the OECD countries have a capacity for industrial innovation? And what are the implications of any differences in this capacity?

An appropriate metaphor for such an exploration may be found in football league tables. First-division countries are those capable of responding successfully to the threats and opportunities presented by the changes in tastes, technology, relative costs, and competitive pressures that have emerged in the 1970s. They can be identified through their relatively high level of innovative activities, particularly in chemicals, electronics, and machinery.

Second-division countries are those that, given the lower level of their innovative activities, have difficulties in making the changes that the first-division countries can. They feel under threat from the third-division countries, which are beginning to move on from exporting textiles, shoes, and clothing to bulk chemicals, steel, and standard consumer durables. Experience has shown that—through precisely the capital-embodied technical change described by

Keith Pavitt is a senior research fellow at the Science Policy Research Unit, University of Sussex, UK, and a member of *Futures* editorial advisory board. He is editor of *Technical Innovation and British Economic Performance* (London, Macmillan, 1980).

The author is grateful for critical and constructive comments on an earlier draft of this article from John Clark, George Ray, Christopher Saunders, and Luc Soete.

Cornwall—it is not too difficult to move up from the third division to the second. Italy, Japan, and Spain have done so in the past 20 years, and there are plenty of other contenders for promotion in Southern and Eastern Europe, Latin America and South East Asia.

The available statistics on industrial R & D activities in OECD countries, and on patents granted in the USA, give a good indication of where the main OECD countries sit in the innovation league tables. Overall levels and trends are shown in Table 1. More detailed sectoral data can be found in reports by the OECD[1] and the Office of Technology Assessment in the USA.[2]

The first division

From these data emerge three undisputed members of the first division: West Germany, Sweden, and Switzerland. All three have relatively high levels of innovative activities that have increased steadily since the mid 1960s. All three have maintained their export positions reasonably well, in spite of relatively high cost increases since the 1960s. Within their high overall levels of innovative activity, West Germany is relatively strong (ie has a comparative advantage) in chemicals, machinery, and motor vehicles. Switzerland is strong in chemicals and machinery and Sweden's strength lies along the whole chain of metal-related products: metal manufacture, fabricated metal products, machinery, motor vehicles, and household consumer durables. However, all three countries are relatively weak in electronics.

US patenting data cannot be used to assess the US position to the same degree of accuracy and detail, but a comparison of industry-financed R & D expenditures suggests that the USA occupies a similar position of strength. It also has a preeminent technological position in aerospace and other defence-related sectors. But the rate of increase of industrial R & D has been relatively low. Some observers argue that the USA has lost its technological lead in many sectors of capital goods and durable consumer goods, because of the opportunity cost of huge military and space expenditures,[3] or because of too much concentration on direct foreign investment.[4, 5] Whatever the merits of these arguments, the USA does not appear to be the technologically predominant power.

This tendency is unlikely to be reversed in future, if only because of the rapid emergence of Japan as a strongly innovative country. As Table 1 shows, Japan, in terms of innovation, was one of the weakest OECD countries as late as 1963. By 1975, it had overtaken Belgium, Canada, France, Italy, the Netherlands, and the UK. Already a first-division country in electronics, Japan also has a comparative advantage in metal production and motor vehicles but a disadvantage in machinery.

Table 1 suggests that the Netherlands was a strong first-division country in the 1960s, but might be threatened with relegation in the 1980s if present trends continue. The rate of increase of innovative activities since the mid 1960s has been slow. This relative decline has been spread across all industries, but has been particularly strong in the sector where the Netherlands has had—and still has—a marked comparative advantage, namely, electrical and electronic products.

TABLE 1. INDICATORS OF INNOVATIVE ACTIVITY IN 11 OECD COUNTRIES

	US patents per capita (UK=100)			Industry-financed R & D per capita (UK=100)		Industry-financed R & D in 1975 (% of 1967)
	1963	1969	1975	1967	1975	
Belgium	27	40	51	56	80	133
Canada	95	82	103	45	46	103
France	53	63	82	61	86	136
West Germany	125	135	180	101	148	138
Italy	20	18	24	24	36	148
Japan	12	37	106	61	113	189
Netherlands	81	76	82	103	110	104
Sweden	150	147	204	83	152	173
Switzerland	341	298	424	124	187	147
UK	100	100	100	100	100	92
USA	na	na	na	128	158	114
Total US patents (10 countries)	7833	15720	23289	na	na	na

Note: na means not applicable.
Sources: See References 1 and 2.

The second division

All the members of the first division in innovation are (not unnaturally) countries with relatively high levels of manufacturing productivity, and the one contender for promotion in the near future, Japan, will soon become one. At least three second-division countries, France, Belgium, and Canada, also have relatively high levels of productivity, in large part reflecting their efficient investment-intensive industries.

The level of innovative activities has increased steadily in France and Belgium since the 1960s. Apart from government-financed programmes in aerospace, France's comparative advantage lies in metal products and in other trans-portation equipment (motor vehicles, railway equipment, motor cycles, and bicycles), and it has improved its position in electronics (mainly military and industrial products). Belgium's comparative advantage lies, as I have already mentioned, in metal production and in stone, clay, and glass products. Since the 1960s, Belgium has improved its relative position in fabricated metal products and machinery.

The data in Table 1 suggest that—given the close proximity of Canada to the USA—the statistics on Canadian patenting in the USA exaggerate the extent of Canadian innovative activities, compared to those of Western European countries and Japan. The R & D statistics suggest that, in terms of innovation, Canada is stuck firmly in the second division, with a relatively low overall level of expenditure. Canada's comparative advantage lies in farm machinery, nonferrous metals, and fabricated metal products. It has a persistent weakness in chemicals and electronic products, although electrical products hold up rather better. Canada is one of the OECD countries where the proportion of manufacturing value added spent by industrialists on R & D activities has fallen since the mid 1960s.

The other such country is the UK, where industry-financed R & D also fell in real terms between 1967 and 1975. In the early 1960s, British industry was a big R & D spender with a low level of productivity, when compared to other Western European countries. Since then, R & D has adjusted relatively downwards rather than productivity relatively upwards—perhaps because British R & D had relatively low productivity, as did British manufacturing investment.

More than any other country in Western Europe (but not more than the USA), the UK has a comparative advantage in innovative activities in aerospace and other defence-related technologies. This advantage has been maintained, and even reinforced, in the 1970s. In most civilian industries, the picture is very different. The strong comparative advantage of the 1960s in electronics and in nonferrous metals has virtually disappeared and R & D in mechanical engineering has been almost halved. In spite of a relatively favourable trend in export prices since the mid 1960s, there has been no marked improvement in export performance: manufacturing imports are increasing rapidly, and competing on nonprice factors. Only the chemical sector has held up reasonably well in innovative activities, and has begun to emerge as a source of UK comparative advantage.

Like the UK, Italy also has relatively low manufacturing productivity. In spite of rapid increases since the mid 1960s, innovative activities remain relatively low, with a strong comparative advantage in motor vehicles, relative growth in machinery, relative decline in chemistry, and continuing weakness in electronics.

International implications

If I am correct about the growing importance of industrial innovation, and about the relative strengths and weakness of the countries I have mentioned, what might be the policy implications for the 1980s? If present trends continue, we can expect Japan to join West Germany, Sweden, and Switzerland as countries with strong capacities for innovation. The Netherlands (and perhaps the USA) may begin to lose some of their strength. France and Belgium will be working their way steadily towards promotion. Italy, Canada, and the UK will be stuck or declining.

The first international consequence of this would be the complete end of any convergence model of economic growth with the USA at the apex. The USA could well be overtaken in productivity and real income per head by countries such as Germany and Japan: the economic and political consequences would be considerable, and their full nature and scope cannot be analysed here. In addition, differences in industrial employment, in economic growth, and in levels of income per head amongst Western European countries could persist and even grow. This process of economic divergence could come to dominate economic and political relations amongst Western European countries.

Relations with the newly industrialising countries could also be strongly influenced. Countries in the second division will find it increasingly difficult with present wage rates to compete on the basis of price in a widening range of standard products. Because of weakness in innovative capacity, they will also find it difficult to move resources into product markets where technical quality is at a premium. Since the work force in such countries is unwilling to accept cuts in real wages, the threat of unemployment will be considerable, and protectionest pressures will be strong. In this context, it is not altogether surprising that the UK and France took obstructive positions on Third-world industrial exports at the Tokyo tariff negotiations in 1979. Entry into the first division could be the only way for the OECD countries to avoid having to choose between falling living standards or unemployment.

A national policy for innovation

But how can entry to the first division be secured? The usual advice favours 'positive' adjustment policies (eg manpower retraining and other measures to encourage workers out of uncompetitive industries), rather than negative adjustment measures (eg subsidies and other aids to uncompetitive industries), which would slow down or stop the necessary process of change. Whilst necessary, such policy prescriptions may not be sufficient, especially if there are few employment opportunities available in the sectors expanding on the basis of successful innovation.

In other words, national policies to promote innovation will assume greater importance: indeed, the recent spate of reports and analyses cited in the first half of this article suggests that they already do. However, many difficulties remain in defining what the content of such policies should be. Over the past 20 years, the promotion of innovation has consisted mainly of government finance for big and sophisticated R & D projects in aerospace, nuclear energy, or computers: these projects often reflected the needs of particular lobbies rather than the opportunities of changing markets.

Specifying a policy for technical innovation is no easy task, although it is relatively easy to identify objectives. West Germany, Sweden, and Switzerland demonstrate that a high level of industrial R & D is not the only characteristic of a strong innovative capacity. These three countries also have a high quality of basic research in universities and engineering schools; and all members of their workforces, including engineers and managers (many of whom are engineers), are highly trained. The government of each country plays a major role in creating an infrastructure of skills and basic knowledge.

A favourable economic climate is not enough

It is much more difficult to identify the appropriate policy instruments. Future requirements for innovation will be dispersed and differentiated widely across firms and industries: innovation must be integrated into an industrial strategy for products and markets. Given such variety, some analysts argue that the best policy for innovation is an indirect one of creating the right economic climate to encourage innovative activities: buoyant demand conditions and high profits to encourage investment and R & D, and a market system that enables strong firms to expand and weak ones to contract. On closer examination, such a policy begs virtually all the questions I am raising here. Because the policy neglects to examine the factors influencing the development of an innovative capacity, it is a prescription that, by itself, is likely to work only in those countries who need it least, namely those already in the first division.

In these countries, precisely because productivity is high and manufacturing products are competitive, profit trends are likely to be relatively favourable and demand conditions buoyant, whilst the reverse will be true in the weak countries. Furthermore, it is in many of the weak or weakening countries that the association between trends in innovative activities and trends in investment are the weakest.

Even if one assumes that the causality runs from buoyant demand conditions through investment to the growth of R & D, investment stimulation is not likely to do much to increase R & D in Canada, the Netherlands, and the UK although it could have an effect in France and Italy (*17*). (The numbers in brackets refer to the rows in Table 2.) It is, as I mentioned in the first half

TABLE 2. SELECTED CORRELATION AND REGRESSION RESULTS

Row	Variables		Countries[a]	r^2	t	Significance[b]
9.1	Increase in industry-financed R & D (1975/1967)	Gross rate of return in manufacturing (1975/1967)	C,G,J, Swe, UK, USA	$+0\cdot05$	$0\cdot439$	ns
9.2	Increase in industry-financed R & D as a percentage of value added (1975/1967)	Gross rate of return in manufacturing (1975/1967)	C, G, J, Swe, UK, USA	$-0\cdot59$	$1\cdot360$	ns
17[c]	Trends in industry-financed R & D (1967, 1969, 1971, 1973, 1975)	Trends in manufacturing investment (1967, 1969, 1971, 1973, 1975)	Canada	$+0\cdot44$ $(0\cdot20)$	$1\cdot534$	20%
			France	$+0\cdot92$ $(0\cdot47)$	$6\cdot073$	1%
			West Germany	$+0\cdot78$ $(0\cdot55)$	$3\cdot222$	5%
			Italy	$+0\cdot95$ $(1\cdot06)$	$7\cdot529$	0·2%
			Japan	$+0\cdot70$ $(0\cdot87)$	$2\cdot647$	10%
			Netherlands	$+0\cdot52$ $(0\cdot09)$	$1\cdot792$	20%
			Sweden	$+0\cdot95$ $(1\cdot69)$	$7\cdot324$	0·2%
			UK	0 (0)	$0\cdot058$	ns
			USA	$+0\cdot15$ $(0\cdot40)$	$0\cdot736$	ns
18[d]	Trends in industry-financed R & D as a percentage of value added	Trends in the gross rate of return in manufacturing	Canada (1967, 1969, 1971, 1973, 1975)	$-0\cdot46$	$1\cdot610$	20%
			West Germany (1967, 1969, 1971, 1973, 1975)	$-0\cdot50$	$1\cdot725$	20%
			Japan (1967–1973)	$-0\cdot35$	$1\cdot645$	20%
			UK (1964, 1966–1969, 1972, 1975)	$+0\cdot23$	$1\cdot237$	ns
			USA (1967–1975)	$-0\cdot78$	$4\cdot959$	0·2%

Notes: [a] Countries: C (Canada), G (West Germany), J (Japan), Swe (Sweden). [b] ns means not significant. [c] Numbers in brackets under r^2 show the percentage increase in R & D for each percentage increase in investment between 1967 and 1975. [d] Numbers in brackets after each country are years for which data are available.
Source: Extracted from Table 2 in the first half of this article, "The new causality", *Futures*, December 1979, *11* (6), pages 463–465.

of this article, unlikely that higher profit rates directly stimulate innovative activities (*9*). Only in the UK has there been a positive association between the trend in profit rates and the trend in the volume of innovative activities (*18*). This association may reflect the tendency of many British businessmen to treat innovation as an expendable activity when times are hard, rather than regarding it as a necessary investment for long-term survival. One may therefore doubt the wisdom of policies to encourage such a belief.

If "letting the market work" simply means letting bad firms fail and encouraging good firms to pick up the pieces, then it too may be a clumsy way of turning failure into success, especially in countries where the bad firms considerably outnumber the good. The consequences of an inadequate policy for innovation in an industrial company are not always immediately apparent. Examples suggest that it is often possible to spin things out for ten years or so before a full-scale crisis and failure. Putting things right can also take a long time. Diffusing good managers and management practice, building R & D design teams, developing a range of products and the related marketing networks can also take ten or more years.

Remedial action, well before failure would happen, can therefore save much time and pain. In some countries and industries, this can perhaps be left to the banks. But in others, supporting government action may be required. Freeman argues that the range of policy instruments used is less important than the widespread acceptance of the strategy which they are mobilised to support.[6] Whatever the precise contours of an appropriate policy for stimulating innovation, three things can be said about it with some confidence.

- It will require considerable patience, given that it will take a long time to have a significant effect: there is no quick or easy way to close the gap in innovation and income amongst Western European countries.
- It will vary considerably amongst countries: West Germany needs few improvements and changes; France and the UK need many.
- It will require an understanding of the factors affecting the firm's capacity for innovation, and of other ways that it might seek to adapt to change.

Innovation and company strategy

It is almost certainly a mistake to base policies for innovation on the assumption that industrial companies react quickly and optimally to clear and unambiguous market signals. In a world of continuously changing tastes, technology, relative prices, and competitive threats, market signals are hardly ever clear and company decisions are hardly ever optimal. As Nelson and Winter have argued,[7] industrialists try to cope or to do better through a continuous process of search, selection, and adaptation. An innovative capacity is obviously an integral and essential feature of the ability to search, select, and adapt. Rothwell has identified what this means for industrial firms:[8] a continuing commitment of resources and attention to innovation; a balance amongst the many inputs into innovation; attention to marketing, user needs, and after-sales servicing; efficient design and development work; good internal and external communication; and high-quality professional management. To a considerable extent, the development of innovative capacity depends on behaviour and strategies within industrial companies.

As Gilpin has shown in his discussion of problems of innovation in the USA,[4] the development of a capacity for innovation is not just a function of the managerial ability to cope, however important this might be. Industrial companies have other options for dealing with the changes that I have identified in the 1970s. A strategy for innovation may have the advantage of being likely to ensure prolonged survival in a rapidly changing world, and of creating high-wage and high-skill employment in the industrially advanced countries. But it is costly and risky, and takes a long time; and there are other strategies available.

Industrial alternatives

The first option is the conservative—or the *status quo ante*—strategy, the main objective of which is to try to make things happen again as they did in the 1950s and the 1960s. This strategy, depending on the industry and products, would consist of increased marketing and advertising of existing product lines, pressures to increase protection against foreign competition, pressures to resist environmental and social legislation, or pressures to keep down or reduce energy prices. Such a policy might succeed in the short term, but it has considerable political and welfare costs—and it may fail in the longer term.

A more effective response could be the 'offshore' strategy, in which existing products and production processes are transferred to countries (usually less developed or newly industrialising) where input costs and/or demand conditions are more favourable. This strategy is more likely to be successful commercially, and could produce considerable welfare benefits. But it has its dangers and its costs. In the short term, it will be resisted by trade unions in the industrially advanced countries. The unions see such strategies as the exporting of jobs, unless there are compensating employment opportunities created, eg through a strategy of innovation. In the longer term, groups and firms in the developing countries will learn the skills and become new sources of competition. If they are not allowed to learn, then the foreign firms will (rightly) be accused of imperialism.

There will also be the danger of loss of technological dynamism. Seeking out regions with favourable costs and markets for existing products may approximate closely to textbook behaviour, but it may have long-term drawbacks. It is a strategy that is likely to give high status and rewards to the accountant, the financial controller, and the diplomat, faced with the problems of running and controlling a worldwide industrial empire. The entrepreneur, the engineer, and the scientists necessary for innovation will have lower status, so that the long-term effects could well be a loss of innovative capacity. Many historians argue that this happened to Britain in the late 19th century.[9] There is evidence to suggest that the same thing might be happening today in parts of US industry.[10]

This description of strategic alternatives is inevitably selective and over-simplified. In the real world, strategies may not be made explicitly, several may coexist at the same time, and they almost certainly change over time. To some extent, the choice is a function of the industry in which the company operates. R & D-intensive industries obviously must innovate to survive. In his study of diversification of large US companies in the 1950s and the 1960s, Rumelt found that firms in most R & D-intensive industries were active and successful in diversifying into new (and usually related) business activities.[11] He argues that firms in chemicals, electrical, electronic, and automobile[12] industries are "extensible technologies" capable of widespread application. The same is not true of textiles, steel, and paper manufacture, although Rumelt does give examples of successful diversification by firms in such industries.

However, a company's product lines are not the only factor influencing strategic choices; at least two others deserve attention. First, national variables may be important in so far as they influence the opportunities and constraints in the economic environment, or the inputs into industrial activities. For example, Albu has argued that lack of innovation in the British engineering industries may reflect the low quality of managers and engineers.[13] Second, even within the same industry and the same country, differences in the emphasis given to innovation may reflect identifiable characteristics of management within industrial companies.

Avenues for investigation

There is now sufficient evidence of the beginnings of a phase change in the rate and direction of industrial innovation, in the explanatory power of related theories, and in the operational power of related policies, to warrant further investigation in a number of directions.

- Systematic data on the rate and direction of technical change in the 1970s should be collected.
- The causal structure of the Schumpeterian model of industrial development should be carefully and systematically specified.
- A detailed statistical analysis should be made of the association between innovative activities and industrial performance: the analysis should include more industrial disaggregation, more countries, longer time periods, and the identification of possible leads and lags.
- The factors in national economic environments that may influence the volume and direction of innovative activities (eg investment, profits, and skills) should be investigated in detail.
- A systematic investigation should be made of the role that innovation plays in company strategies for dealing with the changes in the 1970s.

Notes and references

1. OECD, *Technical Advance and Economic Policy* (Paris, OECD, 1980); and *Trends in Industrial R and D in Selected Member-Countries, 1967–1975* (Paris, OECD, 1980).
2. Office of Technology Assessment and Forecast, *Company Listing and Patent Activity Profiles;* and *US Patent Activity in Thirty-Nine Standard Industrial Classification Categories:* information supplied to the Science Policy Research Unit, University of Sussex, 1977.
3. S. Melman, *Our Depleted Society* (New York, Holt, Rinehart and Winston, 1965).
4. R. Gilpin, *US Power and the Multinational Corporation* (London, Macmillan, 1976).
5. I would also advance the hypothesis that, in many of these sectors, US industry was never technologically preeminent in the first place.

6. C. Freeman, "Government policy", in K. Pavitt, ed, *Technical Innovation and British Economic Performance* (London, Macmillan, 1980).
7. R. Nelson and S. Winter, "In search of a useful theory of innovation", *Research Policy*, Winter 1977, *6*.
8. R. Rothwell, "Policies in industry", in K. Pavitt, ed, *Technical Innovation and British Industrial Performance* (London, Macmillan, 1980).
9. G. Allen, *The British Disease* (London, Institute for Economic Affairs, 1976); E. Hobsbawm, *Industry and Empire* (Harmondsworth, Middlesex, Penguin, 1968); and D. Landes, *The Unbound Prometheus* (Cambridge, Cambridge University Press, 1969).
10. Nason and Steeger, *Support of Basic Research by Industry* (Washington, DC, National Science Foundation, 1978).
11. R. Rumelt, *Strategy, Structure and Economic Performance* (Graduate School of Business Administration, Harvard University, 1974).
12. The analysis given by N. Rosenburg in *Perspectives on Technology* (Cambridge, Cambridge University Press, 1976) suggests that the automobile industry can be extended to all the machinery industries.
13. A. Albu, "British attitudes to engineering education", in K. Pavitt, ed, *Technical Innovation and British Economic Performance* (London, Macmillan, 1980).

THE WORLD FOOD SUPPLY
Physical limitations

N. W. Pirie

The article reviews the present inputs—land, water, light, chemicals—and their possible or likely development. Consideration of the losses inherent in the food-supply chain, eg crop fractionation or conversion, will often lead to a recommendation for a change of policy—if the goal is to maximise food supply from the available resources.

For the foreseeable future, political and psychological factors will be more important restraints on the food supply than physical factors such as the farmed area, water, light, plant nutrients, photosynthetic efficiency, harvest index, and losses entailed in different methods of using crops. The more important restraints operate at all social levels: chronically semi-starved people do not envisage the possibility of better nutrition and so do not strive for it; well-fed planners cannot envisage an agricultural system operating on unfamiliar processes and principles. Even if these psychological barriers can be overcome, we will not get an adequate food supply until we get rid of the political assumption that those working on the dirty side of the farm gate should be paid less than the average for the community. Table 1 shows the situation in a few countries ten years ago; there is no reason to think it is any better now.

The land area

About 1·4 Gha are now being cultivated.[1] Buringh et al divided the world into 222 zones and, after considering the climate and soil characteristics of each, concluded that 3·4 Gha were potentially arable.[2] In reaching that conclusion they did not assume that desalinated sea-water would be used for irrigation, or that land would be managed in unconventional ways. Other authorities do not think the potential arable area is quite so large, but it is clear that there is still much underused land. The potentialities of the 1·5 Gha of land in the wet tropics are the main point of disagreement. Some pessimists say that that land would quickly erode if farmed conventionally; the US President's Science

N. W. Pirie, FRS was head of the Biochemistry Department in Rothamsted Experimental Station, Harpenden, Herts, AL5 2JQ, UK. This article is based on a presentation made to "Applied science for the 21st century", a conference organised by the Society for Social Responsibility in Science and held in London, 12–14 July 1976; see also N. W. Pirie, *Food Resources: Conventional and Novel* (London, Pelican Books, 1976).

TABLE 1

Country	Date	GDP (%)	Labour (%)	Average per capita income (%)
		Agriculture's share of		
Brazil	1950	29	59	49
	1965	30	52	58
Ceylon	1955	54	53	102
	1965	42	49	86
Guyana	1960	27	34	79
	1965	25	30	83
India	1960	50	73	68
	1965	47	70	67
Pakistan	1960	53	75	71
	1965	48	74	65
Uganda	1960	61	87	70
	1965	60	89	67

Advisory Committee[3] argued that much of this soil is no worse than that of Florida 50 years ago. The disagreement illustrates a point that is too often forgotten—good farmland is usually created by skilled farming. The cost of bringing underused land into a fit state for farming would be between \$200–3000 ha^{-1}; Buringh *et al* estimate that $0 \cdot 9$ Gha comes at the expensive end of their scale. However, two or three families can be maintained on 1 ha, if properly farmed: the cost of establishing one workplace in modern industry is more than \$3000.

The water area

Photosynthesis in the oceans is thought to produce 70 Gt of organic matter (dry weight) annually—that is 18 t per head of the world population. In most of the ocean, production is limited by lack of nitrogen (N) and phosphorus (P). Most fish are therefore caught in coastal waters where rivers supply these elements, or in regions where phosphorus-rich water rises. These upwelling areas amount to only $0 \cdot 1 \%$ of the 35 Gha of ocean. It is unrealistic to think of fertilising the open ocean because the fertiliser would spread into the useless unlit depths. There are, however, great potentialities in fertilising and "farming" coastal lagoons; in south-east Asia the potential area is 2 Mha;[4] in the world as a whole the area is probably five times this.

After a period of euphoria in which oceanic resources were assumed to be almost limitless, sober opinion now puts the sustainable annual yield of conventional fish at about 100 Mt, ie less than twice the present catch. Mussels and other shellfish can be "farmed". When protected from predation, annual protein yields as great as 40 t ha^{-1} are claimed.[5] Sites must be chosen carefully, for such a yield depends on products of photosynthesis, including the 1000 Gt of detritus suspended in the ocean, being brought to the molluscs by currents. Now that folly has so depleted the whale population that the catch is only one quarter of that which would be sustainable, an annual harvest of 200 Mt (wet weight) of krill could be taken.[6] It will take time to exploit all these resources; the food supply could be increased more quickly if we ate more of the fish already caught instead of turning 36% of it into animal feed.[7]

Irrigation water

The distribution of water in the world is by no means ideal for agriculture. The ocean contains 95% of the total, and 4% is frozen. Of the remaining 1%, 98·5% is underground, 1% in lakes, 0·2% in the soil and 0·1% in rivers. Irrigation with river water is often easy, and becomes easier still when the river is dammed for hydroelectric power. Pumping is necessary when lake or underground water is used.

The regions that most need irrigation are often windy and always sunny; serious work on wind and solar powered pumps is urgently needed. Between 10–15% of arable land is now irrigated—though sometimes not very efficiently. Buringh *et al* argue that 10–15% of the 2 Gha of unused potentially arable land will also be irrigated.[2] This part of their argument is dubious because it is reasonable to assume that the best sites are already irrigated and that more power, and therefore expense, will be involved in irrigating new land. Excessive irrigation wastes water, but drip irrigation and similar economical methods have ruined land through salinisation.

Overgrazing is an important cause of desert encroachment on arable land. More land is probably being lost in these ways than is coming into use through extended irrigation. With luck, grazing will be controlled before tsetse fly is eliminated, otherwise another 1 Gha will probably be ruined. Irrigation often allows two or three crops to be grown in a year in the tropics; this advantage is offset by the increased hazard from schistosomiasis and from pests which no longer die during fallow periods.

Light

Artificial light is unlikely to increase world food supply by as much as 1%. Any increase would result from such processes as raising seedlings in artificial light for transplanting on to a larger area when the weather is warm. With little prospect of increasing the amount of light, what we get must be used efficiently.

The first step, obviously, is to ensure that as little light as possible escapes interception by a functional leaf. Hence transplanting, which enables land to be used by one crop while the crop that will follow it is confined to a small area while going through the first stages of growth; and intercropping, which uses the space between slow-growing plants that will ultimately become large and intercept all the light. This form of intercropping is unquestionably advantageous and should be distinguished from the cultivation of two or more species growing together at similar rates. The latter technique is probably advantageous[8]—but it complicates harvesting.

The efficiency of photosynthesis diminishes as illumination increases. The more productive crops have a vertical arrangement of their leaves so that leaf area may be six to nine times the ground area with little mutual shading. To a great extent, the superiority of modern plant varieties depends on this "light absorption in depth"; per unit leaf area they photosynthesise little better than primitive varieties.

The rates of photosynthesis of those agriculturally important plants that have been studied are similar in dull weather; but in sunlight, potatoes, sugar beet, and wheat are less efficient than maize, sorghum, sugar cane, and many tropical grasses. The group that uses strong light efficiently tends also to be more economical of water. If water and other nutrients are amply provided and if "light absorption in depth" is catching 95% of the light on healthy green surfaces covering the whole ground surface, the theoretical limit of productivity is about 1 t ha^{-1} day^{-1}. The observed maximum is 0·4–0·6 t ha^{-1} day^{-1} and that rate is not maintained for more than a few weeks because plants get less efficient as they mature. In the tropics annual dry matter yields can reach 70 t ha^{-1} and 100 t ha^{-1} has been claimed; the limit in the UK is 25 t ha^{-1}.

Under ideal conditions, photosynthesis can therefore approach what appears to be the theoretical maximum rate. Practical rates are smaller because, even if protected from disease and predation, plants do not maintain peak performance for long. Senescence is probably part of the flowering process so, if leaf rather than seed is the desired product, there is scope for research on the prolongation of immaturity. There is also scope for research on the control or elimination of photorespiration. This, in normal atmospheric conditions, can turn more than a quarter of what has been synthesised, back into carbon dioxide.

Chemical inputs

Most of the water that a plant needs passes through it. During the period of maximum photosynthesis, most of the carbon dioxide stays inside and is the basis of the accumulation of dry matter. Except on very still sunny days, photosynthesis does not diminish the local supply of atmospheric carbon dioxide, but the rate can usually be enhanced by increasing the concentration of carbon dioxide in the ambient air. Many plants, especially those that use strong light inefficiently, become more efficient if the concentration of oxygen is diminished. These phenomena are physiologically interesting, but it is unlikely that manipulating atmospheric composition will soon be part of large-scale agriculture.

The response curve of a crop to the three main fertilisers—nitrogen, phosphorus, and potassium (NPK)—has the familiar "law of diminishing returns" form. Ideally, a farmer puts on fertiliser until the extra amount costs as much as the extra yield is worth. Practically, the farmer may not get credit to buy fertiliser, and may be unwilling to buy the optimum amount if there is a chance that drought will destroy the crop. Nevertheless, it is obvious from the law of diminishing returns that fertiliser will have most effect on world food supply if it is used in those regions where least is now used. There, the extra weight of

TABLE 2. RICE YIELDS AND FERTILISER PRICES IN DIFFERENT COUNTRIES

Country	Amount of fertiliser bought by 1 kg rice (kg)	Average rice yield (t ha^{-1})
Japan	1·43	5·6
S Korea	0·96	4·55
Taiwan	0·45	4·2
Malaysia	0·44	2·7
Sri Lanka	0·72	2·6
Indonesia	0·30	2·1
Thailand	0·32	2·0
Philippines	0·41	1·7
Burma	0·12	1·7

crop may be 20 times the weight of fertiliser. Unfortunately, it may cost as much to get the fertiliser to such a region as to make the fertiliser. This is illustrated in Table 2 which shows that rice yields tend to be small where the cost of fertiliser, in terms of rice, is large.

Atmospheric nitrogen is inexhaustible because it is recycled. About 1000 Mt of nitrogen is "fixed" annually by biological processes, the oceans contain nearly 1000 times as much, rain and industrial "fixation" each supply 40 to 50 Mt annually. Provided power is available there is no limit to the amount that could be "fixed". However, as things stand, agriculture is likely to depend increasingly on biological fixation by symbiotic microorganisms on the roots of legumes and, as has recently been discovered, on some varieties of maize and other tropical grasses.[9]

Phosphorus is more of a problem. Much of what we use goes wastefully into the ocean which already contains 100 Gt, but it is inconveniently dilute. Rock of mineable grade is thought to contain 30 Gt; globally we use about 13 Mt annually. The position is sufficiently alarming to make it advisable to restrict the amount of phosphorus wasted in detergents etc, but it is not so alarming as some "doomsters" have claimed. They overlook the fact that most of the phosphorus applied to farmland is sequestrated in the soil and is then slowly released to benefit crops for many years. Potassium is slowly leached from clay; oceanic potassium is abundant and could, with a little effort, be extracted.

A great deal of the NPK used in agriculture ends up in sewage and dung. In primitive agriculture these elements are to a large extent conserved: in sophisticated agriculture they are often expensively hurried out to sea. By ensuring that there is adequate arable land near installations where animals are kept, the waste of dung could be avoided. Changes in this direction are inevitable and might as well be started before increased fertiliser prices force change upon us. It will be difficult to use sewage fully because of the extent to which it is contamined by metals such as chromium, nickel, and zinc. A return to the traditional careful recycling of excreta is a sensible facet of the new cult of "organic farming"; another facet, the deliberate growing of crops for compost, is less sensible. The phosphorus and potassium in the crop are simply being restored to the land from which they were taken; much of the carbon and nitrogen is lost through oxidation and denitrification. This is especially true when soil temperatures are high.[10]

The harvest index

The abundant production of dry matter is not the same as the production of food—it is not even the same as the production of fodder. A few leafy vegetables such as chinese cabbage and spinach, in which nearly everything above ground is eaten, come at one extreme; that is why the cultivation of green vegetables is the most productive method of using land.[11] At the other extreme come plants such as corncockle, *Tidestromia* in Death Valley, and *Spartina* on salt marshes, which perform photosynthetic prodigies but for which nutritional roles have not yet been found. Agricultural crops are intermediate, with havest indexes (the percentage of the total dry matter that is useful) ranging from 5–60%.

Improvement is sought both by increasing the index and by using what has previously been wasted.

Hitherto, plant breeders have tended to try to adapt species that are familiar in Europe and USA to increasingly improbable environments. A welcome exception is the recent interest in millet and sorghum. More attention should be given to improving species that are already adapted to tropical climates. This is particularly true of the leafy vegetables that used to be eaten, but that are now losing prestige.[12]

Plant breeders have been remarkably successful in diverting more of the products of photosynthesis into useful parts of the plant. Critics stress the genetic uniformity, and hence risk from disease, of short-strawed wheat, and the susceptibility to drought of sorghums with a harvest index of 40% instead of the traditional 7–10%. But selection is in its infancy. No physiological canon forbids the presence of all the good qualities in the same variety. Physiology does, however, make it likely that photosynthesis will be most active when there is an adequate "sink" into which the product can go. That is why potatoes and sugar beet, in which leaf and root growth proceed together, outyield sweet potato in which leaves are failing when tuber growth is starting. It is unlikely that abundant agricultural by-products will be eliminated: they should therefore be efficiently used.

Crop fractionation

All products of arable land need some form of fractionation—hence the harvest index. Traditional fractionations, such as threshing, peeling, and discarding outside leaves of vegetables need no comment. Other crops need more sophisticated treatments, some of which are traditional. Thus soya beans were fermented to improve flavour and digestibility, or their protein was extracted and coagulated. They are now often heated, or extracted protein is processed into a felt (textured vegetable protein). Attempts are made to mechanise the traditional technique of grating fresh coconuts in warm water so that a protein and oil emulsion can be pressed out. Several other seeds are being treated in similar ways.

To get the maximum dry matter from a field it should be kept in the green, photosynthetically active, vegetative state. Photosynthesis declines as seeds ripen. The yield of protein, edible by people and other non-ruminants, is therefore greater when it is extracted from optimally manured forage crops, than when any other agricultural system is used. About a third of the protein remains in the fibrous part of the leaf for use as ruminant fodder. So much water is pressed out during the extraction that drying this residue for winter feed needs a third or less of the fuel needed to dry the original crop.[13] Protein can also be extracted from leaves that are now wasted: in the UK, potato haulm could yield 50 000 t annually,[14] and sugar beet about the same amount. Water weeds are at present partly controlled, at great expense, by destruction; several of them are suitable for protein extraction. Similarly, one of the more probable approaches to farming tropical rain forest, without causing erosion, would be to grow trees that could be regularly coppiced for leaf and wood-pulp. The methods used for extracting leaf protein are discussed elsewhere.[15]

Conversion

Conversions always involve loss; separations (eg of leaf protein) are preferable because in them there is less loss. During conversion by an animal, the loss is 70–95%.[16] This must be accepted when, as with marine fish, and cattle grazing and browsing on rough ground, there is no other feasible method of using what is eaten. Animal conversion of the whole crop from arable land is unacceptable when food becomes scarce, but many farm and urban wastes (bagasse, haulms, straw, waste paper) are, or could be turned into, ruminant feed, while wastes from food-factory and kitchen are pig and poultry food. Pigs are fed entirely on such scraps in China, and there are four times as many there as in USA—but they do not grow so fast.[17] Although animal products will probably become less abundant, they will not disappear.

The replacement of animals by fermentation tanks is unlikely. Micro-organisms undoubtedly give a larger return of useable products than animals, but the process is more difficult to control. A ruminant is a self-reproducing, mobile, fermentation tank with automatic temperature and pH control; its size is well adapted to farm work. The thought of collecting the material that makes up half the fodder used by ruminants in Britain, and bringing it to fermentation complexes, is intimidating. The cultivation of microorganisms on petroleum and products derived from coal involves even more sophisticated technology than their cultivation on agricultural by-products. It is therefore unlikely to have much impact on the diets of those most in need of more food. This development is however useful because it will increase the prestige of microorganisms and will therefore make their cultivation on local by-products more likely. Many of us have been puzzled at the slow realisation, by those who control funds for development projects, that funds are most usefully deployed when they go to those most in need—that usually means, to those least likely to be able to manage complex technology. However, as Table 3 shows, the point has got across; most of the money now goes to those who need it most.

TABLE 3. THE POOR'S SHARE. The percentage of the money supplied for agriculture by the International Bank for Reconstruction and Development and the International Development Association going to countries with differing gross national product

GNP ($ per head per year)	1964–68 (%)	1969–73 (%)
< $150	24·5	40·4
$151–375	26·6	32·1
$376–700	40·5	20·6
> $700	8·4	6·9

Synthesis

The limiting factor in food production is the supply of carbon in a reduced form. That is why coal and oil are possible sources. The main source is carbon reduced by photosynthesis. However, that depends on atmospheric carbon dioxide: one of the less abundant sources, although it is replenished. If energy should become abundant, food synthesis from limestone will be feasible. In present circumstances, synthesis is likely to be restricted to nutrients needed in small amounts only, eg vitamins. For our bulk foods we will depend on photo-synthesis for many years.

Notes and references

1. 1 Gha = 1 000 000 000 ha; 1 Gt = 1 000 000 000 t.
2. P. Buringh, H. D. J. van Heemst, and G. J. Staring, Publ. 598 Landbouwhoge-school, Wageningen, Netherlands, 1975.
3. US President's Science Advisory Committee, *The World Food Problem* (Washington, DC, US Government Printing Office, 1967).
4. C. P. Idyll, *Ceres*, 1972, *5* (4), page 43.
5. J. Mason, *Oceanography and Marine Biology Annual Review*, 1972, *10*, page 437.
6. Protein Advisory Group, *Bulletin*, 1974, *4* (2) (New York, United Nations).
7. G. H. O. Burgess in *Food Protein Sources*, N. W. Pirie, ed (London, Cambridge University Press, 1975).
8. B. R. Trenbath, *Advances in Agronomy*, 1974, *26*, page 177.
9. J. W. W. von Bulow and J. Dobereiner, *Proceedings of the National Academy of Sciences* (USA), 1975, *72*, page 2389.
10. K. Newton, *Papua & New Guinea Agricultural Journal*, 1960, *13*, page 81.
11. N. W. Pirie, *Baroda Journal of Nutrition*, 1975, *2*, page 43.
12. N. W. Pirie, "Restoring esteem for leafy vegetables", *Appropriate Technology*, November 1976.
13. N. W. Pirie, *Fertiliser and Feeding Stuffs Journal*, 1966, *63*, page 119.
14. N. W. Pirie, in *Food From Waste*, G. G. Birch, K. J. Parker, and J. T. Worgen, eds (London, Applied Science, 1976), page 180; I. B. Carruthers and N. W. Pirie, *Biotechnology and Bioengineering*, 1975, *17*, page 1775.
15. N. W. Pirie, ed, *Leaf Protein: Its Agronomy, Preparation, Quality and Use*, International Biological Program Handbook 20, 1971; N. W. Pirie, in *Protein Nutritional Quality of Foods and Feeds*, volume 2, M. Friedman, ed (New York, Marcel Dekker, 1975), page 341.
16. R. V. Large in *The Biological Efficiency of Protein Production*, J. G. W. Jones, ed (London, Cambridge University Press, 1973), page 183.
17. G. F. Sprague, *Science*, 1975, *188*, page 549.

FORECASTING TECHNOLOGY
Luck and judgement in the chemical industry

H. B. Wiener

The author describes the use of technological forecasting for investment decision making, the five types of forecast generated —process improvement, engineering innovation, new effect product, new process, and new bulk product—and their attendant problems and risks. He illustrates these with recent examples from the chemical industry and outlines the areas where future development will—or should—probably take place.

THE term technological forecasting is hardly ever used in the chemical industry, but it describes exactly what we do to justify an R & D project: we forecast that certain technologies will be in use at a certain time in the future. There is no technique which guarantees that the forecast will turn out to be right.

Someone once said that experts are not more often right than amateurs, they are just wrong for more sophisticated reasons. But this is unfair. By looking at the facts and applying a bit of logic and a bit of arithmetic you can avoid the more obvious blunders. So we do our homework and make two judgements: that the new technology will work, and that the market will accept it. Then we keep our fingers crossed that inventions and discoveries will be made when they are needed, and that nothing funny happens on the way to the market.

We need rather more luck than the world of weapons systems and projects in the public domain. For one thing, in our more modest world the market is absolute master. There is no chance that a product will still be acceptable if it costs several times as much as originally estimated, or that a new process for an existing product will be adopted if it does not save money. For another, though the chemical industry depends heavily on engineering, it is based on

H. B. Wiener is Projects Director of the Anglo-German Foundation for the Study of Industrial Society, previously he was in the Corporate Research Unit of Imperial Chemical Industries, London, UK. The author gratefully acknowledges the help and advice provided by his colleagues.

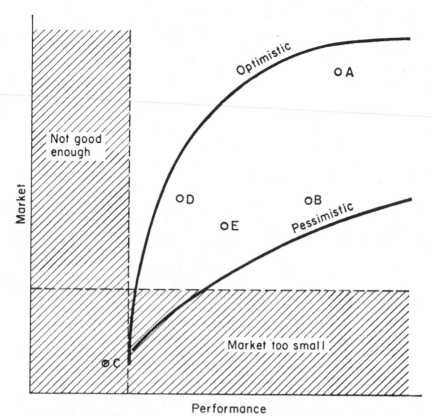

Performance

Figure 1. The sequence of forecasts: **A**, original idea; **B**, realistic reassessment; **C**, technical setback; **D**, technical problem overcome; **E**, case for investment

science, which is a lot less predictable. A catalytic effect or biological activity discovered by chance can outweigh any amount of clever design. But we must still use good judgement to create the conditions for having, and recognising, good luck.

Technological forecasting is science fiction with a difference: it is done quite specifically to persuade someone to spend money. For a project of any size, the money is not appropriated all at once. Usually it has to be asked for in progressively bigger amounts, for bench work, for a bench-scale pilot plant, a proper pilot plant, customer trials, and so forth. Each time a new forecast is required, and each time it has to be more persuasive as more money is involved and more awkward facts have come to light.

In principle, the sequence of forecasts follows the pattern shown in Figure 1. There are some generally agreed ground rules on the minimum to be achieved in terms of technical performance and markets. There is a first rather optimistic forecast made in comparative ignorance; then cold feet and technical setbacks; recovery with hard work, ingenuity, and luck; and, if all goes well, a final forecast which justifies investment in a full-scale plant.

Money is appropriated by people with a good deal of experience in the relevant technical and marketing fields, and with a good many—fortunately usually known—prejudices. Most of them have made technological forecasts themselves, and the chances are that they know the current forecasters quite well. Can you imagine, then, that they will take extrapolations, Delphi, cross-impact matrices, decision trees and risk analyses without a very large pinch of salt?

The techniques in the technological forecasting literature describe the structure of the thought processes rather well. We do extrapolate past data, canvass opinions, consider the effect of extraneous events, spell out alternatives, and test the sensitivity of profitability forecasts to the variability of input data.

The only trouble is that there are never enough undisputed data to make formal deductions credible. And in any case, what would you do with a presentation which says there are six scenarios for the future of which the most likely has a probability of $22\frac{1}{2}\%$? It still comes down to a judgement whether or not to invest the next £100 000 or £10 million.

Technological forecasting, then, at least in our industry, is not mainly the techniques, but a process which involves almost the whole organisation. It is a process of debate by which we form judgements and come to decisions. The process is in two parts: writing general scenarios, and making cases for specific decisions.

Scenarios are usually part of surveys of fields of business and technology by a study team detached from the decision processes, and they are essentially educational. They compete for attention with a barrage of other inputs, and though they are produced with some knowledge of what people in the organisation are sensitive to, we are never very sure what influence they have on the way people react in a decision situation. Certainly, the forecasts made in support of specific decisions carry more weight. Scenarios mostly describe a future which is comfortably far away, while the immediate decision case has specious numerical accuracy. Specious, because the accuracy of the technical cost calculations cannot be matched by similar accuracy in sales and price forecasts. Organisations tend to be cowards and shirk sharp qualitative medium-term judgements.

The document which is put before a body of decision-makers is seldom a complete and objective forecast. It is the product of extensive consultation and, though it does not say so, it represents what the organisation has collectively agreed to believe, despite private misgivings. It spells out those extrapolations, and evaluations of cross-impact and risk, about which there has been most doubt and argument. It leaves out the elements of the scenario about which there is disagreement but which are not felt to be critical to the decision. It leaves out many undisputed assumptions.

Life is too short to state all the common assumptions like the laws of thermodynamics, but most forecasts before 1974 also failed to state explicitly the assumption that nothing drastic would happen to the price of oil. That was an important assumption which turned out to be wrong. Yet, it would have made little difference if it had been made explicit after careful analysis, because that was what the organisation collectively believed. Objections might have been raised, but the consensus would have been the same. Consensus is essential if an organisation is to behave coherently and decisively; but it does lead to forecasts biased towards the conventional wisdom and short-term thinking.

TABLE 1. TYPES OF FORECAST

Process improvement	New process
Engineering innovation	New bulk product
New effect product	

Table 1 lists five types of forecasts leading to R & D expenditure and ultimately investment. Each type presents its own problems, but generally the difficulty increases as one goes down the list, because more commitment of resources is at stake.

Process improvement

This is the easiest to forecast. The market is assured, since by definition the product will be cheaper or better. What is at stake is that one ties up people and money in a quest for marginal gains, and one becomes heavily committed to the old process. It is difficult, at the same time, to believe that the process can be out-flanked and one may become blind to possibilities of more radical innovation. But one has to be very brave or foolish to forecast that further improvement is impossible because it has been possible so often.

An example of a very long run of progressive improvement is methanol synthesis. This is a catalytic process; we do not have very good theories to predict catalyst activity, and almost anything permitted by thermodynamics is worth trying for. Countless research programmes have been based on forecasts that further improvement was possible, and so far it always has been.

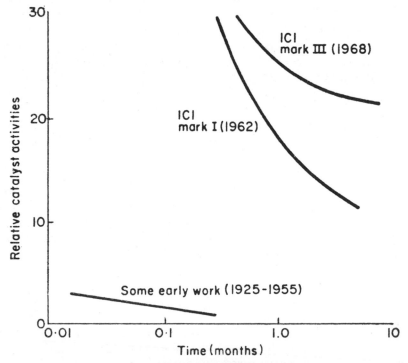

Figure 2. The activity and life of a methanol synthesis catalyst

Figure 2 shows what was achieved between the 1920s and 1968 with copper catalyst which became commercially viable in 1962 and is still the favourite. Before 1962, zinc/chromium oxide catalyst was used and this had to be run at 300°–400°C and 300 atmospheres pressure.

The best combination of temperature and pressure can be calculated for a given catalyst from thermodynamics, and capital and energy costs. It was predictable that with a more active catalyst the technology would move towards lower temperatures and pressures which allow savings in capital and compression costs. Plants are now designed to operate at 50–100 atmospheres and 230°–280°C.

Though the potential of copper catalysts was foreseen a long time before they became viable, the change in technology which actually made them viable was not predicted very long before it happened. This was the switch from coal to oil, and later natural gas, as the raw material for the synthesis gas from which methanol is made. Starting from oil or gas, the synthesis gas can be made much purer, and the purity affects the catalyst life which is quite critical to the economics of the process. We can foresee discontinuities, such as the switch from coal, in principle, but find it difficult to get the timing right. We can already see that we shall eventually switch back to coal; a lot of research is being done now, probably prematurely; will we have the right processes ready when the time comes?

Engineering innovation

In many respects this is fairly easy to predict because it tends to follow developments outside the chemical industry. This is regrettable and the reasons are suspect. We argue that there are few things in chemical processing which absolutely cannot be done with existing engineering technology, and that the industry cannot stand development costs on the scale of nuclear power or aerospace. We adopt and adapt rather cautiously, because teething troubles can lose us more money than the innovation will ever save; there seem to be few prizes for being the pace-setter. Also, inevitably, we work with equipment manufacturers who establish a consensus across the industry as to when an innovation will become standard practice. Too often we have let this consensus become a self-fulfilling forecast.

Fortunately, one can often gain experience in a noncritical application, or adopt a belt-and-braces policy, as in computer control with manual override. Even so, the introduction of computer control has been slower than one would have predicted without considering the dynamics of the industry, that is the rate at which new plants are built and old ones revamped, and the rate at which confidence in new technology is established.

The story did not even begin when we got the first off-line computers in the early 1950s, because it was obvious that they were not reliable enough, and one could not tell when suitable equipment would be commercially available. In 1956 none of the major US journals in the automatic control field carried an article on computer control, though by this time solid-state electronics had arrived in defence applications. The first on-line machine in ICI, which incidentally still works, was installed in 1962. The bold step of

Figure 3. The rate of computer installation in the ICI group

building a plant which relied entirely on computer control was taken in 1968. Today, though some plants are still provided with enough back-up instrumentation to keep going in case of computer failure, practically every new plant is normally computer controlled, and there is a host of minor computer applications. Figure 3 shows how the rate of computerisation has grown since 1962. In 1969 the experts predicted that all new plants would be computer controlled soon, and in fact the take-off came about five years later.

Chemical engineering technology in a narrower sense, for instance crystallisation and filtration, is of course only developed for the chemical industry and sometimes for allied industries such as food and minerals processing. So here we have to forecast our own progress. This is difficult because, as a science, chemical engineering does not yet offer enough powerful generalisations. As engineering, its applications are diverse and scattered and each seems to be specific to a particular chemical system. All one can say for the moment is that some hard thinking is being done and that some progress will follow.

The commitment required to introduce engineering innovation is to set up the appropriate branch of the engineering function, and occasionally to risk some interruption of production. Business policy is hardly affected, and one could well argue that the chemical industry could afford to be more ambitions in the engineering field. The chances are that we will have to be, because the capital cost of plants, and working capital, are ever-increasing burdens. We will have to design for smaller plant inventories, in some cases also to satisfy the health and safety acts. It is fairly safe to forecast that more ingenuity will go into plant design, but not so easy to say how.

New effect products

These range from simple formulations such as cosmetics to highly specific ethical pharmaceuticals. The low-technology end of this range depends almost entirely on market forecasting: when a new marketable product is conceived, the technologists can usually be relied on to develop it. At the other extreme, the *prima facie* assessment of the market is easy: it is known which conditions cannot be adequately treated and how common they are. This does not mean that there are no marketing problems, but they come later, when an effect has been found. The critical forecasting problem is the identification of the targets to which research effort should be committed.

The worthwhile targets are known and more or less agreed right across the industry. Publications and personal contacts generate an on-going Delphi exercise. Back in 1969 the UK Office of Health Economics went further than this and produced a formal technological forecast on medicines in the 1990s by the Delphi technique. Some predictions in this refer to 1975 and these have proved to be only moderately accurate. In general, forecasters tend to be optimistic about work in progress and conservative when it comes to really new approaches. Perhaps the best indication of where people think success is likely is the way they actually spend their money. Some statistics published in the USA are shown in Table 2. Since everyone looks at the statistics they may well be a mechanism of self-fulfilling prophesy.

TABLE 2. RESEARCH STATISTICS: A KIND OF DELPHI
(US applied R & D expenditures, pharmaceuticals)

1974	1973	Product class	Share of applied R & D (%) 1974	1973
1	1	Central nervous system and sense organs	18·5	17·4
2	2	Anti-infectives	17·8	15·8
3	4	Cardiovasculars	15·1	12·8
4	3	Neoplasms, endocrine system, and metabolic diseases	14·0	15·4
5	5	Digestive and genito-urinary system	6·2	6·0
6	9	Respiratory	4·8	3·9
7	8	Biologicals	4·5	4·0
8	7	Dermatologicals	3·5	4·1
9	10	Vitamins	2·1	2·0
*	6	Diagnostics	*	5·1
		Other	6·1	5·8
		Veterinary preparations	6·9	7·2
		Veterinary biologicals	0·5	0·5
			100·0	100·0

However, each individual pharmaceutical laboratory forms a strategy for effort allocation which is based not only on the forecasts of generally fruitful areas, but also very much on what the laboratory thinks it is good at and what leads it already has. The purely statistical chances of success are low. In the decade up to 1973 about 40 new drugs of significant therapeutic value were found. On average this is about one drug in each of about a dozen fields every three years. There are about 60 innovative pharmaceuticals companies around the world and a good many work in each field. Clearly one has to select areas of research where one's chances are much better than average.

The occasional major success in one area must pay for the research in all. What is at stake, however, is not just the cost of the research. Obsolescence of an established drug means the loss of a substantial slice of business if a competitor finds a better one first. One must maintain the capability to forestall this. Good scientists and good luck are essential, but so is good judgement as to where an advance is due.

New processes

Quite different forecasting problems are present here. The starting point is a concept for making an established product by a new route, say from a cheaper feedstock. The basic chemistry will have been shown to work and the market exists. We have to predict the capital and operating costs of the new process; the market growth and hence the time when a new plant will be needed; the development and construction time; the effect of using the new feedstock on its cost; and the competitive developments which may pre-empt our own. If all this adds up to a forecast that the new process will displace the old, development can begin.

New snags emerge at every stage. The original process-cost estimate is almost invariably too low, for instance because a new impurity is found which was not made by the old process and which is expensive to remove; or because the process stream somewhere along the line is more corrosive than had been thought so that a more expensive construction material is necessary. Changes in the market while the development is going on shift the goal posts. The

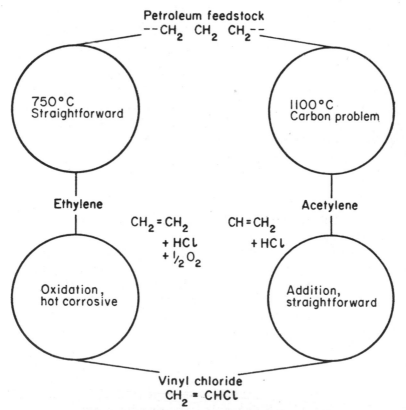

Figure 4. Two alternatives ways to make vinyl chloride

forecast must be re-calculated quite often, and it may well be necessary to call a halt because it becomes clear that the original hopes cannot be fulfilled. If this has to happen, the sooner the better, because the rate of expenditure goes up as the project advances and more and more detailed points have to be checked out. What is more important is the increasing commitment of people to the project, and the widespread disappointment and dislocation if it is abandoned.

An example of a technology that was widely forecast, but which failed to establish itself, is acetylene from oil. Acetylene is one of the few high-tonnage organic chemical building blocks which dates back to the coal days, when it was made from carbide. During the second world war the Germans developed processes for making acetylene from methane but these proved to be uneconomic under peace-time conditions. The development of naphtha cracking then provided ethylene as an alternative feedstock which is cheaper to produce but harder to convert to derivatives such as vinyl chloride. If acetylene could be made cheaply enough from a petroleum fraction such as naphtha it would be preferred to ethylene. Figure 4 shows the two alternative routes in outline.

The technical problem is that, in the equilibrium between a petroleum feedstock and its fragments, acetylene is the main product at much higher temperatures than ethylene. Carbon and hydrogen are the stable products over the whole range, but are formed faster at higher temperatures. The problem of handling the carbon is manageable with ethylene but very difficult with acetylene. Several designs of plant were tried but none has survived. We actually built a full-scale plant but had to abandon it because the problems of economically removing carbon defeated us.

It was perhaps bad luck that this could not have been foreseen. But, with hindsight, it was bad forecasting that we should have tried at all; because the technology is not just the plant but also the storage and handling of the product. Acetylene is unstable and it would never have been possible to store, pipe, and ship it around on the scale on which we now handle ethylene. There is no doubt which is the right technology now. One day it will all change again, when oil gets much more expensive than coal.

New bulk products

The most difficult forecasting problem of all, and the greatest risk of being wrong, are presented by new bulk products.

Here one has to invent and develop a new marketable product and, at the same time, a process that can make it at an appropriate cost on a large scale. Large amounts of money and effort must be committed, not only to development, but to the first (and sometimes the second) production plant before any money begins to flow back. The market will take time to build up, and one may have to go deep into the red for years before the outlay is recovered and the whole venture becomes profitable.

The first step is not so much a forecast as an exercise of imagination. There are no data for a market and a technology which do not yet exist, only an appreciation of the general market area and of technical possibilities. What the market might accept will depend on price and performance as indicated in outline in Figure 1, with a wide gap between optimistic and pessimistic views, depending, for instance on the resistance of the trade to new products and the impact of the new product on the general price structure. In reality, of course, the situation is much more complicated because there is not a single monolithic market but many segments. Thus a new fibre might find a niche in underwear, curtains, carpets or sacks, perhaps in more than one of them; and each is a different trade.

There is one feature of bulk chemicals which makes the market a little easier to visualise than, say, the market for television when it was first thought of. Products of chemistry are nearly always substitutes for traditional products, and so their introduction does not presuppose a fundamental change in the way of life.

However, substitution can have an important cumulative effect: drip-dry fabrics and synthetic detergents enable you to travel with just a briefcase; the whole system of trunks and porters, maids and laundries, has almost disappeared. Such social changes are not usually forecast with any accuracy; but there is probably not much to be gained by being too far ahead of the game. An innovation can easily fall flat. DuPont had a nasty experience with their synthetic leather Corfam.

They were right that a sheet of composite plastic rolled off a machine should be cheaper, better and more uniform than the hide off a pig. But they did not reckon that if the cheap end of the market was going to accept plastic at all it would settle for something that was not so nice—PVC—if it was much cheaper; and that the pig would fight back to hold the expensive end of the market by exploiting the snob value of leather, and cutting prices by maybe charging a little more for the ham.

A nice example of forecasting a new tonnage product and the new process technology that goes with it is the thinking in ICI which led to the recent decision to invest in a plant to make single-cell protein.

Some of this thinking was broad and general, about the fields in which a science-based technological business would find new opportunities. In the mid-1960s it became clear that one such field was biology. Much survey work was done and this may have helped to create a climate in which a rather bold new venture could find support. But the specific ideas were generated in the Agricultural Division from an appreciation of several converging trends and of their own capabilities. Grain, soya, and fishmeal were used as feed, and natural proteins were being imported to meet the needs of pig and poultry factory farming. A market opportunity existed for factory protein.

Predictions had to be made of growth trends in the agricultural industry, and these pointed to the pig and poultry factory-farming business and a demand for protein supplement. One had to judge whether natural products would meet the demand in countries which had to import them, or whether manufactured microorganisms could take over these markets; we decided that they could.

We then had to choose a feedstock. Organisms fed on paraffins were already being developed, and in Britain methane from the North Sea was obviously attractive. Then came an element of scientific forecasting; methanol would be a more efficient feedstock. This, it was reasoned, is because bugs that live on methane, first metabolise it to methanol. The bugs need energy to live, and burn up some of it in the process. So we decided to look for bugs that live more lazily. We would make the methanol for them by a more efficient chemical process. And methanol is a good bet on two other counts: being water soluble it is easier to feed it into the nutrient brew; and since it can be made from oil or coal as well as gas, its future is assured (Table 3).

TABLE 3. THE TECHNOLOGY REQUIRED FOR THE PROTEIN PROJECT

Manufactured microorganisms: yeast, antibiotics	Synthetic methanol process more efficient then bugs
North Sea gas: methane	Solubility of methanol simplifies engineering
Bugs can grow on methane and ammonia	Assured future raw materials for methanol
Bugs metabolise methane to methanol	and ammonia

The next round of forecasts concerned the R & D. One could calculate the technical targets that would make the process economically viable. The bugs had to convert methanol efficiently into protein, they had to do it fast enough, and they had to survive in a dense soup so that the plant would not become too voluminous. All this depended on finding the right strain of bug, and one could not guarantee that the biology would come right. Fortunately it did.

There were also chemical engineering targets to be met. Oxygen had to be absorbed as fast as the bugs needed it, the whole system had to be kept sterile so that strange bugs did not take over, and the product had to be separated from the soup. One could predict with some confidence that with enough ingenuity this could all be done within the target cost. It was, partly through the design of a novel form of aerobic fermenter. This, incidentally, will lead to other new technologies (Table 4).

TABLE 4. RESEARCH AND DEVELOPMENT FOR THE PROTEIN PROJECT

Biological targets	Chemical engineering targets
Methanol conversion efficiency	Oxygen transfer rate
Growth rate of organisms	Sterility
Concentration of organism	Product separation
Achievement not predictable	Achievable through imaginative design

Finally, there were the forecasts that have to be made for any new process: that it will survive the pilot stage, that the long-term market prospects justify the investment in a full-scale plant, and that, when it is built, the inevitable bugs can be ironed out (Table 5).

TABLE 5. PROTEIN PROJECT FORECASTS

1965	Market for protein; tonnage microorganisms
1967	Methanol feedstock; R & D targets will be achieved
1972	Pilot plant justified
1976	Long-term future market; full scale costs and operability

Conclusion

To sum up I would like to quote Dr E G Woodroffe from the 1968 R & D Society symposium:

And yet by far the greater part
Of chemistry is still an art;
In spite of scientific fuss
Research is just a blunderbuss,
Which shoots a monstrous charge of shot
And sometimes hits, but mostly not.

Nevertheless, we are not too bad at forecasting progressive improvement in what we do already. We smell out the areas where novel effects are due to come up, but in looking for biological effects we do indeed fire a monstrous charge of shot. We foresee many of the major social and economic changes which will affect the future of the industry, but we do not predict very accurately when they will happen. Finally, we have been predicting our engineering performance with considerable confidence because we have made most of our advances by adopting and adapting what was first developed for other purposes; and perhaps we have done even this rather conservatively. Chemical plants are clumsy beasts compared with aeroplanes. Now that the industry has moved out of the era of very fast growth, this will not do: the next move forward will be increased elegance and ingenuity in chemical, mechanical and instrument engineering design—you could say in the field of applied physics. This forecast was the message of the recent lecture to the Society of Chemical Industry by Mr Malpas, the technical director of ICI; and a message from such a source is very likely to be a self-fulfilling prophecy.

THE LONG-LIFE CAR

Ernst Fuhrmann

Today, cars last about ten years. This lifespan could be extended to an optimum of 18–25 years. The critical component is the body shell, and more research is needed before all-aluminium bodies could be mass produced. Such a car would consume less material resources in the long run (300 000 km), although it would cost about 30% more than the conventional car. Over a decade or so its production would decrease employment in the car industry by about 4%, while increasing employment in the short term.

THE APPEARANCE, in 1972, of *Limits to Growth* prompted Porsche engineers to make a thorough evaluation of the consequences of vehicle development. One result of this endeavour was the long-life car research project, the initial concept of which was presented some time before the beginning of the energy crisis.

TABLE 1. THE GOALS OF THE LONG-LIFE CAR PROJECT

Conservation of energy resources	Reduction of overall costs
Conservation of material resources	Improvement of operational reliability
Reduction of environmental impact	Retention of established vehicle concept goals

Table 1 shows the goals of this long-term research project, which is supported by the German Federal Ministry for Research and Technology. From the very beginning, it was obvious that the project would reach beyond the technical domain, and would influence the national economy. Porsche therefore obtained the cooperation of two institutions for economic science, which would evaluate the economic aspects of the project.

Component reliability and corrosion

In technical terms, the controlled lengthening of a vehicle's life depends on a thorough knowledge of the reliability of its components. If some components are already reliable, their use would reduce the additional expenditure required to construct a long-life car. However, a survey of the literature did not provide

Professor Ernst Fuhrmann is with F. Porsche Aktiengesellschaft, Postfach 40 06 40, 7000 Stuttgart 40, West Germany. This article, by permission of the Council of the Institution of Mechanical Engineers, is based on a paper presented by the author to a recent conference organised by that Institution. The full conference proceeding are available in a bound volume, *Function Versus Appearance in Vehicle Design* (Bury St Edmunds, Suffolk, Mechanical Engineering Publications Limited, 1978).

an accurate quantitative evaluation of component life. In the literature, the results varied strongly with the application of different objectives, test criteria, and evaluation standards. An additional investigation was therefore necessary to provide the data we required.

To that end, 6500 vehicles of 13 different types were examined throughout the Federal Republic by the German Vehicle Survey Organisation. A specific check list, made up by Porsche, emphasised the importance of the vehicle body, the durability of which determines the entire vehicle's useful life. Figure 1 shows the results obtained for the European medium-size vehicle type, based on an examination of 741 cars.

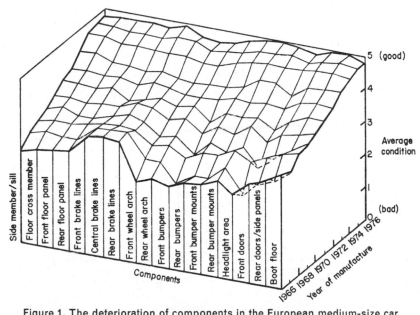

Figure 1. The deterioration of components in the European medium-size car

Obviously the condition of all components deteriorates with age, and over time differences between components become more evident. The brake lines, an important safety feature, remain in relatively good condition, in contrast to other components. This is because vehicle owners pay more attention to the brakes—they are repaired and replaced more frequently than fixed components such as bumpers.

TABLE 2. THE PRESENT LIFE OF CAR COMPONENTS

Satisfactory
Roof structure, firewall (between engine and passenger compartments), bumpers and fixtures, fuel tank, side windows, rear window, seat mechanism, interior locks and hinges, doorlatch mechanism.

In need of improvement
Much of body structure, attachment systems, hinges, paint topcoats, tank-filler lid, windscreen, rear-view mirror, window seals, windscreen wiper, carpets, interior accessories, rear-seat covers, restraint system, ventilation and heating.

In need of much improvement
Welded bodywork flanges exposed to road spray, paint undercoat, water traps (eg bonnet seating), floor sections, door seals, bonnet seals, front-seat covers.

Table 2 lists the components examined in present cars, and classifies them by their ability to sustain a 10-year life span. Wheel arches, bumpers, and front floor panels are especially prone to corrosion.

It is important, particularly in older vehicles, that passive safety features withstand corrosion. Since crash tests are costly, we could not simulate all the kinds of collision which might occur in normal road use. We concentrated on frontal impacts, and over 30 vehicles—most of them with front engines—were crashed. Figure 2 shows the results of crashing three vehicles of the same type, but with different ages and therefore corrosion levels.

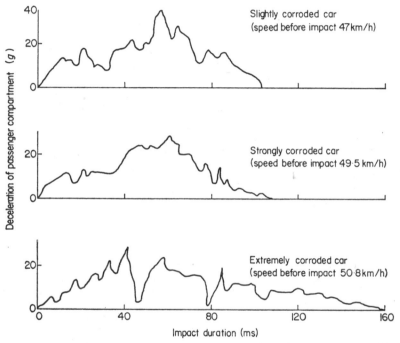

Figure 2. The influence of corrosion on crash behaviour—a frontal impact sustained by a front-engined car

Corrosion markedly affects crash behaviour. The lower deceleration level of the strongly corroded car, which might appear desirable because it reduces the loads on the occupants, proves in fact to be a drawback: it results in increased deformation and thus an unacceptable reduction of the passengers' survival space. Our tests led us to the conclusion that front-engine vehicles with heavily corroded load-carrying bottom assemblies may still be able to show a satisfactory crash behaviour in a frontal impact, as far as conservation of the survival space, energy absorption, and passenger protection are concerned. However, acceptable limits are exceeded in the case of unfavourable design— eg of the steering column—and also in cases of extreme corrosion. Although this conclusion may not be applicable to rear and lateral impacts, it is certain that corrosion-inhibition measures would help to maintain the passive safety of car bodies over an extended lifespan.

The detailed analysis of corrosion occurrence also allowed us to make recommendations for a corrosion-inhibiting design. For example, corrosion of doors and door sills could be reduced by:

- providing nonclogging drain holes in both door and sill;
- locating susceptible parts, such as window cranks and lock mechanisms, within a sealed portion of the door;
- protecting hinges from water with effective door seals; and
- using a flexible strip suspended from the lower door lip to protect the sill from stone chipping and provide a labyrinth seal.

If a part's life cannot be extended, for technical or economical reasons, then its replacement should be simplified. The drive unit in a long-life car, for example, should permit an easy clutch exchange, without removing either the engine or the gearbox. The manifolds, tubes, and silencers in the exhaust system should be connected by flanges, to facilitate the replacement of parts, even after prolonged operation.

Material and energy conservation

The need to conserve raw materials and energy is one of the most important criteria for material selection. Other factors include recycling, production, and— last but not least—durability. We concluded that the long-life car should be made from materials already proven by their use in conventional car construction. New or composite materials should be avoided, in the interest of raw-material preservation and recyclability. It is too early to say yet whether plastics will be able to meet such requirements as recyclability and stability over time.

The next step in our research project was to compare the energy used and raw materials consumed during production, operation, and recycling. Figure 3

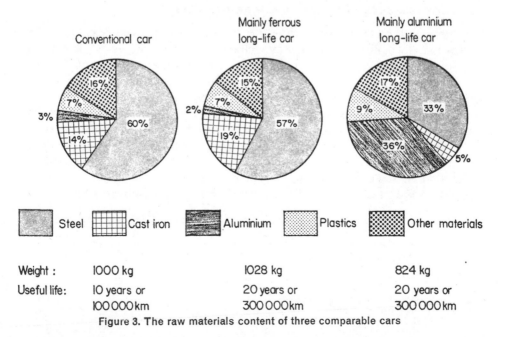

Figure 3. The raw materials content of three comparable cars

shows the different proportions of various materials in three comparable cars—a conventional car, a mainly ferrous long-life car, and a mainly aluminium long-life car.

TABLE 3. THE MATERIALS AND ENERGY REQUIRED TO TRAVEL A DISTANCE OF 300 000 km

	Materials required (%)[a]	Energy required (%)[a]
Three conventional cars	100	100
One mainly ferrous long-life car	45	95
One mainly aluminium long-life car	35	80

Note: [a] The requirement for one conventional car is arbitrarily set at 33·3%.

It can be seen from Table 3 that long-life cars require less materials and less energy to travel a distance of 300 000 km. The impressive saving (of up to 65%) in materials mainly results from the fact that only one long-life car is required, to travel this distance, whereas three conventional vehicles would be required. Losses during scrapping and recycling are therefore reduced. Energy savings, however, are not so pronounced. The figures in Table 3 are based on the overall energy requirements of a car, from production through use to recycling. Since a mainly ferrous long-life car is slightly heavier than a conventional car, it consumes more fuel over a given distance. The large quantity of energy used in the primary production of aluminium keeps the energy requirement for a mainly aluminium long-life car fairly high despite the fuel savings which are a consequence of its lower weight (about 20% lighter than a conventional car). Nonetheless, overall savings are possible, and our calculations are based on typical data—under more favourable assumptions the long-life versions would have shown distinctly better results.

The consequences of adopting a long-life design

Now that the basic considerations are established, it would be possible to produce a long-life version of any vehicle category. However, a European medium-size car, with a planned production of 1000 units per day, is the example we chose, to demonstrate the consequences of adopting long-life designs. Our investigations showed that a long-life vehicle could be largely similar to present-day European medium-size cars. The differences would be mainly in the materials used and in the design of much of the body shell—the remaining components need only small design changes. The large-scale production of improved body shells requires additional development work on the adaptation of deep-drawing and joining techniques. For other components, modifications along the lines of current development would suffice.

TABLE 4. THE LABOUR REQUIREMENTS AND SELLING PRICES OF LONG-LIFE CARS

	Labour required (%)[a]	Selling price (%)[a]
A conventional car	100	100
A mainly ferrous long-life car	107	122
A mainly aluminium long-life car	117	130

Note: [a] The value for a conventional car is arbitrarily set at 100%.

Long-life cars would require a slightly higher labour input and would sell at a higher price than conventional cars (Table 4). The energy costs of aluminium are again reflected in the price rise of about 30%.

Finally, we carried out a benefit–cost analysis to compare the proposed long-life car concept with the conventional vehicle. As there was no generally accepted procedure for private cars, we developed our own. Our analysis takes only technical utility into account, and does not consider that the owner himself might attribute a considerably higher value to his vehicle. Furthermore, the assessment of energy and raw material savings was based on present prices, without taking into account possible shortages and cost changes. For these reasons, the results given in Figure 4 are only a preliminary approximation. The optimum useful life of a long-life car is about 18–25 years, whereas the average car today lasts only about 10 years. If we were to attempt to extend the useful life beyond 25 years, costs would increase progressively, as would the effects of technical obsolescence.

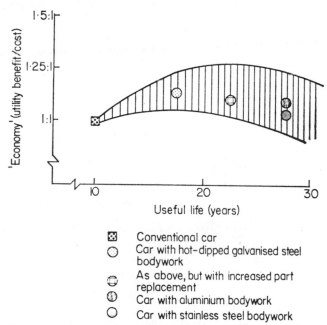

Figure 4. A cost–benefit analysis for four possible long-life cars

Recent forecasts made by Cologne University, and calculations carried out at Mannheim University with a complex system-dynamics model, describe the likely changes in overall passenger-car demand in West Germany up to the year 2010. According to these calculations, demand in the home market will remain constant from 1985 on; and the labour required will decrease slightly as a consequence of industrial rationalisation. These results apply to the production of conventional vehicles rather than long-life cars.

When we added technical data on the long-life car, together with the results of a marketing study, to the Mannheim model, it showed that long-life cars, though 25% more expensive than comparable conventional vehicles, could well reach a market share of 10%. If, however, the long-life car were to be introduced more rapidly and took 50% of the market each year by 1985, the Mannheim model showed that the level of production and the size of the labour force required would initially be about 8% greater than in the case of conventional cars. Subsequently, between 1985 and 2010, the figures would decrease to about 4% less than those for conventional cars (Figure 5).

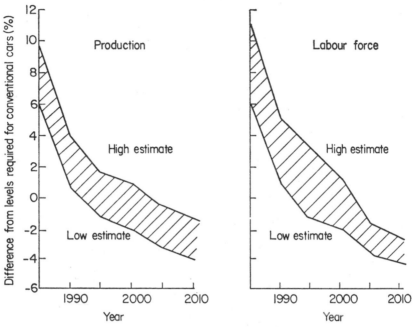

Figure 5. The estimated changes in production and labour force, if long-life cars were to constitute half of all West German new vehicle registration

In summary, the long-life car uses less materials and less energy than conventional vehicles. Since today's vehicles have reached such a high technical level, the development of the long-life car would not entail revolutionary economic changes.

However, a number of problems will have to be solved before the long-life car is ready for series production:
● the detail design of body, engine, electrical, and interior equipment to conserve materials;
● the development of hot-dipped galvanised steel and especially all-aluminium bodies, suitable for large-scale production (this depends partly on the improvement of deep-drawing and welding processes);
● the acquisition of further information on labour requirements, especially for maintenance and repair;
● the adaptation of test methods; and
● establishing the best way of introducing the long-life car onto the market.

The benefits of an extended useful life would apply to many products, in addition to cars. Benefits will be increased if raw material and energy costs increase; if the product in question is based on fully developed technologies resulting from long-term innovation; and if—despite the higher selling price—there are reduced operation costs for the customer.

Quality becomes a priority

Very shortly, a switch-over from the mainly quantitative to a distinctly more qualitative growth will take place. Already, a number of other industries are striving, in various ways, to increase the useful life of their products. We believe that our work to date on the long-life car research project has shown a practical way forward for this industry.

For several years, the mean useful life of passenger cars has been rising slowly. The interval between model changes has increased, and fundamental alterations in automotive engineering are less frequent than they used to be. This tendency is particularly evident in mechanical engineering, which is of special importance for long-life cars. The increasing use of electronic systems in cars can be accommodated by regular up-dating. The risk of technical obsolescence is not therefore a major obstacle to the introduction of the long-life car.

A similar slow-down is observable in styling, where legal regulations have an increasing impact: designs are becoming more 'timeless'. An example of this tendency is the Porsche 911. The timeless basic design of this car has, since its introduction in 1964, been regularly up-dated by small, skillful modifications. And now, as before, there is a strong demand for this Porsche.

In this context, exterior modifications have not significantly reduced the demand for older models on the used-car market. The consumer is increasingly conscious of the futility of a 'throw-away' society, and tends to give the utility value of his vehicle priority over its prestige value.

Finally, because the development towards vehicles with a prolonged useful life will be a continuous process, we cannot expect the immediate introduction of a production vehicle with the full range of long-life features.

CHEMICALS AND ENERGY
The next 25 years

Peter G. Caudle

The chemical industry can no longer rely on a rapid expansion or production based on a single feedstock. New sources of raw materials and energy will have to be used. The uncertainties include costs, social and political factors, new competitors, and the developing botanical and biochemical technologies. The author examines energy use in the OECD area and discusses the factors affecting energy efficiency. He concludes that the chemical industry is likely to maintain a petrochemical base much longer than might be expected. Although competition from Eastern Europe is imminent, OPEC products are unlikely to have a significant impact before 1987. For the next decade the growth rate of the chemical industry in Western Europe will probably be around 5%. Options after petrochemicals include a return to the pathways used 30 years ago, and the new possibilities promised by the use of shale oil, nuclear power, and natural products. At present oil prices, coal is not competitive above about $10/ton, and for the rest of the century the upper limit is around $20/ton.

THE CHEMICAL industry uses, if its raw material requirements are included, over one-quarter of the energy required by manufacturing industry; this proportion will rise as long as chemicals output grows faster than that of manufacturing industry.

The industry's requirements for energy and energy-containing raw materials over the next 25 years are therefore of considerable significance to the development of long-term national, and world, energy supply and demand. Much uncertainty attaches to any forecasts over this period: "Deciding under uncertainty is bad enough, but deciding under an illusion of certainty is catastrophic".[1] Nevertheless, a review of possible trends may be helpful.

The author is Director of Economic Affairs, Chemical Industries Association, 93 Albert Embankment, London SE1, UK. The views expressed in this article are the author's personal opinions.

The uncertainties
What are the major uncertainties? The foremost is, perhaps, the stability of the whole of Western society.

It is clearly unprofitable to try to foresee the effect of social revolutions or military conflicts on our Western economies and industries. However, even if one discounts radical or calamitous changes, one can arrive a decade or two hence with very divergent views on both the quantity and nature of economic growth and change.

The present consensus sees an annual growth in UK gross domestic product (GDP) to the year 2000 of around 3%, with no marked change in lifestyles or social objectives. In fact, the long-term GDP growth rate in the UK, from 1900–1976, was only 1·5% and growth from 1970 has only been at the rate of 1·4%. A 3% assumption is higher even than the 2·8% per year achieved from 1950–1970. So North Sea oil is going to have to offset many other unfavourable features in the UK and international scene if 3% annual growth is to be achieved; 2% seems quite as likely. The uncertain composition of this growth, as between private and public consumption, exports and investment, is also highly relevant to its impact on particular industries, including chemicals.

For the OECD area, estimates for the next few years are being continually revised downwards, eg from the postwar trend of over 5% per year to 4·5% per year in mid 1977, to the latest estimates of 3–4%. Such figures are not claimed to take account of long-term physical resource limitations, or changes in lifestyle, which might begin to have an effect within the next generation. The level of economic activity in the OECD area will have a major effect on UK industries whose raw materials and products are supplied and traded internationally—currently, one-third of UK chemical production is exported.

Alongside these macroeconomic growth uncertainties, there are gross uncertainties about the cost of raw materials, energy, and plant. A recent estimate suggested that by 1987 the world price of oil (in 1977 $) would have risen to between $38–$49/barrel (bbl),[2] whilst other experts (eg Rand) currently suggest an upper limit of $20–$25/bbl, set by the possibility of converting coal or lignite into liquid or gaseous oil-equivalent products. Possibly both views are valid depending on the local situation—eg coal imported into Denmark now costs $35/ton whilst across the border in Schleswig-Holstein the price is $80/ton. Estimates of nuclear-plant costs vary between £400/kW[3] and $3500/kW (~£1800/kW)[4] at 1976–1977 prices. Clearly, uncertainties of this magnitude exclude any attempt to predict future changes purely on the basis of technical economics.

A fourth area of uncertainty is the extent to which the output of chemicals and their derivatives (polymers and fibres in particular) can continue to race ahead of general industrial growth. Before 1973, chemicals growth was almost double that of manufacturing industry, eg annual growth in the OECD area, 1963–1973, was 8·2%, annual GDP growth was 5% (for the UK the figures are 6·7% and 3·1% respectively).

Since the oil crisis, it has been difficult to deduce new relationships, but the general assumption amongst economic experts within the Western European chemical industry is that for the next 5–10 years, chemical growth will be no more than 2 percentage units higher than that of manufacturing industry, depending on GDP growth. This represents a likely annual growth rate for the chemical industry of around 5% in Western Europe; for the UK, a 2·5% per year GDP growth might give a chemicals growth of around 4% per year.

This lower level of 'extra' growth is not the direct result of higher feedstock and energy costs to the chemical industry as compared with competing metallurgical and natural products. Rather, it results from such factors as:

- the inevitable long-term limitation of substitution opportunities;
- constraints arising from concern (justified or otherwise) with the environment and toxins; and
- the limits which lower rates of economic growth impose on rapid technical development, both because of limited capital and research resources and because of reduced opportunities to scrap undersized old plants and build larger and/or improved new ones.

These factors, combined with higher input costs, mean that prices can no longer, as they did in the 1960s, fall in real terms and lead to a rapid expansion of markets.

A further area of major uncertainty arises from the increasing importance of trading areas outside the OECD in the supply of, as distinct from the demand for, chemical products. The impact of Comecon countries is imminent; that of OPEC still in the hazy distance of the late 1980s; the rate of impact of technically advanced Third world countries remains to be determined by decisions yet to be taken on tariffs and quotas.

Taking together all the above factors it will be clear that anything one can say on short- or medium-term prospects for chemicals and energy will be conditional projections, rather than forecasts. In the longer term, ie from around 1990, one can merely identify in qualitative terms some of the factors which, although unimportant at the present time, are already discernable and which may have become significant by the turn of the century.

Short-term trends in energy use
Let us look at the chemical industry in the context of other UK industries and the international scene.

TABLE 1. PRODUCTION AND ENERGY CONSUMPTION
IN UK INDUSTRY, 1966–1976

	All manufacturing (%)	Chemical industry (%)
Output		
Average annual growth of output 1966–1976[a]	1·5	5·0
Overall increase in output 1966–1976	15·6	62·2
Energy		
Overall increase/decrease in energy consumption 1966–1976[b]	−13·0	11·7
Chemical industry's share of all manufacturing energy consumption		
1966[b]		11·8
1976[b]		14·8

Notes: [a] Derived from official production indices; growth rates are trend values; [b] On a heat supplied basis.
Sources: Digest of UK Energy Statistics, Annual Abstract of Statistics, Monthly Digest of Statistics (London, HMSO, 1977 and earlier editions).

TABLE 2. EEC AND US MANUFACTURING AND CHEMICAL INDUSTRIES
(production and purchased energy consumption, 1965–1975)

	All manufacturing[a]		Chemical industry	
	annual output growth (%)	energy consumption output ratio in 1975[b]	annual output growth (%)	energy consumption output ratio in 1975[b]
West Germany	3·4	0·82	6·2	0·73
France	4·6	0·74	6·9	0·69
Italy	4·5	0·96	6·7	0·93
Netherlands	6·1	0·91	9·4	0·98
Belgium	3·1	0·90	6·3	0·99
UK	1·5	0·75	4·5	0·72
USA	2·9	1·05	5·3	0·80

Notes: [a] Industrial production excluding construction; [b] Ratio in 1965 was unity.
Sources: As for Table 1, and see *Eurostat Energy Statistics Yearbook; Eurostat Industrial Statistics; Energy Statistics—1977*, Conseil Européen des Fédérations de l'Industrie Chimique; *Energy Consumption in Manufacturing* (New York, Ballinger for Conference Board, 1974); Federal Energy Administration figures reported in A. P. Christodoulou, *Chemical Industry Energy Usage* (New York, Blyth Eastman Dillon, 1977).

TABLE 3. ENERGY CONSUMPTION IN THE UK CHEMICAL INDUSTRY
(net calorific basis)

	1965 (10³ tce)[a]	1970 (10³ tce)[a]	1973 (10³ tce)[a]	1974 (10³ tce)[a]	1975 (10³ tce)[a]	1976 (10³ tce)[a]
Solid fuels	5017	3635	783	704	588	602
Liquid fuels	2779	4215	6008	5164	4618	4810
Purchased electricity[b]	4128	5652	5741	5508	4933	5307
Gaseous fuels[b]	36	240	2645	3035	3240	3736
Total	11 960	13 732	15 177	14 411	13 379	14 445
Feedstocks[c]	na	9500	13 700	14 800	10 700	14 500
Index of fuel use	*87·1*	*100*	*110·5*	*104·9*	*97·4*	*105·2*
Index of chemical production	*74·6*	*100*	*120·7*	*126·9*	*116·0*	*127·8*
Specific use of fuel per unit of output	*1·17*	*1·00*	*0·92*	*0·83*	*0·84*	*0·82*

Notes:[a] Basic EEC definition 1000 tce (tonnes coal equivalent)=7 Tcal=29 300 GJ. Original data on a heat-supplied, gross-calorific basis have been converted to a net calorific basis using factors supplied by the UK Department of Energy; [b] Purchased electricity in terms of energy output converted to an energy-input basis using average thermal efficiencies for the public supply in England and Wales in each year, and allowing for a 5% transmission loss. Gaseous fuels exclude feedstock use. [c] Net of products returned to refinery; comprises (in 1976) approximately 70% naphtha, gas oil, and LPG, and 30% natural gas.
Sources: As for Tables 1 and 2, and Chemical Industries Association estimates.

In relation to other manufacturing industry, the UK chemical industry accounts for about 15% of total energy use (or over 25% if the energy content of feedstocks is included). The industry's output and energy use has grown much faster than the rest of UK industry (Table 1), but specific energy consumption has improved (Table 2) more quickly than in other industries, and as quickly as any other national chemical industry. The breakdown in use of energy by the UK chemical industry between various fuels is shown in Table 3, which also shows the use of energy-containing raw materials (eg naphtha, gas oil, liquefied petroleum gas (LPG) and natural gas).

The most obvious trend since 1973 is the rapid implementation of energy economies involving better 'housekeeping' and minor capital expenditure. In fact, the UK had been economising in energy well before 1973, and this also applied to certain other European countries. However, Italy and Belgium show a different pattern; this is almost certainly due to the large-scale intro-

TABLE 4. ENERGY CONSUMPTION BY THE US AND
UK CHEMICAL INDUSTRIES

	Energy consumption (10^3 Btu per \$ of sales at 1965 prices)									
	1965	1967	1970	1971	1972	1973	1974	1975	1976	1980 (target)
USA	77·3	78·1		70·4	65·2				58·9	55·5
UK	47·4	46·1	40·6	40·4	38·4	37·2	33·6	34·2	33·4	31·6

Source: Chemical Industries Association estimates.

duction since 1965 of energy-intensive petrochemical processes, in excess of national downstream demand.

In the USA, the low price of energy to the chemical industry has probably been the main factor discouraging economies of energy use; present Western European prices are about 60% higher. Since 1973, the USA has made efforts to improve its energy economy, and had achieved an 11% improvement in energy use per unit of chemical output by 1976 (over 1972 values) and expects an improvement of 15% by 1980. This is a similar trend and projection to that in the UK but, if energy use per unit of chemical output is evaluated for the two countries on a common basis (Table 4), the relatively greater potential for savings in the USA becomes obvious; present UK specific usage is about 60% of that in the USA. Clearly, US chemical plants have been— and still are—as much "gas guzzlers' as their automobiles.

It is unlikely that improvements to date in energy use owe much to changes in process or in product mix, although the present reduced demand for chemicals allows production to be concentrated at the more energy-efficient plants, when a company has a choice. Many older ethylene plants are now mothballed and polymerisation plants, which may vary greatly in energy efficiency, can be selected according to this criterion. Chlorine plants can be run under conditions of optimum cell efficiency—which falls off rapidly at maximum production rates. Taken together, these savings probably offset the generally higher costs of running plants at less than design capacity. However, a rise in demand would bring back into use less efficient plants. Until a further major rise in demand beyond present maximum available capacity can be confidently foreseen, it will be difficult to justify the large expenditure needed for their replacement.

Major changes in processes which led to greater energy efficiency were introduced in the 1960s—eg the almost complete replacement of acetylene as a basic raw material by olefins and paraffins. Changes in products are more difficult; the most energy intensive such as polyvinyl chloride and low-density polyethylene are firmly established as the basic commodities of the plastics industry, while more specialised products are less affected by energy costs. Moreover, even the energy-intensive products of the chemical industry are competitive with nonchemical products—and are therefore unlikely to be displaced.

As new plants are built, they will certainly incorporate energy economy features which were not hitherto economically justified. Nevertheless, the rise in capital costs (tripling between 1970 and 1978) is not far short of that of energy, and given the high rates of return necessitated by high inflation, it is often difficult to sell the case for the more expensive version. Obviously, this is easier if one builds in a rapid escalation of *future* energy costs, but *in the short-term* (1980s) there may not be strong grounds for doing this. After 1990 is quite another matter, but this period will not affect current discounted cash flow calculations very much.

A major source of energy economy within the chemical industry in Europe arises from combined heat and power (CHP) schemes, which can often be balanced within a site, as between electrical or shaft horsepower and process steam, so as to give overall thermal efficiencies approaching 80%, compared with the 30% achieved by the public electricity supply system. Higher utilisation factors (over 90%) can be achieved.

However, while existing schemes are certainly economic to operate, higher capital costs, high distillate-fuel-oil or gas costs, and the higher return needed to justify private-sector investment mitigate the economic benefits of proposed new installations.[5] In addition, there are the more arbitrary problems of commercial relations with the public-supply authorities and some legal constraints which discourage introduction of new schemes in the UK. It is noteworthy that the French have recently introduced measures which, it is claimed, reduce the payback of industrial CHP schemes from 6–7 years to around 2–3 years.[6] In the UK, less than 30% of chemical-industry power is produced by CHP schemes; if this were increased to no more than the present EEC *average* level of 40%, it would represent a saving of 8% (1 million tons of coal equivalent) of the industry's primary energy demand. The long-delayed report of the Marshall Committee on UK industrial CHP schemes will, I hope, give substantial encouragement to such schemes.

Taking all these factors together, a differential of 1% between chemical output annual growth rates and energy use (eg 3% increase in energy use for a 4% output growth) appears sustainable for some further years, followed by a period of slower improvement until massive replacement of existing plants and processes becomes justifiable.

Feedstocks over the next ten years

Over this timespan, one can rely on what is known of present plants, technology, and products, and of concrete plans for new investments.

Downstream, there already exists, to an extent almost adequate for a decade's growth, a complex network of processes yielding intermediates and final products which depend on a few major starting materials and processes, as shown on Figure 1. This diagram omits minor sources and identifies only those primary materials and processes which currently provide the overwhelming bulk of chemicals and polymers; it includes only those inputs which are most important from an energy standpoint, and omits major raw materials such as sulphur and sulphuric acid, phosphate rock, and the sources of metallic radicals.

Figure 1 fails to show the complex and multitudinous range of derivatives of the primary petrochemical products; study of a complete series of charts, such as are published by Stanford Research Institute,[7] demonstrates that the petrochemical industry comprises very much more than a few major olefin

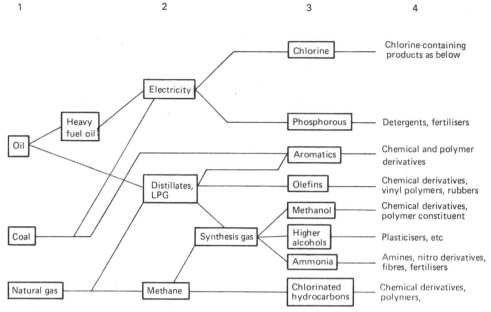

Figure 1. Materials and processes that currently provide most chemicals and polymers

plants, and such a study might correct naive political misapprehensions about the nature of the industry

As far as Europe and Japan are concerned, the most important pathway is the one from oil, through naphtha, to the lower olefins; ammonia and methanol also depend heavily on naphtha though methane is the preferred feedstock, if available, on account of the more favourable ratio of hydrogen to carbon.

In the medium term (the early 1980s), it is widely suggested that the UK chemical industry may develop at a relatively faster rate in the petrochemical and plastics sectors due to the overall security of oil supplies and the particular use, in a very limited number of situations, of gaseous or LPG feedstocks.

The extent of such accelerated development should not be exaggerated; the European and world *market* for such products is the overriding constraint, and the UK share of such markets can only be expected to increase appreciably if there are greater attractions—and fewer disincentives—to international investment in these sectors in the UK compared with elsewhere. Availability of LPG is no particular virtue—for many years the Americans have claimed that the European and Japanese chemical industries have been fortunate to be naphtha-based in contrast to the predominantly LPG base in America. There is certainly nothing new in a technical sense in the use of gaseous/LPG feedstocks for petrochemical manufacture.

The trend of olefin production, and of petrochemicals generally, can be roughly represented by the trend of ethylene alone. Historical data for Western Europe are shown in Figure 2; between 1960 and 1970, an average annual growth rate of about 20% was achieved although the rate fell from about 30% to 14% over the decade. Such data were projected in 1974 by NEDO,[8] leading to an estimate for Western European demand in 1985 of 28 Mtons, nearly

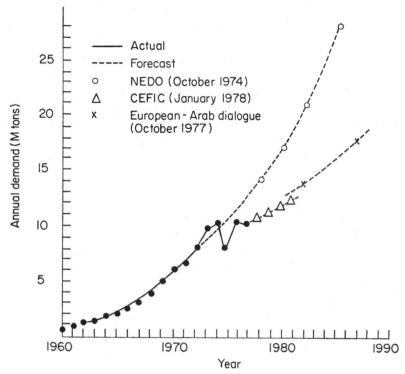

Figure 2. Ethylene demand in Western Europe

18 Mtons higher than 1974 output and 16 Mtons higher than capacity. It was therefore argued that in the period to 1985 Western Europe would need to build at least 30 crackers, and that the UK should make a bid for five of these of which one (the Imperial Chemical Industries/British Petroleum unit at Wilton) was already committed.

However, even in 1974 the industry had little faith in simple trend extrapolations, and events have turned out a lot worse than the somewhat lower estimates the industry expected at that time. The latest forecasts (February 1978) from the Council Européen des Fédérations de l'Industrie Chimique and the figures used in the latest round of the European–Arab dialogue on petrochemicals, suggest that by 1985 demand will be around 16 Mtons— which is almost within the capacity of plant already available or building. Beyond 1985, the top slice of demand will begin to be met by OPEC production, which could possibly be supplying derivatives equivalent to 2 Mtons of ethylene by 1990—although 1 Mtons seems more likely by then.

As to supply of raw material for olefins and other petrochemical products, some experts take the view that there will be by 1990, or possibly earlier, a genuine oil-supply constraint worldwide. At that time, only about 12% of oil produced will be needed for chemicals,[9] and even for the next decade the chemical industry will probably be prepared to outbid the energy industries for supplies, given the existing capital investment and overwhelmingly greater convenience and economy of oil sources for chemical manufacture compared with the possible alternatives. The same applies to natural gas for ammonia and methanol production. The industry can also use the flexibility, which it is currently building into projects, to use gas oil and/or LPG as a feedstock instead of naphtha.

If this is true of the Western world in general, it is even more true for the UK. Department of Energy forecasts suggest that sufficient indigenous oil is available for UK demand until about 1992;[10] this assumes oil production peaking at 125 Mtons—which could be pessimistic, and a 3% per year GDP growth, which seems unlikely. A more likely outturn is that it will be nearer the year 2000 before, in a purely national context, the UK chemical industry has to over-bid for its oil supplies. For gas, the timescale may be even longer; the forecasts show no deficit until the year 2000.

Within OPEC and OECD, OPEC capacity in 1982 will amount, for individual basic petrochemical products, to 0–5% of the two areas' combined capacity, and 1987 seems the earliest that OPEC products will be a significant factor. The European–Arab dialogue studies are currently looking at the need for new capacity in the OECD/OPEC area between 1982 and 1987, and how this might split between the two zones. The sensible position for OPEC countries is to make energy-intensive products which can be readily transported—such as styrene, cumene, and ethylene dichloride—but OPEC countries may have ambitions to make a range of polymer derivatives—in particular polyethylene, polypropylene, and PVC. If so, the impact on the market (particularly on prices) will be greater than would appear from the tonnages involved; already, such destabilisation is arising from Eastern European sales of polymers tied to technical licensing and construction deals, and one can only view with alarm the effect on the chemical industry of such a situation arising on another front.

Pressure to accept OPEC petrochemicals, as and when they become available, could well arise not so much because of a low price—high capital and operating costs will offset their low feedstock and energy input costs—but as a result of the need for the oil-deficient Western nations to accept package deals of oil and petrochemicals. In such circumstances, tariff barriers or fibre-type cartels are unlikely to be accepted as a means of moderating the external competitive pressures on the Western European and Japanese chemical industries, and many companies will increase their dependence on OPEC petrochemical intermediates for their downstream production, despite the political, technical, and commercial risks involved.

Thus, for different reasons, but in both the UK and the wider OECD area, chemical industries are likely to maintain a petrochemical base for a period much longer than would be suggested by the aggregate balance between demand and indigenous oil and gas supply within these areas.

After petrochemicals?

Even though it may be several decades before there is a major shift away from a petrochemical base in the main production areas of world chemicals, it is nevertheless likely that this shift will occur; in some areas, it has already begun.

In certain countries the chemical industry has retained a significant basis of nonpetrochemical raw materials from the previous era of coal and/or fermentation-based chemical production and, in one or two special situations, strategic factors have led to continuing development of indigenous materials other than oil as raw materials. But a move away from oil and natural gas will not in general involve new concepts, on a significant scale, at least for several decades.

In contrast to Figure 1, Figure 3 shows the products and pathways which were important in the pre-petrochemical era, ie up to about 1950. The basic routes then were from coal (via acetylene, synthesis gas, and coal tar), and

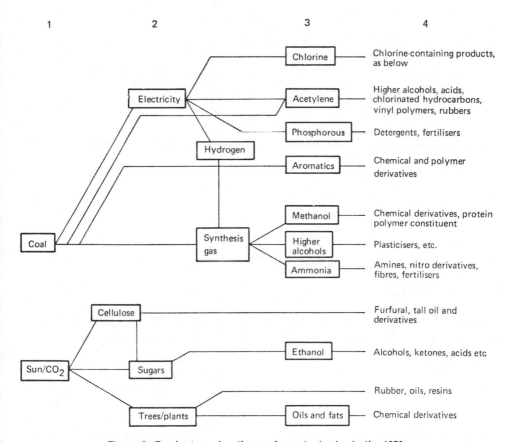

Figure 3. Products and pathways important prior to the 1950s

from sugars (mainly as molasses); however one should also record the early use of refinery gases in the USA as a source of olefins, and the use of natural gas in Germany to produce acetylene, both of which were operational prewar. The other important raw material basis at that time was the range of natural products from plants, in particular natural rubber and other oils and resins from trees.

The combination of Figures 1 and 3 (Figure 4), shows the scope of conventional possibilities to the year 2000, to which have been added a number of potential new routes.

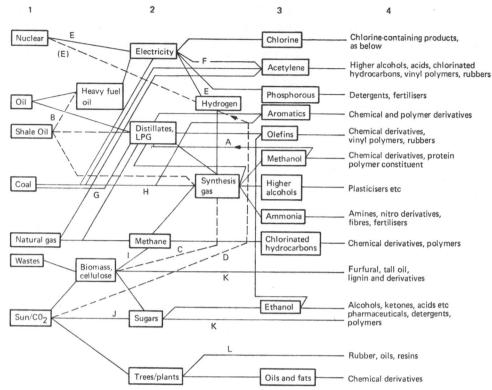

Figure 4. Potential new pathways and their relation to present and previous practice

At present, petrochemical routes are predominant: the use of acetylene has almost ceased; the use of fermentation is restricted to special products (eg citric acid) or special raw-material situations (as in Queensland); the use of coal, except for the by-products of coke production, is limited to South Africa (for strategic reasons) or as a source of electrical energy.

One area, natural products, has retained a significant position, with natural rubber (world production 3·6 Mtons in 1976) still accounting for a third of Western European rubber demand. Natural oils and fats provide, worldwide, around 6 Mtons of chemical raw materials, and essential oil and resins a further significant tonnage. Compare this with world naphtha usage for chemicals which, although around 80 Mtons gross, yields only about 30 Mtons of primary chemical products. Many natural products are much nearer the end of the production chain and provide high performance end-products in high yield, whilst naphtha loses a lot of weight and requires very high downstream capital inputs to produce similar end-products. Natural products of a specialised nature have thus continued to hold a not insignificant place in competition with petrochemicals. In certain cases they provide the only suitable source on a performance basis—eg high-quality brake-lining resins depend for their manufacture on cashew-nut oil rather than synthetic materials.

Perhaps illogically, (and because the statistics are often in a different category) one tends to exclude cellulose from this analysis where its industrial products retain a cellulosic character, eg in fibres and paper; but in both these areas chemical processing is involved and there is a direct market interaction with chemical products. This continuing source of a natural, equivalent, raw material, amounting to about 4·9 Mtons for fibre and chemical conversions,[11] should therefore not be ignored; again, the end-products are obtained in high yield from the raw material, cellulose fibre production being nearly 4 Mtons.

What, then, is new for the post-petrochemical era? Four genuinely novel possibilities, routes A–D, are shown in Figure 4 (see Table 5). There are in addition a number of old routes, E–L, which may gain in importance. As regards these possibilities, there are a number of general principles involved.

TABLE 5. LIKELY ROUTES FOR THE POST-PETROCHEMICAL ERA

New routes

A. The conversion of methanol to liquid and gaseous hydrocarbons

B. The use of shale oil as a substitute in present routes using crude oil and/or coal

C. The aerobic conversion of biomass to synthesis gas

D. The phototropic production of hydrogen in biological systems

Old routes with increased potential

E. Production of hydrogen by electrolysis (use of direct nuclear heat is also being researched)

F. Production of acetylene, possibly via carbide, but more likely through a plasma reactor

G. Coal hydrogenation (which also requires hydrogen or synthesis gas)

H. Fischer–Tropsch type synthesis yielding both hydrocarbons and oxygenated products

I. Anaerobic fermentation of natural and/or waste materials

J. Increased production of sugars either naturally, or by acid or enzymatic hydrolysis of cellulose; and subsequent fermentation or conversion

K. New products (eg lignin) from existing natural materials

L. Increased yields from existing species, and/or new or modified species

Downstream operations

There is a vast range of existing process operations downstream from primary chemicals and first-stage intermediates, and beyond that there are other major industries which expect the raw materials inputs from the chemical industry to match very closely those for which their plants are designed and their markets established. New chemical routes must therefore seek to 'get back on track' as early as possible down the chemical chain of operations— if not in column 3 of Figure 4 then at least in column 4.

Scale

In a paper in 1975,[12] Duncan Davies contrasted large-scale 'coalplexes' with decentralised smaller-scale operations based on carbohydrates. There are intrinsic economic reasons for this distinction, which mean that quite apart from differences in raw-material availability in different areas of the world, the preferred choice may depend as much on geographical, political, and social factors as much as economic ones. Manpower and land availability are clearly very important.

Capital resources

The replacement of European olefin requirements by an acetylene base (ie a reversion, conceptually, to the predominant position in 1950 but at the scale of demand likely in 1990) would cost around £20 thousand million (1977 values), and involve extra electrical generation of around 210 TWh/year (35 000 MW demand);[13] roughly doubling the £20 thousand million needed for conventional development of the remainder of the European petrochemical industry to 1990 and more than doubling the total likely electricity demand of the whole industry under such conditions.

Let us take another, perhaps more realistic example. An olefin plant producing 400 000 tons of ethylene a year, together with immediate downstream and service plant, might cost around £300 M in 1980: a coal conversion plant yielding sufficient chemical feedstock for such a plant (after allowing for some direct products) would cost at the very least £750 M. Even though the additional capital could in part be loaded on to fuel products from the same complex, the sum involved is formidable, especially if one aims to provide for existing olefin production as well as meeting market growth.

Market growth

During the 1950s and 1960s, the annual growth in the OECD of petrochemicals and polymers demand averaged 15% and this, along with the benefits of scale, permitted the rapid replacement of uneconomic techniques and raw materials, eg the switch from acetylene to ethylene as a basis for PVC. With future growth of such products estimated at about 5% and with further economies of scale no longer available, the replacement of petrochemical plant is likely to be much slower than before.

Alternatives to petrochemicals

Although detailed consideration of nonpetrochemical routes would be beyond the scope of this article, I feel comments on the more interesting possibilities would be useful.

Nuclear

Within the timespan under consideration, the only possible contribution of nuclear power to the *feedstock* requirements of the chemical industry is via hydrogen; an electrolytic route can be assumed since anything else is too far away from commercial development to be of interest.

The various possibilities have recently been reviewed by Steinberg.[14] Although he takes an optimistic view about nuclear power costs, his economic analysis does not lead to very encouraging comparisons with alternative routes. Steinberg also considers using nuclear heat as a 'helper' to processes using coal as feedstock.

The juxtaposition or the integration of nuclear and chemical plant raises serious safety questions. Although the Dow chemical company in Michigan is now resuming work with a local utility company on a joint CHP scheme based on nuclear power, Badische Anilin-und-Soda-Fabrik (BASF) who had planned to supply their Ludwigshafen site with steam and power from a fairly conventional nuclear station, appear to have given up a seven-year fight to get approval, and the problems of getting safety approval of an unconventional combined nuclear and chemical installation appear virtually insuperable.

For reasons both of economics and safety it thus seems unlikely that the next 25 years will see any major contribution from nuclear power to the chemical industry, except where conventional electrical needs are met by the nuclear route.

Coal

Up to the immediate postwar period, and in certain countries such as West Germany until somewhat later, coal has been the major source of carbon-containing chemical products, by way of distillation, hydrogenation, or conversion to synthesis gas. Two factors are relevant to the future: physical availability and relative economics. The necessary technology, at least on a moderate scale, already exists or is at an advanced stage of development.

Over the next 25 years the insecurity of coal supplies is likely to be at least as great as that of oil, more so perhaps since the social and political factors involved are on one's doorstep.

In Western Europe, only the UK and West Germany have potential supplies on a large enough scale to be of interest. On a world basis, many hundreds of millions of tons a year *might* be available in the 1980s. However, the diversity of suppliers and transport is less than that for oil, and at least as much subject to interruption by political action or strikes. In addition, coal is much more difficult to handle and store than oil (although the use of a coal–oil mixture may alleviate this problem).

Taking these factors into account, the chemical industry will only return from oil or gas to coal if there is a large economic incentive.

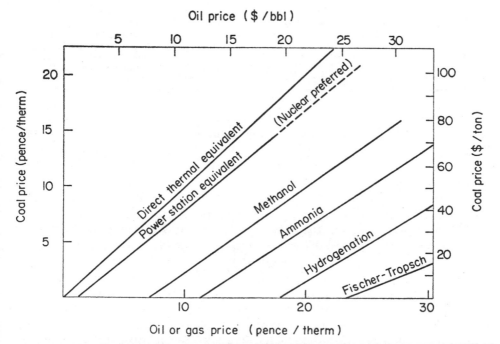

Figure 5. Approximate break-even prices for coal to be able to substitute for oil or gas as a chemical feedstock

Figure 5 shows that if coal prices follow oil on a basis of thermal value, or equivalent costs of power generation, the chemical industry will always choose to use oil or gas. If coal prices are bracketed within limits set by higher production or transport costs, and by the nuclear power break-even[3] to say 15p/therm or £38/ton (in 1977 money) then the oil price break-even for ammonia or methanol production is probably around $30/bbl, and for the hydrogenation route to liquid products even higher; the Fischer–Tropsch route is even less attractive.

At present oil prices, it is only when secure long-term supplies of coal are available locally, priced for one reason or another at around $10/ton, that one begins to look at coal-based chemical operations; for the rest of the century the upper limit is probably around $20/ton, at which price coal would be of interest when oil (or equivalent gas) prices rose to $20/bbl (all in 1977 $).

TABLE 6. TWO COAL-BASED CHEMICAL PROCESSES

Process	Capital cost ($M)	Input (10^3 tons/day)				Output (10^3 tons/day)	
		coal[a]	coal[b]	air	water	waste	useful[c]
Fischer–Tropsch	2200	39	30	106	9	131	13·6
Hydroliquefaction	1500[d]	39	30	3·8[e]	49	66	15·8

Notes: [a] Ex mine; [b] as fed; [c] fuels, feedstocks, and chemicals; [d] excluding oxygen plant; [e] oxygen.

TABLE 7. COMPARISON OF USEFUL OUTPUT

Process	Useful output (10^3 tons/day)					
	synthetic natural gas	hydrocarbons		naptha	sulphur	other
		C_3	C_4			
Fischer–Tropsch	6·59	—	0·34	2·38	1·01	Oxygenated chemicals (0·45), diesel fuel (2·15), distillate fuel oils (0·71)
Hydroliquefaction	3·31	0·45	0·35	1·08	1·05	Ammonia (0·80), fuel oil (9·51)

The present Sasol operation in South Africa provides a guide to what a coal-based chemical operation might look like if the Fischer–Tropsch route is used. Tables 6 and 7 show an operation on a scale currently proposed in the USA. Modern developments of the hydrogenation route would probably now be preferred, even compared with an improved Fischer–Tropsch operation (Tables 6 and 7). The capital cost of a single such scheme (equal to the total 1978 UK chemical industry's investment programme), the considerable production of fuel by-products, and the relatively low thermal efficiencies are all negative factors compared with existing oil- or gas-based schemes.

At present, apart from Sasol which depends for its existence on strategic necessity and coal at about $5/ton, firm plans are limited to demonstration plants of around 2000 tons/day coal input to produce synthetic natural gas and/or ammonia. Consideration, however, is being given to a plant with capital cost of $2 thousand million to produce 25 000 tons/day of methanol from lignite priced at around $6/ton. The methanol would be primarily used as fuel but operation on this scale based on so cheap a raw material could provide fuel-grade methanol at around 40c/US gallon—roughly the present US price—and this could be shipped worldwide as a primary chemical feedstock, or converted by the Mobil process into olefins and aromatic hydrocarbons. Details of another scheme, based on coal, have recently been published.[15]

The other possible route for use of coal as a chemical feedstock is via acetylene, either via calcium carbide or using a plasma reactor. Carbide, flame, or electric-arc processes and downstream operations based on acetylene have a long history; the main objection to them is that as processes they are much less energy efficient in producing the end-products than the petrochemical operations which have replaced them. If there is a world energy shortage, which may develop a decade or so hence, it seems illogical to revert to or develop processes which use more energy to obtain a given result. This could only make economic sense if local coal (or gas) prices were decoupled, by logistic or political factors, from world prices.

Natural products

In contrast to coal and nuclear-based processes which I believe have a very restricted role within the chemical industry, at least until the end of the century, the biological area appears much more interesting in the medium term.

Fermentation of carbohydrates

Fermentation ethanol has remained competitive. In the USA at present, ethanol based on corn is 10c/US gallon cheaper than the petroleum product. The main objections to the fermentation route are the bulk of the primary raw materials, and the loss of weight down the pathway, particularly if one dehydrates ethanol to olefins rather than uses it directly as a source of aldehydes, acids, and esters. The seasonal availability of raw materials may also be an objection, although this does not apply to all sources of starches and sugars.

There is an upsurge of interest in this route in certain areas, and Brazil plans to increase ethanol production from sugar cane and cassava from 16 000 tons/year in 1974 to 550 000 tons/year in 1984. Although a considerable land area is involved, one may note that present world cane-sugar production is 50 Mtons and molasses 27 Mtons; world wine production (31 500 Mlitres in 1976–1977) already contains nearly 4 Mtons of ethanol—although one would hope that this will not all be diverted to chemical manufacture.

Starting with cellulose, rather than sugar or starch-containing raw material, one is faced with an acid- or enzyme-catalysed hydrolysis step before fermentation (see Figure 6). It has been calculated that the farm waste in the USA (550 Mtons/year) is equivalent to 28 Mtons of ethylene (twice the current US production).[16] If only 10% of it were collected and used, this would provide for an appreciable proportion of future increases in ethylene demand.

Expressed in another way, the total weight of carbohydrate and cellulosic *non-food* end-products produced in the USA is 80% of the weight of petrochemical, plastic, and synthetic fibre end-products. A partial shift in the raw material base to natural products cannot be ruled out on supply-limitation grounds. However, for existing petrochemical olefin derivations one must set a long lead time on such developments, since even 'free' cellulose waste is equivalent, after allowing for collection and conversion costs, to a 30c/lb

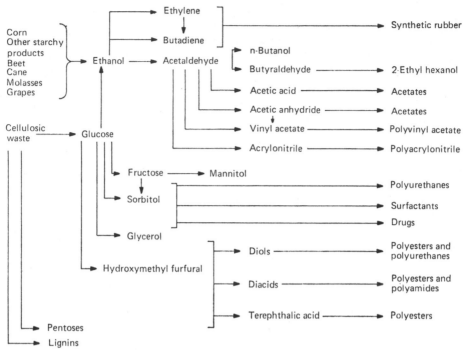

Figure 6. Chemicals that can be produced from cellulose, starch, and sugars

ethylene raw material cost, which is about the total price which petrochemical producers will be looking for in the 1980s.

If, on the other hand, one is aiming at ethanol or furfural, rather than olefins, hydrolysis and fermentation of wood should give a price about 70% higher than present prices, and furfural at prices about 40% higher, which may be of interest a decade hence.

Gas production from natural materials

The conversion of biomass to methane and/or synthesis gas, and the phototrophic production of hydrogen are of considerable research interest. Small-scale methane production from biomass by anaerobic fermentation is, of course, a favourite topic of alternative technologists but it may also offer scope for large-scale development. Papers have been given at various conferences on phototropic production of hydrogen[17] and on pressure conversion of biomass by steam and oxygen to synthesis gas.[18] However, considered as a chemical raw material, there is a major logistical problem, since an economic ammonia or methanol plant requires at least 500 000 tons/year of methane or equivalent.

Natural products for direct use

Since their transplantation to Asia, rubber trees and their mode of exploitation have been developed to give an annual yield of over two tons per acre compared with the original yield of 350 lb;[19] although present prices tend to favour lower-yielding trees with low labour costs in smallholdings rather than the higher-yielding stock in company plantations.

There are 7000 plant species yielding polyisoprene, and many other species yield other hydrocarbons.

Firestone are currently planting 100 000 acres in Texas of the guayule bush which gives an emulsion of low-molecular-weight isoprene-based hydrocarbons, and the Euphorbia tree is estimated to be capable of producing 10 bbl/acre year of hydrocarbons at a cost (including extraction) of $20/bbl.[20] There is clearly large scope for development of such hydrocarbon sources over the next few decades; their use as chemical feedstocks could come ahead of their use as energy sources if the hydrocarbon produced can, as with polyisoprene, be used directly or without serious degradation.

Conclusions

The basic conclusions appear rather dull and conventional—that there will be petrochemicals for a long while to come, with a gradual replacement by raw materials and process routes, most of which were already familiar in the early half of the century.

In fact, the future is far from dull, if only because it is so uncertain. Instead of a steady and rapid expansion of production and techniques based on a single feedstock in plentiful supply, the chemical industry has to grope towards a variety of new sources of raw materials and energy at a pace made uncertain both by supply and by demand factors. It has to base its future development on uncertain capital costs and even more uncertain raw-material and energy costs. It has to take account of a host of social, political, geographical, and logistical factors which it could hitherto almost ignore. And it has to tackle—if my analysis is correct—botanical and biochemical technologies as well as those based on chemistry and physics.

There is no reason why the industry should not solve these problems over the next two or three decades so as to prepare itself for a greater reliance on renewable resources and coal in the 21st century. But it could be thrown off course, nationally and internationally, by politically oriented and oversimplistic pressures which disregard costs, markets, and the complexity of the technical and commercial choices open to the industry. As C. P. Snow put it "Even at the highest level of decision, men do not relish the complexity of brute reality, and will hare after a simple concept whenever one shows its head".[21] For the chemical industry for the next 25 years, only one thing is certain—that there are no simple concepts.

Notes and references

1. K. Boulding, quoted in A. B. Lovins, *Soft Energy Paths* (London, Pelican, 1977), page 110.
2. A. Parker, "Western energy policy after Carter", *Lloyds Bank Review*, January 1978, *127*, page 28.
3. UK Department of Energy, *Energy Commission Paper 6* (London, HMSO, February 1978).
4. A. B. Lovins, *op cit*.
5. P. G. Caudle, "The comparative economics of self-generated and purchased power", *Chemistry and Industry*, 6 September 1975, page 717; and "The chemical industry as a user of electricity", *IEE Symposium—Electricity for Materials Processing and Conservation* (London, IEE, March 1977), page 5.
6. Agence pour les Economies d'Energie, *Decree 77 37/P*, Paris, 31 March 1977, quoted in press release, 20 June 1977.

7. Stanford Research Institute, *Chemical Origins and Markets*, fifth edition (Menlo Park, California, SRI, 1977).
8. National Economic Development Office, *UK Chemicals 1975–1985* (London, NEDO, 1976).
9. N.G.S. Champion, "Oil and gas as chemical feedstocks", *Chemistry and Industry*, 7 January 1978, page 8.
10. UK Department of Energy, *Energy Commission Paper 5* (London, HMSO February 1978).
11. UNESCO, *The Raw Material Requirements of the Chemical Industry*, ECE/Chem/17, UNESCO, Geneva, March 1977.
12. D. S. Davies, "Economics and politics of the return of coal and cellulose", *Chemistry and Industry*, 20 September 1975, page 771.
13. 1TWh = 10^{12} Wh.
14. N. Steinberg, "Nuclear power for the production of synthetic fuels and feedstock", *Energy Policy*, August 1977, *5* (1), page 12.
15. US Department of Energy, "Badger plants study", reported in *Chemical Week*, 22 March 1978, page 32.
16. P. Becher and W. H. C. Rueggeberg of ICI United States Inc., "Glucose isomerisation— possible impact on chemical utilization of carbohydrates", paper presented to meeting of American Chemical Society, New York, April, 1976.
17. R.-P. Owsianowski, paper presented to conference on Bio-energy 12/13 January 1978, reported in *Chemical Age*, 20 January 1978, page 15.
18. Various authors, Institute of Gas Technology Conference reported in *Chemistry and Engineering*, 23 February 1976, page 24.
19. R. L. Schulter, "The odyssey of the cultivated rubber tree", *Endeavour*, 1977, *1* (3/4), page 133.
20. M. Calvin, paper presented to conference on bio-energy *op cit* (reference 18).
21. C. P. Snow, *Science and government* (Cambridge, Mass., Harvard University Press, 1962), page 73.

WORLDWIDE NUCLEAR-PLANT PERFORMANCE
Lessons for technology policy

John Surrey and Steve Thomas

The authors compare the performance of different reactor systems to identify the determinants of plant performance, to examine the evidence of technological maturation, and to discover the principal causes of outage or unavailability. In the light of the findings, they discuss the implications for the UK regarding reactor choice and technology development. They make no judgements about the relative merits of nuclear and fossil-fuel plants, or about safety.

IN SOME senses nuclear power is still an 'immature' industry, characterised by little technical standardisation and limited operating experience of plants embodying current technology and design. There has been little independent analysis of operating performance, particularly on a worldwide basis. Good availability and performance are important requirements for all base-load power plants, particularly for nuclear plants because of their high capital costs. This article should be seen as an interim assessment of some widely canvassed opinions about the maturation of nuclear technologies.

Load factor

Capital costs normally form at least two-thirds of the total cost of nuclear electricity. Load factor expresses the actual output of a plant as a proportion of the potential output obtainable had the plant operated at full capacity throughout the year and is a good measure of performance.[1] Table 1 shows the effect of variations in the load factor on the capital cost per kWh supplied. Besides reducing the capital cost per unit generated, high nuclear-plant availability helps to minimise system operating costs: it avoids having to make

Both authors work at the Science Policy Research Unit, University of Sussex, Falmer, UK. For a more detailed discussion see the Occasional Paper of the same title published by the Science Policy Research Unit, February 1980.

TABLE 1. TRADE-OFF BETWEEN LOAD FACTOR AND CAPITAL COST PER kWh

Construction cost ($/kW)	Annual capital charge ($M)[a]	Capital cost (c/kWh) at a load factor of				
		80%	70%	60%	50%	40%
500	70	1·00	1·14	1·33	1·60	2·00
750	105	1·50	1·71	2·00	2·40	3·00

Note: [a] This assumes straightline depreciation over 25 years and interest at 10% a year.

up a shortfall in base load supply with electricity generated by fossil-fuel plants which have high fuel costs.[2]

Virtually all output losses in 1975–1977 stemmed from unavailability and power reductions (operating below capacity) caused by plant-related factors as opposed to system-operating requirements (eg 'load following').

Plant load factors are sometimes calculated on the basis of the net authorised rating (or maximum dependable rating). A better measure is the design rating. Besides being the basis of the investment decision (on which the plant was planned, built and paid for), it is an unambiguous yardstick of plant operating performance through time. Our use of the design rating has little effect upon the statistical results for most plants now in service apart from British gas-cooled reactors.

Technology development

In 1978 there were 152 commercial nuclear plants, with a capacity of 91·2 GW, installed in 17 countries. These plants were of four types (Table 2).

TABLE 2. THE FOUR TYPES OF COMMERCIAL NUCLEAR-POWER PLANTS

PWRs (pressurised water reactors). Developed in the USA, these are the most numerous in service. They use pressurised water as moderator and coolant and are refuelled when the reactor is shut down (off-load). Because they operate at high pressure they have a strong pressure vessel made of thick steel.

BWRs (boiling water reactors). Like PWRs, these are light-water reactors and refuelled off-load. They were also developed in the USA and have been widely adopted elsewhere. The design is less compact than the PWR but it is simpler and requires no heat exchangers and a thinner pressure vessel.

PHWRS (pressurised heavy-water reactors). Several countries, including the UK, were interested in heavy water reactors up to the prototype stage, partly because of their fuel efficiency; but Canada is the only country to have built a series of commercial PHWRs. The distinctive features of the Canadian design, CANDU, are that the reaction and containment take place in a series of pressure tubes rather than one large pressure vessel and that the uranium fuel does not require enrichment, thus avoiding considerable expense.

GCRs (gas-cooled reactors). Developed by Britain and France in the 1950s and 1960s, GCRs use graphite as the moderator and carbon dioxide as coolant. The first British GCR programme used unenriched uranium metallic fuel elements encased in magnesium alloy (hence the name Magnox); a broadly similar design was developed in France. Partly because of cost, Britain abandoned the Magnox design in 1965 in favour of the advanced gas-cooled reactor (AGR)—a more elaborate design—and France abandoned its GCR design in 1969 in favour of PWRs. The Magnox programme incorporated considerable technical change and the later plants operate at considerably higher coolant conditions than the earlier plants in the series. The Magnox plants have been subject to deratings of about 20% because of corrosion of mild steel parts by the carbon-dioxide coolant.

The reactor market has become increasingly dominated by PWRs and BWRS. In 1967–1970 work was started in 83 light-water reactors, of which 55 were in the USA. Since 1975 there have been many cancellations and postponements and a slump in new orders. However, when the plants on which work had started by December 1978 are completed, installed capacity will rise from 91·2 GW to 218·8 GW. The USA will continue to account for a large proportion of the total number, installed capacity and operating experience of the two principal types of nuclear plant.

Coverage of analysis

This study covers all commercial nuclear plants installed in the non-Communist countries (Table 3).[3]

TABLE 3. CHARACTERISTICS OF THE PLANTS COVERED IN THE ANALYSIS[a]

	PWRs	BWRs	PHWRs	GCRs
Design rating (MW gross)				
Mean (SD)[b]	724 (273)	652 (263)	567 (202)	334 (159)
Range	160–1300	160–1098	220–791	166–676
Age (months)				
Mean (SD)	63·5 (42·4)	70·4 (42·6)	54·0 (31·7)	147·3 (37·5)
Range	12–209	12–220	15–94	77–193
Coolant temperature (°C)				
Mean (SD)	315 (8·5)	286 (6·4)	298 (6·1)	391 (24·7)
Range	278–325	275–302	293–306	319–414
Coolant pressure (kg/cm²)				
Mean (SD)	154 (11·3)	71 (0·9)	97 (9·0)	20 (8·2)
Range	97–175	70–73	87–115	10–43

Notes: [a] Based on plants in commercial operation by 1 January 1978; [b] standard deviation is shown in parentheses.

We identify four causes of 'lost' output, of which the first two are given in IAEA reports and the remaining two are calculated from IAEA output data:

- *Planned outage:* this covers scheduled shutdowns for refuelling, maintenance and repairs.
- *Unplanned outrage:* this covers shutdowns over which the utility has no control, principally equipment failure. Note that the distinction between planned and unplanned outage is sometimes blurred; for example, an equipment failure may result in a long 'planned' outage for repair.
- *Derating losses:* these are the losses incurred if the authorised rating is less than the design rating.
- *Operating losses:* these are the losses sustained in operating below authorised ratings; they arise from less serious equipment failures which do not necessitate shutdown but reduce the possible output, from so-called 'stretchout' operations to ensure that planned outages for refuelling occur at a convenient time (generally when system demand is low), and when a unit is being shut down from, and returned to, full power.

Overview

Average load factors for the years 1975–1978 are shown in Table 4. PHWRs are clearly at the top of the league; but no other type of reactor is achieving the load factors of at least 70% that were widely expected when they were planned and built.[4] GCRs are generally reliable workhorses but their average performance is depressed by the Magnox deratings. The average performance of PWRs is clearly better than that of BWRs.

TABLE 4. OVERVIEW OF NUCLEAR-PLANT PERFORMANCE, 1975–1978

		Load factor (%)		
		mean	SD[a]	range (low–high)
PWRs	1975	65·5	22·3	0–96·9
	1976	61·0	20·4	0–95·7
	1977	67·1	19·6	0–96·2
	1978	67·8	19·9	0–95·2
BWRs	1975	51·8	21·3	0–86·5
	1976	58·8	16·6	13·9–86·9
	1977	50·6	21·7	0–86·6
	1978	60·3	22·0	0–88·1
PHWRs	1975	60·8	27·0	24·3–85·8
	1976	79·5	19·8	44·1–93·3
	1977	74·0	27·6	26·3–95·4
	1978	75·4	26·9	9·2–97·2
GCRs	1975	64·7	16·9	15·3–83·5
	1976	65·2	11·6	36·4–81·7
	1977	65·2	9·6	44·5–78·0
	1978	61·9	11·0	38·2–83·6

Note: [a] SD = standard deviation.

Table 5 shows that unplanned outage is highly variable. Derating losses are small for all reactor systems, except GCRs.

TABLE 5. COMPOSITION OF OUTPUT LOSSES, 1975–1977

	Average number of hours lost per reactor (and standard deviation)[a]			
	planned outage	unplanned outage	derating losses[b]	operating losses[b]
PWR				
1975	1280 (1530)	1020 (1470)	162 (321)	571 (450)
1976	1390 (1360)	1360 (1720)	102 (216)	578 (401)
1977	1480 (1690)	806 (1310)	158 (304)	439 (429)
BWR				
1975	2030 (2020)	963 (1340)	65·4 (112)	1160 (901)
1976	1250 (941)	1150 (1510)	98·4 (361)	1110 (684)
1977	1741 (1760)	1620 (2250)	90·7 (145)	884 (614)
PHWR				
1975	359 (395)	2750 (2340)	8·5 (12·0)	318 (289)
1976	239 (196)	1140 (1340)	18·7 (6·1)	402 (708)
1977	1290 (1210)	803 (973)	−23·4 (95·7)	209 (386)
GCR[c]				
1976	810 (378)	577 (649)	1000 (860)	747 (560)
1977	844 (537)	542 (960)	928 (830)	702 (510)

Notes: [a] Data are shown to three significant figures; [b] expressed as the equivalent number of hours lost had the reactor been shut down; [c] 1975 data for UK reactors not available from IAEA reports.

The chief characteristic of the load-factor data is the extreme variability. Table 6 shows that there is a wide range in performance both from year to year and from reactor to reactor.

TABLE 6. THE DISTRIBUTION OF ANNUAL AND CUMULATIVE PLANT LOAD FACTORS

	PWRs (%)	BWRs (%)	PHWRs (%)	GCRs (%)
Distribution of annual load factors				
> 80%	17·8	7·4	54·1	17·3
70–80%	27·1	17·0	8·1	19·0
60–70%	22·0	22·8	8·1	30·3
40–60%	20·4	35·3	13·5	23·5
30–40%	4·8	10·8	10·8	4·1
< 30%	8·0	6·6	5·4	5·8
Reactor years of operation	*314*	*241*	*37*	*294*
Distribution of cumulative load factors				
> 80%	6·1	—	—	15·4
70–80%	26·5	2·7	83·3	15·4
60–70%	30·6	27·0	—	42·3
40–60%	28·6	59·4	—	15·4
30–40%	6·1	10·8	16·7	11·5
< 30%	2·0	—	—	—
Number of reactors with at least 3 years operation	*49*	*37*	*6*	*26*

Previous analyses have attempted to estimate the effect of a single parameter, eg size, by means of regression analysis.[5] We performed regressions for PWRs and BWRs using the mean load factor over two-year periods for each plant, with age, size and coolant temperature and pressure as the independent variables. Using this method we could explain only a very small proportion of the variability (as shown by R^2). None of the parameters was significant at a 5% level and in some cases the signs of the coefficients reversed from one period to the other.

Hypotheses

A number of hypotheses have been put forward to account for differences and variations in reactor performance.

Refuelling
Other things being equal, we would expect the PHWRs and GCRs, which are refuelled on-load, to achieve consistently higher performance than light-water reactors which are refuelled off-load. Light-water reactors are generally refuelled at intervals of 12–18 months, so performance may fluctuate from year to year according to whether refuelling occurred.[6]

Learning and maturation
It is normally assumed that nuclear plants will have a design life of ~ 40 years and that performance will improve after teething difficulties have been overcome. As the plant matures further, unavailability may rise again as components begin to wear out.

Size and coolant conditions
A major aspect of the rapid technical innovation has been a marked increase in unit size and coolant conditions largely with the aim of reducing the capital

cost per kW and increasing thermal efficiency. Some observers have claimed that the latest plants are not performing as well as the first generation.

Design and quality control
Performance may vary between plants of similar technical characteristics. Problems of quality control may be especially serious during periods of bunching of orders, as occurred, for example, in the late 1960s in the USA.

Safety regulations
The 1970s have witnessed increasingly stringent regulations over safety and engineering standards at nuclear plants. If this has led to more conservative operating regimes, this concern for safety may have caused some deterioration in plant performance.

Vintage effects
The development of nuclear power has been marked by continuous technical innovation which is embodied in successive 'vintages'. Plants of similar age and technical characteristics are said to constitute a given vintage. Performance may be expected to improve not only from vintage to vintage but also between the 'first off' and later plants of the same vintage.

Maturation, size, and steam conditions

The best approach in attempting to disentangle these effects is to group reactors by size, age and steam conditions. For this purpose we use the load-factor data for every plant since it entered commercial operation.

PWRs

There is clear evidence of maturation among PWRs of all sizes (see Table 7); however, the maturation period appears to be around four to five years— rather longer than the two to three years that appears in the technical literature.[7]

TABLE 7. MATURATION AND SIZE EFFECTS AMONG PWRs (1960–1978 data)

Year of operation[a]	Mean load factor by unit size (and number of units)[b]			
	150–399 MW	400–799 MW	800–999 MW	1000–1300 MW
1	60·2 (11)	63·8 (20)	58·0 (22)	50·6 (7)
2	53·6 (11)	67·2 (20)	58·7 (18)	56·0 (6)
3	57·8 (11)	65·4 (18)	57·7 (14)	55·0 (5)
4	54·1 (9)	73·6 (18)	63·8 (9)	66·5 (2)
5	67·8 (9)	70·6 (14)	69·2 (5)	81·0 (1)
6	69·3 (9)	75·2 (9)	60·7 (3)	—
7	69·1 (9)	76·6 (5)	—	—
8	59·4 (8)	76·2 (4)	—	—
9	71·0 (7)	70·0 (2)	—	—
10	83·7 (4)	80·5 (2)	—	—
Overall	62·9	69·4	59·8	56·2

Notes: [a] Only the first ten complete calendar years of operation are given because the data for subsequent years are sparse and therefore less reliable; [b] refers to number of reactors.

Units of medium size (400–799 MW) perform best. Large units (800–999 MW) have been consistently inferior to medium-size units. The smallest size (under 400 MW) consists principally of early units though the two most recent small units (Doel 1 and 2, installed in 1975) have achieved outstanding performance. As yet there is no systematic evidence of declining performance with ageing.

If the group with the lowest coolant temperatures is discounted (since it consists of the oldest, smallest units), load factor falls not only as unit size increases but also as the coolant temperature increases.

A feature of maturation and of the size effect appears to be a reduction in unplanned outage and operating losses in older and/or smaller plants—but often at the expense of some increase in planned outage. Part of the maturation effect is evidently learning by utilities in anticipating equipment failure and remedying it during periods of planned outage.

BWRs

Beyond the fact that 70% load factor is seldom achieved by any group, the picture here is much less clear (see Table 8). There is little evidence of maturation.

TABLE 8. MATURATION AND SIZE EFFECTS AMONG BWRs (1960–1978 data)

Year of operation[a]	Mean load factor by unit size (and number of units)			
	150–399 MW	400–799 MW	800–999 MW	1000–1100 MW
1	62·1 (8)	55·0 (22)	60·7 (7)	40·6 (5)
2	58·5 (8)	52·5 (19)	55·7 (7)	51·5 (4)
3	56·1 (8)	55·7 (16)	53·5 (6)	52·2 (4)
4	62·3 (8)	59·5 (12)	45·5 (4)	70·3 (3)
5	60·6 (8)	64·4 (9)	57·7 (4)	—
6	62·7 (8)	60·4 (9)	64·7 (4)	—
7	61·5 (6)	71·1 (6)	69·0 (2)	—
8	59·3 (7)	55·5 (2)	—	—
9	53·7 (6)	73·5 (2)	—	—
10	45·4 (6)	—	—	—
Overall	58·6	57·9	57·2	51·8

Notes: see Table 7.

Whilst the data suggest some size effect, this may be because the data for very large BWRs (above 1000 MW) are distorted by the cable-tray fire which caused long outage of Browns Ferry units 1 and 2 in their first two years of service.

No pattern emerges when one looks at the causes of lost output in relation to the age of BWRs. However, as for PWRs, large BWRs sustain more unplanned outage, derating losses and operating losses than smaller units.

PHWRs

These must be considered individually rather than in subgroups. The units at the Pickering and Atucha sites have been very reliable, all having achieved high levels of performance from their first year onwards (see Table 9). The Rajasthan unit is an exception, although its poor performance is largely accounted for by factors not connected with the design of the plant as such, eg strikes and external grid disturbance.

TABLE 9. MATURATION AND SIZE EFFECTS AMONG PHWRs
(1960–1978 data)

| Year of operation[a] | Mean load factor and (number of units) | | | |
	Rajasthan 207 MW	Atucha 319 MW	Pickering 515 MW	Bruce 746 MW
1	36·8 (1)	84·4 (1)	70·0 (4)	73·7 (3)
2	33·1 (1)	86·0 (1)	55·2 (4)	—
3	44·1 (1)	55·0 (1)	71·5 (4)	—
4	26·3 (1)	97·2 (1)	87·5 (4)	—
5	9·2 (1)	—	92·5 (4)	—
6	—	—	86·3 (3)	—
7	—	—	84·5 (2)	—
Overall	29·9	80·6	77·4	73·7

Note: [a] Based on complete calendar years.

GCRs

Out of 26 GCRs, 20 are Magnox reactors. Most of the Magnox deratings took place in 1970 when the early plants had been operating for some years. This probably explains the pattern of load factors among GCRs as a whole, which shows maturation in the early years of operation followed by decline and then by partial recovery, with the decline occurring earlier for each successive size group. Although the size range is smaller than for light-water reactors, there appears to be a strong size effect among GCRs: only the smallest size group has achieved 70% load factors and performance drops with each increase in size (see Table 10).

Among the French GCRs there was no evidence that increases in unit size or in coolant conditions affect performance. For the Magnox plants, however,

TABLE 10. MATURATION AND SIZE EFFECTS AMONG GCRs

| Year of operation[a] | Mean load factor by unit size (and number of units) | | |
	138–199 MW	200–399 MW	400–590 MW
1	76·7 (3)	56·9 (11)	37·7 (7)
2	74·0 (3)	63·7 (12)	49·3 (7)
3	76·0 (3)	67·0 (12)	54·4 (7)
4	77·0 (7)	66·7 (12)	51·6 (7)
5	86·3 (7)	55·8 (12)	63·4 (7)
6	83·7 (7)	52·4 (12)	55·9 (7)
7	83·9 (7)	58·5 (12)	42·6 (5)
8	74·4 (7)	62·0 (10)	54·5 (2)
9	63·9 (7)	66·0 (12)	50·5 (2)
10	62·0 (7)	65·5 (12)	59·0 (1)
11	75·0 (7)	64·5 (10)	55·0 (1)
12	74·4 (7)	64·0 (10)	—
13	75·3 (6)	59·6 (8)	—
14	77·0 (6)	68·0 (1)	—
15	70·7 (4)	—	—
16	57·7 (4)	—	—
Overall	74·7	61·8	51·4

Note: [a] Based on complete calendar years. Data for first 3 years of operation are incomplete because some data for the CEGB Magnox plants installed before 1966 are unobtainable.

performance deteriorates markedly both with increases in size and with increases in coolant conditions. Clearly, it is only the early, small Magnox plants that have really worked well; the last two of the Magnox series, which have higher coolant conditions have been poor performers. In this context it is worth noting that all the AGRs, which are a development of the Magnox design, have considerably higher coolant conditions than the last of the Magnox series, and are of the same size range (about 600 MW) as the Wylfa reactors.

Country and manufacturer

Examination of countries that have installed PWRs and BWRs of modern design indicates that plant performance varies significantly from country to country (see Table 11).

TABLE 11. OPERATING PERFORMANCE BY COUNTRY

	PWRs		BWRs		PHWRs		GCRs	
	load factor (%)[a]	units[b]	load factor (%)[a]	units[b]	load factor (%)[a]	units[b]	load factor (%)[a]	units[b]
USA	63·8	39	58·1	22	—	—	—	—
Canada	—	—	—	—	80·5	7	—	—
Belgium	75·8	3	—	—	—	—	—	—
UK	—	—	—	—	—	—	64·2	18
France	74·6	2	—	—	—	—	61·9	5
F R Germany	75·7	5	41·1	4	—	—	—	—
Italy	84·0	1	48·0	1	—	—	60·2	1
Netherlands	78·5	1	—	—	—	—	—	—
Finland	82·0	1	—	—	—	—	—	—
Spain	80·0	1	68·5	1	—	—	77·2	1
Sweden	57·7	1	64·7	5	—	—	—	—
Switzerland	85·7	2	85·7	1	—	—	—	—
Japan	45·8	7	42·1	7	—	—	69·2	1
Argentina	—	—	—	—	80·6	1	—	—
India	—	—	57·5	2	28·0	1	—	—

Notes : [a] Load factors are averages for 1975–1978. [b] Number of units at 1 January 1978.

If 70% load factors indicate satisfactory performance, then many countries are achieving it from their PWRs. Poor BWR performance, however, is common among all countries except Switzerland. Japan stands out in having obtained very disappointing performance from PWRs as well as BWRs.

After reasonable starts, the performance of both BWRs and PWRs in Japan has deteriorated rather than matured. In contrast, Switzerland's two PWRs and one BWR have matured to sustained high performance. Despite achieving good reliability with its PWRs, the Federal Republic of Germany has suffered a severe decline in the performance of its BWRs in recent years. These inter-country differences suggest that nuclear-plant performance may be affected by factors specific to individual countries and individual manufacturers.

Discounting Japan as a special case (which we discuss later), the data show that good performance is associated with low unplanned outage and low operating losses (which may have been gained at the expense of relatively high planned outage).

We also examined the performance of units built by the principal manufacturers (the companies that make reactors). As suppliers of the largest number

TABLE 12. LOAD FACTORS BY PRINCIPAL MANUFACTURERS

Mean load factors, 1975–78 (and number of units)[a]

PWRs		BWRs	
Westinghouse	66·9 (26)	General Electric	55·7 (26)
Babcock and Wilcox	53·7 (7)	ASEA-Atom	63·8 (4)
Combustion Eng.	64·4 (5)	AEG/KWU	43·4 (2)
Siemens/KWU	78·7 (4)	Others	57·3 (3)
Mitsubishi	59·9 (3)		
All suppliers	65·8 (49)	All suppliers	56·1 (35)

Note: [a] Based on units with more than 3 years commercial operation.

of units, Westinghouse and General Electric tend to determine the average load factors for all PWRs and BWRs respectively (see Table 12).

Whilst the industry average for BWRs can hardly be considered satisfactory, the BWRs built by AEG/KWU (Federal Republic of Germany) have performed especially badly.[8] Among the PWRs, those supplied by Babcock and Wilcox are well below the industry average. (Note that the Harrisburg accident occurred in 1979 and its effects upon the load factors achieved by Babcock and Wilcox units are not reflected in our data.) However, PWRs supplied by Siemens/KWU (Federal Republic of Germany) have worked much better on average than Westinghouse units. The cumulative load factors achieved by the PWRs built by Siemens/KWU (Kraftwerk Union) have been better in every size group than comparable units built by Westinghouse (see Table 13).

TABLE 13. PERFORMANCE OF PWRs BUILT BY WESTINGHOUSE AND SIEMENS/KWU[a]

Unit size (MW)	Mean load factors, 1975–78 (and number of units)	
	Westinghouse	Siemens/KWU
200–399	64·2 (4)	79·8 (1)
400–599	76·0 (7)	77·8 (1)
600–799	70·0 (4)	91·8 (1)
800–999	56·7 (5)	—
⩾1000	55·0 (4)	61·1 (1)
All units	66·9 (24)	78·7 (4)

Note: [a] Includes units with more than 3 years commercial operation.

As with the earlier analyses of output losses, analysis by manufacturer shows that the hallmark of good performance is low unplanned outage and low operating losses.

The conclusion we draw is that it is not sufficient to choose reactors of the type and the size which seem inherently more reliable.

Vintages

It proved difficult to identify distinct vintages from the published data. This was because few units have sufficiently similar technical characteristics. Nevertheless, we compared the performance, over identical periods of operation, of duplicate PWRs and BWRs installed in the USA. In eight out of ten cases the subsequent unit performed better than its predecessor, often by a considerable margin. This explains the interest among US utilities, manufacturers, and architect–engineers in developing standardised reactor designs aimed at reducing equipment failures and also licensing difficulties and capital costs.[9]

Equipment failure

The use of planned outage periods to anticipate and remedy potential equipment failure appears to be a feature of maturation. If this is indeed the case, then it follows that equipment failures reported by utilities as unplanned outage are those they did not anticipate. To this extent, the data may not be fully representative of the true failure or malfunction rates.

Main causes

Using IAEA data, we looked at outages that occurred in 1976 and 1977. For all three of the current types of nuclear plant, equipment failure accounts for three-quarters of unplanned outage, whilst three-quarters of equipment failure outage is caused by the so-called conventional subsystems—the main heat removal system, steam generators, the feedwater-condenser system and the turbine generator.[10]

We correlated the failure rate for each main subsystem with unit age, size and steam conditions. That no significant correlations emerged is not surprising since most of the hours lost occurred in rare but prolonged outages. In order to see whether equipment failures can be explained in terms of maturation, ageing or size effects, we calculated the distributions of equipment failure by six major subsystems for 1975–1977.[11]

The main heat removal system accounts for half the equipment failure outage for PHWRs and a smaller but nevertheless significant fraction for light water reactors.

Steam generator and feedwater-condenser system faults are a serious problem with PWRs: these two closely interdependent subsystems contribute almost half of total equipment failure outage. A high proportion of lost output attributable to steam generators consists of outages that last a long time, in several cases more than a year. Turbine generators account for nearly one-fifth of equipment failure for each type of reactor.

We calculated the amount of unit time lost by causal subsystem as a proportion of the time the unit would otherwise have worked had these particular failures not occurred. For BWRs, failures in the feedwater-condenser system are particularly prevalent among poor performers. For PWRs no individual subsystem failure is especially common among poor performers.

Japanese plants

As we stated previously, Japan is a special case in that it has had poor performance from PWRs as well as BWRs. All Japan's nuclear plants have suffered prolonged outages—often more than six months. However, this is not fully reflected in the equipment failure rates because Japanese utilities generally categorise these periods, euphemistically, as planned outage for annual maintenance.

The poor performance of the PWRs is due almost entirely to persistent steam generator tube leaks. For BWRs several subsystems are subject to recurrent problems, including the reactor control rod drive mechanism and leaks in the steam generator and also the feedwater-condenser systems are a common feature.

TABLE 14. SUMMARY OF MAIN FINDINGS

The few PHWRs in commercial operation have consistently achieved outstanding performance

Excluding PHWRs, the main feature of nuclear plant performance is the variability, only a small part of which is explained by the effects we have identified

Among PWRs maturation takes 4 to 5 years on average; over the first 3 years of operation the performance of very large PWRs has been lower than that of medium size ones

BWRs have the lowest average load factor and show no maturation or size effects

The performance of light-water reactors varies according to the country of installation, Japan having a particularly unenviable record. PWRs built by Siemens/KWU have performed appreciably better than PWRs built by other manufacturers, although BWRs built by AEG/KWU have fared worse than most other BWRs

Duplicate units provide some evidence of vintage effects

A large proportion of outage is caused by equipment failures among the so-called conventional subsystems; as with overall performance, however, outage appears to be largely unpredictable

Learning among utilities is reflected in lengthened periods of planned outage to undertake preventive maintenance, which leads to reduced output losses through equipment failures

Our findings carry several implications which are relevant to utilities and manufacturers:

- *Investment risk.* As long as performance remains essentially unpredictable, investment decisions will be correspondingly risky: especially for small utilities, where individual units produce a large fraction of output.
- *Scale and complexity.* Their poorer performance to date implies that investing in very large PWRs (above 1000 MW) is riskier than investing in medium size PWRs (400–800 MW)—though units of the latter size are large compared with many modern fossil-fuel generating units.
- *Standardisation.* As learning is incorporated into design the potential benefits of standardisation are likely to increase. These benefits depend upon how far unpredictable performance stems from genuine weakness, defective metallurgy, substandard sitework, etc, rather than poor design. At present standardisation over a long-term programme runs the risk of 'standardised' design error.
- *Component reliability.* From an economic viewpoint, the claim that 'nuclear core' components function reliably is beside the point. In terms of replacement power costs, an outage of given duration is equally serious no matter whether it is caused by a 'conventional' or a 'nuclear core' component. Good plant performance requires that all components which cannot be replaced easily are equally reliable. This underlines the importance of good operating and maintenance practice and the need to keep spare key com-

ponents. Even keeping a spare turbine or generator may be a worthwhile investment for utilities with a series of similar plants on the same site or in close proximity.

Our analysis also carries implications for technology policy in the UK. Since the early 1970s the British plant supply industry and the Central Electricity Generating Board (CEGB) have advocated building PWRs under licence. Despite this, at least two more AGR stations (Heysham and Torness) are to be built, a decision that owes much to the work shortage facing the plant suppliers. So far the experience gained in building and operating AGRs has been unsatisfactory.[12] With government approval the CEGB has set in hand the necessary design work and negotiations with potential foreign licensors to enable a PWR to be built, starting in 1982. In our view it is sensible to take the preparatory steps needed to switch to another thermal reactor design in the 1980s. The aim must be to facilitate the transition so that the British industry can master the chosen technology and acquire the capability to build a series of reactors efficiently when the need arises.

Since operating reliability must be a major criterion in reactor choice, the CANDU reactor must be given careful consideration. Some of the existing CANDUs will require modification due to problems of creep in the pressure tubes which contain the fuel; but this should not affect new reactors. The superior reliability of CANDU would repay higher construction costs. In addition to having greater fuel efficiency and greater intrinsic safety which, after Harrisburg, probably makes it less vulnerable to public opposition, CANDU has several other advantages. These include the possibility of licensing the CANDU design as part of a package deal which also guarantees uranium supplies; and the possibility of developing the thorium cycle, making CANDU a valuable long-term alternative to the fast breeder reactor in the event of uranium scarcity. Moreover, with surplus heavy-water production capacity in Canada, acquiring heavy-water supplies—at least for one or two reactors— should not present undue difficulty.

Nevertheless, the British government has recently decided to build PWRs under licence, probably from Westinghouse.[13] Worldwide operating experience again provides some relevant lessons.

In spite of the advantages that may eventually flow from design standardisation among very large units, on the basis of current operating performance there is less risk in building a medium-size PWR initially and placing further orders in the light of experience.

Adverse experience in Japan and West Germany suggests that careful consideration should be given to the terms and scope of the licence required, in particular whether continuing access to current research would be available. Thus, there must be a high probability that the proposed licensor will survive as a reactor manufacturer. The superior performance of PWRs built by Kraftwerk Union suggests that, provided the licence fee is acceptable and extensive engineering backup is available, Kraftwerk Union should be considered as the licensor for the British PWR venture.

Above all, we should not make the mistake of believing that choosing a good basic reactor design guarantees reliable operation (eg Japan's light-water reactors). Kraftwerk Union's success with PWRs owes much to the solid foundation of research, development and design engineering laid by Siemens in the 1960s when it was a licensee of Westinghouse.

Major efforts will be needed by the British industry to acquire the necessary design engineering expertise, to ensure quality control over key components and site work and, not least, in launching a research and development programme aimed at reducing equipment failures. As an indication of the scale of British effort likely to be required, it is worth noting that in recent years Westinghouse has spent $100 million on R and D in attempting to overcome problems with the steam generator and related conventional components.[14] If the British industry is to have a genuinely independent capability in reactor technology, it will be necessary to complement any technical licensing arrangement with a substantial R and D programme designed to improve the reliability of the major 'conventional' subsystems.

Mastering a new reactor technology will be difficult for the British industry especially in view of its dearth of orders over the past decade and the 'craft' basis imposed on it hitherto by the large amount of site work in building AGRs.[15] It is unlikely that mastery can be gained if the industry's development and design resources are overstretched with simultaneous work on AGRs and the fast-breeder reactor, or if the industry retains its present structure. Leaving the question of public acceptance of nuclear power on one side, the industry's overriding problem over the next two decades will be to acquire the capability to build thermal reactors efficiently. This will require the choice of a good basic design, a concentration of engineering resources, the emergence of an efficient supply structure, and a workable technical relationship between the industry and its main customer, the CEGB.

Notes and references

1. Load factor is a good measure of performance, unless nuclear plants are *intentionally* operated on an intermittent or 'load following' basis, as might be the case if the amount of nuclear capacity installed exceeds base load demand for a significant part of the year. To cover this possibility we examined the operating record of every commercial nuclear plant in the period 1975–1977 and found that only two units had been subject to occasional periods of intermittent operation when they were available for service at their full capacity or rating.
2. US data suggest that when a 1000 MW unit is unavailable the replacement power costs may be as high as $1 M per day.
3. Apart from readily identifiable prototypes, no plant is excluded on the grounds that its performance might be held to be 'unrepresentative'. Our analysis of nuclear plant load factors and outages concentrates on 1975–1977, the latest years for which comprehensive data were available from the International Atomic Energy Agency (IAEA). Where appropriate for the analysis we also use load factor data for 1978, published in the technical journal *Atomwirtschaft*. The period 1975–1978 covers around 55% of total commercial operating experience and an even higher proportion of the experience with modern plant designs and operating practice. Data on design capacity, steam conditions and manufacturers were taken from the technical journal *Nuclear Engineering International*. However, to give valid comparisons, in a number of cases we have used IAEA load factor data for the years prior to 1975. See *Operating Experience with Nuclear Power Stations in Member States* (Vienna, IAEA, 1975, 1976, 1977).

4. For example, see *Current Status and Future Technical and Economic Potential of Light Water Reactors*, March 1968, WASH–1082, US Atomic Energy Commission, which assumed a range of 70–90% load factors. See also *Fuel Policy*, Cmnd 3438 (London, HMSO, 1967) which assumed 75% load factors.

5. For example, see Charles Komanoff, *Power Plant Performance* (New York, Council on Economic Priorities (CEP), November 1976); Komanoff and Nancy Boxer, *Nuclear Plant Performance Update* (New York, CEP, May 1977); Komanoff, *Nuclear Plant Performance Update 2* (New York, Komanoff Energy Associates, 1978); and P. L. Joskow and G. A. Rozanski, "The effects of learning by doing on nuclear plant operating reliability", *The Review of Economics and Statistics*, *61* (2), May 1979.

6. Electric Power Research Institute, *Refuelling Outage Trends in Light Water Reactors*, EPRI NP–842, August 1978, figures 3.7 and 3.8.

7. For example see Electric Power Research Institute, *Major Outage Trends in Light Water Reactors*, EPRI NP–755, April 1978.

8. Before merging their heavy electrical and nuclear reactor interests into Kraftwerk Union (around 1970), Siemens was under licence to Westinghouse for PWR technology and AEG licensed BWR technology from General Electric.

9. By 'standardisation' we mean a common plant design and identical subsystems, components, materials and procedures for startup. The chief current example is the Standardised Nuclear Unit Power Plant System in the USA, where several utilities have agreed to build four 1150 MW PWRs with Bechtel as the architect–engineer and Westinghouse supplying the reactor. Hitherto standard major components (eg the reactor vessel, steam generators, reactor coolant pumps and fuel assemblies) were commonly used; but the basic configuration, and auxiliary systems design and equipment, varied according to the specifications of the individual architect–engineer or utility.

10. 'Conventional' subsystems in nuclear plants perform similar functions to their equivalents in fossil fuel plants, but they are not necessarily identical.

11. We read the engineering literature to elucidate the reasons for these failures, in particular *Nuclear Engineering International* and various reports by the Electric Power Research Institute.

12. The cumulative load factors at 30 June 1979 of the Hunterston and Hinkley AGRs (after 2–3 years operation) were 23% and 30% respectively. *Nuclear Engineering International*, September 1979.

13. *Nuclear Engineering International*, August 1979 and *Financial Times*, 5 September 1979. Apparently the CEGB has asked the Nuclear Power Company to negotiate with Westinghouse on the supply of an 1100–1200 MW PWR design, so as to enable the CEGB to apply in 1980 for UK government approval to commence building in 1982.

14 R. R. Estes, E. A. Watjen and J. W. Gulaskey, "Retubing for on-site modification on steam generators", *Nuclear Engineering International*, February 1979.

15 D. Fishlock, "World nuclear industries" (survey), and "Where the AGR misses out", both in *Financial Times*, 19 July 1979.

GLOBAL ENERGY STRATEGIES
The implications of CO_2

Jill Williams

The author discusses the uncertainties and shortcomings that surround the current models of the carbon cycle, climatic change, and energy consumption; all are required in predicting the effect of carbon dioxide (CO_2) on climate. Using estimates of energy consumption in 2025 the author defines the boundaries of the problem: a global warming (preponderantly at the poles), and unpredictable (at present) regional climatic variations. The implications for energy policy are discussed, and it is concluded that all options must be kept open at present.

THE GLOBAL climate system consists of five subsystems: the atmosphere, oceans, cryosphere (ice and snow), biosphere, and land. These interact (eg evaporation, wind stress) such that the total system is nonlinear. The climatic state is the average (together with the variability and other statistics) of the complete set of variables over a specified time interval and in a specified domain.[1]

Climate records show that climate has varied and continues to vary on time-scales ranging from the interannual to the geological. The causes of climatic variability have not been determined sufficiently to predict climate. However, important forcing mechanisms for climatic variability can be determined. The system can be considered in terms of an "internal" system of the gaseous, liquid, and ice envelopes surrounding the earth, and an "external" system of the underlying ground and surrounding space. Sufficiently large changes in the external boundary conditions (eg solar flux, the earth's orbit) can change the climate. Climatic variability can also be caused by changes in the internal system—the *feedbacks* among the variables. For example, a change in atmospheric circulation can change ocean-surface temperatures; this change in temperature gradient, can then change the atmospheric circulation, either enhancing (positive feedback) or eliminating (negative feedback) the anomaly. The concept of a feedback mechanism is extremely important in the understanding of climate. Unfortunately the total effect of the many simultaneous feedbacks remains largely unknown.[2]

The author is with the International Institute for Applied Systems Analysis, A-2361 Laxenburg, Austria.

In recent years there has been concern about the potential impact of mankind's activities on climate.[3] At present we cannot predict the climatic changes likely to be caused by different energy strategies, or assess how much man has already changed the climate. We can, however, estimate the impacts of energy conversion using observations and models.

Energy options

In 1974 the total world energy consumption was 7·4 TW (1 TW = 10^{12} W), of which the developed countries (population 1160 million) used 6·15 TW (5·33 kW per capita) and the developing countries (population 2760 million) used 1·25 TW (0·45 kW per capita).[4] If the less-developed countries have a higher energy growth rate in the future and if Keyfitz's population-growth estimates are used,[5] then the world energy requirement (for the year 2025) is about 30 TW.

Apart from the case of solar energy conversion, renewable energy sources (eg wind and tidal energy and including conservation) may have a potential contribution of about 1 TW.[6] In the 21st century there are three energy options, which could produce 30 TW: solar energy, nuclear energy, and (to a lesser extent) coal.

There are constraints associated with the large-scale deployment of any of these options. Each of them could affect the climate.[7] When considering the transition from today's energy system, which is largely based on cheap, convenient fossil fuels, to one, or a combination, of these options, the constraints must be taken into account.

How quickly do primary energy carriers gain or lose their market shares (the market penetration period)? The time taken to gain or lose a 50% (global) market share was 160 years for wood, 170 years for coal, 78 years for oil, and 90 years for gas.[8] In the USA the equivalent periods were shorter, but still about 60 years. The substitution of the primary energy sources follows a regular logistic pattern. The observed, limited flexibility of the global energy system in shifting to new energy sources must be considered.

The large-scale deployment of nuclear energy would influence climate because of the release of waste heat; solar energy conversion (solar-thermal electric, photovoltaic, or ocean-thermal electric conversion systems in particular) could influence climate through changes in the energy balance at the earth's surface.[9] Fossil-fuel combustion (in particular, coal) releases CO_2, other gases, particulates, and waste heat. The release of CO_2 has many implications.

The increase in atmospheric CO$_2$

The atmospheric CO_2 concentration (seasonally adjusted) has risen steadily during 1958–1976.[10] The amount of CO_2 released by combustion of fossil fuels has been computed by Keeling, and by Rotty.[11] This amount is approximately twice the observed increase in atmospheric concentration. The "missing" CO_2 must have been taken up by the oceans or possibly by land plants.

The greenhouse effect

The concern over the increasing atmospheric CO_2 concentration arises because of the radiative properties of the gas: CO_2 is relatively transparent to incoming short-wave (solar) radiation, but absorbs long-wave radiation coming from the earth's surface. An increase in atmospheric CO_2 concentration therefore leads to increased absorption of long-wave radiation from and increased reradiation to the earth's surface, giving an increase in surface temperature; the greenhouse effect.

The carbon cycle

The CO_2 in the atmosphere is a small part of the total carbon circulated between the atmospheric, biospheric, and oceanic reservoirs. The amount of carbon in these reservoirs is reasonably well known.[12] The exchanges of carbon between the reservoirs are less well known but of major importance if estimates are to be made of future levels of CO_2 in the atmosphere. These exchanges can not be measured directly and models of the biogeochemical carbon cycle have been formulated to describe the exchanges. The atmospheric reservoir can be considered as a rather well-mixed reservoir on a time scale of a few years or more (the increases in atmospheric CO_2 concentration are seen in northern and southern hemispheres).

Plants on land assimilate CO_2 from the atmosphere. In greenhouses an increase in the CO_2 concentration leads to an increase in photosynthetic activity, ie to an increase in the size of the biosphere or an increased sink for atmospheric CO_2. Where nutrients and water are sometimes limiting, it has been assumed that a 10% increase in atmospheric CO_2 concentration will lead to a 0–3% increase in the biosphere. This fertilisation effect has to be taken into account in carbon models, but it has recently been suggested that there has, in the last 100 years, been a net decrease of the biosphere due to human influence, resulting in a net flux of biospheric CO_2 into the atmosphere.[13] Estimates vary widely, but it may be as large as the flux of CO_2 into the atmosphere from combustion of fossil fuels.

The exchange of carbon between the atmosphere and the ocean is quite well understood. The buffering action of atmospheric CO_2 with the ocean is due to the presence of carbonate, bicarbonate, and borate ions in seawater and this substantially limits the capacity of the oceans as a sink for excess atmospheric CO_2. If the atmospheric CO_2 content increases by $x\%$, the resulting increase of oceanic CO_2 will (in equilibrium) only be $x/\xi\%$. The value of the buffer factor, ξ, at present is about 10. However, ξ increases with CO_2 pressure so that as dissolved carbonate in the water is used up by reaction with fossil-fuel CO_2, the CO_2 pressure builds up and the water is less and less able to absorb added amounts of fossil-fuel CO_2.[14]

The biogeochemical carbon cycle has generally been described by "box" models, which focus on chemical exchange between various pools of the system. Derivation of these models has been described by several authors.[15] Table 1 lists transfer rates for carbon between the reservoirs. A six-box model is illustrated in Figure 1. The flux of carbon emerging from a box is generally assumed to vary in proportion to the amount of carbon in the reservoir.[16]

TABLE 1. TRANSFER COEFFICIENTS (between reservoirs of 6-reservoir model) [10]

	Transfer coefficient
Perennial biota to troposphere[a]	0
Troposphere to perennial biota	1/75·7
Annual biota to troposphere	1/2·50
Troposphere to annual biota	1/65·6
Stratosphere to troposphere	1/2·00
Troposphere to stratosphere	1/11·3
Troposphere to surface ocean	1/5·92
Surface ocean to troposphere[b]	1/3·02
Surface ocean to deep ocean	1/113
Deep ocean to surface ocean	1/1500

Note: [a] Equals zero because perennial plants are assumed to assimilate as well as respire carbon proportional to their mass; [b] Varies with inorganic carbon in surface ocean layer (buffering factor, see text).

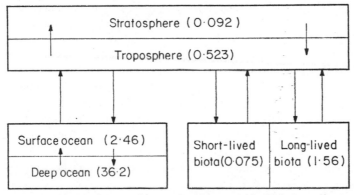

Figure 1. Six reservoir model of the carbon cycle with pre-industrial sizes of reservoirs in 10⁸ g of carbon [12]

The predictions made by existing models of the atmospheric CO_2 concentration (based on projected fossil-fuel combustion) do not disagree significantly over 20–30 years, but beyond 30 years the uncertainties increase rapidly.[17] The role of the oceans is not the major uncertainty in these predictions: it is the role of the biosphere. Forest fires are not significant sources of carbon but tropical forest clearing might be. There probably has been a net global deforestation, compensated in part by regrowth patterns in areas cut over past decades. A major effort is therefore required to study the inventories of biospheric carbon.

Climatic impact of increasing atmospheric CO₂

One-dimensional, globally averaged models have been used to determine the radiational effects of doubling the atmospheric CO_2 content on vertical temperature distribution. Augustsson and Ramanathan showed that the mean surface temperature change for a doubling of CO_2 content would be 2–3°C. Other studies agree, indicating that the purely radiative effects of CO_2 are fairly well understood. However, one-dimensional models of this type are a simplified description, they do not consider all feedback mechanisms or the dynamics of climate.

Observations show that temperature trends in the northern hemisphere winter season are 5–7 times larger in polar areas than in other latitudes,[18] ie the real world climate does not respond equally to change in all areas. Planners and policy makers therefore need to know the likely regional changes of temperature and precipitation.

The results of experiments with a general circulation model show that for a doubling of atmospheric CO_2 concentration the surface temperature increases by 2–3°C in lower latitudes but by 10°C in polar latitudes. This nonlinear response implies that the equator-to-pole temperature gradient would change, and this would lead to shifts in the climatic belts.[19]

The regional impact of an increasing CO_2 concentration can ultimately only be assessed with a model which includes a fully coupled and interactive atmosphere and ocean, and an improved simulation of the ice and snow, particularly in polar regions. The development of interactive ocean models will not be rapid and uncertainties over other feedback mechanisms will also have to be tackled before estimates of regional climatic effects of a doubling in CO_2 concentration can be established.

Until climate models have been developed further we can only make a few generalisations. Parts of the climate system are more sensitive than others; some of the regional changes will be much greater than the global average. In general there will be more rainfall because the warmer atmosphere causes more evaporation from the oceans. This extra rain would probably fall in areas affected by monsoonal circulations and in some mid-latitude regions. A study of paleoclimatic records of periods when it was warmer than now also reveals that there will probably be places where rainfall decreases as a result of altered large-scale circulation patterns.[20]

If the temperature does increase disproportionately at the poles, then it is likely that the arctic pack ice would melt and, once melted, would probably not reform.[21] Climatic shifts would be inevitable.[22] The fate of the ice sheets of Greenland and Antarctica in the event of a warming is undetermined; an increase of precipitation over the ice caps is possible, at least in the early stages.[23] The possibility of a surge of the West Antarctic ice sheet has also been considered.

The climate has its own inherent variability (the climatic noise level). Because of this noise level it is impossible at present to detect in records of surface temperature a temperature rise due to the observed increase of CO_2. A temperature rise of 1°C (which is greater than the natural fluctuations of the past century) due to increasing CO_2 concentration could occur and be detected before the year 2000.

Energy strategies, atmospheric CO_2 and climate

To assess the future atmospheric CO_2 concentration and its implications, three models are required.

- An energy model is used to estimate the future use of fossil fuels, and thus the input of fossil-fuel CO_2 into the atmosphere.
- The proportion of CO_2 that remains in the atmosphere is given by a model of the carbon cycle, which consideres the reservoirs of carbon and the transfers between them.

- The effects of the increased atmospheric CO$_2$ concentration on climate are assessed using a climate model.

Uncertainties must be attached to the results of each of these models. Nevertheless, the model results can currently be used to assess the magnitude of the problem.[24]

Figure 2 shows a strategy for energy consumption based on a 35 TW energy supply scenario for 2030.[25] The energy consumption in 1975 is assumed to be 7·5 TW of which 0·45 TW is not used for energy (eg petrochemicals). The growth rate in energy consumption is assumed to be 3·5% in 1975 decreasing smoothly to 1% by the year 2030 and thereafter. The consumption of oil and

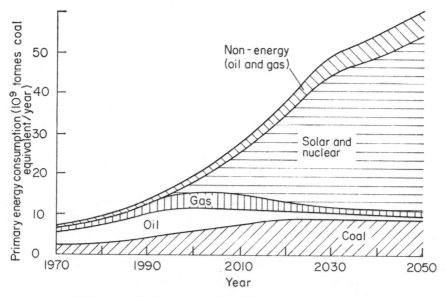

Figure 2. Energy strategy for 35 TW reference scenario

gas for nonenergy purposes is 6% of energy demand in 1975 increasing to 11% by 2030 and constant thereafter. It is assumed that the consumption of oil, gas, and coal reaches a constant level in the year 2020.

Figure 3 shows the atmospheric CO$_2$ concentrations given by the carbon model for the above strategy, together with the CO$_2$ emissions and the estimated global surface temperature change. For this strategy the emissions of CO$_2$ reach a constant level at about the year 2000; the atmospheric CO$_2$ concentration continues to increase, reaching a level of about 510 ppm (by volume) in 2050 and the corresponding mean surface temperature increase is about 1·7°C.

Other strategies can be explored using the same set of models. If energy consumption peaks at 30 TW, with solar and nuclear energy conversion playing a major role (with the consumption of oil and gas stopping by the year 2030 and coal consumption not rising above its present level) then the emissions of fossil-fuel CO$_2$ peak around the year 2000. In this case the atmospheric CO$_2$

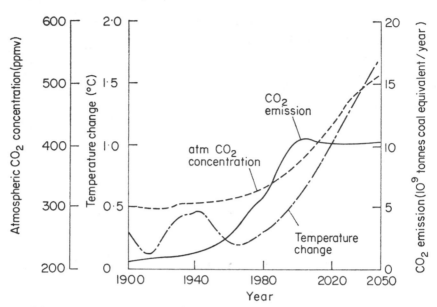

Figure 3. CO$_2$ emissions, atmospheric CO$_2$ concentration, and temperature change for **35 TW** reference scenario

concentration reaches a maximum of 400 ppm (by volume) in about 2020 and the resulting change in mean surface temperature is less than 1 °C.

If energy consumption rises to a maximum of 50 TW, with all of the supply from fossil fuels (coal, oil, and gas until about 2030 and coal thereafter), the emissions of CO$_2$ increase until 2050, reaching a value 3·5 times larger than those in the 35 TW reference scenario, by the year 2050. The atmospheric CO$_2$ concentration reaches about 800 ppm (by volume) in 2050, implying a mean surface temperature increase of about 4 °C.

The results of the models have many limitations and are not predictions.[26] The results show, however, that depending on the energy strategy followed, the climate change could be between <1 °C–4 °C by 2050. Note that the different energy strategies give differing CO$_2$ emission curves. The strategy considered here which gives the smallest temperature change has a peak in 2000 and rapidly decreases thereafter. The CO$_2$ emissions for the strategy with the largest temperature effect increase up to 2050. The substitution of primary energy sources has a time scale of decades.

Implications for energy policy

Combustion of fossil fuels and destruction of the biosphere release CO$_2$ into the atmosphere. Ultimately much of this CO$_2$ transfers into the deep ocean, but the rate of transfer is very slow and thus the atmospheric concentration of CO$_2$ increases. Does this justify changes of energy policy?

Mankind needs and can afford 5–10 years for vigorous research and planning to narrow uncertainties sufficiently to justify a major change to an energy policy which can be more responsive to the CO$_2$ problem than one which relies on abundant and inexpensive fossil fuels.[17] Since quantitative estimates on the rates of increase of CO_2 (and other infrared-absorbing molecules) in the atmosphere and resulting global and regional climate changes are likely to remain uncertain for most of the next decade, it is premature to reduce the use of coal and other fossil fuels. Our present knowledge justifies the comprehensive study of alternative energy supplies but it does not yet warrant a curtailment of fossil-fuel use.

Energy policies which emphasise the use of coal are equally unjustified. Such a policy could be very expensive to reverse; it is important to maintain flexibility in energy supplies. Environmental impact assessments of increased energy use must be performed with greater depth than in the past.

We should devise energy supply systems that do not produce irreversible environmental changes. Such systems would have to be either nonpolluting (or very nearly so) or lead to environmental effects which can be easily mitigated. There are several possibilities: eg a solar or hydroelectric hydrogen economy, or synthetic methanol manufactured at large central facilities with the aid of nuclear (breeder) reactors, or a "hard" solar energy supply,[25] or a highly decentralised solar-energy supply system (this would be unlikely to provide sufficient energy to maintain the global economy at a satisfactory level). Systems employing a short-time recycling of carbon through the atmosphere can be considered eg the use of biomass as a fuel with prompt and rapid regrowth. Stripping CO_2 from exhaust stack systems and even from the atmosphere itself is now technically feasible and the manufacture of methane or methanol from the carbon thus obtained would be an effective short-term recycling system. The carbon could also be stored in the living biomass by planting more trees or in the deep ocean, by locating and using areas of sinking ocean waters[27] or in old oil and gas wells. These techniques may prove to be costly.

No less important than efforts to maintain supply are those to reduce energy demands. Energy demands can be reduced globally without causing unacceptable changes in economic well-being.

Finally, the question of CO_2 and its impact is very complex. It involves detailed study of nonlinear biological, chemical, physical and social systems. There is a need for a continued international and interdisciplinary research effort.

Acknowledgements

The IIASA Subtask on Energy and Climate is supported by the United Nations Environment Programme. The IIASA Workshop on "Carbon dioxide, climate and society" was cosponsored by UNEP, the World Meteorological Organisation and the Scientific Committee on Problems of the Environment. I would like to thank Ingrid Baubinder for her help in preparing this paper.

References and notes

1. US Committee for GARP, *Understanding Climatic Change* (Washington, DC, US National Academy of Sciences, 1975).
2. S. H. Schneider and R. E. Dickinson, "Climate modeling", *Review of Geophysics and Space Physics*, 1974, *12*, pages 447–493.
3. SMIC, *Inadvertent Climate Modification, Report of the Study of Man's Impact on Climate* (Massachusetts, The MIT Press, 1971); NAS, *Energy and Climate* (Washington, DC, US National Academy of Sciences, 1977).

4. C. Riedel, "Zero order evaluation of the supply/demand situation in the various world regions, 1975–2025", paper presented at IIASA workshop on "Energy strategies, conception and embedding", Laxenburg, Austria, 1977.

5. N. Keyfitz, "Population of the world and its regions", working paper, International Institute for Applied Systems Analysis, Laxenburg, Austria, 1977.

6. W. Häfele, "Energy options open to mankind beyond the turn of the century", paper presented at conference on "Nuclear power and its fuel cycle", Salzburg, Austria, 1977.

7. J. Williams, "Global climatic disturbance due to large-scale energy conversion systems", in M. Glantz, ed, *Multidisciplinary Research Related to the Atmospheric Sciences* (Boulder, Westview Press, 1978).

8. C. Marchetti, "Primary energy substitution model. On the interaction between energy and society", *Chem Econ Eng Rev*, 1975, *7/8*, pages 9–15.

9. J. Williams, G. Krömer and J. M. Weingart, eds, *Proceedings of a Workshop on Climate and Solar Energy Conversion* (Laxenburg, Austria, International Institute for Applied Systems Analysis, 1977).

10. C. D. Keeling and R. B. Bacastow, "Impact of industrial gases on climate", *Energy and Climate* (Washington, DC, US National Academy of Sciences, 1977).

11. C. D. Keeling, "Industrial production of carbon dioxide from fossil fuels and limestone", *Tellus*, 1973, *25*, pages 174–198; R. M. Rotty, "Present and future production of CO_2 from fossil fuels—a global appraisal", paper presented at ERDA workshop on "Significant environmental concerns", Miami, Florida, 1977.

12. R. B. Bacastow and C. D. Keeling, "Atmospheric carbon dioxide and radiocarbon in the natural carbon cycle: Changes from A.D. 1700 to 2070 as deduced from a geochemical model", in G. M. Woodwell and E. V. Pecan, eds, *Carbon and the Biosphere* (Washington, D.C., U.S. Atomic Energy Commission, 1973).

13. G. M. Woodwell, "The carbon dioxide question", *Scientific American*, 1978, *238*, pages 34–43.

14. U. Siegenthaler and H. Oeschger, "Predicting future atmospheric carbon dioxide levels", *Science*, 1978, *199*, pages 388–395.

15. B. Bolin, "A critical appraisal of models for the carbon cycle", *GARP Publications Series*, 1975, *16*, pages 225–235.

16. A different treatment of the ocean boxes can also be taken by considering a well-mixed atmosphere and well-mixed ocean surface layer coupled to a diffusive deep ocean: H. Oeschger, U. Siegenthaler, U. Schotterer and A. Gugelmann, "A box diffusion model to study the carbon dioxide exchange in nature", *Tellus*, 1975, *27*, pages 168–192.

17. These conclusions are taken from a recent workshop on the state of the art in the modelling of the carbon cycle; see J. Williams, ed, *Proceedings of the IIASA Workshop on Carbon Dioxide, Climate and Society* (Laxenburg, Austria, International Institute for Applied Systems Analysis, 1978 in preparation).

18. H. van Loon and J. Williams, "The connection between trends of mean temperature and circulation at the surface: part I. Winter", *Monthly Weather Review*, 1976, *104*, pages 365–380.

19. S. Manabe and R. T. Wetherald, "The effects of doubling the CO_2 concentration on the climate of a general circulation model", *Journal of Atmospheric Science*, 1975, *32*, pages 3–15. The general circulation model simulates the three-dimensional atmospheric circulation, but it still has many shortcomings. It considers only one continent, has fixed cloud amounts (ie the cloudiness-atmosphere feedback is not considered) and simulates a swamp-like ocean (ie no ocean circulation is coupled to the atmospheric circulation).

20. W. W. Kellogg, "Global influences of mankind on the climate", in J. Gribbin, ed, *Climatic Change* (Cambridge, Cambridge University Press, 1978).
21. M. I. Budyko, *Climate and Life*, English edition D. H. Miller, ed, *International Geophysical Series, 18* (New York, Academic Press, 1974).
22. M. Warshaw and R. R. Rapp, "An experiment on the sensitivity of a global circulation model", *Journal of Applied Meteorology*, 1973, *12*, pages 43–49.
23. R. G. Barry, "Cryospheric responses to a global temperature increase", in *Proceedings of the IIASA Workshop on Carbon Dioxide, Climate and Society* (Laxenburg, Austria, International Institute for Applied Systems Analysis, 1978 in preparation).
24. An example of the use of the combined use of energy, carbon, and climate models is given in F. Niehaus and J. Williams, "Studies of different energy strategies in terms of their effects on the atmospheric CO_2 concentration", *Journal of Geophysical Research*, 1978, in press. The global surface temperature response was assumed from T. Augustsson and V. Ramanathan, "A radiative-convective study of the CO_2 climate problem", *Journal of Atmospheric Science*, 1977, *34*, pages 448–451.
25. W. Häfele and W. Sassin, "Resources and endowments: an outline on future energy systems", Contribution to NATO Science Committee Twentieth Anniversay Commemoration Conference, Brussels, 1978.
26. For example, the mean surface temperature change, as derived from a simple one-dimensional atmospheric model, only has been considered rather than the response of the total climate system. Similarly, the input of CO_2 from other sources (eg the destruction of the biosphere), has not been taken into account.
27. C. Marchetti, "On geoengineering and the CO_2 problem", *Climatic Change*, 1977, *1*, pages 59–68.

CARBON

The real limit to growth

P. Kelly

Under preindustrial conditions the quantities of animal and vegetable life on Earth were fixed by the rate at which animals and microorganisms could restore carbon to vegetation through atmospheric carbon dioxide. The combustion of fossil hydrocarbons has disturbed this balance by bringing "new" organically useable carbon into the ecosystem. The biomass and free carbon dioxide on the Earth has accordingly increased since the industrial revolution and will continue to increase until and beyond the cessation of hydrocarbon-based technology. The author presents arguments in support of this hypothesis and indicates in the Appendix how the carbon cycle and its response to disturbances might be treated mathematically.

The pollution of the Earth's atmosphere by the by-products of industry has received much attention in recent years, a social phenomenon which though not historically unique is comforting—it is reassuring to know that mankind is not prepared to impose great changes on the world system without proper caution.

Unfortunately when the proper caution of the scientist is transmuted into the high fashion of the weekly magazines, the result tends to be something of an overkill, a process illustrated most vividly by the vilification to which carbon dioxide has been subject. The carbon dioxide concentration in the atmosphere increased from 312 parts per million (ppm) in 1958 to 321 ppm in 1970, an increase which has been universally interpreted as evidence of "carbon dioxide pollution" by man.[1]

The author is a writer and teacher; he lives in Tonbridge, Kent, UK.

The figures are incontrovertible, as is the contention that the increase is due to the production of carbon dioxide in the most fundamental of industrial processes, the combustion of fossil hydrocarbon.

The unlikely pollutant: CO_2

What is surprising is that the gas which forms the bubbles in the beer we drink should be bracketed with Freon-12 and hydrogen cyanide as a pollutant, for if carbon dioxide is a pollutant then everybody since Adam and Eve has been polluting the atmosphere with every exhalation. As it does not seem likely that God intended that we should pass our three-score and ten years holding our breath we are forced to the conclusion that either the industrial production of carbon dioxide does not constitute pollution of the atmosphere or that there is a fundamental difference between a molecule of carbon dioxide in an exhaust pipe and one in a wind-pipe.

The test of such an hypothesis should be found in the subsequent history of those two molecules, a history which would presumably be best known to that section of the world of living things to whom carbon dioxide is bread and butter. To date it does not appear that the stomata of even the most environmentally aware vegetable species instantly close in horror on the approach of a molecule of carbon dioxide whose central member has enjoyed a lengthy rest some miles beneath the surface of Saudi Arabia.

Photosynthesising plants are indeed quite indifferent to the origins of their sustenance, are as happy as creatures without a nervous system might ever be to consume as much carbon dioxide as they can; and the more carbon dioxide there is the more they will consume, the more they will grow and reproduce, the more vegetation there will be and accordingly the more animals there will be living off it.

It happens, though this has never been man's intention, that the best way of converting fossil hydrocarbon into living things is by burning it.

The word pollutant has been used most frequently to signify the user's disapproval of some material rather than in an etymologically definitive sense; however, if we accept that a pollutant is a material produced by man which is in some way inimical to life in general and human life in particular then carbon dioxide is certainly an unlikely candidate for such a pejorative title. The rate-determining factor in the production of all living tissue is the carbon dioxide content of the atmosphere, in which case life can only benefit from an increase in that content.

The obvious rejoinder that any benefit can be overdone is pertinent, but ignores the fact that the hydro-carbons we have been busily burning over the past 200 years or so did not come from Mars; they came from terrestrial vegetation. Nothing new and noxious has been introduced into the world ecosystem though something old and beneficial has been restored to it.

And yet, there is no doubt that in this restoration we have disturbed the ecosystem or at least have altered the normal chronological progress of that system. To understand the nature of that disturbance and its conse-quences for the future it is necessary that we understand the nature of the system we have disturbed.

The equilibrium carbon cycle

The crucial point in any consideration of the role of carbon dioxide in the system of living things is reflected in the units of measurement (ppm): the essential atmospheric link between animals and vegetables is maintained at a vanishingly small level of carbon dioxide.

The complete combustion of one gallon of high octane petrol produces (approximately) 12 pounds of water and 25 pounds of carbon dioxide and consumes in the process 28 pounds of oxygen. We do not hear of water pollution from internal combustion engines, much less of the oxygen deple-tion they are causing, simply because those materials are already super-abundant near the surface of the earth; it is the carbon dioxide that makes the difference and for the simple reason that there is precious little of the stuff about.

When Joseph Priestley first described carbon dioxide in the late eighteenth century the atmospheric concentration of the good doctor's "fixed air" was probably about 290 ppm. During the Carboniferous age it would have been around 450 ppm. The relationship be-tween the carbon in the atmosphere and the carbon in the tissues of living things is neatly demonstrated by the process of carbon loss which caused this diminution, for carbon dioxide was not lost to the atmosphere *as such* during the hundreds of millions of years before Priestley burnt the coal in his fireplace. It was lost as vegetable and animal tissue which, by virtue of being by some means abstracted from the ecosystem in the process of fossil-fuel formation, was denied its more usual fate of being recycled back to the atmosphere as carbon dioxide and ultimately back into living tissue via photosynthesis and the benign provision of the energy deficit by the sun.

Thus, as organic carbon (in the sense of carbon bound up with life) was lost to the system, less carbon was oxidised in the tissues of animals (and vegetables of course), simply because less was available, and accordingly less carbon dioxide was supplied to the atmosphere.

The carbon cycle is a closed chain and no link is more essential than any other yet it is tempting to cast photosynthesis as the key link, if only because it is the least understood. But there is nothing magic about photosynthesis, it is a chemical reaction and like all chemical reactions its rate is related to the product of the concentrations of the materials reacting; where one of these materials is scarce compared to the others the rate of reaction is effectively proportional to the concentration of that material alone. As animals produced less carbon dioxide vegetation consumed less and the carbon cycle was maintained in a constant state of equilibrium in which each of its three main parts were and must always be in a state of mutual dependence on the other two.

The rate of production of vegetation is proportional to the concentration of carbon dioxide in the atmosphere; the rate of production of animals is proportional to the rate of production of vegetation; the rate of production of carbon dioxide by animals and

plants less the rate of consumption of carbon dioxide by plants dictates the concentration of carbon dioxide in the atmosphere.

Over a time period as short as that of man's existence on the Earth each of these quantities remains more or less constant. During the period between Homo Habilis and Joseph Priestley the total mass of carbon moving around the carbon cycle was fixed and the constituent parts of this mass were fixed in atmospheric carbon (carbon dioxide), in vegetable carbon, and in animal carbon.

Under such conditions there is no way in which, say, the total mass of animals can increase or decrease. The only way in which a particular animal species can increase its share of the total animal mass is at the expense of other animal species either directly (and temporarily) by consumption or indirectly (and permanently) by intruding into other food chains. The most proficient animal species at expediting such processes are those which can live almost anywhere and eat almost anything; man, rat, and starling are examples. It is clear that the (apparent) slow increase in human population up to about 1800 was thus achieved; more to the point, it could not have been achieved in any other way.

The biosphere is a chemical reactor and it proceeds in accordance with the laws of chemistry.

The industrial revolution

During the sixteenth century England was afflicted with a severe energy crisis, reflected in the growing scarcity and soaring price of firewood.[2]

With considerable reluctance the English were forced to discover the dubious benefits of heating their homes with coal, a begrudged transformation which besides creating an industry (coal) without which the industrial revolution could not have taken place, also gave rise, in the mid-seventeenth century, to some remarkably modern-sounding treatises on pollution, although they tended to concentrate on soot pending the discovery of oxides of nitrogen.

From that time mankind has burnt fossil hydrocarbon of one form or another in ever-increasing quantities and in so doing has effectively introduced a new form of animal into the world system, one which while it sows, does not reap. When we smelted iron by burning wood or charcoal derived from wood we were taking carbon recently fixed from the atmosphere by photosynthesis and restoring it to the atmosphere as carbon dioxide. The carbon cycle was not disturbed by such activities though where the burning of wood increased the survival rate of humans, be it through winter warmth or the manufacture of ploughshares, the distribution of animal carbon would indeed have been altered in humanity's favour.

The new animal, however, the combustion machine—whether fireplace, furnace or F-16—is an unequivocal carbon plus; no food chains are disturbed by the raising of coal or oil because nothing depends on these materials for sustenance; the oxidation of fossil fuels produces carbon dioxide which enters the carbon cycle and stays in it (less, of course, the process of fossil fuel formation, which is slow enough to be discounted).

True, the carbon oxidised in using fossil fuels was originally fixed from the atmosphere by photosynthesis, but it has been out of the system for a long time, it is carbon that the world has learnt to do without; as far as any extant species is concerned it is new carbon; it is new material from which to construct new life.

Although precise figures are unobtainable, it appears that the carbon dioxide content of the atmosphere has increased by about 10% over the last 200 years, and the rate of photosynthesis must have increased accordingly.

This means that the rate of production of vegetation is greater now than it was then, that the available quantity of vegetation for conversion to animal tissue was greater during 1976 than it was during 1776. Furthermore this happy circumstance has not come about, as is often supposed, because we can fix atmospheric nitrogen to fertilise the earth; it has come about because we have provided vegetation with an increased supply of its limiting food component, that is carbon dioxide.[3]

Vegetable growth has responded blindly and predictably to the increase in the supply of carbon dioxide with which we have provided it and equally blindly the mass of animals supported by vegetation has increased as a consequence; there are lags in the system, of course (see Appendix).

Who benefits?

The particular type or types of animal which would benefit most from such an increase in the overall supply of carbon to the biosphere is immaterial. Were there no intelligent species on Earth and a passing interstellar traveller happened to squirt a trillion or so tonnes of carbon dioxide into the terrestrial atmosphere the ensuing development of life on the planet would not be dissimilar to that which has occurred over the last two centuries.

First, vegetable growth would increase, producing a greater supply of reduced carbon compounds; next, animals would increase in numbers and therefore total mass, producing a greater quantity of oxidised vegetation, carbon dioxide in particular; ultimately a new equilibrium would be obtained, and sustained in fixed proportions by a new and fixed concentration of carbon dioxide in the atmosphere. Any overshoots which occurred would be local and temporary and balanced by undershoots, equally local and temporary, elsewhere. Overall the system of life would move smoothly to its new equilibrium level.

What has actually happened, of course, is that the animal species which has benefited most from the increase in the total mass of vegetation is the most dynamic and adaptable species on Earth, along with its dependent and associated fauna.

Indeed, this is doubly unsurprising because man and by association cattle, sewer rats, gum protozoa, and intestinal bacteria may be regarded, not wholly fancifully, if somewhat ungrammatically, as symbiotic with the new animal: the combustion machine.

Man provides the machine with hydrocarbon to oxidise, the oxidation product is recycled through vegetation to enable man to produce more of his kind to build more machines; by the by the process also enables man to travel from London to Washington in three and a half hours.

The causes of the spectacular growth in human population in recent times have been the subject of much debate which, for all the learned borrowings from servomechanism theory and studies of bacteria in jars, has consistently ignored the inescapable fact that human beings have got to be made of something. What human beings are made of is about 91% of water (bound and unbound), 8% of carbon and 1% of other things. Water and the other things are abundant, carbon is the limiting component.

The carbon dioxide figures quoted at the beginning of this article have a hidden interest because calculation based on the actual consumption of fossil hydrocarbons between 1958 and 1970 shows that the 1970 figure for atmospheric carbon dioxide concentration should have been 326 ppm, not the 321 ppm actually recorded (partition into the oceans has, of course, been accounted for).[1]

Thus, 5 ppm of carbon dioxide or about a thousand million tonnes of elemental carbon are "missing"; missing from the atmosphere that is, but present in the biosphere as living tissue.

The increase in human population during this period was something like 400 million people, equivalent, were they all verging on obesity, to some 4 million tonnes of carbon. As we were at the same time carrying on the more traditional process by which animal species increase their numbers, that is by supplanting other animal species, we need not be unduly concerned by such a population increase; we are actually taking rather less out of the system than we are putting in.

The role of synthetic fertilisers

I have mentioned synthetic fertilisers; I shall examine the impact of this class of compounds on the biosphere more thoroughly, if only because they figure so large in the popular conception of the burgeoning of the earth.

Modern man, particularly in the developed countries, might be excused for thinking that plants are composed of a selection of minerals headed by ammonium salts, phosphoric acid, and potassium carbonate.

The fertiliser companies, perhaps not unwittingly, help to foster this illusion by giving their products such names as "plant food"; plant food is carbon dioxide and water. Nitrogen, phosphorous, potassium, magnesium, boron and a host of other elements are all essential to plant growth, principally because of their inclusion in the compounds associated with genetic consistency, metabolism, and respiration. But the mass requirement of plants in terms of these "inorganic" materials is extremely small compared to the total mass requirement; plants, like animals, consist almost entirely of carbon, hydrogen, and oxygen.

Nitrogen is the most important of the nutrient elements required by vegetable and in the equilibrium system this element is obtained from nitrogen-fixing soil bacteria, some living in a state of symbiosis with certain vegetable species, as well as from organic detritus.

After an increase in the supply of vegetation's limiting food component, carbon dioxide, the population of nitrogen-fixing bacteria will grow in concert with the new increased growth potential of vegetation and so ultimately will the quantity of detritus from animals feeding, at some remove, on the vegetation, until a new equilibrium is attained.

We must beware of taking too anthropomorphic a point of view in this analysis; unless the animals which rely on cereals for sustenance are unusually ingenious (which as it happens they are) it would not be such innately nitrogen-limited plants as cereals which would initially benefit from this process, it would be the leguminous plants with which the nitrogen-fixing bacteria live as symbiotes; but this does not affect the general tendency, only its specific rate of progress.

The nutrient limit

The important point to bear in mind here is that, like oxygen and water, nitrogen is abundant in the biosphere and the net input of nitrogen to the global ecosystem through the nitrogen-fixing bacteria is not limited by the supply of nitrogen but by the supply of carbon from their symbiotes, the carbon-dioxide fixing plants.

The other components in the inorganic soup required by vegetation, principally phosphorus and potassium, are provided in the equilibrium system by organic detritus and in the disturbed system by inorganic sources.

The inorganic sources of these materials are vastly in excess of the requirements of any possible (ie limited by carbon supply) level of vegetation on Earth. That these sources are not evenly distributed is irrelevant; left alone, vegetation would ultimately secure them and they would be spread across the world by the motion of

animals, in the tissues of an albatross as well, if somewhat less quickly and selectively, as in the hold of a ship.

The application of fertilisers to arable land has been practised by man since the discovery of agriculture and has been governed by the basic principle that what is taken out of the soil must be returned to it; the barrels on the outskirts of the traditional Chinese village were the village latrine and when a barrel became full it was carted off to be emptied on the fields. The principle is sound and in an equilibrium ecosystem such a process will occur anyway, with or without the deliberate intervention of any particular animal species.

The process, however, cannot be perfectly efficient in terms of human agriculture if only because even the most diligent community of subsistence farmers cannot entirely recycle their detritus to the place where they want it, though nature as a whole is indifferent to where it ends up and the overall balance is maintained.

The inevitable loss of nutrients to the human agricultural system is made up by other animal detritus and from inorganic sources and a static human population is thus maintained by a fixed amount of land (= vegetation), or a slowly increasing population is facilitated by a gradual extension of the supporting land area, which amounts to the supplanting of other animal species.

Now, following an increase in the supply of carbon dioxide to vegetation, the rate of photosynthesis will increase and accordingly the rate of consumption of "inorganic" nutrients will increase, the sources of fresh nutrients being those described above.

However, this is a slow process and through the eyes of a particularly intelligent and voracious animal species it will appear that the rate of production of vegetation has come up against a nutrient limit. Whereas some of the insects which feed on the leaves of a date palm in Morocco might be eaten by wintering swallows, some of whom might ultimately defaecate in Wiltshire, the wheat farmer in Wiltshire might be reasonably supposed to prefer that his Moroccan phosphate arrive in hundred-weight sacks bearing the name of a reputable shipper.

The apparent nutrient limit to the rate of production of vegetation appears to have been perceived by man at about the turn of the present century, whereupon he set about making up the shortfall by synthetic fixation of nitrogen and by redistribution of the inorganic sources of nutrient.

The shortfall, however, is one perceptible, and indeed relevant, only to man.

There is no shortage of the minerals required for plant growth, nor is there any reason to doubt the breeding capacity of nitrogen-fixing bacteria. Vegetation will expand to its carbon limit; man has simply accelerated the process in responding in his own uniquely intelligent way to the increase in the carbon supply with which he has unwittingly furnished it. When all the fossil carbon has been burnt and all the lagged responses have smoothed out an entire planetload of National Growmore fertiliser will not make the planet Earth produce any more vegetation than it is by then producing; the quantity will be fixed, as will be the quantity of animals living on it and oxidising it.

After the revolution

Had the industrial revolution been powered by the Newcomen fast breeder reactor, later superseded by the Daimler–Benz hydrogen–deuterium fusion process, the animal mass of the world would now be the same as it had always been during historical times.

The population of man would probably have increased following his taming of nuclear energy as the ability of his fission-powered bulldozers to

clear forest and of his fusion-powered tractors to plant the land with vegetation suitable to his own palate would greatly have improved his powers of converting other animal tissue to his own.

It is unlikely, however, that it would have increased anything like it has, if only because the variety of animal and vegetable species works against too great a concentration of animal tissue in any one species. In equilibrium man may seek to alter the distribution of animal life, but alter it too far and the balance will restore itself; one blue whale less may be a thousand or so people more, but the people had better learn to eat krill when all the blue whales have gone because something will be profiting from the krill surfeit (possibly even krill) and if it proves to be unpalatable to man then there will be a thousand or so people less.

If, on the other hand, the industrial revolution had never taken place but all the coal and oil we have burnt during it and its aftermath had by some miraculous means been simply burnt off into the atmosphere then the animal mass of the world would have increased to that which we now have (neglecting lags).

Man, being the most adaptable and successful animal species even in pre-industrial times, would no doubt have increased his population accordingly, perhaps even to something like the real present figure. Eventually he would almost certainly have done so; the most successful species does, after all, tend to win out—though the proportion of the carbon cornucopia going to other animal species would initially have been greater than has appertained in the real circumstances of recent history, where man has at the same time achieved high technology and supplied large quantities of organically usable carbon to the biosphere.

The principal ecological consequence of man's employment of packaged

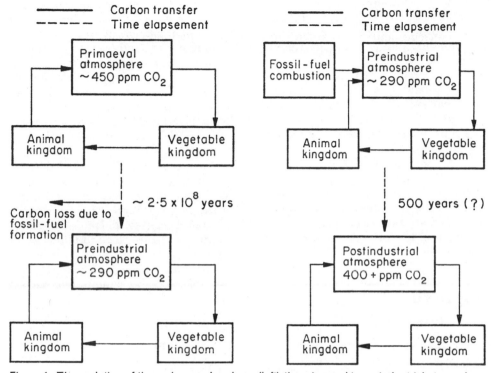

Figure 1. The evolution of the carbon cycle: above (left) the primaeval to preindustrial atmosphere and (right) the preindustrial to postindustrial atmosphere

energy in the form of fossil hydrocarbons has been an increase in the biomass of the Earth, and nothing we can now do will make the carbon go away. As we will doubtless continue to oxidise fossil hydrocarbon until it is all used up, the biomass of the Earth will continue to increase until that time when, after the lagged responses have smoothed out, the interaction between the vegetable and the animal kingdoms will be such as to support a new equilibrium system, sustained by a new and higher level of carbon dioxide in the atmosphere.

This is the real limit to growth and no amount of farsighted social and economic legislation or earnest cerebration in university bowers can have the slightest effect on it or our blithe progress towards it.

Were we to accept the wisdom of those philosophers of the future who point to the advantages of substantially reducing human population, then the ecological niche left vacant would simply be filled by other animal species, with or without backbones. If every human being on Earth were to drop dead at this moment the total mass of animal life on this planet would be back to its precatastrophe level within years.

When the fossil hydrocarbon has all been burnt and we have (hopefully) switched to a technology based on a constantly available energy source in human terms, such as fusion reactions, then we will cease to increase our numbers—where "we" means not just humanity but all animals taken together. The system of living things was stable in the Carboniferous age and it will be stable then, though it need not necessarily contain human beings.

The world of living things is always full and the material balance of the carbon cycle assures that it cannot be otherwise; it was full two hundred years ago, it is full now with an extra ten thousand million tonnes of carbon going the rounds between one life form and another, and it will be full when we have restored the remaining fossil carbon to the biosphere; not overfull, not crowded, just full—whether it be of men and corn or silkworms and mulberry trees.

J. M. Keynes said, "In the long run we're all dead". Wrong. In the long run we're all recycled. Now, thanks to the ingenuity and the avarice of mankind, the same can be said of the lost life of some hundreds of million years ago.

Appendix

System lags

The carbon cycle is a dynamic system and when the cycle is disturbed the material quantities in each of its sectors will change in a lagged fashion. In the following analysis I indicate what form these responses might take rather than predict actual numerical values; indeed the lack of numerical data precludes the latter.

The element carbon is the limiting material component on the quantity of living things present in the biosphere. Thus the total mass of vegetable life is proportional to the mass of carbon incorporated into vegetable life; similarly for animals. Further, as the atmospheric concentration of carbon dioxide is small and the mass of atmospheric carbon bears a constant ratio to the mass of atmospheric carbon dioxide, we may regard the mass of atmospheric carbon as being proportional to the atmospheric concentration of carbon dioxide.

We ignore carbon loss from the biosphere; thus we are concerned with a period of thousands of years rather than millions. We ignore stochastic flicker; in other words we consider the vegetable kingdom (green plants) and the animal kingdom (things which eat green plants at some remove, including fungi and bacteria) as homogeneous entities and temperature, water supply, nutrient supply, intensity of sunlight etc as constants; thus we average over all space (the whole biosphere) and, as a moving average, over a fairly long period in human terms, say 50 years.

We ignore nonlinearities due to limiting; thus we suppose that over the range of atmospheric carbon dioxide concentration with which we are concerned (say, 250 ppm–500 ppm), carbon remains the limiting component.

The basic equations governing the dynamics of the equilibrium carbon cycle are:

$$\frac{dA}{dt} = aV - bA, \qquad (1)$$

$$\frac{dC}{dt} = bA - cC, \qquad (2)$$

$$\frac{dV}{dt} = cC - aV, \qquad (3)$$

where A is the mass of animal carbon (M),
C is the mass of atmospheric carbon (M),
V is the mass of vegetable carbon (M),
t is time (T), and
a, b, c are rate constants (T^{-1}).

At steady state all the derivatives are zero and:
$$aV = bA = cC,$$

ie the rate of conversion of vegetable carbon to animal carbon is equal to the rate of conversion of animal carbon to atmospheric carbon is equal to the rate of conversion of atmospheric carbon to vegetable carbon. Which, of course, defines the steady state.

Because the characteristic matrix of the model is singular, none of these quantities may be determined by observation of the steady-state carbon cycle. Like most physical systems, and one suspects most social systems, the carbon cycle will only yield its secrets when it is disturbed.

The form of disturbance with which we are concerned is an input, $U(MT^{-1})$, of carbon into the atmosphere. Equation (2) then becomes:

$$\frac{dC}{dt} = bA - cC + U, \qquad (2a)$$

Solving the system of equations in the Laplace domain we obtain:

$$C = \frac{U(s + a)(s + b)}{D(s)}. \qquad (4)$$

$$V = \frac{Uc(s + b)}{D(s)}, \qquad (5)$$

$$A = \frac{Uac}{D(s)}, \qquad (6)$$

where

$$D(s) = s[s^2 + s(a + b + c) + ab + ac + bc],$$

s is the Laplace operator, and
C, V, A now have the significance of the Laplace transformations of $C(t) - C(0)$, $V(t) - V(0)$, $A(t) - A(0)$.

The eigenvalues of the model are thus:

$$E1 = 0,$$
$$E2, E3 = -\tfrac{1}{2}\{(a + b + c) \pm [a^2 + b^2 + c^2 - 2(ab + ac + bc)]^{1/2}\}.$$

Had we numerical values for a, b, c we could proceed further to solve the model equations, plot graphs, and so forth. As we do not have these numerical values we must content ourselves with algebraic interpretations.

The zero eigenvalue represents the integrator implicit in the model structure and indicates mathematically what was said in the main text, that fresh carbon entering the system stays in

it. Thus a sudden sharp burst of carbon into the system becomes a constant increase in the level of carbon within the system.

Such an input began its rise phase about the time of the industrial revolution and it is still rising; ultimately it will fall back to zero, no doubt in the same fashion as it rose from zero, that is imperceptibly. Human consumption of fossil hydrocarbon is not rising on an exponential curve, it is on the front side of a normal distribution curve.

The net result of this brief eruption of "new" carbon into the system will be that this quantity of carbon is back in the system, forever.

The two nonzero eigenvalues represent the lag terms in the response of the system. Firstly we note that whether or not these eigenvalues are real or complex their real parts must be negative for, given a, b, c all positive, then:

$$- (a + b + c) < 0,$$

and, given

$$[a^2 + b^2 + c^2 - 2(ab + ac + bc)] > 0,$$

then

$$[a^2 + b^2 + c^2 - 2(ab + ac + bc)]^{1/2} < (a + b + c).$$

Thus, the response terms dependent on these eigenvalues are decaying terms, there is no indication of an unstable (ie growing) response. Once the input has switched off the system will move to a finite equilibrium state.

The term under the square root sign may be positive or negative, depending on the numerical values of a, b, and c. If it is positive then both eigenvalues are negative real and the lagged terms are fully damped, ie the system moves smoothly to the final state.

If it is negative then the eigenvalues are a complex conjugate pair and the system response is accordingly oscillatory, ie during the transition to the final state each of the three sectors of the carbon cycle will go through a series of peaks and troughs. The frequency of these oscillations is, of course, also fixed by the numerical values of the parameters and is the same for each of the three sectors.

The phase of the putative oscillations is a different matter and brings us to consideration of the numerators of the right hand expressions of equations (4)–(6). We note, as would be expected, that the atmospheric carbon sector leads, that the vegetable carbon sector follows and that the animal carbon sector comes in the rear.

Given negative real eigenvalues and a smooth input function such properties are probably most favourable, in a cautionary sense, to animals, who always lag.

Given complex eigenvalues the difference between each of the three sectors may be stated more precisely as a 90 degree phase lag, that is a quarter cycle between each sector with the atmospheric sector leading. In other words, given an oscillatory response, the peak in animal carbon comes a quarter cycle after the peak in vegetable carbon, and so forth.

We can go no further with this analysis in the absence of experimentally determined parameters or indeed of reliable estimates of the quantities of living things with which we are concerned. The reader may draw his own conclusions from the analysis presented above.

Notes and references

1. *Energy*, volume 1. A survey of US energy requirements past and present, published by the US Government (1974). The figures on CO_2 concentrations are also quoted in D. Meadows *et al*, *The Limits to Growth* (New York, Universe Books, 1972). The original source was the Mauna Loa Observatory in Hawaii.
2. Alan D. Dyer, "Wood and coal: a change of fuel", *History Today*, 26 (9), September 1976, pages 598–607.
3. The comment in N. W. Pirie, "The world food supply", *Futures*, December 1976, 8 (6), pages 509–516, that "it is unlikely that manipulating atmospheric composition will soon become part of large scale agriculture" is apposite here, for this is precisely what we have done.